A Social Contract for the Coal Fields

A Social Contract for the Coal Fields

The Rise and Fall of the United Mine Workers
of America Welfare and Retirement Fund

Richard P. Mulcahy

The University of Tennessee Press / Knoxville

Parts of this book originally appeared as:

"'They Shall Walk Again!': The Physical Rehabilitation Program
of the UMWA Welfare and Retirement Fund," in *The Journal of
the Appalachian Studies Association* 6 (1994). © 1994 by Center
for Appalachian Studies and Services. Used with permission.

"Partitioning the Miners' Welfare State: The Destruction of the
UMWA Welfare and Retirement Fund," in *Mid-America: An
Historical Review* 77, no. 2 (spring–summer 1995). Used with
permission.

The paper used in this book meets the minimum requirements of
ANSI/NISO Z39.48-1992 (R 1997) (Permanence of Paper). The
binding materials have been chosen for strength and durability.

Library of Congress Cataloging-in-Publication Data

Mulcahy, Richard P.
A social contract for the coal fields : the rise and fall of the
United Mine Workers of America Welfare and Retirement Fund /
Richard P. Mulcahy.— 1st ed.
    p. cm.
Parts of this book originally appeared as: "'They Shall Walk
Again!': The Physical Rehabilitation Program of the UMWA
Welfare and Retirement Fund," in *The Journal of the Appalachian
Studies Association* 6 (1994) and in "Partitioning the Miners'
Welfare State: The Destruction of the UMWA Welfare and
Retirement Fund," in *Mid-America: An Historical Review* 77,
no. 2 (spring-summer 1995).
Includes bibliographical references and index.
ISBN 1-57233-100-3 (cl.: alk. paper)
1. United Mine Workers of America. Welfare and Retirement
Fund—History. 2. United Mine Workers of America—History.
3. Miners—Medical care—United States. I. Journal of the
Appalachian Studies Association. II. Mid-America. III. Title.
HD6515.M62 U556 2000
. 362.1'088'622—dc21   00-009341

For my Father and Mother:
Patrick Francis Mulcahy and Frances Catherine Bell Mulcahy

Contents

Illustrations

Acknowledgments

No project such as this is ever truly the work of a single person. Therefore I would like to gratefully acknowledge several of the people who helped make this book a reality. First, I would like to thank the scholars at West Virginia University who first suggested this topic to me and guided me through it: Drs. Ronald L. Lewis, George Parkinson, and Ronald Althouse.

Next, I wish to thank Dr. Richard Couto for his constructive and helpful commentary on my work when it was in its final stages of preparation. In the same vein, I would to thank my wife, Michelle, whose help, interest, and patience proved invaluable.

Finally, I wish to thank the surviving members of the United Mine Workers of America Welfare and Retirement Fund's staff that I interviewed. Some not only took the time to speak with me several times but also sent me written materials. In this regard, I would especially like to recognize the contributions of Dr. John Newdorp; Mr. Henry Daniels; Ms. Susan Jarworski Rodenbaugh; Mr. Domanic Raino; Ms. Ada Kruger, R.N.; Dr. Paul Cornely; Mr. W. Philip Palmer; and the late Drs. Lorin E. Kerr and John Winebrenner.

Introduction

This book is a general treatment of the United Mine Workers of America Welfare and Retirement Fund from its creation in 1946 to the termination of its medical service in 1978. When I began this project, I believed it would be a study in conflict of interest and abuse of power. My beliefs were conditioned both by my reading and memories. I watched avidly as UMWA president W. A. (Tony) Boyle fell from power between 1969 and 1972. Being from the Pittsburgh area, I was exposed to both national and local coverage of the event. Pittsburgh was the headquarters for the union's fifth district, and the news was full of the power struggle there between Joseph Budzanowski, a Boyle stalwart, and Louis B. Antal, leader of the district's opposition.

As the story unfolded, Boyle and his associates were thoroughly discredited. Moreover, John L. Lewis's reputation suffered tremendously, since Boyle was regarded as Lewis's hand-chosen successor. On the level of personal experience, the connection between Boyle and Lewis was difficult for my family to accept. My mother's people had been coal miners, and she always looked to Lewis as the one man who cared about them. Her admiration was further reinforced by the successes scored in the 1930s by Lewis's creation, the Congress of Industrial Organizations (CIO). Now, Lewis suddenly appeared to her in a new and less attractive light.

A similar reappraisal of Lewis has also taken place in the more recent scholarship about him and the UMWA. From the 1930s to the 1950s, authors lauded Lewis for his accomplishments.[1] However, with the revelations made about the UMWA during the Boyle era, scholars began to reevaluate Lewis. While admitting Lewis's contributions as a labor leader, historians have become highly critical of him. They point out that Lewis craved power, was undemocratic in his administration of the UMWA, and refused to tolerate criticism. A good example of this is Melvyn Dubofsky and Warren Van Tine's book, *John L. Lewis: A Biography.* The study begins with a recounting of the events leading to the murder of Boyle's rival in the UMWA's 1969 presidential election, Joseph A. (Jock) Yablonski. Immediately thereafter, the authors turn to their analysis of Lewis, giving special attention to the tactics he used to gain control of the UMWA, and to keep it. The reader is left to draw the conclusion that Lewis created the preconditions which ultimately lead to Yablonski's murder.

The weaknesses Lewis displayed as a union leader are undeniable, and they appeared in his stewardship of the Fund. From its inception, Lewis used every means at his disposal to ensure his control over it, in violation of the Taft-Hartley Act and the estate and trust laws. It is also true that the Fund was intended to serve purposes other than simple humanitarianism, and that its relationship with the union constituted conflict of interest. However, these facts are only part of the story. On closer examination, a far more complex picture emerges.

As the Second World War came to a close, there was an effort to revive and continue the process of economic and social reform started by the New Deal. This was marked by President Roosevelt's call for an "Economic Bill of Rights" in 1944.[2] Unfortunately, neither Roosevelt nor Truman could get the idea past the conservative coalition that had taken control in Congress. The election of a reactionary Congress in 1946 complicated matters further and made passage of any other social policy initiatives an impossibility.

For its part, organized labor, especially the CIO, was prepared to make good on its commitment to continuing a program of liberal reform when the war ended. This included a massive effort to organize southern workers known as "Operation Dixie," support for a renewed attempt at passage of a national health insurance bill, as well as the postwar strike wave.[3] According to Nelson Lichtenstein, CIO president Phil Murray hoped to win a program of social democracy, which not only expanded the government's role in social policy but also gave organized labor a say in how corporations were managed. It was only after these efforts failed that the CIO, around 1948, began opting for a privatized and divided system of fringe benefits which varied from union to union and from employer to employer.

It was during these same years that John L. Lewis moved in his own direction. Rather than joining with his colleagues in 1945 in the quest for additional reform, Lewis demanded the creation of a welfare fund for the nation's coal miners. Aside from death and educational benefits, the program's major offerings would include complete health care and retirement pensions. Although Lewis was moved to action in this area in part by the UMWA's membership, he probably also believed that the renewed drive for governmental reform would fail. Whatever his reasons, Lewis made the creation of a miners' welfare fund an all-consuming issue in his negotiations with the major coal operators. This culminated with the establishment of the United Mine Workers of America Welfare and Retirement Fund in 1946.

The Fund's creation was not conceded easily. As will be seen, it came about only when the government seized the nation's coal mines and negotiated with the UMWA in the operators' name. In addition, a struggle ensued between Lewis and the coal operators after 1946 for control of the Fund. What ultimately came out of this dispute was a three-way social contract between the miners, the union, and management.

In return for being a disciplined workforce and following the union's orders, the miners received a generous set of benefits. In return for providing a disciplined workforce, and for not opposing mine mechanization, the union received control of the Fund. There was also an end to the combativeness that had marked the union's relationship with management. In fact, not only did the union and the major coal operators move from being adversaries, they became quasi-partners in an effort to remake the coal industry. Management, although it had conceded much, gained as much, particularly the union's quiescence in a number of areas, especially mechanization.

For Lewis, this appeared to be a win/win situation since he supported mechanization as part of an overall program he had to rationalize coal production. Thus, while the new relationship was semicollusive, the problem of its contradictory nature did not immediately manifest itself. In fact, what became *the* major problem for Lewis was making good on his promise of providing an extensive social service system in what turned out to be a declining industry.

These issues aside, the Fund's creation anticipated the rise of, and organized labor's eventual acceptance of, the divided fringe benefit system mentioned above. Yet, what made the Fund unique in this setting was that, unlike programs sponsored by other unions, it kept the spirit of social democracy alive. Staffed by people who had either worked for the United States Public Health Service (USPHS), the Farm Security Administration (FSA), and the military, the Fund became, in effect, a privatized version of the Social Security Administration. In making the miner social contract a reality, the Fund's staff innovated and pioneered in a number of areas.

Most union-sponsored programs were financed, either in whole or in part, by membership contributions. Moreover, these programs did not address pension issues and confined their health care work to paying bills. In stark contrast, the Fund was financed by a royalty assessed on every ton of coal mined for sale or use, thereby making it fully noncontributory. In addition, aside from offering a pension that was paid over and above Social Security, the Fund sought to go beyond simply paying its beneficiaries' medical bills by working to secure the best treatment possible. In so doing, the Fund's staff hoped not only to show that the program was efficient and workable, but also to offer the federal government a model for national health insurance.[4]

Taking all of this into account, the Fund's story is an important one. This point takes on even greater significance when one considers the impact the program had in the coal fields, as well as the lessons the program can offer in the area of social policy formation. Unfortunately, scholarship on the program until now has concentrated exclusively on its medical program.[5] This study not only covers the Fund's work in the area of health care but also its pension program, as well as how it related to the UMWA and the problems involved with that relationship. Its purpose it to present the Fund's complete story.

In pursuit of this goal, this study is based on the Fund's records and on private papers not available before, as well as on an extensive set of interviews with surviving members of the Fund's staff. These include people who served at the Fund's headquarters and those who worked in the field. As a result, this study covers not only the problems the Fund had with fulfilling the miner social contract but also its successes. Moreover, this study shows how the Fund was an exemplar of the New Deal Order, how it anticipated that order's fall, and how it may provide insights into where social policy is currently heading.

Chapter 1
Establishing the Fund

From beginning to end, the United Mine Workers of America Welfare and Retirement Fund was John L. Lewis's unique creation. Although Lewis did not micromanage the Fund's day-to-day operation, he was undoubtedly the final authority, promulgating the program's overall goals and fighting to protect it from outside interference.[1] Lewis intended the Fund to fulfill several different goals. These goals ranged from rationalizing the coal industry to establishing a three-way social contract between the union, the miners, and the operators. While these various goals often complimented each other, they also conflicted. It was in these conflicts that Lewis's personality as a labor leader emerged. He had an unyielding faith in his ability as an administrator who could bring conflicting points together and thereby solve problems.

Although he is dryly characterized as a conservative by labor historian Alan Derickson, this view of Lewis as a successful opportunist does not present the complete picture.[2] Lewis's primary goal was to permanently stabilize the coal industry. Party affiliations and various belief systems were simply tools to achieve that end. Thus, Lewis began his career as the UMWA's president as a confirmed Wilsonian. During the 1920s, however, he switched sides and supported the Republicans and purged leftists out of the union. But, in 1933 he switched sides again and joined with Roosevelt and the New Deal, only to break with FDR in 1940 in favor of Wendell Wilkie. During these same years Lewis not only stopped persecuting the UMWA's left wing, but also willingly used Communist labor organizers when he founded the Congress of Industrial Organizations (CIO). Far from being a simple opportunist, Lewis was a skilled pragmatist.

When he assumed the UMWA's presidency in 1919, coal demand was plagued by constant boom/bust cycles. Lewis attributed this to the industry producing more coal than needed.[3] In addition, most coal companies were small and constantly underbid each other. Forced to reduce their expenses to the bare minimum, these companies cut wages, which represented the largest portion of total costs.[4] Lewis sought to alleviate this situation by consolidating coal production into the hands of a few large firms. By restructuring the industry in this way, Lewis hoped to regulate coal output in a corporate manner, with producers and the union working together. This would level out the business cycle and end the related problems of overproduction and unemployment. Under Lewis's leadership, everything sought by the miner's union reflected his agenda.

This included higher wage demands, mine mechanization, and the strict enforcement of seniority clauses in union contracts.[5]

In tandem with his policy of rationalization, Lewis also remade the union by concentrating power in his hands. Prior to his presidency, the UMWA had been decentralized with considerable authority resting on the district level. Lewis saw the arrangement as ineffective and decided to centralize the union. This meant breaking the power of the district unions. Lewis accomplished this during the 1920s by various methods, including divide and conquer, patronage, and abuse of administrative procedures. By 1928 Lewis had absolute control and firmly held the UMWA's presidency until his retirement in 1959.[6]

Although he won his fight, Lewis paid a heavy price, since breaking the districts was synonymous with breaking the union. By itself, such a policy should have been disastrous. But, while Lewis was in-fighting, coal demand fell dramatically. Coal operators who had once cooperated with the union now broke their contracts in a scramble to cut costs.[7] The combination of these factors resulted in a dramatic decline in the union's membership between 1919 and 1929 and the loss of its powerful position within the American Federation of Labor (AFL).[8] Two events, however, saved the union from ultimate destruction. First, the federal government, using the National Industrial Recovery Act and the Guffey-Snyder Act, took an active role in shoring up both the coal industry and the UMWA as part of the New Deal. These laws promoted collective bargaining and the creation of market/pricing agreements among the operators. Second, in 1937 the coal industry began to recover from its depression with a demand for increased production. This marked the beginning of the industry's second great boom, which lasted until 1948, primarily due to the demands created by the Second World War. By 1946 both Lewis and the union were at the height of their power and influence.[9]

Despite victories the UMWA had won for its membership in terms of hours and wages, two issues remained to be addressed: health care and retirement. Both concerns were especially important to the union's rank and file. As early as 1920, Great Britain had addressed these concerns through the Mine Industry Act, which created an industrywide welfare fund for its miners. No comparable system existed in America.[10] Coal producers ignored retirement, and what medical care existed for many miners in the bituminous coal fields was poor. Bituminous coal lagged behind all other basic industries in such areas as preventative medicine, industrial hygiene, and the maintenance and analysis of employee health records.[11]

Health care problems were particularly acute in the Appalachian coal fields, illustrated by the fact that infant mortality rates in the region were the highest in the nation.[12] A further complication was the danger involved with mining. An average of 1,000 miners a year were killed due to accidents, and work in the mines ranked as the most hazardous in basic industry.[13] Yet, management insisted that it had made great strides toward providing a safe workplace despite these facts.[14] To cope with this situation, the only medical insurance available to most miners were company-sponsored "check-off" schemes to pay doctor bills and hospitalization. Financed by a deduction or check-off from the miners' salaries, these plans generated deep dissatisfaction.[15] First, many check-off physicians were incompetent, and most of the miners regarded them as agents for the company.[16] Second, company doctor and hospitalization plans did not cover treatment for such things as tuberculosis, venereal disease, or obstetrical services.[17]

Hostility to the check-offs ran deep within the union's membership, and the system was damned by a union official as the bastard of American medicine.[18] Lewis, however, had not shown a consistent interest in either health care or retirement benefits prior to World War II. One of the few times where he touched on either subject came in 1921, when he ran for the AFL's presidency. Lewis endorsed national health insurance not only as part of his platform, but also as an overall program of social democracy.[19] In this instance, Lewis was more progressive than most of his colleagues in the AFL, who opposed such measures. But in the years which followed, Lewis made no further statement concerning social policy as he moved back and forth on the political spectrum.

Ironically, while the UMWA became a tightly run organization during these years, the impetus for change came from the rank and file. As the union grew and recovered its former strength, the membership became increasingly vocal at the union's conventions about its anger over the check-off system.[20] Demands from union locals became so numerous and strident, a rebellion against Lewis could have been possible if these concerns had not been addressed. Confronted with this situation, Lewis probably decided to demand a welfare fund's creation as a method of co-opting this movement, and so turn it to his advantage. Thus, with the conclusion of the Second World War, Lewis made a welfare fund's creation the centerpiece of the union's demands.

The program he envisioned was to be industrywide and noncontributory, financed by a royalty paid on every ton of coal mined for sale or use.[21] The fund would provide the miners with retirement benefits, as well as comprehensive medical care. While achieving these ends, the fund would also assist Lewis in meeting his long-term goals for the industry. Older union members would be enticed to retire by the opportunity to draw pensions and so cut the mining workforce. Royalty payments would mean an additional expense for marginal operators, forcing them out of business and further concentrating the industry.[22]

This was too much for coal producers to concede willingly. The costs from financing such a fund would be enormous, and Lewis's prestige among the miners would be enhanced by his managing large sums of money for welfare purposes. Therefore, the nation's coal operators refused to even discuss creation of a fund. Despite such uniform opposition, Lewis would not drop the demand. Depending on the federal government's attitude, he would still have room to maneuver. Even a policy of benevolent neutrality could strengthen his hand. However, all hope of creating a fund in 1945 evaporated when Secretary of Labor Frances Perkins sided with the operators during the coal negotiations that year.[23]

The Labor Department's lack of support for the fund idea was not surprising since no union had ever attempted something so extensive. Organized labor's health care arrangements varied widely. The International Ladies Garment Worker Union (ILGWU) had pioneered in the area by organizing its New York Union Health Center in 1917.[24] By 1938 the ILGWU had created a unionwide welfare fund covering health care, but it was decentralized and administered through each of the union's local offices.[25] Finally, in 1943, the ILGWU created a retirement fund financed by employer contributions equal to 3 percent of their weekly payroll. The minimum retirement age was sixty-five, with each retiree receiving a monthly payment of fifty dollars.[26] A similar program was established by the United Hatters, Cap, and Millinery Workers. [27]

The situation was different in heavy industry. These unions were taking a minimalist approach when it came to fringe benefits. The reason, in part, was that between 1945 and 1948 the CIO concentrated its efforts on achieving a social democratic legislative program that included a drive for national health insurance.[28] Because the federation was also sponsoring a major organizational campaign for the South known as "Operation Dixie," duplication of effort had to be avoided. Also, each member union had to take into account the various company-sponsored programs that already existed.

In December 1943, the United Electrical Workers (UE) passed a resolution encouraging its locals to include group insurance as part of their contract talks.[29] Several varieties of insurance were discussed at that time, including coverage for basic health care and hospitalization, life insurance, and accident protection.[30] Local unions made insurance arrangements with their employers, using a sample contract clause issued by the international union.[31] Employers would then be obligated to assume the premium costs under this clause while subscribing to a group contract negotiated between the international and an insurance company.[32] Although this method was fairly complex, the UE's leadership did not see the plan as a primary source of health insurance for its members. Rather, the plan was meant to supplement a government-sponsored program.[33] The UE did not address retirement concerns.

The opposite was true with steel. Whereas health care arrangements were next to nonexistent in the industry, steel had some of the nation's oldest company-sponsored pension programs. U.S. Steel's Carnegie Plan was a good example. Under the plan, a pension amount was determined using a basic formula: each award was pegged to a steelworker's average monthly earnings for his last ten years. This figure was then multiplied by a percentage equal to the worker's years of service. [34] The resulting figure represented the maximum payment the worker was entitled to receive. In a hypothetical case, a steelworker whose monthly earnings averaged $229.17 and who had thirty years of service with the company was eligible for 30 percent of that average: $68.75 a month.[35] However, this was the maximum the steelworker could receive. Receipt of any Social Security payments meant the pension would be reduced accordingly. This requirement was changed slightly with the 1949 United Steel Workers (USW) contract. Under the agreement, steelworkers could receive a combined pension/Social Security benefit without any reductions in the pension, provided the combined figure did not exceed $100 a month.[36]

Hoping national health insurance would pass, thereby making a union plan unnecessary, the USW took no action on health care until 1949. When national health insurance was defeated, the USW made provision for its members by negotiating the first national Blue Cross contract ever written.[37] Premiums were covered through a joint employer/employee contribution.[38] While there was no deductible, nor other specific out-of-pocket expenses, the plan did have coverage limitations, including a ceiling of seventy days per year for hospitalization.[39]

As for the population outside organized labor, health insurance was available from commercial organizations or Blue Cross. In either case, comprehensive coverage did not exist. Commercial plans operated on an indemnity basis whereby money benefits were paid directly to the policyholder. However, benefit rates were set according to what the company believed a given procedure was worth. Because there was no physician negotiation, payment usually fell short of the actual charge. [40]

Blue Cross and Blue Shield were organized during the 1930s. Established in 1934, Blue Cross was designed to cover hospital expenses. Blue Shield came into existence five years later and covered doctor bills. [41] Both groups were decentralized and operated on a franchise-style basis, with each plan working independently of the others. A national office conferred Blue Cross/Blue Shield affiliation based on certain benefit and premium criteria. Benefits were not portable from one locale to another.

Despite these flaws, cost was the biggest problem with all private insurance. Most people could not afford the premiums. During the 1930s, out of a total population of 130 million to 140 million people, only 2 million had any sort of health coverage.[42] National health insurance was meant to address this problem. Dating back to the Progressive Era, social workers, labor theorists, public health specialists, academic physicians, and other advocates for national health insurance characterized it as an investment for the nation.[43] This reasoning held that public spending for health care was far cheaper than the continuing drain placed upon the economy by the presence of chronic sickness and ill health.[44] Although their original drive between 1916 and 1920 for health reform had failed, this coalition remained actively concerned about the issue.

The fight for national health insurance was renewed with the New Deal. FDR, however, offered only tepid support. In August 1935, he created the Interdepartmental Committee on Health and Welfare Activities, whose purpose was to study the full spectrum of welfare needs in the United States and make recommendations.[45] The committee concentrated most of its attention on health reform, despite its broad mandate, and its efforts culminated in 1938 with a major conference on national health insurance. While various speakers presented their ideas, the committee unveiled its own plan for a joint federal/state effort.[46] The plan, which offered complete coverage for all, was eventually put forward as a bill sponsored by Sen. Robert F. Wagner of New York. The measure died, however, when FDR withdrew his support after extensive lobbying by the American Medical Association (AMA).[47]

Organized in 1855, the AMA had been created to protect the professional interests of physicians. During the first half of the nineteenth century, mainstream physicians, or "allopaths," were an embattled group. Not only did they face competition from alternative healing systems, such as homeopathy and the water cure, but many states opposed licensure. To many Jacksonian politicians it appeared that university-trained physicians were attempting to make themselves into an aristocracy.[48] The AMA tried to counter such attitudes by showing that its membership represented competence and quality in medical practice. By 1900 its efforts were having an effect. After making peace with homeopathy, allopaths worked to eclipse other healing systems. At the same time, due to AMA lobbying, most states regulated the practice of medicine by imposing licensure.[49] In conjunction with these successes, the AMA promoted one, and only one, model for health care delivery in America: complete free choice of physician by the patient, and fee-for-service payment. The association's ideal of medicine was the solo practitioner working independently as a free-standing professional. They opposed any and all proposals which diverged from this model.[50]

Despite claims to the contrary, the AMA found itself acting as one of the health reform movement's principle opponents. Certainly, no AMA spokesman ever advocated that anyone needing treatment should be denied care due to an inability to pay. But the association opposed previous plans, as well as the 1938 initiative referring to them as bureaucratic medicine. The association's alternative was a decentralized system where its county affiliates would set prices, with the federal government simply paying bills. Barring this solution, the association had nothing to offer other than a call for further expansion of existing insurance plans.[51]

The AMA clung to this particular line with increasing tenacity during the Second World War. Although the New Deal's original health insurance bill had failed, it was soon revived. The catalyst for this resurrection was the Selective Service Act of 1940. The act authorized a call-up of one million young men. While these first draftees were being processed, examining physicians made a shocking discovery: approximately 40 percent were found medically unfit for military service.[52] According to the examining physicians, many of these young men would have been fit if they had received timely medical treatment for past ailments.[53] In response, Senator Wagner reintroduced his health insurance bill in 1943, with two cosponsors: Sen. James Murray of Montana and Rep. John Dingell. The bill's supporters now presented the health reform issue as a matter of national security, rather than one of social policy. They now asked the question: "How could America expect to defend herself when such a major portion of her young men were physically incapable of shouldering their responsibilities as citizens?"[54]

The debate this question generated outlasted the war and continued until the end of the 1940s. Unlike Roosevelt, President Truman supported the health insurance concept, and the Gallup poll showed most Americans favored the idea.[55] Despite broad-based support, the bill was bitterly opposed by the new Republican majority that took over the Congress after the 1946 election. Interestingly, while the rest of organized labor directed its efforts at winning passage of the Murray-Wagner-Dingell bill, the changed political landscape may have prompted John L. Lewis to seek a fund's creation once again only a year after his defeat on the issue.

The conservative tenor of the new Congress, with its overt hostility to the New Deal's legacy, negated any chance of expanding the country's social welfare efforts. Because Truman was friendly to health reform, Lewis probably assumed that his proposals would receive a more serious hearing than before. At the same time, the nation's coal stockpiles were low and the country was still reconverting to a peacetime economy. A protracted coal strike could derail government reconversion plans. From Lewis's perspective, now was the time to act. Because of this, when the 1946 contract negotiations began, not only did Lewis renew his demand for a welfare fund, he made it a make or break issue and called a national strike over it.[56]

Once again, coal operators were unanimous in their refusal to consider the proposal. Against this backdrop, Lewis presented himself to the public as the spirit of reason and compromise. He denied in a press statement that he was adamant about financing the fund through a coal royalty. A payroll deduction method would be acceptable if coal operators agreed to a fund in principal.[57] Such disclaimers notwithstanding, the royalty issue was the main bone of contention in the negotiations, with Lewis calling for an assessment of five cents a ton. The money would be used for medical services and hospitalization. Lewis was also interested in rehabilitation for injured miners, economic assistance for victims of the industry, and educational/cultural aid to miners and their families. He made no mention of a pension program at this time, possibly hoping to bring a fund into existence first.

The strike came close to becoming a national crisis. On May 22, 1946, the federal government intervened by seizing the mines under the War Labor Disputes Act. They were placed under the control of Secretary of the Interior Julius A. Krug, who began immediate and direct negotiations with Lewis. A week later, on May 29, Krug and Lewis signed the National Bituminous Coal Wage Agreement of 1946. The United Mine Workers of America Welfare and Retirement Fund of 1946 was thereby created, with the contract mandating that the Fund be financed by the five-cent tonnage royalty Lewis had sought.[58]

Although the Fund became a reality, it did not actually begin operating for almost eleven months.[59] Part of the delay involved organizing the program's administration. The contract stipulated that the Fund would be overseen by a board of trustees composed of three persons: one representing the union, the other the government, and a third neutral trustee.[60] The contract also called for a medical survey of the bituminous coal industry to establish empirically whether or not a union medical program was necessary.[61] The Fund could not be activated until this survey was completed.

The study was directed by the surgeon general of the navy, Rear Adm. Joel T. Boone, and conducted under the auspices of the Department of the Interior.[62] Although Boone was a public health specialist, he was familiar with the coal industry. He was a native of St. Clair, Pennsylvania, located in the heart of the nation's anthracite coal field.[63] Eventually known as *The Boone Report,* the survey listed all of the health and medical care deficiencies in the coal fields. Investigative teams who concentrated on remote Appalachian areas were appalled by the poor conditions found in many hospitals. Operated on a proprietary, or for-profit basis, most of these institutions were understaffed and deficient in every way. Moreover, the survey uncovered medical incompetence, as well as cases of medicine practiced by unqualified persons.[64] The report also called attention to the shocking living conditions found in many Appalachian mining towns or coal camps. Describing the problem, the report stated: "If it is custom and tradition that miner families shall exist in squalor, it is time for custom and tradition to be abolished."[65] If anyone had doubts concerning the Fund's necessity, the survey report laid them to rest.[66]

Organizational work on the Fund began in earnest with the new year. Lewis had already appointed himself as the union's trustee in June of 1946.[67] The following January Capt. Norman H. Collisson, the coal mines administrator, appointed himself as the government trustee.[68] A neutral trustee still had to be found, and Lewis attempted to use this matter to establish his control over the board. Lewis sent Collisson a list of twelve nominees for the neutral position soon after he became the government's trustee. Among the persons recommended were noted progressives such as Sen. Burton K. Wheeler, and the Most Reverend Bernard J. Sheil, archbishop of Chicago. One person, however, stood out: Miss Josephine Roche.[69]

Roche, the daughter of Colorado's largest coal operator, was a graduate of both Vassar College and Columbia University. While at Columbia she met and became friends with the future secretary of labor, Frances Perkins. Immersed in an environment of social concern, Roche became a Progressive and took part in the early social work movement. While other future New Dealers such as Miss Perkins and Harry Hopkins worked with the Settlement House movement, or in labor relations, Roche became a juvenile justice officer in Denver.[70] This was in keeping with Roche's research interests, which focused on the causes of delinquency among immigrant girls.[71]

Roche's focus changed when she inherited control of the Rocky Mountain Fuel Company from her father in 1927. True to her liberal convictions, she became the first major coal operator west of the Mississippi to sign a UMWA contract. This established a lifelong friendship with Lewis.

With the implementation of the New Deal, Roche threw her support behind FDR and even ran for Colorado's governorship on the slogan "Roche and Roosevelt" in 1934. Losing the Democratic primary, she was then appointed as assistant secretary of the Treasury. Although she coauthored the Social Security Act, health reform was her primary niche within the New Deal administration.[72] The United States Public Health Service (USPHS) was part of the Treasury Department at this time and was overseen by Roche's section. Because of the relationship between public health physicians and the health care reform movement, Roche herself became immersed in the issue. As a result, she was appointed to head the interdepartmental committee mentioned above and organized the 1938 health reform conference.[73]

Taking these facts into account, Roche was valuable to Lewis as a trustee for two reasons. First, she would loyally support him in all of his decisions and so give him control over the Fund's board. Second, because of her previous experience, Roche was familiar with health care delivery and knew people who could make a health program work. Unfortunately for Lewis, his initial effort to place Roche on the Fund's board was rebuffed when Collisson appointed New York businessman Thomas Murray to fill the post.[74] As for Roche, she joined the Fund's staff in December 1947 as assistant director. From there she was eventually promoted to director and finally to neutral trustee. [75]

The trustees held their first official meeting on April 9, 1947. Thomas Murray was elected as the board's chairman at this meeting, and the Fund's assets, amounting to $18 million, were formally transferred from Navy Paymaster Gen. Walter Burk.[76] The only other item the board addressed at the meeting was the creation of a $1,000 death benefit for miners' widows, retroactive to June 1, 1946.[77] While assistance for widows was a fine gesture, the board had other more important matters to settle. An application procedure had to be worked out, as well as the question of eligibility and what benefits to provide. Eligibility was addressed first and would be based upon whether the applicant was a member of the union in good standing. Medical and death benefits aside, the Fund would aid approved applicants whose problems came under headings ranging from permanent to temporary disability.[78] These payments were to be handled by the Fund's distress benefit division that had been organized by Percy Tetlow.

An army major with longstanding ties to the union, Tetlow was responsible for processing all distress claims coming to the Fund. To expedite processing, he allowed the union's local and district offices to act as clearinghouses for all applications.[79] Godfry P. Schmidt, Murray's lawyer and personal advisor, endorsed the idea as a way to clear the backlog of assistance requests.[80] Tetlow's system became the standard method of applying for all Fund benefits, including health care and hospitalization. It required that a client's application bear the signature of an officer of the local union and the union's seal. In disability cases a certified copy of the applicant's medical record or a statement from his doctor also had to be included.[81] This final requirement was dropped some time later.

The decision to use the union's bureaucracy for processing claims was a creative solution to a difficult problem. However, this method had a major flaw: it created the appearance that the Fund and the UMWA were a single organization. The appearance was reinforced by the fact that many people on the Fund's staff had originally worked for the union. The most influential person of this group was William L. P. Burke, the Fund's general counsel.[82] Prior to his joining the Fund, Burke had served in the UMWA's legal department.[83] Where Lewis had failed to co-opt the 1946 Fund's board, he now had considerable influence over the program's administration.

As 1947 opened, Lewis's fortunes appeared to be reaching new heights. The Fund was a reality and the northern coal operators had reconciled themselves to it for the moment. [84] Moreover, while the 1946 Fund was still being organized, Lewis negotiated a new one-year contract for the bituminous industry. The agreement increased coal royalties from five to ten cents a ton and created the Fund's pension system.[85] While the 1947 contract was certainly a victory, its creation presented certain problems—not the least of which was writing it in conformity with the Taft-Hartley Act.

Taft-Hartley came out of the antilabor atmosphere that pervaded Washington immediately after the 1946 elections. Myriad legislation was introduced by Republicans seeking to limit organized labor's influence. Several of these bills would have outlawed all union-sponsored welfare programs. The beliefs underlying these proposals were incorporated into Taft-Hartley, especially the need to prevent labor racketeering. Taft-Hartley addressed this concern by demanding the joint administration of all union welfare programs by labor and management.[86] Lewis railed against the requirement when he testified before the Senate Committee on Labor and Public Welfare on March 7, 1947. He characterized Taft-Hartley as a union busting-measure based upon false notions concerning collective bargaining. He also informed the committee that the UMWA recognized the rights of coal operators to manage their property, including their prerogative to hire and fire workers. Moreover, he ridiculed union racketeering as a popular misconception without basis in fact.[87] Lewis's pleading fell on deaf ears, and the act passed over President Truman's veto.

Taft-Hartley notwithstanding, Lewis resented any encumbrance on his authority and went to great lengths to avoid "outside interference." This was illustrated by his decision to maintain the 1946 and 1947 Funds as separate legal entities. While Lewis was negotiating the 1947 contract, Captain Collisson was concluding his work as a Fund trustee. Collisson was anxious to leave government service, especially since the War Labor Disputes Act was set to expire on June 30. After his resignation, he would be replaced by the newly elected industry trustee.[88] The only business involving Collisson was a formal audit of the Fund and his court application to be relieved of his responsibilities. But, a legal technicality interfered with his plans.

According to Burke, who handled Collisson's request, the captain could resign if the board unanimously petitioned the court to allow the arrangement.[89] Burke cautioned that if the trustees petitioned the court, they could end up getting more than they expected. Owing to the nature of estate and trust law, the 1946 and 1947 Funds were two distinct legal entities. Under these circumstances, Collisson's resignation and the appointment of the new trustee in his place constituted a merger of the two trusts. The newly merged Fund would come under the court's jurisdiction and direction as a ward.[90] Burke added that Chancery courts have extensive discretionary power relating to charitable trusts, and that it was impossible to predict just what the court might do in this case.[91] Burke ended his warning by citing a precedent of similar intervention in the case of *Smithson* vs. *Callahan*.[92] For Lewis, such a possibility had to be avoided. Therefore, the 1946 and 1947 Funds remained separate, each with its own board of trustees.

Despite this maneuvering, the only major change was the election of the new industry trustee. Under the contract, coal operators voted for their representative, with each company having a number of votes proportionate to its output. The man chosen was Ezra Van Horn, a fellow coal operator.[93] From the beginning Van Horn's relationship with Lewis was tense. This was not surprising.

According to author Ivana Krajcinovic, Van Horn was told by his colleagues to obstruct the Fund's operation in any way possible.[94] This he tried to do with great élan. Soon after joining the board, Van Horn expressed dissatisfaction over the Fund's organization. He also complained that he was being prevented from exercising the powers of his office.[95]

As chairman of the 1947 Fund's trustee board, Lewis was in a position to make Van Horn extremely uncomfortable and was prepared to retaliate in kind. Lewis denied or delayed any and all information to which Van Horn was entitled as industry trustee.[96] Just how far Lewis would take this tactic is seen in a refusal he made to Van Horn's request for a minor piece of data: "In further consideration of Mr. Van Horn's request . . . I have this to say: As one trustee I object to the furnishing of this information to Mr. Van Horn until his request has been considered in a meeting of the trustees and satisfactory showing has been made by Mr. Van Horn to justify his personal use of this material."[97] This situation did not improve after Miss Roche became the Fund's director in 1948. Roche cooperated with Lewis through her office to undermine Van Horn.[98] He reacted bitterly to such treatment and came close to accusing Lewis of dishonesty.[99]

Although Van Horn's complaints in these instances were justified, his overall behavior gave Lewis and Roche more than adequate cause to be disgusted with him. One glaring example of Van Horn's poor conduct were his comments concerning activation of the Fund's medical program in the summer of 1949. Van Horn protested in a letter to Lewis that the Fund spent large sums of money for health care without the board's approval.[100] Roche read the letter and reacted angrily, since she had presented a detailed progress report on the medical program at a previous trustee meeting. The report outlined the program's organization under the Fund's new executive medical officer, Dr. Warren F. Draper, and the favorable reception it received from the medical community. The minutes of the meeting also showed that after the report was presented, the trustees discussed it and were impressed with its contents. The trustees then congratulated Dr. Draper for his work. Going further, Roche added that both her report and the medical program were topics of conversation at subsequent trustee meetings.[101]

While these differences did hamper the Fund's smooth operation, they paled in comparison to the confrontation between Lewis and Van Horn over activation of the Fund's pension program. When the 1947 Fund's board held its first meeting in July of that year, Lewis was elected chairman and a depository was selected.[102] The board did not meet again until September, when it appointed Dr. Royd R. Sayers as the first director of the Fund's medical program and Mr. Thomas Ryan as comptroller.[103] After making these appointments, the board turned to the question of activating the pension system.

The 1947 contract creating the pension program contained two major stipulations. First, the trustees had to agree on a detailed written plan as to how the pensions would be paid. Second, the plan had to be firmly grounded on accepted actuarial computations.[104] Lewis allowed Van Horn to choose the actuary, possibly as a gesture of good faith. As part of the task, Van Horn asked Lewis to give him a general outline of the program. Lewis responded that he wanted to provide a $100-a-month pension to all members of the UMWA who had retired at age sixty or over and who had a record of twenty years' service in the mines. After further discussion, the trustees agreed that the proposal was a fair standard and that it would be used as a basis for the study.[105]

Despite the appearance of consensus, there were major differences of opinion. While the board of trustees agreed to expedite the choice of an actuary, Van Horn delayed making his selection as long as possible. Lewis did not lose his patience, but the trustees were pressed to take action by Murray's legal advisor, Godfrey P. Schmidt. In Schmidt's opinion, the trustees could begin investing the Fund's holdings without an actuarial study because the Taft-Hartley Act did not apply in this case.[106] The union's legal staff disagreed with Schmidt's analysis and advised that nothing should be done with the Fund's money until after the study had been completed.[107]

Not long after the board considered Schmidt's suggestion, Van Horn chose an actuarial firm: Towers-Perrin, Forster & Crosby, based in Philadelphia.[108] Lewis approved the choice, and in late September the company began working on its study.[109] The results of these efforts were contained in two reports: a preliminary assessment presented in November 1947 and a final version given in March 1948.[110]

From Lewis's perspective, neither assessment was acceptable. The preliminary report stated that the Fund could not finance Lewis's proposal and remain solvent. It added that even if Lewis's plan was feasible, other factors made it inadvisable.[111] According to the firm's calculations, a total of 400,000 miners were eligible for benefits, with the majority of these men aged forty years and over.[112] Although these men composed the bituminous industry's active workforce, the figure did not include the large number of inactive or retired miners who could also be eligible for pension benefits.[113] The actuaries also claimed that the statistics indicated a low future mortality rate among working miners and a low employee turnover rate.[114] Any interest income from the Fund's investments would be negligible, and administrative costs represented a major hidden expense.[115]

In addition to these costs, the report stated that there would be a high rate of retirement among working miners. Although the study did not assert that every miner who reached age sixty might retire immediately, it suggested that the majority would. By providing a $100-a-month pension over and above Social Security, the Fund offered every miner a strong incentive to retire as soon as possible.[116] Estimating future costs to the Fund if the Lewis plan was accepted, the firm claimed the pension cost would be $91 million per year by 1952 and $138 million per year by 1972.[117] Even if the retirement age was raised to seventy, pension costs would have climbed to $57 million a year by 1962. These amounts were unacceptable since the firm projected that the Fund's annual income would never exceed $50 million, and in future years it could be substantially less.[118]

After outlining the objections, the firm offered its recommendations. First, the retirement age had to be raised to sixty-five. Second, the maximum monthly payment should be set at $50, and possibly at a lower figure when a beneficiary began collecting Social Security, so that the sum of both did not exceed $100 a month.[119] This plan would be less expensive and within the range of feasibility.

Aside from the financial aspect, the firm argued that a $100-a-month pension was undesirable from the position of social policy. Even the most liberal pension systems did not exceed 50 percent of a recipient's base salary. If the Lewis plan was implemented, miners would receive a total benefit from the pension and Social Security amounting to 70 or 80 percent of their former income. This was too generous.[120] In its summation, the preliminary study suggested the creation of an actuarial reserve. To achieve this goal, the firm recommended that upon the pension's activation, the initial retirement age be set at seventy and lowered gradually over the course of five to ten years to sixty-five.[121]

In its second study, the firm listed various organizational/payment methods the Fund could use. The two most important were the disbursement, or "pay-as-you-go," and the actuarial reserve systems. Pay-as-you-go involved distributing the Fund's monies as needed without maintaining an untouchable reserve of investments earning income.[122] The firm claimed that no long-range pension program could successfully be financed on such a basis.[123] With this, the report argued strenuously for the creation of an actuarial reserve accumulated over a number of years.[124]

The actuaries made a strong case, but their reasoning was flawed by skewed statistical references and assumptions. To begin, their assertions concerning the inadvisability of offering a $100-a-month pension on the basis of social precedent was similar to the thinking behind the British poor law and workhouses. Their claims that the pension, plus Social Security, would provide 70 to 80 percent of a miner's preretirement income was highly questionable. In 1947, the average monthly wage in the mining industry was $239.56 (based on a weekly average of $59.84).[125] For this same time, a high-end Social Security payment ran between $35 and $40 a month.[126] Taking these figures into account, Social Security plus the $100-a-month pension Lewis sought was, under the best of circumstances, closer to 57 percent of the average monthly salary given above. Moreover, no evidence existed to substantiate the assertion that most eligible miners would quickly retire under the Lewis plan.

Finally, the firm based its estimation of miner mortality for both of the reports upon the "Life Table for White Males in the United States, 1939–

1941."[127] Created by the U.S. census, the table presented average mortality levels of all white males. No mortality statistics specific to the coal industry were used. The survival rates the studies presented were grossly inflated as a result and did not reflect reality.

Showing his disappointment, Lewis disputed the preliminary findings. He refused to consider any funding method other than pay-as-you-go and displayed considerable hostility to the suggestion of an actuarial reserve.[128] His attitude was understandable since pay-as-you-go afforded the least restriction on trustee authority. After the actuaries presented their findings at the fourth trustee meeting, Lewis offered his pension plan for the board's adoption. Disregarding the firm's objections, he told the board the report was wrong and should be ignored. However, Murray opposed this idea, saying the trustees were obligated not to adopt an unsound plan.[129] Finding himself outvoted, Lewis retreated by asking the trustees to authorize another report, this one done by the Social Security Administration.[130] Unfortunately for Lewis, this second study endorsed the firm's conclusions.[131]

Shaken and desperate, Lewis now changed tactics. Ignoring all of the reports, he opened the trustee meetings with William L. P. Burke presenting the original pension resolution and then reminding the board of its obligation under the 1947 contract to adopt some sort of a plan.[132] Rather than convincing the other trustees to act, this tactic only antagonized them and created a stalemate.[133]

With the calendar year coming to an end, Murray intervened at the last minute by offering a compromise.[134] His program would set aside $20 million for pensions and place retired miners into two classes. The first group consisted of men sixty years old and over who had twenty years' service in the mines and had not retired prior to July 1, 1947. The second class contained those who met the first three qualifications, but who had retired between July 1, 1942, and July 1, 1947. All miners in the first class would receive a $100-a-month pension automatically. Men in the second class would be considered if, and only if, sufficient funds existed to meet the needs of the first class.

After that, the program became increasingly complex. Miners in the second class would be placed in ascending order on the basis of pension points. Each man in this class received two pension points for each year of age over sixty and one point for each year in a senior mining position. But, one point would be deducted for each year a miner had been retired prior to July 1, 1947.[135] After he presented his plan, Murray asked the other trustees not to make any rash decisions, but to take their time and study the proposal. Van Horn and Lewis, however, rejected the plan out of hand. There is no record of their objections, but they probably considered the plan too cumbersome.[136] Moreover, neither man was likely to compromise.

As the new year opened, the Lewis/Van Horn stalemate continued. Disgusted with the situation, Murray abruptly resigned his trusteeship, citing his failure to bring the board together.[137] Activation of the 1947 Fund now seemed farther away than ever. A replacement for Murray had to be chosen before anything else could be done, and the method for choosing a new impartial trustee required that Van Horn and Lewis agree on a candidate.[138] Since their views differed so widely, the likelihood of their agreeing to a new board member looked impossible. For the moment Van Horn appeared the victor. He had managed to fight an effective rear-guard action. But, while Lewis may have been frustrated by Van Horn in the short term, Lewis was further ahead in realizing his goals than he had been a year earlier. He had come to this point through a determined persistence and was not about to retreat the field with the culmination of goals so clearly in sight. Despite Van Horn's obstructionism, Lewis had many resources at his disposal and would soon begin using them to realize his vision.

Chapter 2
The Struggle for Control

Although Lewis had asked Van Horn to present a nominee list in order to find a replacement, Lewis actually attempted to break the stalemate by taking his case to the nation's two largest coal operators.[1] The first was United States Steel chairman Benjamin Fairless, who controlled the U.S. Captive Mine Group. The second was George Humphrey of Pittsburgh Consolidated Coal.[2] These men could speak for the industry if they wanted and so force Van Horn to back down. Unfortunately for Lewis, both men rebuffed his overture.[3]

Undaunted, Lewis sent a circular letter to all operators who had signed the 1947 contract. In it, Lewis hinted that unless something was done to bring Van Horn to terms, the union would take independent action to enforce the contract. Here again Lewis's efforts to bypass Van Horn failed, this time in the form of a nonresponse. Lewis waited for two months for a response after sending the letter and received none.[4] With his options running out, Lewis moved cautiously to avoid the appearance of the UMWA violating the contract. A strike was becoming a real possibility.

To meet the challenge, he sent a memo to all district and local union offices informing the membership about his conflict with Van Horn.[5] While avoiding the word "strike," the notice instructed all union members to discuss the issue and then decide on possible action. This allowed Lewis to deny later that he had called the union's membership out of the mines.[6] The notice had not been a formal strike call, but it had the same effect. The miners walked off their jobs three days after it was sent, and coal production fell by 1.25 million tons a day.[7]

Response to Lewis's action was swift. President Truman created a special commission to investigate the problem five days after the walkout started.[8] When the commission called Lewis, he refused to appear. Van Horn reacted by damning Lewis to the commission, saying that problems with activating the pension were due to union intransigence. He also complained about Lewis's failure to return messages, call a trustee meeting, or decide on a new impartial trustee.[9] Topping off the list, he accused Lewis of attempting to break the Taft-Hartley Act by forcing the creation of a pension plan that was unsound and thereby illegal.[10]

While Van Horn ranted, Lewis finally received some notice from the industry's leadership. The major operators reiterated Van Horn's claims, albeit without his belligerence. They insisted that they had fulfilled the 1947 contract's letter and spirit and pointed to their continuing royalty payments as evidence of good faith.[11] They concluded by stating that they were willing to talk once the miners went back to work.[12] Lewis ignored the suggestion.

As the walkout continued into April, the federal government finally took action to deal with the problem. At the government's request, the Federal District Court of Washington issued an injunction ordering an end to the strike.[13] While the union's lawyers fought this demand, Rep. Joseph Martin, Speaker of the House, intervened.[14]

As a major figure in the Republican party, Martin was a prime candidate for the 1948 presidential nomination. Anxious for the attention that being peacemaker would bring, Martin arranged a meeting with Lewis and Van Horn. At this meeting, Martin suggested a neutral trustee: Sen. H. Styles Bridges of New Hampshire.[15] The choice was interesting. Bridges stood out as a minor McCarthyist because of a number of his earlier statements.[16] Yet, his name had been included on the original nominee list Lewis presented to Captain Collisson during the organization of the 1946 Fund's board.[17] Whatever his other political views were, Bridges was not hostile to organized labor. Van Horn did not object to Bridges, and so the senator took over as the Fund's neutral trustee.

The new board met the day after the senator's appointment. Van Horn opened the meeting by restating his objections to the Lewis plan, and Bridges questioned the two trustees about the board's options. Overwhelmed, Bridges requested a day's recess so he could study the situation and make a decision.[18] The senator crafted a compromise resolution in that time, which he presented the following day. All union miners who had worked twenty years in the industry and had retired at age sixty-two would receive a $100-a-month pension. Eligibility would be limited to those miners who were working when the Krug-Lewis agreement was signed.[19]

To legitimize the plan, Bridges declared that the nation's security was at stake. It would be unconscionable to place the country in jeopardy by demanding a narrow reading of a labor contract.[20] Bridges added that he would not attempt to settle the actuarial issue, but would commission another study. Because the trustees were entitled to change their position on the pension settlement if necessary, it was better to take some risks now than endanger the country.[21]

Bridges was probably influenced by an actuarial study which Lewis had presented the day before.[22] The study's author was Murray W. Latimer. A graduate of Harvard Business School, Latimer came to Washington during the 1930s to work for the Bureau of Labor Statistics. He had done a massive study of private social insurance arrangements while in this position, as well as serving as chairman of the First and Second Railroad Retirement Boards.[23] In addition, Latimer authored a study concerning the feasibility of a guaranteed national wage near the close of World War II. After the war's end, he left the government and went to work in the labor movement, like a number of former New Dealers. He eventually joined the United Steel Workers' benefit staff and was responsible for negotiating the nation's first national Blue Cross contract. Latimer remained with the USW until the 1970s.[24]

In the study Lewis commissioned, Latimer summarized the Towers report and then systematically refuted each of its major claims. First, he said that Towers had given an inflated figure for the total number of working miners. Latimer estimated there were 328,000 men in the mines, not 400,000.[25] Second, while the age distribution Towers presented was correct, Latimer said it had been distorted by forces outside the industry. The Philadelphia actuaries had failed to take into account that the median age of miners had risen because of the war. As younger men left the mines for military service, older men, many of whom had never worked in the mines before, filled their places. These men would soon leave the mines for other jobs, and the vast majority of them had not spent twenty years in the industry.[26]

Third, Latimer ridiculed Towers's statistical basis for miner mortality as too wide an average. According to his information, the accident and related death rate in the coal industry for 1937–39 was 248 percent larger than the accepted rate for all other industrial occupations. This figure was determined by the Metropolitan Life Insurance Company.[27] In addition to the high mortality rate, the industry was also marked by a high job turnover rate.[28]

Fourth, Latimer disagreed that most miners would retire as soon as they were eligible. He cited his experience with the railroad retirement system to prove the point. The statistics showed that most men continued working long after they were able to take their retirement.[29] The only apparent explanation was that most men preferred ongoing employment for more money, rather than retiring for less. Latimer concluded his study by saying that no foolproof insurance system existed. Indeed, pension and insurance programs could spend years gathering statistical evidence and still be mistaken in their predictions. The only way a pension program could be tested as far as its costs were concerned was through a provisional activation for a few years.[30]

This was probably what Bridges had in mind when he presented his resolution. Lewis supported it as an appropriate compromise. It provided a cutoff date for eligibility and raised the minimum retirement age by two years. Van Horn opposed the resolution, but it passed by a vote of two to one. However, the industry trustee refused to let the matter rest. He complained that the senator's plan was not substantially different from Lewis's. Further, there had not been any clear determination on what portion of the Fund's monies would be used for the pension system. He also objected that the trustees had not met the 1947 contract's stipulation for a detailed agreement to serve as the pension system's foundation.[31] Lewis ignored these comments and prepared to contact the Fund's depositories about investment strategies.[32] Shortly thereafter, Lewis and Bridges hired Josephine Roche, again over Van Horn's objection, to replace Francis Fitzgerald as the Fund's director.[33]

Infuriated, Van Horn struck back soundly. Without Lewis's knowledge, Van Horn wrote all of the Fund's depositories and instructed their officers not to honor any checks from the Fund which did not carry his signature.[34] At the same time, he filed suit with the Federal District Court of Washington, asking the court to block activation of the pension system. To ensure further that none of the Fund's monies were spent, Van Horn included a clause in his petition stipulating that Lewis and Bridges should be held personally liable for any disbursements while the suit was pending.[35]

Lewis was incensed by the maneuver and demanded that the banks honor all checks signed by Bridges and him.[36] Bridges, however, took a different stance. Frightened by the suit, the senator was not interested in testing Van Horn's resolve.[37] Lacking a united front, Lewis would have to fight Van Horn in the courts rather than calling his bluff. This was not going to be easy, since Judge Allen Goldsborough had been appointed to hear the case.[38] Although Goldsborough would probably be impartial, he nevertheless had found Lewis in contempt of court over his calling an unauthorized strike two years earlier.[39]

Van Horn's lawyers repeated to the court the same points their client raised at the trustee meetings. They added that failure to activate the pension fund was not their client's fault, but that of his fellow trustees, since Bridges's pension resolution violated Taft-Hartley and the 1947 contract.[40] The board had not accepted any of the actuarial studies as a basis for the pension, nor had it mapped out a written plan.[41] Believing that a sound actuarial study was vital to the Fund's future solvency, they charged that the 1946 Fund had been mismanaged. They claimed the trust was nearly exhausted and still owed about $14 million in unpaid bills.[42] Van Horn even offered his own interpretation of the regulation of charitable trusts. According to him, the neutral trustee only served as an umpire. Real authority rested in the hands of the interested trustees alone. Policy decisions had to be settled between the representatives of the industry and the union before the Fund could take any action.[43]

Lawyers for Lewis and Bridges argued that this final claim was a fundamental misreading of both estate and trust law and the 1947 contract. Taft-Hartley's inclusion of a neutral trusteeship implied that its framers expected conflict between labor and management and so intended trusts to be administered equally by the three trustees.[44] Edward R. Hale, who represented Bridges, added that it was not Congress's intent to thwart the administration of any welfare fund through a failure of the interested trustees to agree. The presence of a neutral trustee indicated that such stalemates were expected and should thereby be settled by the neutral member's vote.[45]

The union's lawyers also denied that the pension resolution violated any federal labor laws. They cited the Latimer report's endorsement of the original Lewis plan.[46] Lewis would have allowed all union members with twenty years' service to draw a pension, regardless of when they had retired. The lawyers reasoned that if the original scheme was prudent, then the Bridges plan was even more so, due to its limitations, and Van Horn could not truthfully claim otherwise.[47]

As a last resort, the union's counsel turned to a technicality within the Taft-Hartley Act. The law did not refer to a "union" as the agency creating a welfare fund, but an "employee representative." The lawyers declared that the term implied that the representative conferred with the rank and file and acted with its explicit consent. Because the UMWA had not consulted the membership about the Fund's establishment, the union did not act as an employee representative in this case and was not bound by the law's stipulations.[48]

Although some of these arguments had merit, they did not entirely negate Van Horn's position. While Van Horn's claims about trustee authority were questionable, his lawyers had the findings of both the Towers and the Social Security studies to cite as authorities for their contention that the Bridges plan was unsound.[49] Because of this, the situation appeared to be a stalemate, with the final outcome uncertain.

Here, Lewis may have tried to tip the scales in his favor by giving Judge Goldsborough additional evidence. While both sides were still arguing their cases, Lewis sent the judge a confidential affidavit. It presented another aspect of the controversy the lawyers had not addressed: Van Horn's obstructionism. The affidavit included all minutes of Fund trustee meetings held July 1947 and April 1948. From the record it was apparent Van Horn never intended to cooperate with his fellow trustees. Lewis also stressed that for all of Van Horn's objections he had never presented a plan of his own to the board.[50] As such, however, the affidavit and its attachments would have constituted an ex parte communication between Lewis and the judge and was thereby improper. There is no evidence to indicate the judge ever received the affidavit or read it.

Judge Goldsborough handed down his decision on June 23, 1948. He ruled in Lewis's favor, interpreting that Taft-Hartley and the 1947 contract allowed all of the trustees to administer the Fund coequally. The neutral trustee, therefore, was an equal partner and could legally cast his vote to break a tie.[51] The judge also wrote that Bridges's resolution fulfilled the contract's stipulation that the trustees agree to a written and detailed basis for the pension system prior to activation.[52] As far as the actuarial studies were concerned, Goldsborough cited his own business experience. He recalled how a senior actuary once told him that a report could be done to validate any set of beliefs, depending upon what a client wanted to hear. He concluded his ruling with this statement:

There seems to be nothing that shocks the mind at the idea that members of the United Mine Workers who have worked for 20 years under the ground, and are 62 years old, and were employed on May 29, 1946 should get a $100 a month pension. . . . it is meager. It is enough to keep them from being the objects of charity in their old age; it is just enough to give them a little dignity; it is some thing to make them able to hold their head up. The court doesn't think, gentlemen, that there is any justification in law or in sound reason for this [Van Horn's] petition, or complaint, as it should be called.[53]

Goldsborough's decision came just in time. While the case was pending, the 1947 Fund was temporarily suspended. This meant that all benefits had to be covered by the 1946 Fund, and it was nearly depleted. The 1946 Fund's board approved a plan to meet the crisis by continuing coverage only for those beneficiaries already receiving hospital care. All other benefits, and applications, would be suspended.[54] The decision came just days before the suspension notices were to be mailed.

Goldsborough's timing also favored Lewis in his talks with the coal operators. At the time when Van Horn filed his suit, Lewis initiated negotiations for a 1948 contract and demanded that producers increase their royalty payments to twenty cents a ton. The operators resisted, and Van Horn's suit placed them in a strong bargaining position.[55] The operators claimed that no one wished to deny eligible miners their benefits and that the industry accepted its responsibility to pay royalties.[56] But they added Lewis's demands were irresponsible and that some control had to be placed upon Lewis and Roche.[57] Lewis could do nothing until Goldsborough made his decision, and if he ruled for Van Horn, loss of the Fund to operator control was a real possibility. The judge's decision gave Lewis the leverage he needed to press his demands.[58] With Van Horn's suit out of the way, the operators acquiesced and signed the 1948 contract on Lewis's terms.[59]

With the controversy over, the Fund started processing applications, and by September the pension system was ready to begin operation. The first check was presented personally by Lewis at a special ceremony.[60] By early November, more than five thousand miners had already received their first pension checks. According to the Fund's statistics, the median age of these miners was sixty-six, with each having an average of thirty-seven years in the mines.[61]

Through the problems with Van Horn, and with their successes, a spirit of cooperation appeared to exist between Roche, Lewis, and Bridges. However, this amity was superficial. The difficulty involved how the senator viewed his responsibilities as a trustee. Bridges was willing to cooperate with Lewis, but not without question. The senator was determined to exercise his duties independently, always working within the letter of the law and thereby protecting himself from any liability. This created an uneasy relationship, but that relationship did not break down until the Fund went into suspension again in 1949.

Earlier, in her office memos to Lewis, Josephine Roche had expressed her dissatisfaction with Senator Bridges's behavior. Her position on issues concerning the Fund amounted to institution worship of the UMWA and reflected an infinite faith in Lewis's ability. Roche believed that the interests of the miners and those of their union were one and the same. To advance the cause of the miners, one advanced the UMWA, and to advance the union, one supported Lewis. Roche fought anyone whose point of view did not coincide with hers on these matters.

Roche first exhibited the vehemence of her beliefs by opposing the senator's effort to sponsor another actuarial study. Roche opined to Lewis that most actuaries were suspect because they disliked the pay-as-you-go system on general principle. She added that another study was unnecessary. Bridges either had to accept the original Latimer report or commission Latimer to do another based on the pension's eligibility restrictions.[62]

William L. P. Burke also advised not to do another study. Burke claimed Goldsborough's decision nullified the 1947 contract's stipulation of an actuarial basis for the pension program. The decision had the force of law, and Burke interpreted it to mean the trustees could legally use the pay-as-you-go method, and were even obligated to use it.[63] Commissioning another study would be illegal due to the expenditure of the Fund's monies for something invalidated by the law and contrary to the interests of the Fund's clients.[64]

Lewis gave no indication as to whether he agreed with this analysis or not. Even if he did, his hands were tied. Lewis wanted to lower the retirement age to sixty, and he needed the senator's support to do so. Lewis approached Bridges about the matter during a trustee meeting held in late June of 1948. Although the senator believed the request had merit, he wanted to wait and commission another study to see if the revision was feasible.[65] The senator's comments reflected the legal advice he received at the time.[66] The result was that another study had to be conducted if Lewis was to have any chance at lowering the minimum age. Like it or not, the search for a new actuary began.

At first, Roche hoped that Bridges and his lawyer, Edward R. Hale, would hire an actuary recommended by Latimer. The man was named Lipton, and his experience centered primarily on studies commissioned by union-sponsored systems. While Hale praised Lipton's work, he objected to the actuary's youth and narrow professional experience. Hale preferred an older man whose attitudes better reflected management's beliefs, and he recommended Russel B. Reagh.[67] Reagh was a member of the Board of Actuaries for the U.S. Crude

Steel Fund and regularly consulted for the U.S. Treasury.[68] Reagh also worked independently for clients like Du Pont.[69] Unlike Hale, Roche was not impressed with Reagh's qualifications, and she was especially put off by his business experience. Commenting about Reagh, Roche quipped that the last thing the Fund needed was another actuary representing the "U.S. Steel point of view."[70]

Once hired, Reagh immediately went to work and brought in an assistant named Lowell Mayberry. In the meantime, both Latimer and Roche conferred with Reagh, hoping to convince him that Latimer's projections were correct. Reagh disagreed, especially with Latimer's claim that $50 million a year was sufficient to finance a pension allowing retirement at age sixty, with no cutoff date for eligibility. Reagh believed this figure would be adequate only if the exceptions contained in the Bridges resolution were continued.[71] Reagh estimated that the maximum cost for the system that Lewis hoped to establish actually ran between $66 million and $74 million a year.[72] These figures were based on the assumption that most miners would retire once they became eligible. Latimer argued with Reagh on the point and believed he convinced Reagh this would not happen.[73]

Reagh presented his preliminary findings in November of 1948, but did not submit a final report until the following year.[74] He estimated annual pension costs would hover between $76 million to $82 million, if the retirement age was lowered to sixty.[75] To finance the system, Reagh recommended establishing a dual funding scheme: simple reliance upon the pay-as-you-go method would be a mistake. He proved his point by citing the experience of insurance society programs that went bankrupt due to sole usage of this approach.[76] However, Reagh did not recommend that pay-as-you-go be discarded entirely. Instead, he devised a plan which he called the single premium method.

According to Reagh's estimates, the Fund would have a large annual surplus during the early years of its operation. This surplus could be invested to create a reserve while the Fund's early clients were served through the pay-as-you-go plan. Eventually a sound financial basis for the Fund would be created. This would ensure the program's continued operation when payments to retired miners exceeded its income. The Fund would also be protected from bankruptcy if royalty payments declined drastically due to a depression in the industry or other problems.[77]

Reagh's report was a compromise between the divergent claims made by the Latimer and Towers studies. Contrary to what he originally believed, Reagh disputed Towers's assertion that most miners would retire once they became eligible. He also differed with both Towers and Latimer about the industry's turnover rate. He estimated that at the end of twenty years, 47.6 percent of the people who entered the mines in a given year would still be working. The Towers estimate was 87.4 percent, while Latimer's was 11.6.[78] Finally, Reagh's report did not contain Towers's contention that a $100 pension was undesirable because the sum of it and Social Security exceeded 50 percent of a miner's base salary.

Lowell Mayberry's initial report reiterated Reagh's recommendations. His premise was that exclusive use of the pay-as-you-go method was forbidden by the 1947 contract.[79] An actuarial plan was also out of the question, since such an approach was based upon computations of a person's life expectancy and projected income. The Fund's income could vary from year to year, and too many factors affected projections on miner mortality to make exact calculations.[80]

Both Reagh and Mayberry tried to be fair to all parties in the pension debate, despite their alleged conservatism. Roche, however, disparaged their findings. She charged that Reagh used the same assumptions as the Towers study, while taking a less strident tone for the sake of appearances. She further charged that Reagh's report showed all of the orthodox actuarial thinking favored by Van Horn and the operators. She also damned Reagh's study as highly speculative and complained that it ignored Latimer's input.[81]

Roche's opposition to Reagh and Mayberry went deeper than disagreeing with their findings. She suspected that Mayberry planned to force an actuarial reserve system on the trustees. Although Mayberry said the creation of an actuarial reserve was not possible, he placed great emphasis on the 1947 contract's stipulations in his report. In December of 1948 Mayberry was anxious to meet with Burke about the report. Roche suspected that Mayberry hoped to speak to Burke as one lawyer to another and convince him that an actuarial reserve was mandated by the contract, even if it was not desirable.[82] Strange as her suspicion was, Roche took it very seriously. Since neither Reagh nor Mayberry advocated the sole use of the pay-as-you-go system, Roche disbelieved everything they said, and she regarded both men with disdain.[83] Yet, for all of Roche's distrust, neither Reagh's nor Mayberry's reports were ever presented to the trustees for their consideration.

Aside from Bridges's insistence on another actuarial study, Roche was also upset by the senator's curiosity about the Fund's administrative expenses. In one instance, Bridges asked Roche for detailed information concerning large and unspecified costs listed on the financial report.[84] Incensed, Roche crafted a response which took every opportunity to make Bridges appear foolish. For example, Roche presented an itemized list to clarify office expenses which included the prices of trivial things such as air-conditioners and adding machines.[85]

The irony was that the senator's curiosity in no way reflected a suspicious attitude toward either Lewis or Roche. In fact, Bridges was impressed with Roche's accomplishments as the Fund's director. He was especially impressed with her efficiency and the spirit of élan she established with the staff.[86] From available evidence, Bridges clearly saw himself as Lewis and Roche's ally and acted accordingly. One example was the question of lowering the pension retirement age from 62 to 60, which came before the trustees in April 1949. Roche and Lewis discussed the matter a few days before the meeting in order to anticipate any problems. They believed Bridges would support the change but feared he would oppose retroactive payments to miners who had retired earlier.[87] Bridges, however, made no such objection and lavished praise on the program.[88]

Bridges was even more supportive of Roche a few months later when the Senate Committee on Banking and Currency investigated the Fund's operations. Roche was called to testify and Bridges decided to find out the reason behind the committee's sudden interest. When Bridges discussed the investigation with the committee's chair, Sen. John Roberston, Roberston protested that the committee was only examining the UMWA's position within the coal industry. Bridges was not convinced, and believed that Roberston had been coached on certain points. Bridges suspected that the investigation was in retaliation by the coal operators against Lewis for his declaration of a three-day work week.[89]

Lewis did this unilaterally on July 5, 1949, in response to a sudden drop in coal demand.[90] Although statistics indicated later that the second great coal boom was over, the problem at the time appeared to be a cyclical readjustment.[91] Operators sought to cut wage and other costs to cope with the situation, and contract negotiations for a 1949 agreement bogged down as a result. Lewis responded by creating the three-day week rather than calling a strike.[92] This would express the union's dissatisfaction while spreading out the available work.

In an attempt to head off any problems with the committee, Bridges met with Roberston and tried to convince him to abandon any investigation of the Fund. Bridges stressed the program's humanitarian goals and that it prevented the miners from seeking government help. Roberston refused to be persuaded, and alleged the program was running on a deficit.[93] Since Bridges could not dissuade Robertson, he decided to assist Roche in preparing her testimony. Not only did Bridges advise her on what to say before the committee, he added that he would make a statement on her behalf, if necessary, before she testified.[94] As a result of these precautions, Roche made a good impression when she appeared, even to the point where Van Horn was pleased with her performance.[95]

While problems with the government were avoided, Lewis's conflict with the coal operators became more acute during the spring and summer of 1949. This would eventually disrupt the Fund's operation as all-out war broke out between the two sides. The first skirmish concerned the Fund's audit. All union welfare programs had to be audited once a year, as mandated by Taft-Hartley. The Fund's initial audit had been started in 1948 by the accounting firm of Haskins & Sells, but was never completed. The firm had asked for permission to review the union's contracts with individual coal companies as part of its procedure. Roche and Lewis decided the request was inappropriate and refused.[96] After finishing with Haskins & Sells, Lewis and Roche hired Wayne Kendrick, Inc., a Washington-based accounting firm, to conduct a new study. The study was completed in April 1949.

Joseph Moody of the Southern Coal Producers Association (SCPA), in the meantime, publicly accused Lewis of never having commissioned such a study and thereby breaking the law. Lewis answered the charge by inviting Moody and his associates to a special meeting, where he presented them with a copy of the 1949 report. After reading it, Moody agreed that everything appeared to be in order.[97]

The meeting was a minor victory for Lewis, especially since it thwarted the SCPA's accusations of impropriety. But other problems began to appear which could not be dispatched so easily. Starting in the late summer of 1949, the Fund's trustee board was racked by a number of simultaneous conflicts which culminated in the Fund's suspension. Among these were the following: the lack of a new contract, Van Horn's abrupt resignation from the board, various lawsuits, and the breakdown of cooperation between Bridges and Lewis. The most important was Lewis's failure to win a new contract.

Although the 1948 agreement expired on July 1, 1949, the Fund continued working, since many of the signatory coal operators continued paying their royalties. In addition, the operators agreed to an extension of the old agreement until a new contract could be ironed out. However, they protested the three-day week, asserting it was a violation of the existing contract. The operators also reminded Lewis that they could legitimately end their payments at any time and hinted they would hold the Fund hostage in the negotiations.

For its part, the SCPA took more drastic action by ending all royalty payments on June 30.[98] Melvyn Dubofsky and Warren Van Tine assert in their biography of Lewis that the SCPA's action placed the Fund's programs in jeopardy. This is not quite true. The Fund could have continued operating, but Van Horn insisted that no monies collected after July 1 could be legitimately used.[99] Van Horn was correct from a legal standpoint, and a danger existed that if any of the Fund's assets were unlawfully disbursed, the trustees would be personally liable. The result was that the board voted on September 16, 1949, to suspend all Fund activities until a new contract was concluded. The only clients who would continue receiving treatment were emergency medical cases.[100]

It was at this meeting that Roche said things which brought her into conflict not only with Van Horn, but with Bridges as well. Roche stated in the director's report that the Fund still had certain unpaid bills as of August 31. She hastened to add that this was not a problem since a backlog of cases always existed from month to month.[101]

Upset, Van Horn sent Roche a threatening letter complaining that this information never appeared in any of the monthly financial statements. He also quoted Roche's testimony before the Senate Committee on Banking and Currency, where she said: "the Fund had no unpaid obligations, bills are paid currently."[102] These two positions were contradictory, and he demanded an immediate explanation, along with the figures for the Fund's medical and pension balances, which he had been denied earlier. Van Horn concluded by hinting that if he was not given a satisfactory answer, he would join a suit that had been filed against the Fund by a miner named George Livengood. Livengood claimed that be had been unjustly denied Fund benefits.[103] This action was eventually dismissed when the Fund proved Livengood falsified his application.[104]

Bridges also contacted Roche demanding an explanation about the unpaid bills.[105] Roche did not respond immediately, but eventually sent a memo to both men offering clarification. According to Roche, the trustees had always been told that the monthly financial reports contained estimates of payments, since it was impossible to determine the Fund's exact costs from month to month.[106] This must have satisfied Bridges and Van Horn, since neither raised the issue again.

However, the problem with the financial reports was one aspect of a growing concern over the Fund's solvency, which arose in the later half of 1949. Bridges was the first to express concern maintaining that spending was too high for emergency cases. True to form, the senator was especially fearful about any personal liability if the Fund was mismanaged. This concern was evident in a series of resolutions he proposed which sought to suspend all Fund payments. These resolutions were never considered, since the senator was confined to his home with a severe illness when they were presented.[107]

Opposed to what the senator was attempting, Lewis used Bridges's absence as a pretext to delay action.[108] While Lewis engaged in this obstructionism, Bridges received no help from Van Horn. Still angry over Bridges's earlier cooperation with Lewis, Van Horn now adopted a vindictive posture. Van Horn wrote to Bridges and lectured the senator at length that, because he had ignored earlier protests about how the Fund was being managed, he could now look elsewhere for assistance.[109]

Bridges resented being lectured and protested that he had done everything possible to see to the prudent operation of the Fund.[110] His counterarguments were useless. Van Horn harbored a deep-seated animosity for Lewis, as well as frustration over his loss on the pension issue. Believing he had been victimized by Lewis, Bridges, and Roche, he now displayed the great depth of his frustration when he wrote Lewis concerning the Fund's audit for 1949.

Van Horn wanted the report to present a month-by-month list of the monies collected by the Fund, including all sums paid by coal companies who signed the union's contract. Following this, he wanted a complete list of all of the Fund's employees, their salaries, as well as a list of all beneficiaries, their addresses, the sums paid to them, and the nature of the payments.[111] Not only were these demands impracticable, they were inappropriate. They violated the privacy of everyone involved.

As a result, the final report for the fiscal year of July 1, 1948, to June 30, 1949, contained none of the information Van Horn demanded. It simply listed the Fund's total income and expenses. In addition, the auditors tested and verified the Fund's administrative procedures for collecting delinquent royalty payments, the cash-receipt system, and other administrative functions. The report concluded that the Fund was solvent and that all of its financial and administrative procedures were sound.[112] Van Horn was livid over the report when he received it. He called it wholly inadequate, saying it amounted to nothing more than a balance sheet. Deeming the report useless, he hired a group of accountants to conduct his own audit.[113] To do such a study, however, he needed access to the Fund's financial records, a privilege which Lewis and Bridges refused to grant. Although Bridges had broken with Lewis, he agreed that it would be wrong to turn the Fund's records over to people that the Fund had not hired. Plus, he did not think another study was necessary.[114]

Sadly, Van Horn's demands on this matter amounted to nothing more than petulance. While making this fuss over the audit in late October 1949, Van Horn had secretly resigned his trusteeship in September.[115] Although the record does not provide Van Horn's specific motive for doing this, it is reasonable to assume that he hoped to leave Lewis in an awkward position now that the Fund was once again in disarray. Keeping his decision from Lewis and Bridges, Van Horn continued in his position until November 3, when the news was released that Judge Charles I. Dawson had been selected by the operators as a replacement.[116]

A former federal district court judge for western Kentucky, Dawson had been appointed to the federal bench by President Coolidge in 1925. Dawson resigned his judgeship after serving in the post for ten years and became general counsel for the Harlan County Kentucky Coal Operators' Association.[117] This group had distinguished itself by its vehement opposition to unionization during the Great Depression. From 1930 to 1938, these operators waged an all-out war against the UMWA that displayed some of the ugliest labor violence of the decade. The situation became so bad in Harlan County that conditions there were finally investigated by the Senate Committee on Civil Liberties, chaired by Robert LaFollette Jr.[118]

Although Lewis disputed the legitimacy of Dawson's appointment, he did allow the judge to attend the next scheduled trustee meeting. At this meeting, Dawson voted with Bridges to suspend all Fund payments.[119] The judge then sent a telegram to Roche informing her of the decision, adding: "I shall consider any disregard in violation of that resolution [to suspend all payments] as an act of insubordination to the authority of the trustees and of subservience to the Chairman, and I shall move for the immediate removal and discharge of any employee or officer of the Fund so offending."[120] This message amounted to Dawson throwing down the gauntlet. Lewis responded by withholding recognition of Dawson's appointment.[121] Retaliating in kind, Dawson filed suit to compel his being seated on the board.

Dawson's argument was simple: Van Horn could resign at any time, provided the selection of a replacement was carried out in strict conformity with the provisions of the 1947 and 1948 contracts.[122] The union's lawyers countered that a trustee could not resign whenever he wanted. A letter of resignation alone was not enough. By law, a trustee could legitimately resign in only one of three ways. He could do so by court order, by a formal resignation in accordance with the terms of the trust, or by gaining the consent of all the trust's beneficiaries.[123]

Gaining the consent of all the trust's beneficiaries in this case was out of the question. A formal resignation in accordance with the terms of the trust could not be done either. The contract, which specified the terms of the trust in this case, did not include any procedures for a trustee's resignation. The union's lawyers concluded that Van Horn's only option was to receive permission to resign from the courts, which he failed to do.[124]

By itself, the union's position was weak since Murray had been allowed to resign without court permission. To prevent Van Horn's use of this precedent, the union argued that he continued to play an active role as a trustee after his resignation, rather than behaving as a caretaker.[125] Van Horn's cross-claim in the Livengood case was cited as evidence in support of this contention. He joined in Livengood's case against the Fund's administration by filing the claim, and could only have done so as a fully empowered trustee.[126]

As the Dawson case unfolded, the Fund's situation worsened. Angry over Lewis's disregard of his concerns, Bridges refused to attend any more trustee meetings unless Dawson was seated.[127] Worse, the *Indianapolis Times,* a member of the Scripps-Howard syndicate, published an investigative story on the Fund that made specific charges of mismanagement.[128] It appeared as if this mess was unsolvable and would continue well into the new year as 1949 came to a close. But, Lewis had a ray of hope. While the various controversies played out in the courts and press, he quietly negotiated a new contract with Kentucky's "truck" mine operators. The agreement covered a total coal production of only two million tons, as opposed to the hundreds of millions covered by the national contract; but it gave Lewis a start toward gaining control of the Fund and ending his legal problems. Aside from raising wages, and the prevailing royalty, the contract listed Roche as the neutral trustee and appointed an entirely new person to represent the industry.[129] If a new national contract could be negotiated along these lines, Dawson's case would be rendered moot.

With the Kentucky agreement in hand, Lewis focused on winning the same concessions from the major operators. Lewis's principle adversary here was George Love, who spoke for both the Northern Coal Operators' Association and the U.S. Captive Mine Group. In November, a long steel strike was settled, which prompted Love to make an offer of serious negotiations with the UMWA. Lewis ignored the offer, however, because the steel workers' contract was not as generous as the National Bituminous Coal Wage Agreement of 1948.[130]

Love and his associates attempted to pressure Lewis by filing unfair labor practice charges with the National Labor Relations Board. This touched off a number of small strikes that eventually mushroomed into a national walkout. Lewis claimed the strike was unauthorized and was able to show he had attempted to end it.[131] Nevertheless, the strike forced the two sides together. President Truman became impatient with what he saw as the parties' criminal disregard for the public welfare by all parties involved. He had decided to seize the mines once again to break the deadlock, but in a manner hostile to both the union and the operators. Facing an outcome neither side wanted, Lewis met with Love on March 3. At this meeting, the two men crafted an arrangement that became the basis of the National Bituminous Wage Agreement of 1950, two days before the planned seizure.[132]

Using the Kentucky agreement as a model, the new contract increased royalties to thirty cents a ton and gave Lewis control of the board by appointing Roche neutral trustee.[133] In return, Lewis agreed not to oppose increased mechanization of the mining industry.[134] This did not appear to be a major concession at the time, since Lewis saw mechanization as one method to rationalize coal production and decrease the number of working miners.[135]

Another breakthrough came in July of 1950 with the creation of the Bituminous Coal Operators' Association (BCOA). This organization spoke for both the northern operators and the captive mines, whose combined output represented half of all coal tonnage produced in the United States.[136] Acting as one, they were in a position to set the standard for the industry relative to wages and coal prices. Lewis had achieved his long-sought goal: instead of dealing with myriad operator associations, he would now only deal with one. The UMWA would be the sole representative of labor. In this way, the industry could be managed in a truly corporate fashion. The union and the major coal companies in the BCOA ceased to be true adversaries and entered into a quasi-cooperative/collusive arrangement.

Although this was seen as a major achievement, not everyone was happy about it. The SCPA accused Love and the northern operators of betrayal.[137] However, the SCPA could do little more than complain. The agreement was a reality, with Lewis the apparent winner. A three-way social contract was forged, with its contradictions present, if not apparent. First, its legality was questionable. Josephine Roche was

hardly a neutral party. Second, the belief that the union and the major coal operators could work together, having more interests in common than not, was dubious
at best. Yet the fact remains that this arrangement gave Lewis, Roche, and the
Fund's staff the freedom to make the program work. As one retired staff member
recalled, Lewis's attitude was summed up by this statement: "Tell me what you
need, and I will pay for it."[138] The staff never had to worry about any interference
and was able to experiment in areas of social policy and industrial benefits.

Unfortunately, while the Fund became a leader in these areas, it was constantly bedeviled by the coal industry's decline after 1948. There were long-
term consequences to the 1950 agreement which no one foresaw, such as the
wholesale layoffs arising from mine mechanization. Finally, the manner in which
Lewis and Roche implemented decisions concerning those problems, while
understandable, eventually hurt the union and the Fund by diminishing both in
the eyes of the miners.

Chapter 3

Retreat and Advance: The Thirty-Year Rule and the Creation of the Miners' Hospitals

Although the National Bituminous Coal Wage Agreement of 1950 was only to be effective until 1952, it served as the base agreement between the UMWA and the BCOA for the next twenty-two years. During that time, negotiations were simply a matter of extending the contract and revising its relevant portions. Under the terms of the National Bituminous Coal Wage Agreement of 1950, the Fund was declared an irrevocable trust, which was an important distinction not found in earlier contracts.[1] Under those previous contracts, the Fund's life was not guaranteed beyond any one agreement. Conceivably, if the Fund became too much of a burden, the operators had the option of revoking it. With the 1950 accord, the Fund's continuation was assured, leaving the royalty as the only matter for discussion. As an added bonus, the 1950 contract liquidated the 1947 Fund, vacated all operator reimbursement claims, and turned over all assets to the new trust.[2]

One problem the new contract did not address was responsibility for the legal fees arising from litigation involving the 1947 Fund. Lewis had complete discretion over the matter as chairman of both the 1947 and 1950 trusts. The primary litigants were Dawson, Bridges, and Van Horn. Dawson's costs did not present a problem since his appointment as trustee was rendered moot by the 1950 contract. Senator Bridges and Van Horn were in a different position because both men had actually served on the board.

At first, Lewis was inclined to cover the senator's expenses only. Bridges had once been an ally, and Lewis apparently could not resist giving Van Horn a parting gesture of ill-will. However, Lewis did not carry through with this. In spite of Van Horn's threats of a discrimination suit, Lewis came to his own understanding that he could not have it both ways. Moreover, covering Van Horn's costs was a small price to pay to be rid of him once and for all. After payment was made, the two men never corresponded again.[3]

With Van Horn out of the picture, the operators chose a new representative: Charles Owen, president of the Black Diamond Coal Company. While Owen's views were similar to Van Horn's, his style was far less combative. His position on the board, though, amounted to little more than window dressing. With Roche serving as the neutral trustee, Owen never had any hope that his ideas would be considered. Nevertheless, during his first year in office, he tried to have an impact on the Fund's management.[4]

His plans were ambitious. First, Owen wanted to do a general census of the Fund's beneficiaries.[5] Such a study was necessary to place the pension program on a sound footing.[6] He added that the census would also help determine who was entitled to receive other Fund services.[7] Next Owen wanted pension eligibility rules tightened so that a miner would have to be working full time for two years prior to retirement. Moreover, he wanted all of the UMWA's Canadian members dropped from the program. He also sought to reduce the basic pension from $100 a month when a retiree reached sixty-five and began collecting Social Security.[8]

In the area of death benefits, Owen suggested replacing the Fund's flat $1,000 survivor's payment with a graduated approach. The proposal offered a $2,000 benefit for a working miner's widow and $1,000 to his family if unmarried. Upon retirement, however, the amount received by both categories would fall to $500.[9] Owen also wanted to decrease disability payments and limit hospitalization expenditures to $75 per stay.[10] Owen further suggested that to assure overall efficiency, the Fund had to end direct administration of all services, except pensions, and place them under the control of an insurance company.[11]

Owen did not confine his interests to restricting the Fund's organization and programs. He was also deeply concerned by Lewis's decision to deposit the Fund's liquid assets in a union-owned institution: the National Bank of Washington. Lewis had purchased the bank in the union's name during the Fund's suspension crisis. This was a conflict of interest, and Owen demanded that it be stopped.[12]

Looking at Owen's suggestions in totality, there is no question that some of what he said had merit. Most notable was his concern about the Fund using the union's bank. Not only was the action improper, it created the false impression that Lewis sought to misuse the Fund for corrupt purposes.[13] To see what Lewis was doing, however, one must also understand his frame of reference.

According to a member of the Fund's senior medical staff, Lewis's attitudes about money and investing had a distinct nineteenth-century quality. Despite his apparent sophistication in such matters, Lewis distrusted banks. Depositing in the union's bank, therefore, amounted to an institutionally acceptable version of keeping the Fund's assets in a mattress. This also might explain why so much of the Fund's resources were invested in government securities prior to the late 1950s.[14] In addition, while Roche's presence on the Fund's board gave Lewis absolute authority, use of the union's bank placed the trust's holdings farther out of management's reach. There would be no repeat of Van Horn's attempt to block activation of the pension program.

Turning to the remainder of Owen's plan, the overall quality of what he had to say varied. His ideas about the pension system reflected the same beliefs found in the Towers report. Lewis and Roche found this unacceptable. Within a few years though they would have to come to terms with declining demand for coal. Some benefit reductions would be made, but they would not be as extensive as those Owen originally proposed.

The most questionable of Owen's suggestions was turning the Fund's medical and health-related programs over to an insurance company. Although the Fund's medical program is covered in chapter 5, some facts must be presented here. As mentioned before, most of the Fund's staff had worked for various government agencies, including the USPHS, Farm Security Administration, and the military.[15] These people as a group, from Dr. Draper on down, had a wealth of experience in the areas of health care delivery and social welfare. Confident they could devise a cost-effective system, they sought to create a privatized version of national health insurance. They hoped the government would eventually adopt it as a model for health reform.[16] Working from this premise, the staff wanted to create an all-out program with no coverage limitations. Suggestions that the Fund should work through an insurance company were unwelcome. Their attitude also fit nicely with Lewis's determination to keep outsiders from interfering with the Fund's operations.

From Owen's perspective, this amounted to subordination of fiscal responsibility to ideology. He was seeking to combat the impression that the Fund was extravagant.[17] However, the experience of the Progressive Mine Workers of America, a smaller rival of the UMWA, showed that it was fiscally sound to keep the Fund's programs independent.

The Progressives were founded on September 1, 1932, with a major portion of UMWA District 12 in Illinois seceding over dissatisfaction with Lewis's authoritarianism.[18] Unfortunately for the Progressives, their creation came on the eve of the UMWA's revival. Rather than overshadowing the UMWA and discrediting Lewis, the Progressives were overshadowed. The organization was permanently set in the position of being a minor dual union.[19] Even more galling was the fact that to keep their membership they had to win concessions similar to the UMWA's. It was no surprise that the Progressives and the Coal Producers' Association of Illinois agreed to create their own fund less than a month after the Krug-Lewis agreement was signed.[20]

The Progressives' fund was almost identical to the UMWA's. The similarity even extended to charging the same tonnage royalty and increasing it whenever the UMWA's increased.[21] But, unlike the UMWA, the Progressives originally administered their medical program through an insurance company. To do this, the Progressives received bids from a number of different corporations, including Aetna, The Travelers, John Hancock, and Prudential. They eventually awarded the contract to General American Life Insurance in September of 1947.[22]

Ironically, when this agreement was concluded, the Progressives canceled its contract with a different company, which administered their death benefit system. They began operating their program directly, claiming it was more cost effective.[23] It remained independent thereafter. Moreover, the Progressives canceled their contract with American General after only one year and began following the UMWA's example.[24] There is no evidence that the Progressives ever out-contracted their health program again. Based on these facts, it is reasonable to assume the Progressives discovered they could offer effective programs for as much, or less, than what it cost to work through an insurance company.

It is not clear if Lewis or Roche was aware of the Progressives' experience, or if they bothered to show Owen where he might have been mistaken. It is clear that Roche reacted to Owen's commentary with extreme hostility that bordered on outright hatred.[25] She retaliated by stonewalling Owen much in the same way she had Van Horn.[26] The most overt example of this behavior was displayed during trustee meetings. Whenever Owen made a resolution, neither Roche nor Lewis would second, allowing it to die without discussion. Owen protested that he should at least be allowed a hearing before his suggestions were rejected.[27] These pleas went unheeded.

By late 1951, Owen began to accept his marginal position as industry trustee. Gradually, his correspondence with Roche and Lewis ceased to have any real substance and dealt only with where and when trustee meetings were to take place. Further reinforcing Owen's attitude was the fact that the major coal operators would not seek to assert any authority relative to the Fund again until 1969.

While Lewis and Roche demonstrated their absolute control over the program, the Fund prepared to restart operation. The suspension period ended in June 1950, when all payments were resumed. Although there were minor changes in the Fund's medical program, there was little alteration in the eligibility requirements for most Fund services. In fact, eligibility for hospitalization was extended to a miner's adult dependents, which was part of a broader plan to end company hospitalization check-off schemes.[28] As far as pensions were concerned, the 1947 requirements remained in force. The trustees decided against making any retroactive payments to compensate pensioners for lost income.[29]

Local administration of the Fund changed little, if at all. The medical program was operated through ten area medical offices, which Dr. Draper had organized. All other benefit applications were handled by the UMWA's district and local affiliates. To facilitate this work, benefit application procedures were further refined, especially with the introduction of a new set of forms.[30] The new methods were accepted with little difficulty. However, one official objected: A. O. Lewis, secretary treasurer of UMWA District 17.

District 17 was centered in the southern counties of West Virginia, with its headquarters located in the state's capital, Charleston. This region had been witness to some of the most intense struggles between labor and management in an industry noted for violence. Coming out of this experience, the district had a history of refractory behavior.[31] As pointed out earlier, Lewis had ended district autonomy. His argument was that centralizing the union brought greater rewards to the membership. Restoring district autonomy, on the other hand, would render the UMWA impotent in its dealings with employers.[32]

This reasoning notwithstanding, certain members chafed under the system. One representative of District 17 went so far as to make an impassioned plea against centralization during the union's 1936 convention, when Lewis's prestige as a labor leader was near its height.[33] Lewis successfully defeated such challenges. But, the Fund offered a possibility for district offices to exercise some control over policy, instead of acting as the program's field network.

With this, there were two other factors that had to be considered. First, although the union's staff was professional, its officers had risen from the rank and file and had little formal education. Some district officials resented the Fund's college-trained staff, regarding them as dilettantes.[34] Second, there was the problem of Roche's personality. While she was devoted to the Fund and the union, she could be abrasive when dealing with people she regarded as subordinates. For example, she often lectured the Fund's administrators at length whenever there were disagreements on policy. According to the late Dr. Lorin E. Kerr, who was an officer in the Fund's medical program, Dr. Draper came out of Roche's office after meeting with her on more than one occasion muttering, "That woman!"[35] Considering the attitudes of many district officials, strained relations between the two sides were inevitable.

Unfortunately, the two sides were not able to compromise on forms and application procedures. The major hurdle in this case was form 85 HS (Health Services). The 85 HS and other forms were sent to the district offices for distribution to the locals under their jurisdictions. A union miner, whether he was working, unemployed, or retired, could then request the form and complete it. It was then certified by his local and sent to the district for approval. From there it was referred to the Fund's headquarters, where the staff determined the applicant's eligibility. A record of the application was kept on all levels. In addition, another set of forms was used to revise the information on the original if the miner's family or work status changed, or if the information he gave on the original was incorrect.[36]

Once the application process was completed, the Fund issued the miner an 85 HS health card. This card was presented to participating doctors, clinics, and hospitals whenever he or his dependents needed treatment. The bill was then paid through the appropriate area medical office. The system was devised to prevent fraud and was the only way a miner and his family could receive Fund medical benefits.

Transition to the new system had been smooth. But Roche discovered in late December 1950 that almost half the 85 HS forms sent to District 17 had not been distributed.[37] This meant that many union members could not apply for their medical benefits. Roche received an even more disturbing report from Dr. Draper informing her that District 17 had been derelict in its other duties. Not only had it failed to distribute the forms effectively, but it had not processed any of the benefit applications it had received. Moreover, the Fund's area medical office in Charleston was swamped by people requesting information on how to apply for their benefits. Draper believed the situation was out of control. Action by the appropriate authority was needed to make sure the miners were able to get their forms and to ensure that they were processed correctly.[38]

At Draper's suggestion, Roche contacted the district officers. The president of district 17 at this time was William Blizzard. Blizzard had worked as an organizer in West Virginia during the 1930s and had been part of the march on Logan in 1920. Ten thousand miners rebelled against the state's pro-operator authorities during this event, the single largest insurrection since the Civil War.[39] Roche told both Blizzard and Lewis that the Fund was aware of the district's poor record in getting the forms distributed. She added that she understood the forms meant extra paperwork for all district offices, but pointed out that the work had to be done if the miners were to get the help they needed.[40]

Roche obviously hoped this gentle prodding would move the district office to action. It did not. A week after she sent her notice, Dr. Draper reported that due to the district's mishandling of application forms, a sick child nearly died. According to the story, the child's mother, a widow of a miner, completed the necessary papers for medical assistance, but they had not been processed by the district office. By chance, Charleston's area medical administrator was able to intervene and had the child hospitalized.[41]

This was too much for Roche to ignore, especially since it struck a resonant chord with her approach to social welfare. Owing to her Progressive background, Roche had certain opinions concerning those characterized as the deserving poor. At the center of this construct were those who found themselves in desperate straits through no fault of their own, particularly widows and minor children.[42] Roche therefore decided to investigate the matter personally. This pitted her against A. O. Lewis. As secretary treasurer of the district, Lewis was responsible not only for distributing the forms but also for making sure completed applications were processed.

The situation would have been difficult under ordinary circumstances. However, further complicating matters was the fact that Secretary Lewis was John L. Lewis's younger brother.[43] Roche had to pick her way carefully here and avoid pulling rank unless absolutely necessary. The meeting with the younger Lewis did not go well. He was argumentative and aired his dissatisfaction with both the Fund and the international union. He claimed that because of the additional paperwork from the Fund, no one in the local unions wanted to serve as secretary anymore. He also complained that he did not have enough financial support from the UMWA to run his office correctly, demanding $250,000 to $300,000 more a year. Lewis made it clear that he intended to "pester" the union's main office until he received it.[44]

When Roche questioned him about the incident involving the child, Lewis retorted, "That's your problem."[45] He refused to accept any responsibility for mishandling the forms, and took the opportunity to outline a procedure that he favored. Instead of a system where the Fund's Washington office made the final determination of eligibility, Lewis wanted the task done by the districts. Each district would issue a series of cards to the union's members four times a year, with the names taken from dues check-off lists.[46] If implemented, the basic processing work would shift from the local unions to the district offices.[47]

Roche countered that the plan was impractical for several reasons. It increased the workload for the district offices and it did not fit the legal requirements of the 1950 Fund. Also, the proposal made no provision for unemployed miners and their dependents.[48] Roche's objections did not dissuade Lewis. He continued to demand that the Fund should implement his proposed changes, and he went so far as to try to get around Roche by writing a letter to John Owens, the union's secretary treasurer.[49] Owens turned over the letter to Roche, who, in her turn, made a point-by-point refutation of Lewis's claims.

Most of what Roche wrote was similar to what she told Lewis during their meeting, except for emphasis on one point. Here, Roche insisted that "authorization of benefits by the trustees of the 1950 Fund cannot be made *on the basis of membership alone* [italics Roche's]; determination of eligibility rests solely with the trustees."[50] Thus, to counter Lewis's arguments, union membership and eligibility were decoupled. To receive help from the Fund, a miner needed to belong to the union. But his membership did not automatically entitle him to anything.

Roche's statement about eligibility was not simply a convenient argument to outmaneuver an adversary. She believed the trustees needed unlimited power to act in order to meet any eventuality. Because of this requirement, Roche refused to consider allowing the districts to play a larger role than the one given to them.[51]

It is not clear from the correspondence how the problem with District 17 was finally resolved. As district president, William Blizzard was in a position to discipline the secretary treasurer. Blizzard decided to stay out of the matter, saying that all questions concerning the forms were Lewis's responsibility.[52] More than likely Lewis realized he was in a weaker position relative to Roche, despite his relationship to the union's president, and dropped the matter. None of the officers in the union really dared question Roche's authority because of her long association with John L. Lewis. Moreover, other avenues of appeal, such as the union's convention or International Executive Board, were closed since they were under John L. Lewis's absolute control. On the other hand, Roche may have won her point, but she could not antagonize A. O. Lewis or any other district official too much. The international depended upon the district unions to enforce discipline within the rank and file. The importance of this role became evident when the trustees decided to tighten the pension eligibility rules a few years later.

Although coal was still a major fuel source in 1950, there was no question that the industry was declining. Lewis sought to limit the effects of the process, and his decision to allow mechanization of the mines appeared to dovetail with this goal. As stated previously, Lewis hoped to see a measured concentration of the industry into fewer and larger firms. Steady employment for working miners and regular coal output could be assured through this restructuring. Lewis knew that the change would mean increased unemployment by job displacement, but he believed distress could be limited. Younger men could find work in other industries, while older men now had the Fund's pension for their support.

Unemployment among coal miners rose, just as Lewis foresaw, but he underestimated its extent and how quickly it would happen. The figures presented in tables 1, 2, and 3 tell the story. From 1950 to 1959, the industry's workforce fell by more than half. Areas dependent upon the industry as a major source of jobs were hit especially hard, particularly Pennsylvania and West Virginia.

Throughout this period, the Fund carried all union miners and their families on its medical program regardless of employment status. This was unusually generous. Other major programs, such as that offered by the United Steel Workers, had major restrictions in this regard. In the USW's case, a laid-off worker lost his coverage after ninety days.[53] In 1960, this maximum was extended to six months.[54] The Fund's pension system, however, was another matter. Lewis and Roche had argued for a liberal program on the grounds that most miners would continue working when they became eligible, rather than retire. The statistical information the Fund kept on the pension system proved their argument. Cumulative pension figures as of January 1949 showed the average retirement age for union member was 66.3 years. Also, each retiree had served an average of thirty-five years in the mines.[55] Even more important were the monthly and cumulative age breakdowns the Fund gathered. Of the 11,000 pensions granted by December 1949, half of them were taken by retirees falling into the 64 to 67 age bracket. Smaller percentages were almost evenly distributed between the 60–63 and 68 and above categories.[56] Gradually, this trend changed when a greater number of miners began taking early retirement as unemployment in the industry increased.

By December 1951, this change was already becoming evident. The Fund was now carrying a total of 45,780 pensioners. According to the cumulative figures, 54 percent of the men who retired after 1950 fell into the sixty to sixty-two age group, with an increasing share retiring at sixty to sixty-one. More significantly, this group constituted 35 percent of all pensioned retirees, and the trend was continuing.[57] This shift placed a considerable strain on the pension system. Not only was it serving a larger number of retirees, but the largest group of recipients fell into its youngest age category.[58] Because these people left the mines earlier, they probably would remain on the Fund's pension roles

Table 1

Number of Bituminous Miners Working in United States, 1950–1959

1950	400,000
1952	350,000
1955	225,000
1959	179,600

SOURCE: National Coal Association, *Bituminous Coal Facts, 1960* (Washington: National Coal Association, 1960), 116; idem, *Bituminous Coal Facts, 1964* (Washington: National Coal Association, 1964), 100; idem, *Coal Facts, 1978–1979* (Washington: National Coal Association, 1979), 56.

Table 2

Number of Bituminous Miners Working in Pennsylvania, 1950–1959

1950	93,000
1952	75,900
1955	47,900
1959	36,000

SOURCE: National Coal Association, *Bituminous Coal Facts, 1960* (Washington: National Coal Association, 1960), 116; idem, *Bituminous Coal Facts, 1964* (Washington: National Coal Association, 1964), 100; idem, *Coal Facts, 1978–1979* (Washington: National Coal Association, 1979), 56.

Table 3

Number of Bituminous Miners Working in West Virginia, 1950–1959

1950	120,000
1952	102,000
1955	62,000
1959	54,000

SOURCE: National Coal Association, *Bituminous Coal Facts, 1960* (Washington: National Coal Association, 1960), 116; idem, *Bituminous Coal Facts, 1964* (Washington: National Coal Association, 1964), 100; idem, *Coal Facts, 1978–1979* (Washington: National Coal Association, 1979), 56.

longer because of an increased life span. Yet, while pension costs were increasing, the Fund's income remained static.

The problem is illustrated by the figures presented in table 4. Whereas 1947 was a banner production year, coal output had fallen off sharply by 1952.[59] The tonnage figures, multiplied by the prevailing royalty, represented the Fund's potential income. That potential could only be realized if the union had managed to organize 100 percent of the industry. Obviously, this was not the case. In terms of the royalty, each successive contract after 1946 included an increase, with the royalty rising to forty cents a ton by 1952.[60] It stayed there for the rest of the decade. Taking into account inflation, production fluctuations, and the economy's overall strength, the Fund's annual income was very uncertain from year to year. Additionally, by 1952 the Fund was irrevocably committed to building a chain of modern hospitals in south-central Appalachia. The project turned out to be far more expensive than originally estimated.

By late 1952 it became apparent that if the Fund was to avoid a deficit, benefits would have to be reduced. Judging from what was done first, the Fund's administration attempted to make the cuts as painless as possible. To begin, the death benefit was reduced from $1,000 to $500 in early 1953.[61] Not long after, regulations concerning workman's compensation and the Fund were also changed. The Fund originally paid all hospital expenses for injured miners, regardless of whether or not their employers contributed to the state's workman's compensation program. The Fund now demanded that all union operators pay into their state systems. Failure to do so would result in their employees losing Fund benefits.[62]

Sadly, these changes did not provide enough savings to meet the Fund's needs. Therefore, the trustees voted on January 28, 1953, to initiate the pension system's thirty-year rule. All of the other eligibility requirements remained the same under this new regulation, except that a miner now applying for his pension was required to prove that he had worked steadily for twenty years within a thirty-year time frame.[63] Although the new rule did not categorically disqualify any miner whose twenty years did not fall within the thirty-year limit, it presented a new obstacle. A miner wishing to retire who did not meet the requirement would have to continue working until he met the 20/30 formula. It also meant that an older miner who lost his job before meeting the requirement, and who could not find new employment with a union operator, could lose his eligibility entirely. Continuous employment as a miner now became the criterion.

Pension application forms were adjusted to meet the new demand. Not only was the miner required to have his membership certified by the local and district offices, he also had to list all of the companies where he had been employed during his twenty years. He also had to include his length of service with each company. All of the forms contained a listing sheet, and failure to complete it voided the application.

Table 4	
Coal Tonnage, 1947–1952 (in Millions)	
1947	630.6
1950	516.3
1952	466.8

SOURCE: National Coal Association, *Bituminous Coal Facts, 1960* (Washington: National Coal Association, 1960), 80.

Opposition to the cuts within the union was muted. A handful of resolutions calling for restoration of full pensions rights to miners now deemed ineligible were presented at the union's 1956 convention.[64] However, major grassroots opposition began stirring in District 17. Local union representatives from the Logan and Kanawha coal fields met in Smithers, West Virginia, to protest the changes and to plan a strategy.[65] The two most prominent groups involved were Locals 6013 and 677. Both sponsored meetings and invited all interested locals to attend.[66] Local 6013 had already succeeded in getting the cooperation of seven other local unions in this drive.[67] The district office was able to nip the opposition in the bud. But, it underscored the fact that the Fund had raised expectations among the union's membership. Disappointments arising from what appeared to be the Fund's leadership going back on the social contract would not be quietly accepted.

What added to the dissension was how the thirty-year rule was created. Lewis and Roche acted on their own, in consultation with the Fund's staff, and handed down the rule with little or no warning. The decision was unpleasant, especially since it appeared to vindicate the Towers report. Also, while it eased the crisis, it fostered the impression that Lewis and Roche were indifferent to the miners.

Ironically, drastic as the thirty-year rule appeared to be, it only diminished the rate of growth in pension awards. This is clearly shown by the figures in table 5. Chances are that if the thirty-year rule had not been established, the pension approval rate would have been much higher. The statistics for 1954 also showed that the rule had not stopped the trend for early retirement. By the end of 1954, the cumulative percentage share of pensioned miners in the sixty to sixty-two bracket had risen to 39 percent.[68] Therefore, the cuts were a necessity if the Fund was to continue operating.

Despite this partial retreat, the Fund was moving aggressively to further expand its benefits, particularly in relation to the medical program. One example of this expansion was building the chain of hospitals in south-central Appalachia. On one level, the decision was questionable because the Fund would be assuming a major commitment at a time when the coal industry was contracting. However, there were several factors which impelled the Fund to

Table 5

Pensions Awarded by the Fund, 1950–1954

1950–51	9,000 (avg. of two years)
1952	8,557
1954	7,023

SOURCE: *Statistical Abstract, Welfare and Retirement Fund United Mine Workers of America,* Jan. 10, 1951, 10; Jan. 10, 1952, 10; Jan. 10, 1953, 12; Jan. 10, 1954, 11; Jan. 10, 1955, 11, box 1 of 7, Statistical Reports, Series V, Office of Research and Statistics, UMWA Health and Retirement Funds.

undertake the project. With improvements in health care technology, hospitals had become the centers of medical practice in the United States.[69] This was further enhanced after the close of World War II with the passage of the Hill-Burton Hospital Construction Act. In such a setting, hospitals were the very symbols of medical progress.[70] Moreover, the presence of adequate hospital, laboratory, and other facilities was an absolute requirement if a given area was interested in attracting qualified physicians.[71] Added to these considerations was the fact that the Fund was a payer for hospital services. As such, it had a vested interest in assuring that its beneficiaries were receiving the best possible care at a reasonable price. Therein arose a major problem.

When the Fund's medical program began operating in late 1948, the availability of hospital facilities in the coal fields was uneven. Miners living close to cities such as Pittsburgh, Knoxville, and Louisville had access to excellent facilities. But, the situation was far different in the more remote areas of Appalachia, especially the southern region. According to the *Boone Report,* most of the hospitals in this area were small institutions operated on a for-profit basis and consequently offered substandard care.[72] Because these institutions were for profit, their owners, usually physicians, sought to increase income while limiting costs. Thus, each had an incentive to give minimal service for an inflated rate, which translated into the Fund being overcharged for poor work.[73] The deficiencies were appalling. At the time the *Boone Report* was published, only a third of these hospitals had any X-ray facilities, many of which were antiquated. Almost 50 percent of these institutions lacked specialist services, while 60 percent were understaffed, and failed to meet minimum AMA requirements concerning delivery rooms and obstetrical facilities.[74]

The *Boone Report* recommended construction of new community hospitals through the Hill-Burton Act as the remedy to the situation.[75] Unfortunately, several obstacles made the recommendation impractical. Hill-Burton limited the government's role in hospital improvement to providing matching funds. A locality seeking to upgrade its hospital facilities had to provide the primary funding. Many southern Appalachian communities were unable to raise such large amounts of money. Another flaw in the recommendation was the suggestion that the UMWA join with operator associations to provide the start-up funds.[76]

Operator/union antagonisms aside, the UMWA was reticent about joining any project unless it controlled it. This was due primarily to Lewis's authoritarian nature. A telling example of this reticence involved the Raleigh-Boone Association of Whitesville, West Virginia. This organization was formed in 1948 to create a modern hospital for Whitesville. By the spring of 1949, it was in the middle of a fundraising campaign.[77] According to its brochure, the association had already secured a promised grant from the federal government for $500,000.[78] The association still needed to collect another $1.5 million to complete the project. In an effort to show that the hospital had broad community support, the brochure said that the association had the public endorsement of UMWA District 17.[79]

The endorsement had been given jointly by District President William Blizzard and Dr. John Morrison, a member of the Fund's medical staff. Morrison had been approached by the association for advice concerning its bylaws. Favorably impressed by what he saw, he asked Blizzard to lend his support. After their meeting, both Blizzard and Morrison attended a fund-raiser sponsored by the association.[80] But, soon thereafter, Blizzard received a telegram from the international union ordering him not to send the letter of endorsement he had written.[81] On the same day, Lewis sent a letter to Blizzard which outlined his objections. In it, Lewis stated that Morrison had overstepped his authority and that the UMWA should not endorse any local projects unless it planned to formally participate.[82] That ended the union's involvement with the Raleigh-Boone Association. Blizzard apologized for his mistake, adding that he would keep local unions from being involved with the project.[83] Lewis's refusal to allow union cooperation with other groups on hospital improvement in Appalachia placed a great responsibility upon the Fund. Under these conditions, it was the only organization in the region that was capable of undertaking such a large venture.

No doubt, this fact played a part in convincing the Fund's leadership to develop a hospital project of their own. The primary cause, however, was the Fund's difficulties with the region's proprietary hospitals. Because these institutions were operated on a closed staff basis, Fund patients were denied their free choice of physician.[84] This particular requirement was a cornerstone of the AMA's approach to health care.[85] In addition to poor service, these institutions were also charging exorbitant prices and including mortgage costs, and other nonmedical charges, in their bills.[86] Disgusted by these and other fraudulent practices, Dr. Draper arranged for a preliminary investigation of medical conditions in the region.[87]

Anxious to avoid the appearance of partisanship, Draper hoped to do the study through the AMA's Council on Medical Service. But, the association was reluctant to do anything viewed as controversial. Not to be put off, Draper then decided to conduct the study through the Fund's Medical Advisory Board.[88] The Advisory Board did not have any formal power. Rather, it was intended to provide a channel of communication between the Fund and the AMA. Its membership included some of the most noted figures in contemporary organized medicine.

A complete investigation of the Appalachian region was out of the question, so one portion was selected for an intensive look: southeastern Kentucky. The tour was arranged through the Fund's area office in Knoxville. During the tour, which lasted for three days, they visited a number of facilities, including seven hospitals. The institutions were in uniformly poor condition. Most were understaffed, dirty, and even smelly.[89] At the same time, many of their pharmacies were filled with bottle after bottle of brightly colored placebos.[90]

The tour set several events into motion. The AMA's Council on Medical Service, concerned by what was uncovered, joined with its Council on Industrial Health to create the Committee on Health Care for Industrial Workers. Also, they planned for a second survey in 1952, which would cover a much wider geographic area.[91] Meanwhile, the Fund's leadership decided to go ahead with its own hospital project. The project's institutional framework was officially voted into existence on October 10, 1951.[92] While Roche did not hold any particular office in the new structure, she nonetheless oversaw its initial operation.[93] It was clear during this time that the Fund's leadership decided against building or owning the hospitals directly. Instead, it opted to create hospital associations incorporated in the states where the institutions would be located: Kentucky, West Virginia, and Virginia. After the associations received their charters they could request construction loans from the Fund's board.[94]

This method did not appear to be unnecessarily complex at the time. Fund chief counsel Val J. Mitch and other attorneys reviewed all of the laws concerning charitable trusts for the three states.[95] The lawyers agreed that the incorporation of separate associations was the best method available to secure a tax-exempt status. The articles of incorporation were filed, therefore, under the generic name of "The Memorial Hospital Association," in order to avoid any reference to either the Fund or the UMWA. Once incorporated, the Fund would assume control of the associations and appoint the same board of directors for each. They would then function as a single unit with central administration in the Fund's Washington office.[96]

This facade eventually proved to be too elaborate. Whenever they requested the Fund's help, the associations' board members were legally required to go through the same process for each organization. This was an unnecessary duplication of effort. The problem was solved by allowing the Kentucky association to assume the duties for the entire hospital project and chartering it to operate as a foreign corporation in the other two states.[97] The only other change came in 1955, when Roche ordered the renaming of the Kentucky association. After some inquiries, they agreed to a new title: the Miners' Memorial Hospital Association (MMHA).[98]

Simultaneous with these legal maneuvers they began to choose construction sites, as well as assemble a staff. The program's senior directors, with a few exceptions, were taken from the Fund. They included Edward L. Carey, a Fund lawyer who was designated as the MMHA's secretary, and Henry Combs, the Fund's assistant controller, who served as the chain's treasurer.[99] Heading the chain were two physicians: Frederick W. Mott and John Newdorp.

Both men had worked in the area of public health and had a broad range of experience. Mott had served not only in the USPHS, but also as deputy minister of health for Saskatchewan Province, Canada.[100] He had also coauthored an in-depth study of the state of rural health care in the United States, published by McGraw-Hill in 1948, entitled *Rural Health and Medical Care*.[101] Such was

Mott's eminence in this field that he was appointed a panel member of President Truman's Commission on America's Health Needs.[102] The only other Fund staff member who had this same distinction was Dr. Draper.[103] Sadly, while Dr. Mott had a great deal to offer, he was wedded to one particular hospital model: the urban teaching institution.[104]

Dr. Newdorp was an obstetrician, and had served in the USPHS during World War II. As part of his service he worked as state health officer for Alabama and actively supported health reform during his tenure there.[105] Of greater significance was Newdorp's having been a principle author of Alabama's postwar plan to use Hill-Burton funding effectively.[106] The plan outlined a blueprint whereby Alabama's hospitals would be organized around one or two major medical centers, with a network of smaller community hospitals serving as satellites for the larger institutions.

Such an approach represented contemporary mainstream thinking relative to hospital development. Dubbed "regional hierarchy" by Prof. Daniel Fox, the model postulated the integration of hospitals and clinics into a single health delivery network. The medical center would be at the network's top. Not only would it treat illness, it would also serve in a research and teaching capacity. Community hospitals, more or less in the middle of the hierarchy, would treat more common varieties of illness, while referring complex cases to the medical center. Clinics and solo practitioners would be at the bottom of the hierarchy and would serve as the first point of service. With this, any advance in medical techniques would be filtered down through the hierarchy by the medical center.[107] This model was eventually adopted by the health reform movement and represented that movement's approach to reorganization of health care delivery in America. Considering the influence of this model, it is little wonder that both Newdorp and Mott adopted it as the basis for the Fund's hospital project.

In order to determine where the hospitals would locate, and how many to build, the Fund conducted a census of south-central Appalachia from eastern Kentucky to southwestern Virginia. The study's purpose was to determine the composition of the population base in the area.[108] It was crucial that enough people, especially beneficiaries, resided in the region to make the hospitals economically viable.[109] The census, based upon information gathered in 1952, appeared to show that an adequate population base existed. Assuming the situation would not change, a plan was developed which called for the creation of ten hospitals. Three of the institutions would serve as medical centers, with the remaining seven acting as community facilities.[110] The choice of sites was determined, in part, by the information derived from the census, as well as discussions with the various AMOs involved.[111]

The hospital chain would stretch over 250 miles, ranging from Bell County,

Kentucky, to Wise County, Virginia, and Raleigh County, West Virginia, to Cumberland, Maryland. The chain's western portion consisted of a medical center at Harlan, Kentucky, with four satellite institutions at Hazard, Whitesburg, and Middlesboro, Kentucky, and Wise, Virginia. The chain's central portion would consist of a medical center at Williamson, West Virginia, served by three community hospitals in Man, West Virginia, and Pikeville and McDowell, Kentucky. The chain's eastern portion consisted of a medical center at Beckley, West Virginia. Cumberland, Maryland, would be served by an outpatient clinic. In looking at the plan, Dr. Draper did not believe that the ten new institutions were enough to meet all of the region's needs. He hoped, however, that the chain would force proprietary hospital operators to upgrade their facilities and so improve the overall quality of care available.[112]

Construction of the hospitals did not begin until the spring of 1953. In the interim, time was spent securing agreements with architectural firms, working out preliminary building designs, and hiring a contractor. The search for a construction company began in the fall of 1952. Dr. Mott recommended hiring a single contractor for the entire project. His reasoning was that using one construction company would cut costs and establish a single standard of performance. Because the architects and the contractor would work as a team, the general outlay of the buildings could be uniform, allowing similar equipment to be used when the buildings were completed.[113]

Contracts were bid on an open basis. Each company filled out a questionnaire on its background, including a list of completed projects. They were also given a prospectus which outlined the program and the intended methods of payment by the Fund.[114] While the bidding was in progress, Lewis received several requests from interested parties suggesting certain construction companies. Among the people who contacted Lewis were Benjamin Morell, chairman of the board of Jones & Laughlin Steel, and John R. Steelman.[115] Steelman wrote from the White House and was a pro-labor official who had served as a government conciliator in previous mine disputes.[116]

Despite whatever influence Morell and Steelman had, their suggestions were ignored, and the contract was awarded to the J. A. Jones Construction Company. Roche told Lewis that all of the Fund's officials connected with the hospital project agreed that Jones met the desired qualifications, particularly the ability to build all ten of the hospitals simultaneously at the desired cost.[117]

Roche required the contractor to use union-made materials and labor, especially labor belonging to UMWA District 50.[118] District 50 was a general organization that Lewis created during his stewardship of the CIO. While originally intended to represent coke and coal by-product workers, Lewis eventually used it to raid the memberships of other unions.[119]

The Jones Company wanted to cooperate as much as possible. Their representatives told Roche that they planned to use District 50 members wherever they could, but they wanted to avoid any jurisdictional problems with the AFL [120] Jones's equivocation on the matter caused much discussion between Dr. Mott, Dr. Newdorp, Roche, and Mitch. Thomas Davis, a District 50 official, told them that his organization was already sending out work notices to its unemployed members in the areas where the hospitals were being built. Without actually saying so, Davis's plan was to mobilize the district's membership and have it ready to work, thus outmaneuvering any AFL affiliates.[121] The plan would only work if the Jones Company did not have a blanket agreement with the federation. The district's members would have no other choice but to temporarily join the AFL.[122] Roche and her associates discovered later that Jones had never made such an agreement, and soon the contractor agreed to hire only District 50 members. Roche was overjoyed.[123]

While Roche and Lewis had been very careful to ensure that the UMWA exercised the maximum possible control over the hospital project, one aspect eluded their authority: the program's costs. As mentioned above, part of the rationale for building and operating the hospitals was that it would be cheaper for the Fund to do so, rather than subsidizing the low-quality hospitals already in existence. When the hospital associations were formed, the Fund's trustees granted a loan of $15 million through the National Bank of Washington. That amount was considered adequate to cover all expenses, except staff and equipment.[124] By the time the hospitals were nearing completion in 1956, that figure had risen to more than $30 million.[125]

Although inflation accounted for part of the increase, Lewis, Roche, and their associates underestimated the costs involved with building an urban-style medical complex in a remote area. Before construction began, plans had to be revised. Due to the difficulty in acquiring land, the bed distribution between the hospitals had to be adjusted. The new plans also increased the bed space available from 1,000 units to 1,040.[126] Another problem arose concerning the size of the outpatient facilities. Dr. Mott maintained that this was the heart of hospital care, and adequate space had to be provided for it. To achieve Mott's goal, the plans were revised to set aside 60,000 square feet for outpatient facilities, rather than the 45,000 square feet originally allotted.[127]

Design modifications were not the only problem. Even more important were the questions of acquiring staff, housing them, and providing nurse's training. In order to attract competent people, they had to offer competitive salaries. At the same time, housing facilities were substandard or unavailable in nearly all of the areas where the hospitals were being built. It became evident that the Fund had to fill the housing void. If it failed to do so, the hospitals faced a chronic shortage of nurses and technicians, which meant the quality of care would suffer. Dr. Mott recommended including an apartment building with each hospital, instead of a dormitory, which could be used by single or married people.[128]

Training facilities for nurses also had to be provided. This was very much a part of a teaching hospital's function, and they ensured a supply of personnel. Because the miners' hospitals made up a single system, they could conduct nurse's training at the regional medical centers at Beckley and Williamson, rather than at all of the community hospitals.[129]

These changes represented a substantial increase in costs over the original estimates, but the Fund could readily accommodate them because the project was still in the planning stages. Once construction began, another unforeseen difficulty arose related to building in an underdeveloped area: the lack of water and sewage treatment services. The Fund's policy was to work with the various communities in providing essential services and to proceed on its own only as a last resort.[130] In some cases, the Fund entered into agreements in areas which could not meet water and sewage needs. Under these agreements, the Fund built the facilities with the guarantee that the communities would pay for them later.[131] After the facilities were built, several of the communities defaulted, forcing the Fund to cover the expenses.[132]

Of all the problems increasing the Fund's costs, construction delays accounted for the largest share. One source of delay involved labor trouble. While the hospitals were under construction, a total of forty-nine strikes were called at individual sites, with the Hazard area witnessing thirty-four of them.[133] Clearly using District 50 organizations for the project did not produce as disciplined a labor force as anticipated. Feelings at Hazard became so bitter that in July 1954 a car belonging to the site's general foreman was dynamited.[134] Immediately after the incident, there was a flurry of activity between Roche, Dr. Draper, and District 50 officials.[135] The perpetrators responsible were never found, but the cause involved the general foreman's layoff and recall decisions.[136] No other acts of violence were ever reported after the incident, but relations between the Jones Company and District 50 remained strained.[137]

These problems aside, the project's completion schedule proved overly ambitious. While the project was still in its early stages, the Fund's leadership planned to begin construction in May of 1953 and finish in the late fall of 1954.[138] Dr. Mott, for example, envisioned the following scenario for the Beckley hospital: the final designs were to be done by February 1953, and all subcontract bidding completed by the following May. The hospital's construction would end in November of 1954. After staffing and other final arrangements had been made, the Beckley facility could open for patients on January 1, 1955. Unfortunately, the plans failed to take into account the myriad major and minor problems that appeared. Construction proceeded at an uneven pace, and the final inspection of all the hospitals by the Fund's consultants did not take place until April 1956, more than a full year later than the date originally anticipated.[139]

A central figure in the building program was E. Todd Wheeler. Wheeler was an independent architect who specialized in hospital construction. He was hired in 1952 to assist Dr. Newdorp with some of the planning. Newdorp was pleased with Wheeler, and the Fund retained him.[140] Wheeler eventually became Dr. Draper's advisor on the hospital program and wrote a series of detailed weekly reports between August 1954 and April 1956. By the time Wheeler began writing his reports, the completion schedules had already been pushed back by several months. Only four of the hospitals were now slated to be opened by the end of 1955, with the rest delayed until the new year.[141] Meeting the completion dates became Wheeler's primary goal. This brought him into conflict with Newdorp and other MMHA board members. Because he reported to Draper, Wheeler acted as a detached expert and did not pay close attention to the personal conflicts which resulted from his criticisms. These problems, however, came up during the latter part of his tenure.

At first, Wheeler directed his attention to avoiding construction delays, which caused budget overruns. In an example Wheeler cited, new budget limitations required a change of materials used, which involved a readjustment of wall thicknesses in several of the buildings. As a result, all door frame specifications had to be revised to meet the new design. However, the single set of architect's drawings for the door frames used the old design only, and the supplier did not have any updated drawings for reference. The new plans were finally approved and given to the supplier, but fabrication took eight weeks.[142]

Wheeler's example showed how one comparatively minor change could hold up completion for weeks and increase construction costs. He admitted that there were similar difficulties in other projects. He criticized the Fund's lack of foresight in not allowing time for delays in its completion schedules. The major cause was that final cost decisions were not made until well after construction had begun. If such behavior continued, the hospital project was going to be plagued with similar mistakes.[143] Wheeler believed, however, that the program was now being managed with greater care, and future deadlines could be met. His statement proved too optimistic, and as the hospitals neared completion, more difficulties appeared. Wheeler became so obsessed with opening the hospitals on time that he broke with the association's doctors over which course of action to take.

The controversy began in June 1955, when Wheeler reported to Dr. Draper that the Williamson hospital could not be completed on time. Wheeler was concerned because this was the first indication that a deadline could not be met. He wanted Dr. Mott to ask the contractor to provide a revised schedule for all construction. Mott had not received any notice from the Jones company that it was having any difficulties, and the contractor was confident about meeting deadlines.[144] By the end of the summer, it was obvious that completion would be delayed because of two major problems. First, most of the subcontracted work, such as the electrical, heating, and phone systems, was only half finished. Second, none of the kitchen equipment was installed, or even delivered, because of a supplier's strike.[145]

Wheeler feared that if decisive action was not taken the Fund would lose control of expenses and the completion times.[146] To prevent this, he suggested that staff training programs begin while the hospitals were still being finished. He maintained that the nurses and other personnel would not bother the workmen, and it would allow the hospitals to open immediately upon completion. Wheeler then commented that the training period was too long and should be reduced from forty-two to twenty-eight days.[147]

Mott and the other doctors disagreed and reminded Draper of an earlier statement he made about adequate staff training to ensure quality care. Mott insisted that the consensus of opinion indicated that a minimum of four weeks was needed for basic orientation, and to establish work relationships for staff teams and between different departments. He concluded that while cost containment was important, training was not the area to implement it.[148] By December 1955, Mott was complaining to Draper that Wheeler was pushing too hard to meet the deadlines.[149]

Through the fall of 1955 Wheeler became increasingly disgusted with the situation. Although he understood that part of the difficulty revolved around the completion of support facilities, he insisted that the association bore the rest of the responsibility. In a memo he sent to Draper in October, Wheeler wrote that a pattern for failure was being set due to the association's inability to keep the schedules.[150]

While Wheeler believed that he was acting in the Fund's best interest to press for an early opening, even at the expense of training, Mott's arguments prevailed. Draper had ordered Mott to begin hiring and training the hospital staffs in anticipation of an early opening. Mott complied, but when the opening was further delayed, the association had to contact the people it hired and ask them not to report for duty. People preparing to leave their employers had to retract their notices. Other people had already severed their ties, and the association was obligated to provide them with some form of work in the interval.[151] Because of the delays involved with finishing the support systems, there was no way to hasten the opening of the hospitals, and they were not completed until April of 1956.

Although the internal dynamics of building the hospitals were marked by chaos, the image presented to the public was one of efficiency and humanitarianism. Articles about the hospital system appeared in trade and popular magazines and covered how the Fund was creating the nation's first integrated hospital system. They also pointed to how it was improving medical conditions in Appalachia.[152] Sometimes this praise was more trouble than it was worth. In one instance, *Reader's Digest* carried a favorable article about the hospitals, but presented it in the context of the popular view of Appalachian medicine.

The new system would end the pervasive usage of so-called granny doctors and other types of folk healing once and for all.[153]

While Dr. Draper thanked editor DeWitt Wallace for the favorable coverage, he also wrote an apology to Dr. Wallace E. Vest, a senior member of West Virginia's Board of Medical Advisors. Vest had worked with Draper in the past. Drawing on this relationship, Draper asked Vest to apologize on the Fund's behalf to his associates. Draper asked Dr. Vest to stress that the Fund had nothing to do with writing the article, and that its author had not interviewed any Fund employees.[154] Nevertheless, the piece caused considerable controversy and was damned as an insult to the region.[155]

In addition to the articles, the hospital program received some publicity through speaking engagements given by both Draper and Mott. Draper once gave a presentation before the Rip Van Winkle Foundation of New York. This was a group which sponsored hospital and clinic improvement, and among its members were corporate officers of Yale University and ITT. Dr. Benjamin Spock also appeared on the program the day Draper spoke.[156] At another point, Mott was the principle speaker at the Fourth Annual Group Health Institute of the Cooperative Health Federation of America. The meeting was opened with a speech given by Sen. Hubert Humphrey.[157]

But, not all of the publicity was favorable. When construction of the hospitals began in 1953, Joseph Moody of the SCPA gave a speech at the University of Kentucky attacking the project, and he accused the Fund of mishandling its assets. He went on to say that the coal royalty was a major burden to operators, but they were willing to pay it out of a sense of responsibility for their workers. The hospitals were a different matter. Because they were supposed to serve the entire public and not just the miners, part of the cost should be handled by the men and not just the operators.[158] Moody's line of reasoning was picked up by an editorial writer for the *Pineville (Kentucky) Sun,* who asked rhetorically why the Fund was building these new hospitals when so many adequate facilities existed in Appalachia's coal fields.[159]

Roche wanted a definite response to Moody's comments, and Draper agreed to give it as part of his remarks for the groundbreaking ceremonies at the site for the Man hospital in October 1953. The Fund also received some unexpected help from Jane Jacobs, who wrote a lengthy letter to the *Pineville Sun* refuting its editorial. Jacobs had written an extensive article on the hospital project for the *Architectural Forum* and was shocked by the substandard hospital facilities in the region. She detailed what she had seen and emphasized that the Fund was powerless to force the existing institutions to improve.[160] Jacob's letter was beneficial because it appeared to be unsolicited and spoke from authority. The combined effects of Draper's remarks and Jacob's letter ended all public debate over the necessity of the hospitals.

The hospitals were officially opened with a dedication ceremony held on

June 2, 1956.[161] The booklet the Fund printed for the occasion gave a general description of the new system and its goals under the title "A New Era Begins." [162] The title reflected a confidence in the future that Lewis, Roche, and their associates must have felt. The goal had been reached. The hospitals might have cost more than originally estimated, but now it seemed that the worst was over because they were open and ready to operate.

However, the Fund's leadership would soon discover that the hospitals would continue to be a major expense and source of trouble. Building the hospitals was only half the battle. Once opened, they became a source of controversy within the Fund itself and contributed to problems the Fund was having with organized medicine. In addition, the hospitals did not become self-supporting, which meant the Fund had to underwrite their operation. The Fund's leadership would soon discover that, while it could act as a medical third party, being a direct heath care provider was beyond its reach.

Chapter 4

The Noble Failure: The Miners'
Memorial Hospital Association

When the hospitals were dedicated in June 1956, the Fund's officers looked to the future with satisfaction and confidence. The Fund had been operating for ten years, celebrating its anniversary three weeks earlier on May 26, and there was cause for celebration.[1] The Fund moved to a new level of service while successfully weathering various setbacks, especially the 1953 benefit cuts. *U.S. News and World Report* had claimed that the Fund was near bankruptcy when the cuts were made.[2] Although the situation had been serious, *U.S. News* exaggerated the story. The thirty-year rule and the reduction in widows' payments had alleviated the situation. By 1956, royalty income was rising, and it appeared that the Fund was on solid footing.

When the hospitals opened, 80 percent of all coal tonnage produced in the United States came out of mines under contract with the UMWA. The Fund recorded a total income of $127.9 million and spent $119.1 million of that on health care, pensions, and other services. The $8.8 million surplus was the result of the benefit cuts.[3] Pensions and medical benefits now accounted for 86 percent of the Fund's obligations, with pension costs exceeding those of the medical program. The difference was substantial. While the Fund paid out $42.8 million a year for all medical and hospital assistance, the pension system spent close to $70 million year.[4] Despite the program's size, administrative costs were kept to a minimum, averaging a total of $3.54 million for any given year in the 1950s.[5]

By any account, the Fund's performance was impressive. Articles appeared in several magazines pointing to the program as *the* example of an efficiently managed and effective private welfare system.[6] While these articles gave welcome support, the most authoritative piece of good publicity came from the U.S. Congress. A subcommittee of the U.S. Senate's panel on Labor and Public Welfare held hearings on the administration of various labor welfare programs in 1955. The subcommittee, under the chairmanship of Sen. Paul Douglas of Illinois, spent much of its time investigating the Fund and took testimony from several of its officers.

The committee issued its report in April 1956 and lauded the Fund's work.[7] The report stated that the Fund had set a new standard in good administration. While offering complete coverage for severe illness "without limitation," it secured the best quality medical care available at the lowest possible price. This was due to the Fund's staff, who were praised as "an outstanding group of individuals."[8] In reference to the hospitals, the report concluded that the decision to build the chain demonstrated the vigor and imagination of the Fund's administration.[9] The Fund and its staff received a further honor in 1956 when it was presented with the prestigious Lasker Award by the American Public Health Association (APHA). Named for Dr. Albert Lasker, the award was in recognition of the Fund's efforts to bring a higher standard of medical practice to the coal fields.

Hand in hand with this, the union's overall sense of achievement was prominently displayed in the *United Mine Workers Journal*. The paper's January 1, 1956, edition ran a special statement from Lewis about the industry's future prospects. His comments read like a chamber of commerce release. Expansion of overseas demand for American coal offered greater investment opportunities than ever before. Lewis referred to the industry's restructuring into fewer "physical plants of larger capacity" with great pride. He also claimed that lower production costs now enabled the industry to meet the needs of expanding markets.[10]

By itself, the statement was not unusual since it was consistent with Lewis's overall program for the industry. Its distinctive feature was Lewis's self-satisfaction. He appeared to be saying that his program was becoming a reality just as planned. While job displacement occurred at an alarming rate, Lewis probably convinced himself that employment and demand would soon stabilize. If this happened, then the Fund's earlier problems would prove to be only an aberration.

Ironically, despite the hospital program's importance as a tangible sign of the Fund's work, the chain did not receive much attention in the *UMWA Journal*. In the months before and after dedication of the chain, only a handful of articles appeared. Most of these consisted of human interest stories. In one case, the journal ran a medium-sized article about a young mother whose first child was delivered at Beckley, West Virginia's, facility. The story focused on the family's plan to name their new baby girl after Roche, and not on the high quality of treatment received.[11]

Also, while the dedication took up most of the journal's June 1 and 15, 1956, editions, coverage of the event in the wider press was almost nonexistent. This was no accident. Although the Fund and union staffs had worked constantly to publicize Fund activities, Roche was always an obstacle. She had a nearly absolute aversion to the mass press. The reason dated back to her service with the Treasury Department. According to Roche, reporters never appeared to be interested in the real issues, such as health reform. Rather, they always questioned her about the nature of her relationship with Lewis.[12] Viewing the mass press as vulgar, Roche would have nothing to do with it, and she sought to shut it out whenever possible.

This was a terrible mistake. Roche had done the same thing back in 1938 with the conference she chaired on national health insurance, with disastrous results.[13] Regular press coverage of the Fund's work, including the hospital program, would have built goodwill with the general public as well as the miners. Such goodwill would have been invaluable later.

Yet, for the moment, it appeared that the industry had reached a new plateau of understanding and cooperation. Industry trustee Charles Owen was featured as one of the principal speakers at the chain's dedication ceremony. One would have never guessed, judging from his remarks, that there had ever been any conflict between the industry and the union about the Fund, or any other issue. Owen gushed with praise for Roche, Lewis, and the Fund's other officers. Going further, Owen reflected upon his fifty years in the industry and his sense of pride with the progress which had been achieved during that time.[14] The individual miner's quality of life had improved, while production methods had modernized. Dedication of the hospitals represented another milestone in the industry's development, and he felt proud to be part of the program.[15] The tone of Owen's statements went beyond the public courtesies associated with such an event. By 1956 he had not only accepted the reality of his position as industry trustee, but also actually began to cooperate with Roche and Lewis.

About a year after dedication of the chain, Owen became seriously ill and died. The new industry trustee was not appointed until March 1958. This was done only after the president of the Bituminous Coal Operator's Association, Edward Fox, conferred with Lewis over the appointment.[16] The man chosen was Henry G. Schmidt, president of the North American Coal Company.[17] As a trustee, Schmidt continued and expanded the cooperative relationship that had developed among the trustees and viewed himself as Lewis's and Roche's collaborator. He worked enthusiastically with them until his resignation from the Fund's board in 1968.

While Roche and Lewis no longer faced operator interference, new problems emerged concerning the hospital chain that were equally as serious. Ironically, the first disagreement appeared within the Fund itself and involved a jurisdictional dispute between the medical service and the MMHA. Technically, the Fund's entire medical apparatus came under Dr. Draper's control. Prior to the MMHA's creation, the medical program was administered via ten area offices throughout the bituminous coal fields. These offices were located in Johnstown and Pittsburgh, Pennsylvania; Morgantown, Beckley, and Charleston, West Virginia; Knoxville, Tennessee; Louisville, Kentucky; Birmingham, Alabama; Denver, Colorado; and St. Louis, Missouri.

Each area office was headed by an area medical administrator (AMO) who was a physician. Under the system, the AMOs acted as purchasing agents for medical services. They had the responsibility of ensuring that the Fund's beneficiaries received quality care from both physicians and hospitals.[18] This structure was Dr. Draper's creation. Having served in the USPHS for most of his career, he drew upon his experience and modeled the Fund's health program after it.[19] Because the chain operated within the jurisdiction of four of these offices, the AMOs involved insisted they should examine the MMHA's performance as they did that of other institutions.[20]

As pointed out in the previous chapter, the reason the ten hospitals had been placed under the control of a nominally separate corporation was to ensure the chain's tax-exempt status. However, Roche and her advisors failed to consider the possibility of administrative conflict. Such a situation could not be avoided. Although the Fund had uniform eligibility rules and the pension program was administered in Washington, the area offices had autonomy in securing health care for the miners. The availability and quality of health care providers (physicians, group practice clinics, and hospitals) varied from place to place. Thus, the area offices needed discretion to make judgments on how the medical needs of the Fund's beneficiaries were best served. Since they worked on site, the AMOs understood local conditions better than anybody else.

The MMHA's administration, on the other hand, worked out of the Fund's headquarters in Washington, D.C. The association's board of directors was nominally at the top of the chain's hierarchy. Appointed by the Fund, the board did not deal with much of the association's day-to-day activities. This responsibility was left to the association's medical administrator, who ran the entire chain. He appointed the administrators for each of the hospitals and was responsible for carrying out the purposes and objectives of the association. Although officially an employee of the association's board, the medical administrator actually reported to Dr. Draper and was subject to his orders.[21] Immediately under the medical administrator was the association's clinical director, who oversaw the chain's medical services and assured their quality. Dr. Gordon Meade filled this position for the eight years the association operated the hospitals.

The power structure in the individual hospitals became more complex. Each hospital was headed by an administrator who handled daily matters and who prepared the institution's annual budget. Medical matters for each hospital were handled by the chief of clinical services. These individuals reported to the clinical director, and their authority was broader than the hospital administrator's. They directed the medical staffs and held the power of reprimand, suspension, and recommendation for dismissal.[22] Since the chain was divided between three central hospitals and seven smaller institutions, both the administrators and the chiefs of clinical services for each of the seven answered to their counterparts at the three central facilities.[23]

As early as 1953, Dr. Mott and others attempted to determine the MMHA's relationship to the Fund's medical program and how they would be integrated.[24] Concern over the matter continued and became the subject of a two-day conference held for the area offices and the association on May 23 and 24, 1955. The only clear division of jurisdiction which came out of this meeting was that the area offices alone acted as the Fund's representative to the UMWA's district and local unions. Also, the meeting stressed the need for friendly relations between the association and the area offices due to the similar goals of each. While the area offices offered quality medical care at a reasonable price, the chain was built to provide the Fund's beneficiaries with needed hospitalization. Therefore, both the hospital chain and the medical service were different parts of the same team, with similar goals and ideals.[25]

Unfortunately, the outline presented at the May 1955 meeting never came into being. Before the end of 1956 all four of the area medical administrators who dealt with the hospitals directly were expressing concern to Dr. Draper about the chain's operation. The first concern involved how the chain's medical staff was paid. All staff physicians were hired by the association and worked for a salary. Such an arrangement was seldom used, and the only other hospital system which used it was the Veterans Administration.[26]

As a rule, the medical profession sanctioned fee-for-service payment only, where a physician charged his patients for each treatment received. In some cases, the AMA's commitment to this system engendered bitter feelings toward any program that deviated from it. For example, organized medicine fought with the Blue Cross insurance plans at various times about the matter.[27] Although the plans did not limit a patient's free choice of physician, which the AMA regarded as sacred, they did set limits on how much a participating doctor could charge for common procedures through the use of a fee schedule.

At the same time, the medical profession even viewed group practice with suspicion. Group practice was usually done by a set of physicians working through a clinic. While fee-for-service was used as a payment basis, the idea was to keep medical prices down through pooling the group's income and paying the member physicians a percentage of the proceeds. Such cooperation ran counter to the AMA's ideal of solo practice.[28] While not condemned by organized medicine, and even endorsed by the AMA's national office, local medical societies in many places treated group practice physicians as pariahs. In the case of a clinic in Bellaire, Ohio, which served union miners in the Pittsburgh area, the participating doctors were denied staff privileges at local hospitals and were excluded from all professional activities.[29] It was clear that the medical profession deemed any payment arrangement which deviated from fee-for-service as unacceptable.

At the time the chain was dedicated, the Fund's relations with various state medical societies, and with the AMA itself, were strained. The Fund originally paid all medical bills presented to it without restrictions. By the early 1950s, however, Dr. Draper realized that a great deal of unnecessary work was being done at inflated costs, and he sought to limit it. His actions brought a swift response from the AMA, causing Draper to back off.[30]

It was in this context that Dr. Asa Barns, AMO for the Louisville office, expressed his doubts about the wisdom of using a salaried staff at the hospitals. In addition to working with the union, Barnes insisted that the area administrators had the duty to establish and maintain cordial relationships with the medical community. This was to ensure good care for the miners. The hospitals offered quality treatment and granted visiting staff membership to anyone who sought them. But, the presence of salaried doctors placed the chain in direct competition with physicians and other medical institutions who participated in the Fund's programs. Also, Barnes claimed a salaried staff mitigated against a beneficiary's free choice of physician.[31] According to Barnes, free choice was important to people in Kentucky, since their sense of individualism would not allow others to make decisions for them.[32]

In terms of the jurisdictional issue, the AMOs insisted the hospitals could not be integrated into the Fund's program so long as they operated under the direction of a separate body. Because the medical staffs were responsible to the association's officers only, the AMOs could not do their job of overseeing standards. By November 1956 some AMOs agreed the problem could be solved by dissolving the association and reorganizing the hospitals as a set of autonomous institutions. Although the Fund would prepare the budgets of the various hospitals, their staffs would be autonomous from Washington and would be self-directing. Such autonomy would ensure good care and reorient the staffs toward viewing the patients as individuals, rather than as clinical cases.[33]

From the correspondence it is obvious that the issue here was similar to one which troubled the union: local versus central authority. The AMOs were convinced they had a better idea about what the Fund's beneficiaries needed than the people in Washington. Such an attitude was understandable and defensible since these men worked in the field and possessed a firsthand knowledge about local conditions. But, Draper could not possibly consider such a change, let alone suggest it to Roche or Lewis. Aside from the tax issue, he had to take into account the opinions of the association's officers.

Attempting to solve the problem, Draper issued a lengthy memo in December 1956 to everyone concerned. It outlined the duties of the ten area offices and those of the association. But, when he mentioned the hospital chain's integration with the medical program, his statements became contradictory. While he admitted that the hospitals came under the authority of the AMOs, that authority was limited by the association's distinct structure within the Fund.[34]

Instead of clarifying matters, the memo made them worse. Not only were the AMOs dissatisfied, but Dr. Mott refused to allow them any input in what he regarded as the association's affairs.[35] He believed that to do so meant divided responsibility and possible failure. His concern centered particularly on the physicians hired by the association. These people came to work for the chain as a result of an extensive recruitment campaign, attracted by the challenging work the chain offered.[36] As a group, the physicians were committed to industrial medicine and understood the Fund's goals.[37] Moreover, Mott argued that an AMO at a desk a hundred miles away should not be in a position to tell a hospital staff member how to practice medicine. The doctor in question probably knew what was the best form of treatment for a given case, and his discretion had to be trusted.[38]

The tone of Mott's correspondence indicated his anger with Draper and hinted broadly that Draper had somehow caved in to the AMOs. What Mott refused to understand, however, was that the AMOs presented as strong a case as his. Moreover, Draper could not simply exempt the chain from scrutiny by the area offices while demanding complete accountability from independent providers. Such a double standard would have further strained the already bad relations the Fund had with organized medicine. Mott's reaction to Draper's memo played a major role in his decision to resign from the MMHA in June of 1957.

The clash between the chain and the four area offices was costly. It failed to solve anything and worked against the Fund's efficient operation. In a plea for unity, Dr. Morrison circulated a memo in which he attempted to define the duties of the area offices and the hospitals. The area offices acted as the purchasers of medical services, and the hospitals as the providers of those services.[39] Harmonious relations between the two offered great possibilities for both the Fund and union miners. If factions developed, however, both the medical service and the chain would be too expensive for the Fund to support.[40]

Unlike previous conflicts, Lewis and Roche did not become involved. Owing to her position as both trustee and director, it would have been Roche's responsibility to make a final decision on a solution. Apparently, she did not care to risk alienating either side by trying to craft a compromise. To avoid a permanent rift, Roche left it to Dr. Draper to gloss over these differences as best as he could. Draper managed to do so because of the high regard in which he was held by the Fund's staff.[41] Nevertheless, the leadership's failure to find a solution to the problem was regrettable. Although the immediate crisis was settled by 1957, it left hard feelings on both sides, thereby making it more difficult for the Fund to present a united front.

Sadly, a united front was necessary due to the intense hostility the chain faced from the county and state-level branches of the AMA in its operating areas. Although this problem occurred in the wider context of a dispute between the Fund and the AMA's national office, the problem with the hospital chain was strictly of a local nature. As mentioned in chapter 3, relations with the medical community in the chain's area of operation had been hurt when *Reader's Digest* published a favorable article about the chain, saying it would end the common use of granny doctors and home cures. Obviously, the author relied upon popular perceptions about Appalachian medicine which had little basis in fact.

The reality was that most people in the region had access to an M.D., but the quality of these physicians varied greatly. Although Appalachia had qualified and capable practitioners, some even working as coal camp physicians in company check-off practices, it also had a high proportion of incompetents practicing medicine. According to a profile prepared by Dr. Asa Barnes, most local doctors were general practitioners whose average age was fifty-nine. They were graduates of medical schools that had disbanded and they usually resorted to surgery more often than needed.[42]

In all of the things Barnes said here, his use of the word *disbanded* in relation to the medical schools these physicians had attended was the most significant. In 1910, the American Medical Association commissioned a study by the Carnegie Foundation on the state of medical education in the United States. The study was conducted by educational theorist Prof. Abraham Flexner. Of the schools examined, forty-six were identified as substandard and forced by the AMA to close by 1925.[43] Yet graduates of these schools were grandfathered and allowed into the medical profession. Without exception, these schools had offered a two-year medical degree rather than a four-year graduate program. As will be seen in chapter 5, this was only the tip of the iceberg in terms of the poor state of the medical profession the Fund uncovered in Appalachia.

Despite this, the Fund attempted to foster good relations with local practitioners, especially by operating its hospitals on an open-staff basis. Regardless of the Fund's courtesy, problems began to appear even before all of the hospitals opened. In December 1955 the Fund's Louisville office discovered that four county medical societies in eastern Kentucky had filed new articles of incorporation.[44] These documents outlined the goals of the various societies, but each contained a clause limiting membership to persons approved by the directors.[45] This meant the directors could deny membership to anyone on any basis.

Organizationally, the AMA represented the sum total of its parts on the state and county levels. If a physician wanted to belong to the AMA, he first had to be accepted by his county medical society.[46] After the society approved his application, the state and national associations automatically granted membership. If an AMA member moved to a new location outside of his original county, the rules required him to join the new county's society. In such cases, the AMA gave the member a two-year grace period before it pulled his name from its list.[47]

Denial and/or loss of AMA membership was a serious matter. But, if the ramifications had been limited to a physician's being shunned by his peers, the Fund could have lived with the problem and sought a solution. However, the AMA at the time was still the touchstone for the entire medical profession. Although it did not license physicians, leaders of AMA state affiliates were in some cases the same people who made up the state licensing board.[48] It was conceivable that a shunned physician could see his right to practice jeopardized.

The most intense opposition to the Fund's efforts came from the Lecher, Perry, Pike, and Floyd County medical societies in Kentucky, as well as from the Kentucky State Medical Association (KSMA).[49] While these groups justified their actions by invoking high ideals of medical practice, the societies, including the KSMA, functioned as if they were business associations.

The MMHA's open-staff policies notwithstanding, the Fund was accused of denying patients a free choice of physician by using the hospitals as teaching institutions.[50] According to the critics, resident doctors who examined the patients during their rounds made additional diagnoses and recommendations for treatment without the knowledge or consent of the attending physician.[51] In addition, several of these residents discussed individual cases and freely gave their opinion about the quality of care the patient received.[52] Such behavior was unprofessional, and it placed the local doctor at a disadvantage. He would always feel he was being watched while working in the hospital and so lose the satisfaction he derived from practicing medicine.[53]

Although the critics were correct to protest the residents' behavior, their claim that the hospitals denied their patients a free choice of physician was patent nonsense. Moreover, the denial of free choice of physician had been the modus operandi of medical practice in eastern Kentucky for many years through its system of closed-staff proprietary hospitals. Invocation of free choice in this instance was merely a cover for the KSMA's real concern: stopping unwanted competition. The only legitimate doubts expressed about using the chain as teaching and research hospitals came from within the Fund itself, and were made by Knoxville AMO Dr. John Winebrenner. While he lauded the ideals behind resident training, he believed it was an expensive luxury.[54]

An even more pressing issue concerned the MMHA's use of salaried staff.[55] On that point, the critics offered the same arguments advanced by some Fund AMOs: a salaried staff stifled competition, and a fee-for-service system offered the best guarantee of quality care. What disturbed the critics the most, however, was the office care procedures used by the specialists the chain employed. In addition to their work for the chain, the specialists maintained offices in the hospitals for consultation with patients referred to them.[56]

Because some of the referrals were nonbeneficiaries who paid fees for their visits, physicians outside the MMHA claimed the chain's staff was engaging in unfair competition. If a specialist wanted to do private practice over and above his hospital service, the critics demanded that he establish an office outside the hospital and not be subsidized to an extra income. The critics failed to mention, however, that doctors working for the chain were obliged to turn these proceeds over to the MMHA, which in turn used them to finance retirement plans for the staff.[57] The striking thing about these particular complaints against the chain and its physicians was that not one of the refusing county societies made any statement concerning their competitors' competency to practice medicine, the quality of care offered, or anything remotely resembling concern for a patient's welfare in a clinical setting.

Such outright discrimination angered Draper, Newdorp, Meade, and others, but they were powerless to take any action other than the appeal procedures offered by the KSMA or the AMA itself. As head of the Fund's legal department, Val J. Mitch decided against any litigation.[58] Unjust as the refusals were, county medical societies did have the prerogative to bar any doctor applying for membership. If the Fund sued the societies, the cases would have been heard in the Kentucky courts, and the climate of opinion in the state at the time did not favor the union.[59] The only alternative open to the Fund was a direct appeal for reconsideration to the KSMA. The process was slow and complicated and did not offer much hope of a favorable outcome. Several influential doctors in the state society fanatically opposed any accommodation with the chain.[60]

The Fund appealed only one refusal case, that of Dr. Fred Zuspan. It is likely that the Fund's leadership hoped to use any favorable decision in the case as a guide to future action. Dr. Zuspan joined the chain's staff in 1956 and specialized in obstetrics and gynecology.[61] In December 1956 he applied for membership in the Floyd County Medical Society, which rejected his application on the grounds that he was a salaried physician.[62] Dr. Zuspan decided to appeal the decision to the KSMA's governing council. He still needed final certification in his chosen specialization, and that could only be done by joining the appropriate specialist's society.[63] Much to his disappointment, the council rejected the appeal. According to its executive secretary, Dr. J. P. Sanford, the council believed the MMHA operated in violation of the AMA's suggested guidelines on medical ethics, thus, an appeal could not be considered.[64]

Zuspan refused to be put off so easily. He retained legal counsel, and in November 1957 he wrote the KSMA's president demanding that an appeal be granted.[65] Zuspan reminded the president that chapter 13 of the KSMA's bylaws allowed any qualified physician to join, if he practiced nonsectarian medicine. Moreover, sections 6 and 7 allowed any physician the right to appeal and to present evidence to support his case.[66] This time the council relented, and Zuspan appeared before it on December 12, 1957.

After listing the facts of his case, Zuspan testified that the only reason the Floyd County society rejected him was his employment as a salaried physician.[67] Ostensibly, the condemnation of such an arrangement was designed for the physician's protection, to prevent his exploitation. Zuspan pointed out that the general rule applied to for-profit hospitals and not to his case, since the chain was a nonprofit organization.[68] Zuspan also stressed that all sections of the Fund operated within the guidelines adopted by the AMA's House of Delegates in 1949 and its 1955 "Guiding Principles" for union health centers.[69] He concluded by saying, "The free choice principle is not an ethic. It is not part of the 'Principles of Medical Ethics' of the AMA and is not part of public law. It is merely an *excuse* [italics his] for disciplinary action, which, without the excuse, would be plain economic boycott."[70] The council did not take any action on Zuspan's appeal until the new year, and not until it recalled him to answer some questions. Most of these questions concerned the use of the extra fees charged by staff doctors for office care, how the chain was organized, and whether the hospitals allowed the patients a free choice of physicians.[71]

In the meantime, Zuspan's case became a rallying cry within the AMA and anyone hostile to medical third parties. The rhetoric became particularly heated, as shown by the following statement which appeared in the February 10, 1958, edition of the AMA's *Washington Report on Medical Services:* "Dr. Zuspan's appeal is merely the opening gun to turn the Sherman Anti-Trust Act into a sword rather than a shield. Evidence of this is found in the fact that 14 of 25 UMWA doctors applied for admission to the Pike County Medical Society and withdrew their applications the following day, were forced by the UMWA to resubmit their applications upon pain of dismissal."[72] Asa Barnes protested the report's contents and asked rhetorically, if the hospital chain was as exploitative as the statement claimed, how did it manage to keep so many well-qualified physicians on its staff?[73]

Even more upsetting was a move on the part of the Kentucky legislature to outlaw medical third parties from operating in the state.[74] Subsections of the act raised free choice of physician to legal status, allowed the courts to enjoin any out-of-state medical program from operating in Kentucky, and threatened any participating doctor with loss of his license.[75] If passed, the act would have forced the Fund to cease all operations in the state. Although it did not gain approval, the act's supporters were able to keep it alive in the legislature as a viable threat until 1960.[76]

After Zuspan made his second appearance before the council in March 1957, he did not hear anything again until August, when the council approved his appeal.[77] Because the Floyd County society voted unanimously to refuse Zuspan's application, the KSMA determined that it could not force the society to accept him. Instead it allowed Zuspan to apply for membership in an adjoining county's society.[78] Zuspan followed the KSMA's directive and applied to the Johnson County Medical Society, only to be denied admission again.[79]

The second denial prompted Dr. Meade to demand more aggressive action against the KSMA by filing a lawsuit. Owing to the nature of the laws, the only grounds available were restraint of trade. In this setting, all of the precedents rested on organized medicine's side. Val J. Mitch cited a recent decision to prove the point. A ruling by the Federal District Court in Arkansas on a similar case held that the antitrust laws did not apply in such cases.[80] Shortly after his second rejection, Dr. Zuspan left his position with the MMHA and became head of obstetrics and gynecology for the Chicago Lying-in Hospital of the University of Chicago. Subsequent to this, Dr. Zuspan was recruited to serve as chief of Obstetrical Services for the Ohio State University.[81]

The frustration the impasse caused moved several people within the Fund's structure to use more aggressive methods. In one instance, Dr. Barnes attempted to pressure an influential physician into giving his support by threatening to drop him from the participation list. Barnes's clumsiness was underscored by the fact that the doctor in question had supported the Fund's program and now intended to work against it. Upset, Dr. Meade made a note of the affair to his file under the heading "Asa Barnes Does It Again."[82]

While such directly coercive tactics were useless, Dr. Draper suggested a more subtle method: turn the KSMA's own bylaws against it by the formation of rival county societies. Chapter 12, section 4 of the KSMA's rules clearly stated that when two rival societies existed in one county, the state association had the responsibility of bringing them together into one body.[83] Dr. Meade took up the suggestion enthusiastically and approached one of the hospitals about forming a rival society for Lecher County, Kentucky.

Although it was a dangerous step to create an open division within the medical community, the benefits here outweighed the risks. The recognized county society had only eight members, while the proposed rival had seventeen. Meade was confident that the KSMA would be forced to bring the two organizations together, since the rival body represented the majority of practicing doctors in the county.[84] Much to Meade's disappointment, the hospital's staff decided not to pursue the idea.[85] No record exists of the staff meeting during which the decision was made, but it is reasonable to assume that the hospital's staff wanted to avoid poisoning their future relations with organized medicine.

Pikeville Memorial's staff, though, did not have the same fears. Between 1956 and 1959, forty-four of their physicians sought entry into the Pike County Medical Society, and all of them were rejected. With no alternative, they formed a rival society and requested a charter from the KSMA. The state society refused on the grounds that a recognized body already existed. The rival organization responded by pointing out that it represented the majority of practicing physicians in the county and reminded the KSMA of its own rules in such cases.[86] The KSMA refused to take any action by claiming it lacked jurisdiction in the matter.[87] As a last resort, the rival society appealed to the chairman of the AMA's board of directors.[88]

These events took place between December 1959 and May 1961, and during that period the rival society sponsored a series of lectures given by outstanding leaders in the medical profession. Among the speakers were Dr. Jonas Salk; Prof. Alan M. Butler, director of clinical services at the Metropolitan Hospital of Detroit; Dr. Harvey Crule, director of the Cleveland Clinic; and Dr. Isador Radain, professor of surgery at the University of Pennsylvania Hospital.[89] Although never explicitly stated in the correspondence, the purpose behind the lecture series was obvious. The Fund wished to demonstrate that its medical society, rather than the recognized KSMA local, acted in greater conformity with AMA ideals of scholarship and improved medical service. By 1962, however, acceptance of the MMHA by organized medicine had become moot. The Fund had decided earlier that it could no longer afford to operate the entire hospital chain, and it directed its attention to finding buyers.

In terms of its impact, the KSMA's boycott of the chain's physicians did not keep the hospitals from operating; but it further complicated matters in a setting where attracting physicians was already difficult. While these institutions offered young doctors a chance to practice a challenging form of medicine, working for the association required sacrifice. It was a hardship for most doctors to live and work in an isolated, rural area under the best of circumstances. Organized medicine's disdain added to that problem and made it harder for the chain to retain good staff members. Dr. Zuspan's case clearly demonstrates that fact. Through their actions, the members of the county societies and the KSMA showed they were not concerned about promoting good health. They were concerned about protecting their incomes.

While organized medicine's hostility had been a serious problem, the biggest concern was to ensure that the Fund's beneficiaries used the new institutions. Dr. Mott stressed the importance of a good rapport between the staff and the miners. He hoped that once the hospitals established an operating pattern all of the MMHA's physicians, general practitioners, and specialists alike would be regarded as family doctors.[90]

Dr. Meade placed emphasis on the chain's role in preventive medicine.[91] Because of their attitudes concerning quality medical practice, in particular their adherence to the regional hierarchy approach, the MMHA's leadership attempted to bring an urban hospital model to a rural area. For example, Dr. Newdorp believed that research was as important a function for the professional staff as handling cases. He also maintained that the opportunity to conduct clinical research was an important factor in the chain's ability to attract and keep high-caliber people.[92] Newdorp's arguments were convincing, and the association budgeted $130,000 annually for research grants, which it continued to do until the hospitals were sold.[93]

The same reasoning also accounted for the decision to use the hospitals as teaching institutions. Despite the doubts of some area administrators, residency training programs were established throughout the chain. They were centered in the Harlan, Beckley, and Williamson hospitals.[94] Also, the hospitals operated various nursing schools.

The association's experience with this aspect of its work was mixed. In one instance, the chain was forced to close its practical nursing school at Beckley because Williamson's program was large enough to meet local needs. But, at the same time, the Fund established relationships with local educational institutions by making the chain's facilities available for clinical training.[95] The best example was an arrangement with Moorehead State College of Kentucky, which enabled the college to offer clinical experience for its Bachelor of Science program in medical technology.[96]

A more practical concern for the association was its salary structure. Many distinctions existed in this area. First, pay scales for physicians were based upon the doctor's training and position. Second, payment for all physician service classifications was not uniform. Nevertheless, the physician salaries offered were more than competitive with similar positions across the country.[97] In 1959 the salaries for the chiefs of clinical services at the three central hospitals ranged from $20,401 to $27,692 a year, and between $17,654 and $24,750 at the other seven.[98] By 1962 payment for this position in the entire chain ranged between $24,000 to $30,000. However, several of the hospitals had reduced the position to part-time status because of budget limitations.[99] Payment for general practitioners during these same years was considerably lower. In 1959, a general practitioner earned between $12,400 and $13,600. Three years later, the highest salary of the group had risen to $15,356, with most still earning between $12,000 and $13,000 a year.[100]

Nurses were in a different position. All of them were organized into UMWA District 50. Salary scales for these positions in 1956 were as follows: $370 a month for general duty nurses, $270 a month for practical nurses, and $216 a month for unskilled workers. Although regular salary increases were given to the staff, the starting salaries were never increased between 1956 and 1961.[101]

District 50's weak representation was underscored about a year after the chain's dedication when the support staff sought to create a grievance committee. Although the idea had been endorsed by two hospital administrators, District 50's president rejected the request. The reason for his decision was that Local 13410, which handled the support staff, also represented the association's managers. As such, they were forbidden to work under a union contract by the Taft-Hartley Act. Without a contract, a grievance committee could not be created.[102] In essence, District 50 functioned as a company union. This sort of scheme offered the appearance of worker participation in decision making while keeping real unions out. The irony was that through District 50 John L. Lewis was using the same mechanism within the MMHA which he had fought against when he organized the CIO in 1935. Underlying all of this was a constant budget problem caused by the chain's beneficiary usage level. A year after the dedication, the chain's leadership discovered that the hospitals were not being heavily used by the Fund's beneficiaries, except for the outpatient clinics. Figures for 1956 and 1957 showed that the chain's monthly inpatient census was slightly less than half of full capacity, falling between 615 and 722 people.[103]

As time passed, improvement in the usage figures was uneven. According to the MMHA's reports for fiscal year 1958, the central hospitals at Beckley, Harlan, and Williamson were running at 86.3, 75.6, and 83 percent of capacity, respectively. Performance at the seven other institutions for the same period was much more erratic. Pikeville and Hazard reported usage levels just above 76 percent. Meanwhile, Man and Middlesboro operated at only 60 percent and brought the chain's average down to 73.3 percent.[104]

Meanwhile, during the same period, more than half a million people passed through the outpatient clinics.[105] The high level of patient turnover for these clinics offered some consolation. But, if the hospital program was to succeed, the inpatient facilities had to show a higher level of usage by the Fund's beneficiaries. This situation placed the Fund into a position where it paid twice for the same services. If union miners residing in the MMHA's operational area chose to be treated at a competing institution on the Fund's participation list, the Fund had no choice but to pay. Forcing people to use the chain was out of the question. It would confirm AMA accusations that the Fund was engaging in corporate medicine and denying patients a free choice of providers. Yet, despite these facts, the Fund was compelled to maintain the hospital chain and its services at a level of full readiness, even if facilities remained idle.

While the chain was distinct from the Fund in a legal sense, it never became self-supporting. Its expenses were subsidized by the Fund from the dedication until the chain's transfer in 1963–64. The figures are not complete, but judging from those which are available, the Fund's subsidy amounted to roughly $12 million a year.[106] If the hospital program was to be less of an expense, beneficiary occupancy had to be increased.

Solving the problem of beneficiary occupancy became the Fund's most pressing concern. Generally, the cause lay in beneficiary dissatisfaction with the chain's patient services. In one instance, Leon Rayburn, the administrator for Man Memorial, wrote that he could not handle a number of the cases which came to his facility for treatment because of high staff turnover. For example, he had been forced to refer the cases of four children to a competing institution because his pediatrician had found another position.[107] Rayburn's predicament, however, was only part of a much wider set of difficulties. These came under two general headings: misunderstandings about the extent of the Fund's coverage and a clash between rural and urban attitudes about medicine. Although the Fund offered comprehensive coverage for hospitalization and office care rendered by specialists, it did not cover routine treatment given by general practitioners outside of a clinical setting. Many beneficiaries did not understand the distinction.

Payment for prescription drugs was another major source of misunderstanding. The Fund's general policy was that it paid for drugs prescribed during a beneficiary's stay in the hospital. Also, it paid for medications used for the treatment of chronic conditions, such as diabetes.[108] Beyond that, prescription payment varied in the ten area offices, and there was no coordinated policy established with the MMHA on the matter. Consequently, some of the chain's hospitals assumed responsibility for drug prescriptions, while others did not, which prompted confused beneficiaries to complain.[109]

The lack of a set policy for prescription payment embarrassed the Fund, but the single-most important area of dissatisfaction centered on the chain's admission and treatment procedures. After the end of the association's second year of operation, the Fund polled its beneficiaries who resided in proximity to the hospital chain to determine the source of the problem. No one received low quality care. Many people complained though that they had been forced to wait too long to see a physician. In some cases people left an association hospital in disgust and sought treatment at other institutions.[110] The problem was not confined to the chain's inpatient system. In a number of cases, beneficiaries expressed a wish that the outpatient clinics would be open on Saturday for their convenience.[111] From the point of view of these beneficiaries, the MMHA's doctors and support staff were indifferent to their needs.

In fact, indifference was not the problem. Rather, the staff followed the techniques used by urban hospitals. The patient made an appointment and the attending physician developed a complete workup, consisting of X rays, lab reports, and diagnostic aids. Most of the miners the hospitals treated, however, were accustomed to a much less thorough method.[112] The local physician, usually a company doctor, treated his patients on a walk-in basis and worked out of a black bag. People simply came to the doctor's office when they had a complaint, and he made a diagnosis based on the symptoms reported. Accustomed to this form of practice, many beneficiaries walked in, either to the clinics or the hospitals, without regard to schedules or appointment regulations. Dr. Newdorp realized the difference in expectations and stressed the need to educate the beneficiaries that appointments were for their own good, and not designed to put them off.[113]

To facilitate this understanding, Pikeville Memorial distributed a small pamphlet explaining the hospital's services and their limitations. It emphasized that its outpatient clinic operated on a regular schedule and could not be open at all times since the physicians also treated people staying in the hospital.[114] The pamphlet failed to explain why appointments were necessary, though, and a problem with walk-in patients continued throughout the chain.

Ever conscious of the need to increase occupancy and make the hospitals attractive to union members, Dr. Newdorp explored different methods of accommodating beneficiary needs. One of these was for the chain to keep its clinics open on Saturdays and to end charging additional fees to beneficiaries who came after hours for outpatient care. Neither of these decisions were popular with the staff.

By November of 1958, three of the chain's hospitals were maintaining Saturday hours at their clinics. Newdorp liked the idea and made inquiries about it with the rest of the chain's staff.[115] The consensus of opinion was as follows: the association's doctors would resent giving up their Saturdays, since these were usually reserved for their families. No evidence existed to show that Saturday hours would increase usage. Finally, Monday was always the day with the heaviest service load.[116] Newdorp answered these criticisms by saying the chain needed the goodwill of the miners, and Saturday clinics were the best option available to win it. The heavy service load usual for Mondays resulted from the fact that it was the first operation day after the weekend, not because there was anything special about Monday itself. If the five-day schedule were shifted to Tuesday through Saturday, Tuesday would be the busiest day.[117]

Newdorp used the same argument to end the fee differential. Although miners received free treatment at the hospitals, they were charged two dollars for the physician's time in the clinics. Several of the hospitals such as McDowell and Pikeville charged an additional three dollars for patients seeking treatment after service hours to discourage walk-ins. While the fees did not penalize an individual beyond his ability to pay, Newdorp wanted the after-hours charge lowered to one dollar.[118] He agreed that the schedules had to be respected, but he added that most of these visits were made by people who sought emergency treatment. It did not matter if the attending physician knew that no emergency existed; the prospective patients believed it and should not be penalized for their fears.[119] In the end, the arguments became moot when the Fund's leadership decided in February 1959 to keep the clinics open on Saturdays as part of an overall program designed to increase the number of miners treated by the association.

Owing to his work as Alabama's state health officer, as well as a principle author of that state's postwar hospital plan, Newdorp understood the sensibilities of the rural population the MMHA served. In attempting to bring urban medicine to this area, he wanted to continue the personal touch traditionally associated with rural practice. But the staff as well as the chiefs of clinical services for Hazard, Middlesboro, and Pikeville resisted his efforts. It is reasonable to assume, therefore, that the reluctance to accommodate standard procedure to a rural setting was one of the major sources of the chain's ultimate failure.

Near the end of 1958, Roche became concerned about the low beneficiary census levels the hospitals reported. She denied that the problem proved the chain had been a mistake, but stressed that it demonstrated a need to ensure the fullest usage possible. According to Roche's statistics, 17.4 percent of the people the chain had treated during the first nine months of 1958 were not Fund beneficiaries. This amounted to a loss for the Fund of fifty cents on every dollar paid for each of these cases.[120] Roche did not offer any clear explanation as to how she arrived at this figure. The cause was probably connected to the Fund's maintaining its own hospital system while continuing to purchase a large volume of hospital care from competing institutions.

During the same nine months, the Fund purchased hospital care at competing institutions for 31 percent of the eligible union miners who resided in the chain's service area. Something had to be done about the imbalance, and Roche concluded that the chain's usage could be increased by dropping competitors from the participation list.[121] She believed that the move would not overburden the chain, because the statistics showed the association had a large number of patient days open. The same figures indicated that the average stay of a union miner at an association hospital was longer than a private patient's. Roche hoped to find some way to lower the average.[122]

No easy solutions could be found, however, and Newdorp's first response was to question the statistical evidence Roche used. The figures and tables involved had been prepared by the Fund's comptroller, Thomas Ryan. Dr. Newdorp admitted they were mathematically correct, but did not truly reflect how much space the chain's hospitals had available at any given time. Ryan's formula produced a total figure taken over a period of time and created the impression of considerable unused space. The figures showed that Beckley and Pikeville were operating at 80 to 85 percent of capacity, but in reality these two facilities were usually full. Newdorp admitted that some of the chain's hospitals were underused, such as Man and McDowell, but this was due to problems with high staff turnover and not competition. [123]

As far as usage of the chain by nonbeneficiaries, Newdorp explained that some of the people listed under the heading were eligible miners. Treatment in these cases was being paid by either workman's compensation or another third-party carrier.[124] Poor transportation and referral of seriously ill patients by the area offices accounted for the higher-than-average stay among the union members using the hospital chain.[125]

Originally, when Roche made her inquiries, she approached Dr. Draper about the matter. As the Fund's chief medical officer, he was the most logical choice. When Draper made his final report to Roche six weeks later, he cited all of the arguments which Dr. Newdorp presented and other information which had been gathered by Dr. John Morrison, who was serving as the association's president. Several months before Roche spoke with Draper, Dr. Morrison had conducted a study of the competing hospitals in the MMHA's operating area to see if they could be discontinued. A total of ten operated in the immediate vicinities of Man, Wise, Middlesboro, Pikeville, McDowell, and Whitesburg, seven of which were "general" or community hospitals: Holden, Logan, Madison, Norton, Pikeville Community, and Sharon Heights. The other three were sectarian: Methodist Hospital, St. Mary's, and Our Lady of the Way.[126] Morrison based his analysis on several factors. These included geographic conditions and available transportation, referral patterns of the local physicians for hospital and specialist services, and the physical capacity of the chain to care for an increased load.[127] In every case, one of these concerns, or a combination of them, prevented the Fund from tightening the participation list.

At first, Madison General Hospital appeared to be a good candidate for elimination. It was a small fifty-bed facility and fit the description usually associated with an Appalachian proprietary hospital. But, it served a population working for a large mining operation located in Wharton, Barrett, and Broadtown, West Virginia. No paved access road existed in the area, and the communities it served were too isolated to enable residents to seek care elsewhere.[128] Logan General Hospital was a one-hundred-bed facility which served Fund beneficiaries south of Blair Mountain. On the map, Williamson Memorial was not far away, but ambulances could not cross the mountain, which necessitated a twenty-five-mile detour. Norton General Hospital had to be continued because of the large number of pediatric cases it treated. Wise Memorial was Norton's closest rival, but it did not have the facilities to handle this type of patient load.[129]

Both Morrison's study and Roche's inquiry pointed to a growing anxiety concerning cost containment. Under normal circumstances, the Fund might have been able to absorb the chain's expenses without difficulty. Unfortunately, a severe recession during the latter half of President Eisenhower's second term was taking a huge toll. The period from 1958 to 1961 were the Fund's bleakest years financially. As always, the Fund's income was subject to production levels and demand for coal. The industry's performance during these years was poor, marked by a sharp drop in sales.

The immediate effect upon the Fund's income was obvious. However, there was an additional problem to address: the refusal of many smaller companies to continue royalty payments when faced with bankruptcy.[130] There were two reasons why these smaller operators could get away without paying. First, the men they employed were glad for the opportunity to work and did not protest the decision, despite pro-union sympathies. As Lewis had foreseen, when mechanization displaced these miners, they left the coal fields to find work in other industries. But many returned when their searches for alternative employment failed. This was partially due to the recession. In addition, the creation of new manufacturing jobs had stopped growing at an appreciable rate by the middle 1950s.[131] Confronted with this situation, many people took jobs with smaller operators who were either nonunion or had broken their contracts.

Second, the larger companies, which Lewis depended upon to discipline the industry, were incapable of forcing these smaller mines out of business. Because they had no royalty obligations and paid lower wages, the small companies could undercut the larger firms. The large operators could not meet the challenge by cutting their own prices, still abide by their union contracts, and remain solvent. Thus, the union was powerless to intervene directly, since neither its membership nor the large operators could cope with the challenge.[132]

The only alternative available to the Fund's leaders was to cut services. The first step was to reduce all pensions to seventy-five dollars a month in 1961. To enforce contractual obligations, the Fund canceled the 85 HS cards held by union members working for defaulting operators. The most important action taken in terms of its impact upon the MMHA was the cancellation of medical benefits in July 1960 for all union members unemployed for one year or more. Prior to that decision, the Fund covered everyone in the union regardless of employment status. The reduction was the most extensive of all actions taken at the time; it dropped 59,550 union miners, about 25 percent of all 85 HS card holders in the union.[133]

These emergency measures may have kept the Fund solvent, but, as will be seen later, they occasioned a major outpouring of criticism from the union's membership. They also created the preconditions for the hospital program's final collapse. Ironically, the needs of the Fund and those of the MMHA worked at cross-purposes. For the MMHA to succeed, it needed a consistently high beneficiary census level. But the Fund could no longer afford to maintain the union's unemployed members, who made up at least 25 percent of the potential users residing in the association's service area. Without the patronage of the unemployed miners, the hospitals became even more expensive to maintain, placing a greater burden on the Fund. This resulted in the decision to sell or close four of the hospitals. Reductions not withstanding, Roche and Draper were committed to saving the hospital program, and they attempted to martial the Fund's resources for that purpose between 1959 and 1962.

After reviewing information sent to him by Morrison, Newdorp, and Ryan, Draper drew up a three-part plan in February 1959 to shore up the chain. First, referrals to competing institutions would be restricted whenever possible. Second, all ten hospitals would now maintain Saturday hours for the outpatient clinics. Third, the Fund attempted to the solve morale and turnover problems at some of its institutions. At McDowell Memorial, where physician turnover was the highest, all members of the medical staff were given a financial incentive to remain. The Fund offered each physician a $1,000-a-year bonus for each year worked, payable at the end of his service. Also, a physician received an additional $1,000 for each of his children, with a maximum of $3,000. To deal with similar problems at Man Memorial, and to provide direction for its medical staff, Charleston area administrator Dr. Riheldaffer was appointed as Man's chief of clinical services in addition to his other duties.[134]

At best, these steps only palliated the situation and did not offer a long-term solution. As time passed, the sense of urgency within the Fund increased. Out of desperation, it eventually dropped almost every competing hospital from its participation list, including St. Mary's and Norton General.[135] In conjunction with these actions, the Fund's leadership attempted to increase the chain's usage by bringing in beneficiary patients from outlying medical areas. The idea was originally discussed during a general meeting held between the Fund's central staff, the area administrators, and the MMHA's officers in April 1960 to prepare for benefit reductions.[136] Subsequently, the area administrators were ordered to compile lists of all cases that could be sent to the chain for treatment.[137] The idea was innovative but unworkable. It required that at least 150 additional patients a month had to be brought in from the other areas.[138] The Fund simply no longer served enough beneficiaries to keep the association afloat. To make matters worse, after the 1960 benefit cuts went into effect the nonbeneficiary usage share increased at all ten of the hospitals.

Newdorp remained hopeful that a solution could be found, but few of the Fund's officers shared his optimism. Before the end of 1961, even Draper became convinced that the Fund could no longer afford to keep the entire chain open. He suggested to Roche that the entire chain should be sold before the Fund closed one or more of the institutions.[139] Roche did not like the idea, but by the spring of 1962, she informed Draper that the Fund was no longer committed to supporting the entire chain indefinitely.[140] The beginning of the end came almost as an anticlimax. On August 14, 1962, Newdorp sent a memo to Draper about another idea to save the chain. Draper responded the following day with this short note: "Doctor Newdorp, In the common mode of expression, 'Let's face it' What do you think? [signed] WFD."[141] Shortly thereafter, the Fund decided to sell or close four of the ten hospitals: Hazard, Whitesburg, McDowell, and Middlesboro.[142] The cutoff date set for sale or closure was July 1, 1963. All of the remaining facilities were to remain open.

The Fund announced its plans on October 12, 1962, but it did not publicly commit itself to closing the four hospitals if they were not sold. Roche had been advised against making these plans known, since the uproar would disrupt the medical service's activities.[143] To say anything about closing any of the hospitals would hurt morale among the association's medical staff. Roche was advised simply to mention the chain's successes in upgrading the quality of care in eastern Kentucky, and that the Fund decided to divest itself of some of its institutions and make them available to their communities.[144] Nevertheless, rumors had been circulating about the Fund's financial condition and plans to dispose of the chain since the previous December.[145]

Even before the announcement, the Fund began its search for a buyer. In September 1962 Harlan's chief of clinical services, Dr. David McL. Greely, made inquiries on the subject through some of his friends in the University of Kentucky medical school. Among Greely's friends here were the medical school's dean, Dr. William Willard, and Kentucky's director of state and local services, Dr. Robert Johnson. Dr. Johnson was also an assistant professor of community medicine. With Dr. Willard's help, Dr. Greely managed to air his views with Dr. Robert Long, senior delegate of the Kentucky State Medical Association to the AMA. Surprisingly, Greely made a good impression with Dr. Johnson, whose attitude toward the Fund seemed comparatively generous for a ranking member of the KSMA. While protesting that he admired the associations' work, Dr. Johnson disapproved of its organizational methods. If, however, the Fund's institutions became true community hospitals, he hinted that the KSMA would be more reasonable in its attitude. He recommended that the Fund try to sell the hospitals to their respective communities. Greely believed Dr. Johnson's suggestion was the most logical step to take and endorsed it in his discussions with Newdorp.[146]

The idea may have been logical, but none of the towns which hosted the four hospitals could afford to purchase them. Therefore, the Fund requested the assistance of Kentucky's governor, Bert T. Combs. Combs was fairly liberal and part of the Democratic political machine built by the state's leading New Dealer: Senator and former Vice-President Alben W. Barkley.[147] With Mr. Combs's help, an informational meeting was scheduled to discuss the problem and possible solutions.[148] Prior to the meeting, the Fund's officers were guardedly optimistic about the outcome since Combs had called a special session of the state legislature. Officially, the session was intended to address the state's reapportionment, but the governor's message added that the state should help find a solution to the crisis with the miner's hospitals.[149]

After a great deal of preparation, the meeting was held at Harlan on January 10–11, 1963. Instead of arriving at a workable method for transferring the four facilities, the delegates took it as an opportunity to express their pent-up anger at the Fund and the union. Dr. James B. Holloway, chairman of the KSMA's standing committee on hospitals, said that the hospital chain had driven many smaller institutions into bankruptcy with its unfair competition. Now, after suffering this loss, the Fund dared to ask the taxpayers of Kentucky to pay again by purchasing the four institutions. Instead, he demanded that the Fund simply give the hospitals to their communities, which would generously take them off the Fund's hands.[150]

Holloway's speech represented the consensus of the meeting. Dr. Newdorp, who attended, made it clear that he would entertain a reasonable price, probably at a loss, but would not give the facilities away. The Fund had a duty to its beneficiaries to see that its resources were handled carefully. If the four hospitals could not be sold, the Fund planned to close them down until it received a reasonable offer.[151] Immediately after Newdorp made his remarks, Sen. Nick Johnson blurted out that the richest union in the world was "thumbing its nose" at the people of Kentucky. He added that the courts would order the union to keep the facilities open. The senator was then informed that the courts could do no such thing.[152] Although Johnson's hostility for the union was probably real, his attitude at the meeting was fueled by his political allegiances. Whereas Governor Combs was a Barkley man, Senator Johnson was an associate of Barkley's conservative rival: former Gov. Albert B. (Happy) Chandler. Thus, in this case, the chain was simply another political football in a bitter feud dating back almost thirty years.[153]

The meeting's failure killed any chance of transferring the hospitals to their communities. Offers from other potential buyers turned out to be equally disappointing.[154] The best prospect at the time appeared to be the Kaiser Health Plan. Financed by Kaiser Steel, the plan provided full medical coverage for all of the company's employees and had also created its own chain of hospitals. The Fund's had a longstanding relationship with the Kaiser plan. Shortly after the Fund was organized, its physical rehabilitation program was started. The program was designed to treat miners disabled in work-related accidents. Many of these men were sent by the Fund to the Kaiser physical therapy center in Vallejo, California, headed by Dr. Herman Kabat. This association had been successful and resulted in mutual respect between the two programs. In the end, however, Kaiser decided against the purchase because the local population was not large enough to provide a steady flow of patients.[155]

In economic terms, the Fund's position in January 1963 was a liquidity trap, where the Fund owned valuable property but could not convert it into cash. Press coverage further complicated the Fund's position by emphasizing that a crisis was in progress through such headlines as "Chaos in the Coal Fields" and "Private Welfare State in Trouble."[156] The press's reaction was understandable. For years, the Fund was regarded as the premier union benefit program. Now, suddenly, it was overextended and its leadership appeared to be moving with disillusioning haste to retrench.

Further, writers like Dan Wakefield, who wrote about Appalachia and economic issues, made matters worse by presenting misinformation. For example, upset over the benefit reductions, Wakefield informed his readers that the union had $100 million in its treasury and that the Fund's assets were the same.[157] From how Wakefield presented it, the reader was given the impression that the

Fund's and union's assets were commingled. They were not. The union's treasury would not be tapped to cover the Fund's expenses. Second, the Fund's various holdings were meant to serve as a barrier against a major loss of income. Considering the large amounts of money the Fund spent on the services it offered, keeping a reserve made good sense, especially since royalty income was erratic.

Despite these problems, however, the Fund accidentally found a buyer for the hospitals. When the Fund announced that it intended to close four of its institutions, Rev. McMaster Kerr, pastor of a large Presbyterian congregation in Harlan, contacted the union's Washington office. He was concerned that the Harlan hospital would be closed as well.[158] Roche assured him in a terse form letter that the Fund did not plan to close any of the other hospitals. Although relieved, Reverend Kerr remained interested in the association's future and arranged a meeting with Dr. Greely. After speaking with Greely, Kerr conferred with the Board of National Missions of the Presbyterian Church U.S.A. about acquiring the ten hospitals. After the Harlan meeting, the missions board interviewed members of the association's medical staff, and by the end of January 1963 the board expressed a definite interest in purchasing the entire chain.[159]

Agreement was one thing, final action was another. Between January and June 1963, the Fund and the church worked to create an arrangement where the chain could be successfully transferred and all problems settled. The actual negotiations were handled by the Reverend Robert Barrie, who headed the mission board's health and welfare division. Under his direction, the church retained Dr. E. D. Rosenfeld to appraise the chain.[160]

Dr. Rosenfeld made an exhaustive study of the chain's reimbursement rates, bad debt accounts, physical plant, land, and operating costs.[161] Based upon his information, Rosenfeld determined the price according to a set formula: any hospital became obsolete twenty-five years after its construction, and since the chain had operated for seven, one-third of the original building costs had to be deducted from the purchase price. Another third was similarly deducted on the basis of the population decline witnessed in the association's operating area since its dedication in 1956. According to Rosenfeld, the original building costs for the ten hospitals was $28.69 million which was $2 million less than the amount listed in the Fund's records. After the deductions, the church made a final offer of $9.5 million.[162] Although this represented a considerable loss for the Fund, compared with the other offers that had been made, the amount came the closest to matching the Fund's original investment.

The mission board, however, did not have the resources available to it to raise the necessary monies. The federal government was the only possible source for obtaining the funding, and it was the best choice as well. President Kennedy made a commitment to Appalachian redevelopment during the 1960 campaign, and the hospitals were a valuable resource for the region. Assistant Secretary of Labor Daniel Patrick Moynihan had contacted the Fund about its future plans for the association and expressed his concern that the institutions should continue to function. Although Moynihan's department did not become involved with providing the monies for the transfer, his interest proved valuable in subsequent negotiations. The funding agency the chain and the Presbyterians turned to was the Area Redevelopment Administration, which functioned under the Department of Commerce. This office was responsible for making monies available for local improvement projects, but its emphasis involved developing businesses.[163]

On April 26, 1963, the Board of National Missions finally took the organizational step necessary to facilitate the sale and formed a nonprofit corporation similar to the association: Appalachian Regional Hospitals, Inc.[164] At the same time, the Fund was using its contacts in Washington to arrange an initial meeting with Marjorie Heston, the ARA's administrator.[165] From the beginning, the Fund's relationship with the ARA was precarious and nearly jeopardized the arrangement with the church. While the Fund had originally approached the ARA, Roche, Draper, and Newdorp intended Appalachian Regional Hospitals to do the actual negotiating in Washington. While talks progressed, the Fund planned to work out an agreement with Governor Combs about amending the Kentucky welfare laws to cover people who were medically indigent. This had been a source of trouble for the association beginning in 1959.

The ARA, however, refused to negotiate with the Appalachian Regional Hospitals. The agency based its decision on the opinion that since the Fund would ultimately receive the grant money, it was the real client seeking the award. Therefore, the Fund had to justify the amount of money requested in the grant proposal. The ARA's purpose was to force the Fund to reduce its sale price for the hospitals. But the Fund's leadership refused to consider anything less than the amount determined by Dr. Rosenfeld. Upon receiving the Fund's refusal, Undersecretary of Commerce Franklin D. Roosevelt Jr., who oversaw the ARA, suspended the case and informed Governor Combs about it. Combs, in his turn, immediately stopped all work on amending his state's welfare laws. The entire transfer was now in serious trouble.

Roosevelt's motive for his hard attitude in all probability was a vindictiveness spurred by John L. Lewis's break with Roosevelt's father in 1940. Although Lewis and President Roosevelt had been allies for most of the 1930s, their relationship was always strained and fell apart in 1938. Roosevelt withheld his support for Lewis after a police riot resulted in an attack upon striking Republic steelworkers. That year the steelworkers were organizing through the CIO. During the next two years, Lewis became increasingly critical of the president and actively campaigned for Wendell Wilkie in 1940. Now the undersecretary had the opportunity to repay the wrong done to his father by

Lewis twenty-three years before. But, at no time did Roosevelt ever reveal his true motives. Throughout the process, he assumed the posture of the dedicated public servant guarding the government's money.

To try to break the impasse, a special meeting was held in Roosevelt's office. Present at the meeting were representatives of the Fund, including Dr. Newdorp and Fund Comptroller Thomas Ryan.[166] As the meeting progressed, it became obvious that Roosevelt intended to disapprove the grant.[167] According-ing to Joseph E. Finely in his book *The Corrupt Kingdom*, Roosevelt was stopped by Undersecretary of Labor Daniel Patrick Moynihan. Supposedly, Moynihan saw what Roosevelt was doing and left the room to inform President Kennedy by phone about what was happening. Whereupon, Kennedy, who was return-ing on Air Force One after meeting with the U.S. Conference of Mayors, called Roosevelt and ordered him to make the grant.[168]

While this story has made for fascinating reading, it has problems. First, Finley never documented it. Second, Moynihan has never confirmed it. Third, its veracity has been flatly disputed by one of the meeting's participants.[169] In actuality, while Moynihan was instrumental in securing the grant, his partici-pation was done behind closed doors.

Regardless of how it was done, the news that the grant had been secured came none too soon. The Fund had already developed contingency plans to close the four hospitals if the grant was denied. Because of the uncertainty the situation created, some of the chain's professional medical staff had left to seek more secure employment. With the grant's approval, however, the arrangement between the Fund and the Board of National Missions could be implemented immediately. First, the hospitals would be transferred gradually between 1963 and 1964, five institutions at a time. The chain's central purchasing office would continue working with both sets of hospitals. The Fund also agreed to keep the ten institutions on its participation list. Secondly, the Kentucky legislature passed the changes in the state's welfare laws. Finally, the hospitals changed their payment system for their physicians. Instead of a salary, each hospital would be organized on a group practice basis, with each doctor working as a member of the group.

These changes helped to ease the opposition of organized medicine, and there is no question that the Kentucky state government became more coopera-tive now that the chain's ownership was shifting from a union to a church. By the fall of 1964, all ten hospitals were transferred and the Fund's experiment with the chain came to an end.

As for ARH, due to the creation of Medicare, the chain managed to break even between 1965 and 1969. However, in 1970 the chain once again began running at a deficit. Ironically, the problem was related to unforeseen conse-quences that arose out of the Medicare system. Although Medicare did not provide comprehensive coverage to its beneficiaries, the system did not have any mechanisms to prevent medical fraud and overcharging. This, in turn, ignited an inflationary spiral within health care that was much higher than the rate of inflation seen in the rest of the economy.[170]

The situation changed, however, in 1978 with the accession of Robert Johnson as ARH's president. Through a combination of budget cuts and increases in state funding, ARH began showing a budget surplus in 1979. Shortly thereafter, ARH's name was changed to Appalachian Regional Health Care, and the chain itself was further expanded. Continuing with the regional hierarchy model, the chain as of 1993 consisted of the ten original hospitals, with an eleventh opened in Sommers County, West Virginia.[171] In addition, the hospitals were served by a network of fifty-one smaller affiliated institutions, ranging from clinics to home health agencies.

In light of these facts, the question must be asked whether the hospital program was a mistake. Certainly, what ultimately became ARH represented a major contribution to Appalachia. Moreover, the poor quality of hospital conditions in the region at the time the Fund undertook the project was undeniable.[172] But, while the project started in 1952, the chain did not start taking patients until late 1955. By that time, other initiatives the Fund was taking through its area offices to improve the quality of care, such as the development of freestanding outpatient clinics, were beginning to have an effect.[173]

Hand in hand with this, a great deal of effort was expended in understanding the region's demographics so that the chain's size would be appropriate to local needs.[174] Unfortunately, because of the state of the coal industry, as well as the American economy as a whole during the 1950s, population levels in south-central Appalachia were in flux. By the time the hospitals opened, the region's demographic profile had changed, leaving the chain overcapitalized. These factors, combined with other problems covered earlier, led to the inescapable conclusion that the Fund had overextended itself.

This is further illustrated by the expenses the Fund had in maintaining the chain. The $31 million spent to build the hospitals was only the beginning. After the chain was dedicated, the Fund's operating costs for the chain between 1957 and 1962 amounted to $12 million a year. When the operating costs for 1956, the 1963–64 transition period, and the building costs are added in, the grand total for the project exceeded $110 million.

Yet, did the hospital project constitute a mishandling of the Fund's assets? The answer is no. When it was originally proposed, the hospital project appeared to be a sound venture. Because the Fund was interested in quality care and wanted to do something immediately to improve hospital conditions, the Fund's leadership was almost compelled to create its own hospital system. While the Fund's leadership underestimated the original and continuing costs involved with the project, their mistakes were understandable. No institution, public or private, had ever attempted such an undertaking. Moreover, the Fund was powerless to control coal demand and production levels.

As for the MMHA, it was not formally dissolved until 1968, and its directors continued to meet regularly until that year. Most of its business involved selling former staff members' homes it had purchased. Considering all that had been done, as well as the purposes for which the MMHA had been created, this was indeed a sad ending for it.

John L. Lewis in 1948. Lewis had been a giant in the American labor movement, but soon went into obscurity as other fuels displaced coal. Courtesy of the West Virginia and Regional History Collection, West Virginia University Libraries.

Rear Adm. Joel T. Boone in 1947, at the time the Boone Report was written. Admiral Boone was a native of St. Claire, Pennsylvania, and thus had a firsthand understanding of living conditions in the coal mining industry. Courtesy of the West Virginia and Regional History Collection, West Virginia University Libraries.

Josephine Roche in 1958. Roche, the Fund's director for ten years when this photograph was taken, spent a lifetime in public service. Courtesy of the West Virginia and Regional History Collection, West Virginia University Libraries.

Dr. Warren F. Draper in 1948, when he was appointed the Fund's executive medical officer. Assuming the position at the age of sixty-eight, Draper was starting a second career. Courtesy of the West Virginia and Regional History Collection, West Virginia University Libraries.

A meeting of senior Fund and MMHA personnel sometime in 1957/58. Dr. Draper is seated in the foreground at the table's head. To his right are Dr. John Morrison, Dr. John Newdorp, Kenneth Pohlman, Dr. F. W. Mott, Gen. Paul Henry Streit (U.S. Army Medical Corps), Harold Mayers, Henry Daniels, Dr. Lorin Kerr, unidentified, Josephine Roche. Courtesy of the West Virginia and Regional History Collection, West Virginia University Libraries.

Dr. John Newdorp in 1958. An obstetrician by speciality, Dr. Newdorp served as state health officer for Alabama during World War II. He was also a principle architect of the state's plan to use Hill-Burton funding for hospital development. Dr. Newdorp eventually became head of the Fund's hospital chain and later succeeded Dr. Draper as executive medical officer. Courtesy of the West Virginia and Regional History Collection, West Virginia University Libraries.

Dr. Lorin E. Kerr at the time he joined the Fund's staff in 1947–48. A public health specialist, Dr. Kerr came to the Fund from the USPHS and was originally AMO for Morgantown, West Virginia. He later joined the Fund's Washington staff and became the program's expert on coal workers' pneumoconiosis, or black lung. Courtesy of the West Virginia and Regional History Collection, West Virginia University Libraries.

Dr. John Winebrenner in 1958. A public health specialist, Winebrenner came to the Fund after serving for six years (1942–48) in the U.S. Army Medical Corps. He served as AMO for Knoxville, Tennessee, for most of his career with the Fund. Courtesy of the West Virginia and Regional History Collection, West Virginia University Libraries.

The American Public Health Association's Albert Lasker Group Award. Named for Dr. Albert Lasker, this award was given to the Fund in 1956 in recognition of its efforts to bring high-quality health care to medically underserved areas in the coal mining industry. Courtesy of the West Virginia and Regional History Collection, West Virginia University Libraries.

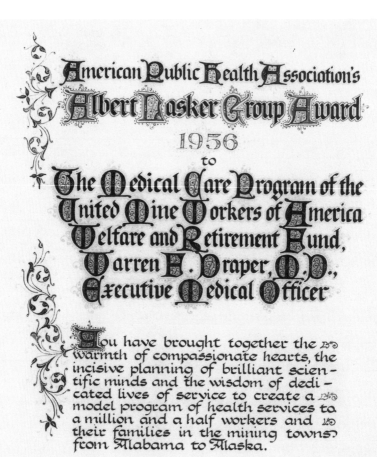

American Public Health Association's
Albert Lasker Group Award
1956
to
The Medical Care Program of the
United Mine Workers of America
Welfare and Retirement Fund,
Warren F. Draper, M.D.,
Executive Medical Officer

You have brought together the
warmth of compassionate hearts, the
incisive planning of brilliant scientific minds and the wisdom of dedicated lives of service to create a
model program of health services to
a million and a half workers and
their families in the mining towns
from Alabama to Alaska.

The scroll presented with the Lasker Award. Courtesy of the West Virginia and Regional History Collection, West Virginia University Libraries.

Dr. Draper accepting, on behalf of the Fund's medical staff, the Lasker Award from Mrs. Albert Lasker. Courtesy of the West Virginia and Regional History Collection, West Virginia University Libraries.

Hazard Memorial Hospital shortly after its opening in 1956. Courtesy of the West Virginia and Regional History Collection, West Virginia University Libraries.

Williamson Hospital under construction in 1955. Courtesy of the West Virginia and Regional History Collection, West Virginia University Libraries.

Chapter 5

The National Conflict: The Fund and the American Medical Association

Although the hospital chain was the Fund's most visible and well-known project, it was only one part of the Fund's health care program. Unlike the MMHA or the pension system, the medical program served every family in the union. Moreover, it had the distinction of being the first industrywide, noncontributory, health care system ever devised. As a health services purchaser, the Fund came closer to offering access to comprehensive care than any other medical third party in existence at the time, including Blue Cross.

Because of the program's size, its actions were of major interest to the medical profession, since whatever the Fund did might influence other payers. The Fund's leadership was determined to provide the program's beneficiaries with the best care available for the best possible price. As a result, the Fund's medical service eventually came into conflict with the AMA over what the nature of health care delivery ought to be. The argument's central point was how to best serve the interests of the patient: free choice of physician with fee-for-service payment, or a closed panel/managed care model.

After the Krug-Lewis agreement was signed in 1946, the Fund only existed on paper for its first eleven months. Work on creating the medical service did not actually begin until after the first trustee board was organized in 1947. During this interim, the Fund's medical staff was assembled.

While each member's story was unique in its details, there was a general trend which most seemed to share. Between 1946 and 1947, word spread within a set of interlocking networks that the UMWA was creating a new health program. These networks consisted of personal contacts between health professionals in three different, yet allied, organizations. These included the American Public Health Association (APHA), the USPHS, and the Farm Security Administration (FSA). Through these connections, the Fund acquired such people as Dr. John Newdorp, Dr. Lorin E. Kerr, Mr. Henry Daniels, Mr. Kenneth Pohlman, and others.[1] Shortly thereafter, another source of trained professionals appeared: the U.S. Army Medical Corps. Almost without exception, these people had either supported or been involved with the health reform movement. This determined the methods the Fund would use to fulfill its mission.

While the medical staff was being assembled, John L. Lewis attempted to find a physician who had the administrative experience necessary to put a program together. The person had to be knowledgeable in the area of public health, but also had to understand the needs of the bituminous coal industry. The first man Lewis appointed to head the medical program appeared to combine these qualities and more: Dr. Royd R. Sayers.[2] A resident of northern Virginia and Lewis's longtime neighbor, Sayers had spent most of his career in the U.S. Bureau of Mines as chief surgeon, heading its health and safety branch. In 1940, primarily on Lewis's recommendation, Sayers was promoted to the bureau's directorship.[3] During his years with the bureau, Sayers had conducted extensive research into the problem of carbon monoxide poisoning. His work later provided the design basis for the ventilation systems used in the Holland Tunnel.[4]

What probably pleased Lewis most, however, was Sayers's apparent pro-union sentiments. Although the record is not completely clear, Sayers had been forced to resign his position as bureau director. Ostensibly, this was in retaliation for his criticism of a tough stand President Truman assumed with the union when Lewis attempted to force a renegotiation of the 1946 contract several weeks after it was signed. Lewis failed in his efforts and was humiliated. At the same time, Sayers's comments and subsequent dismissal were noted in the *United Mine Workers Journal*, with the union newspaper broadly hinting that Sayers was being persecuted.[5] Five months later, Lewis announced that Sayers had been appointed as the Fund's chief medical officer.[6]

Sayers served in the position for approximately one year and made little progress in activating the medical service. Part of the reason was Sayers's cautious nature. Despite his thirty-year connection with the industry, and the positions he had held, most of the work Sayers had done was clinical, meaning he had no real administrative or organizational experience. But, an even greater problem was Sayers's conservatism. This was evident in several contexts. Despite a growing body of evidence to the contrary, he denied that coal workers' pneumoconiosis (black lung) was an actual disease afflicting coal miners. Instead, he upheld a reductionist view which held that silicosis was the coal industry's one and only work-related respiratory disease.[7] (This argument will be more thoroughly explored in the next chapter.) Even more upsetting was that Sayers had never worked in private practice, yet he endorsed the AMA's beliefs on the subject. This included accepting its wishes relative to health insurance.

Sayers attempted to create a program that was a verbatim copy of the AMA's counterproposal to Roche's 1938 national health insurance plan. The program would be thoroughly decentralized, operating through the UMWA's district offices. AMA county medical societies would set prices, practice standards, and monitor professional conduct.[8] The Fund would fill the role the AMA had originally envisioned for the government: simply paying bills.[9]

Understandably, Roche opposed Sayers's plan.[10] But, undermining Sayers in Lewis's eyes was going to take some doing, and just pointing to the similarity between Sayers's plan and the AMA's 1938 counterproposal might not be enough. Roche opted to make an appeal to Lewis's pocketbook. Joining the Fund's staff in 1947 as assistant director, she had unlimited access to Lewis. Roche claimed in her correspondence with Lewis that Sayers's plan would be needlessly expensive. Sayers had already estimated that his approach would cost the Fund $60 million a year. Using this fact, Roche painted a lurid picture of an AMA–coal operator conspiracy to keep medical costs high in order to block the Fund from offering pensions.[11]

Certainly, this idea was far-fetched and Roche knew it. But, it moved Lewis to act. Shortly after Roche made the claim, a medical advisory committee for the Fund was created, and Dr. Sayers was "promoted" to this body. Although the committee reported directly to Lewis, it had little or no real authority.[12] In the meantime, Sayers's former position became vacant. Retitled "executive medical officer," a search began for a replacement. By September 1948 the *United Mine Workers Journal* announced that a new man had been hired: Dr. Warren F. Draper.[13]

Because of Draper's longstanding connections with organized medicine, many staffers did not believe at first that his opinions would be substantially different from Dr. Sayers's. Dr. Draper not only belonged to the AMA, but also had been a senior member of its ruling body, the House of Delegates, for twenty years.[14] But on closer inspection, Draper's experience and ideas matched what the Fund needed at the time. First, Draper had been trained as a public health specialist, with an emphasis on preventive medicine. Second, for most of his career he had served in the USPHS and had worked with Roche during the 1930s.[15] Rising to chief deputy surgeon general, Draper had needed administrative experience, which was augmented during the Second World War, when he transferred to active duty in the U.S. Army.

Assigned to the Supreme Headquarters Allied Expeditionary Force (SHAEF), Draper was given the rank of major general and oversaw all Allied military hospitals in the European Theater of Operations.[16] In addition, Draper's work within the AMA had demonstrated a concern for the medical needs of working people. In particular, he was a cofounder and charter member of the AMA's Council on Industrial Health, which had been organized in 1938.[17] Judging from his professional activities prior to joining the Fund, it appears Draper viewed medicine as a public service, not a private enterprise.

Immediately following his appointment, Draper began to organize the Fund's medical system, and Lewis and Roche agreed with his ideas. Instead of following the pattern Sayers had used, Draper borrowed the USPHS's organizational model. This was clearly seen with the creation of the ten area medical offices mentioned in chapter 4. Each was headed by a physician who served as the area medical officer. It was an AMO's responsibility to arrange for treatment of Fund beneficiaries with local health care providers. Part of this meant paying bills, but it also meant monitoring the quality of care and guarding against fraud.[18] Although the AMOs reported to Draper and worked within a uniform set of guidelines relative to benefits, they were given the autonomy necessary to tailor Fund medical benefits to meet local conditions.[19]

By the end of 1948 all of the area offices had been organized, and each AMO made an extensive six-month report to Draper in August 1949. Judging from the reports, relations between the area offices and the local branches of the union were good. The only difficulty was that some local union officials did not understand the Fund's regulations, which contributed to confusion among the miners over what benefits they were entitled to receive.[20]

Another problem was that company doctors were generally hostile to the Fund's program and refused to cooperate with it.[21] Despite their opposition, these physicians failed to prevent the medical service from functioning. In one case, Dr. Allen Koplin, who ran the Birmingham office, informed Draper that the coal operators controlled most of the doctors in his area and were openly hostile to the Fund. Regardless of this fact, Koplin reported that there were enough interested physicians available who cooperated out of their desire to see the medical service succeed.[22]

Aside from reporting the hostility of company doctors, the reports described the fees local physicians charged and the quality of service rendered. From the start, Draper attempted to cultivate good relations with organized medicine. As a result, the Fund's general policy followed the AMA's basic principles for medical practice. Each beneficiary was allowed a free choice of physician, who was paid on a fee-for-service basis. The term free choice in this context meant that a beneficiary could use any licensed physician for any treatment required and paid whatever the doctor charged. To facilitate individual choice, the Fund offered all licensed doctors the opportunity to participate, including general practitioners.

While most of the offices reported that they had already received some excessive fees, a clear picture on the matter had not yet emerged. For example, Dr. Lorin Kerr, who originally headed the Morgantown office, wrote that most of the fees charged in his area were reasonable, although a few surgeons were charging excessive prices for their work.[23] On the other hand, the fees presented to the Johnstown office had been set by the county medical society and were in line with local standards. But the Johnstown administrator added that the set prices were high, and that attempts to lower them were fought vigorously by the county society. To prove the point, the report cited the fact that a bitter controversy had arisen within the society when one of its members attempted to perform tonsillectomies for under the set price of fifty dollars.[24]

In terms of the quality of care, the record was mixed. None of the AMOs reported any cases of gross malpractice. However, problems were already beginning to appear which would have an impact later. Among the Fund's basic rules of participation was a strict policy of not paying for surgical work unless it was performed in a hospital.[25] Yet some physicians insisted that they should be allowed to deliver babies in a patient's home, while others claimed that simple operations could be performed effectively in their offices.[26] Also, medical incompetence among certain physicians was already being noticed.[27]

After the AMOs concluded their description of medical standards, each turned to the progress being made by the Fund's physical rehabilitation program in their areas. The rehabilitation project was the first of the Fund's major services and graphically demonstrated a determination to improve the quality of life for the miners. Throughout the bituminous coal fields, but especially in Appalachia, there were miners who had been disabled by severe job-related accidents. These miners had not been given adequate care or physical rehabilitation by local medical facilities. Most of these cases had only received some preliminary treatment and were left medically neglected. The results of the neglect were appalling.[28] In one instance, the Fund assisted a man whose back had been broken some time in the 1930s. Bedfast since that time, the man suffered from severe pressure sores and acute muscle atrophy. Before he could be given any basic physical therapy, the man received thirty operations over the course of two months for procedures ranging from leg straightening to skin grafts.[29]

Strangely, the rehabilitation program did not originate as part of any coherent plan determining what medical benefits should be offered. Rather, during the program's early period under Dr. Sayers, a union official named Albert Pass contacted George Titler, then president of UMWA District 29, headquartered in Beckley, West Virginia, about getting medical attention for a disabled miner. This request was eventually referred from Titler's office to Dr. Sayers.[30] Understanding the industry as he did, Sayers did not view this as an isolated plea for help. He thought it was probable that there were other disabled miners in need of treatment.

As mentioned in chapter 2, coal mining was the most dangerous occupation in all of basic industry. According to the Metropolitan Life Insurance Company, the job-related injury rate in mining was 248 percent greater than the average accident levels reported in other occupations. In addition, between 1906 and 1939 a total of 8,049 men had been killed in mining disasters. The majority of these accidents were caused by either methane or coal dust explosions.[31] Further, the accident rate increased when coal production rose to meet the energy needs created by the Second World War. Mining disasters, thus, were not unusual, and some ranked as the worst industrial accidents in U.S. history. The most infamous of these were the Monongah, West Virginia, mining disaster in 1907, where 361 men were killed; the 1947 Centralia, Illinois, mine explosion, which killed 111 men; and the explosion at West Frankfort,

Illinois, which killed 119 men in 1951. Except for momentary outrage, mine safety did not concern the general public, and nothing was done about the medical needs of those men who had been injured on the job and permanently disabled. Taking these facts into account, Sayers decided to mount a major effort in the area of physical rehabilitation.[32]

This decision was not one to be taken lightly. Physical rehabilitation as a part of medical science was still in its infancy. However, there had been a number of advances made in the field as a result of the demands created by World War II.[33] Although they had been preceded by others, the two leaders in the field were Drs. Howard Rusk and Herman Kabat. Rusk in particular had pioneered the idea of combining treatment of the physical problem with vocational retraining. Rusk maintained that it was central to a patient's recovery to know that he would be self-supporting.[34] As it was, the physical problems these men were treating were the same disabilities the Fund would encounter in its search for injured miners. Aside from amputations, there were myriad paraplegic and quadriplegic cases.

From the outset Sayers realized that the miners who needed physical rehabilitation would have to be sent to special medical facilities. Thus, he developed a list of the various hospitals offering major rehabilitation programs at the time.[35] Meanwhile, the Fund began searching for disabled miners. Neither process was complete when Dr. Draper took over, but the record shows Sayers had started sending disabled miners to special centers for treatment.[36]

Dr. Draper completed arrangements with various special centers, and the Fund established working relationships with nine major hospitals throughout the United States. The list included the George Washington University Hospital; the Kabat-Kaiser Institutes located in Washington, D.C., Vallejo and Santa Monica, California; the Kessler Institute of Physical Rehabilitation in West Orange, New Jersey; the Institute of Physical Medicine and Rehabilitation in New York; the Woodrow Wilson Rehabilitation Center in Fishersville, Vermont; and the Bay State Medical Rehabilitation Clinic in Boston.[37] Each of these centers varied in terms of the procedures they offered. While proximity to the institutions might have been a consideration for sending a disabled miner to a specific hospital, the most important factors in making the choice were related to the successful outcome of the rehabilitation regimen: the patient's physical condition and mental attitude.[38]

Also facilitating a smooth transition from Sayers to Draper was the appointment of Kenneth E. Pohlman as the Fund's rehabilitation director in 1948. Formerly employed with the Farm Security Administration, Pohlman managed to set the rehabilitation program's goals very early. It was the Fund's responsibility to go out and find paraplegic and other disabled miners in need of help. Also, once a patient was in the early stages of recovery, it was necessary to determine what his interests were and to develop them. A disciple of Dr. Rusk, Pohlman also believed that physical rehabilitation would be worthless unless the patients were interested in being, and trained to be, self-supporting.[39]

Pohlman's emphasis on finding the miners who needed help might have seemed like a statement of the obvious, but the task was vital and difficult. Many of the men who had been disabled in the mines were confined to their homes and forgotten. While some cases were readily accessible in several of the union's districts, finding them in the more isolated areas of eastern Tennessee, Kentucky, and southwestern West Virginia was an enormous problem. In order to locate the disabled miners, the Fund sent out teams of physicians to conduct a search.[40] Any and all available membership lists from the union's district and local offices were used, as well as information provided by people residing in the coal camps. Generally, a coal camp resident would remember an individual who had been injured in the mines but whose name did not appear on the union's lists or medical records.[41]

Finding miners who needed treatment was only half of the battle. Apart from any emotional or psychological considerations, it was necessary to devise various means to get the patients out of the more remote mountain areas and to transportation facilities. Because of a lack of ready access in such cases, the patients had to be hand-carried out of the hills by stretcher teams. Once a paved road had been reached, the patients were sent by ambulance to rail stations, where they were placed aboard specially outfitted trains that took them to the rehabilitation centers. For those who participated in it, the work was deeply satisfying and inspirational. Eight years after the initial search had been completed, Dr. Draper received a letter from Dr. Rusk which detailed this sense of moral uplift.[42]

Because of the nature of the rehabilitation project, the Fund could not be concerned about purchasing health care only; it also had to invest part of its efforts into counseling both the patient and his family. Each paraplegic miner who was contacted had to fill out a questionnaire before he received the Fund's assistance. The questionnaire was designed to determine which center should be used in a particular case and to give the patient an idea of how extensive his recovery would be.[43] The questionnaire alone, however, was insufficient to meet emotional problems a patient could experience as a result of his treatment.

In September 1949, Dr. John Morrison and William H. Timer presented a lengthy outline on how disability, especially paraplegic, cases should be processed. The two men stressed that paraplegic rehabilitation was a process that addressed not only the patient's physical condition, but also his psychological needs and those of his family.[44] If the patient did not receive the right counseling, the Fund's efforts could be wasted. Initially it was necessary to visit each patient in his home and ask if he wanted treatment. The miner was told that he would receive the best medical care available. Although he would probably never be able to walk again on his own, and would have to accept physical limitations, his general health would be greatly improved.[45] If the miner was bedfast and wanted to be treated, every effort had to be made to respect his privacy.[46]

Once the patient gave his consent to treatment, the area office's focus shifted from the miner to his family. In most cases, the trip to a special center was an emotional strain for everyone involved, because the miner was probably going farther from his home than he had ever gone before. Thus, it was important for the patient's family to be there to see him off when he was placed on the train. After the miner had left for the center, the area administrator kept in contact with the patient's family through regular home visits and provided news about the patient's recovery progress.[47]

At the same time, the family had to be prepared for both how to correctly deal with the miner and his needs when he returned home and for a reordering of roles. In southern families especially, the father was the head of the household and, as the wage earner, he symbolized physical strength and power. Disciplining the children was usually his responsibility, and he made all final decisions.[48] Due to his physical limitations, there was a risk that the miner could enter into clinical depression, since he was no longer fully able to fill his traditional role. Therefore, Morrison and Timer recommended that each patient be trained to do a manual or "man's" job as a method of maintaining his self-esteem.[49]

In order to foster the patient's feeling of self-worth, his family needed to be informed about what he could and could not do for himself before he returned home, to avoid disappointment and an overprotective attitude. Overprotectiveness, while an understandable reaction, was counterproductive. If the miner was made to feel that he was not capable of doing anything for himself, he'd become submissive and a total invalid.[50] Finally, Morrison and Timer suggested that the union should maintain a representative at the various centers. For most of the miners being treated, the union's presence represented security and a link with home. It also reassured the men that the union was making sure that the doctors were doing everything in their power to help.[51] Overall, the report provided the Fund with a method to deal with any problems that could arise in a miner's home and might be detrimental to complete rehabilitation. Dr. Draper reacted enthusiastically to the report and showed it to Roche. He also asked Dr. Morrison if Timer could be persuaded to work for the rehabilitation project, for a short time at least, since it appeared that he had a firm understanding of what the miners required.[52]

Despite the report's strengths, some of its claims were questionable, especially its idea about the position of the father in the household. It is obvious that Timer and Morrison were not concerned about southern families per se, but about families from southern Appalachia. Although what they had to say about a father's position in the home was probably true, it is doubtful that this feature was confined only to the South or the southern Appalachian coal fields.

Such a bias within the report raises a basic question about the rehabilitation project: were its efforts concentrated in southern Appalachia? The available literature covering the Fund, such as Finley's *The Corrupt Kingdom,* gives that impression. This is understandable, because the Fund's records show that the effort to find forgotten miners was concentrated in union Districts 17, 19, 20, 28, and 30, all of which were located in the south-central area of the region. A high proportion of the men sent for treatment came from these districts. The records also demonstrate, however, that many miners were brought to the centers from other parts of the country, such as District 12 in Illinois and Districts 2 and 5 in Pennsylvania.[53] So, it should be noted that the rehabilitation project had an impact on the union as a whole and was not solely an Appalachian concern.

Part of that impact was the effect the program had upon the prestige of both the union and John L. Lewis with the miners and the general public. By 1952, more than 1,200 cases had been, or were being, sent to the special centers, with half that figure already discharged successfully.[54] The miners felt a deep sense of gratitude to Lewis for their treatment, and petitions expressing their thanks came to the union's headquarters from the various centers. One such petition read in part: "and to you, John L. Lewis, our beloved President, we wish to affirm our loyalty and our sincerest appreciation of your great leadership in our behalf. We wish you the fullest measure of success in your outstanding fight to obtain continuing welfare and pension benefits for our union."[55]

Similar sentiments were expressed in a lengthy telegram which came from the Kabat hospital in Vallejo: "We . . . want to congratulate our great President and all the men who worked with him . . . to obtain the greatest victory in the history of the coal industry. Although we were not present to help, our hearts were with you at all times. We know our brothers went through much hardship to obtain this victory which means so much to crippled miners all over."[56] In addition, the Fund's work in rehabilitation received favorable notice in the popular media through such articles as "The Gate to Bright Hope," which appeared in the July 8, 1950, edition of Collier's magazine.[57]

Once a miner's physical rehabilitation was completed, the Fund addressed his vocational retraining. The Fund's policy was that it could not handle the problem alone. It sought the assistance of state authorities by referring disabled miners to public vocational rehabilitation facilities.[58] As the men went through their retraining, they remained eligible for the Fund's medical benefits and received small cash payments as a temporary income.

The largest obstacle to this policy was that state vocational agencies were badly underfunded.[59] Draper realized that the Fund was in direct competition with other referral authorities for the limited resources offered by the state programs, but he insisted on using the vocational offices.[60] The Fund's experience showed that appropriations for the vocational offices were steadily increasing each year, because the agencies were able to document a rising demand for vocational rehabilitation services.[61] With Draper's policy, the Fund was able to establish a working partnership with the state vocational offices and could offer disabled miners the chance to be self-supporting.

To facilitate the completion of the rehabilitation process, the Fund sponsored regular screening clinics designed to bring representatives of the Fund, union, and state vocational authorities together into one place. At these clinics, miners could inquire about what benefits and assistance they were eligible to receive from both the state agencies and the Fund. If a miner was having medical difficulties, he could also make arrangements at the clinics for further treatment.[62]

The Fund's performance in returning disabled miners to economic self-sufficiency was good, and in some cases impressive. One man's physical recovery was so nearly complete that he became sheriff of his home county.[63] From the case studies available, most of the rehabilitated miners who returned to the full-time workforce were self-employed in skilled positions as electricians, lens grinders, and watch repairmen.[64] Unfortunately, after 1953 the Fund did not monitor the progress of its disabled beneficiaries as closely as it had before, and the statistics for completely successful reemployment only extend to that year. According to the figures, 970 patients had been discharged from the various special centers. However, 570 of these cases needed additional treatment. Of the 337 remaining, 224 had reentered the workforce; 101 of them were paraplegics.[65]

A possible explanation as to why the Fund did not monitor its rehabilitation cases so closely after 1953 is that most of the men seeking treatment after that year were recent injury victims. The majority of the neglected men had been found and treated. Despite the demographic change, Draper remained committed to the program. Although nothing exists in the records to explain why he took this attitude, it is reasonable to assume that it grew out of his general view of medicine as a public service. As long as coal was mined, people would continue to be injured, and the Fund had a duty to help them build a new life. His views on the subject were so strong that he was willing to defy Roche's authority on this issue.

Like other services the Fund offered, the rehabilitation program needed to be scaled back in the 1950s because of budgetary limitations. At one point, Draper directed the discontinuance of the Fund's original cash maintenance benefit. The benefit had been designed to give some temporary income to disability cases while they sought vocational assistance. Regardless of the Fund's intentions, records showed that disabled miners were becoming dependent on the grant and not seeking to become self-supporting.[66]

Draper recommended replacing this benefit with another more limited payment, which would be discontinued once an individual ceased to be completely disabled. The new benefit required the miner to periodically reapply to maintain his eligibility, which allowed the Fund to make a status determination. According to Draper, the change would save time and money since the area administrators no longer evaluated eligibility through expensive interim checkups.[67] Dr. Draper's motivation was twofold, while seeking to cut expenses, he did not want the reductions to impair the rehabilitation program's effectiveness.

But, the effectiveness of the rehabilitation program was endangered in February 1956 when Roche decided to discontinue all medical assistance to unemployed miners who were either attending college or were undergoing retraining. This included men who were receiving such training as part of the rehabilitation program.[68] As mentioned before, until 1960 the Fund provided unemployed miners with medical assistance until they left the industry. No one ever clearly stated what leaving the industry meant, but it had been generally regarded as the point when a beneficiary found employment outside of the mines. Now, in order to cut costs, Roche decided that leaving the industry included any form of retraining.[69]

Draper was livid over the decision. The Fund's medical service had invested considerable effort in building its partnership with the rehabilitation agencies of the mining states. Roche's decision threatened to break that partnership while hurting the beneficiaries who needed the help. [70] Draper also believed that the Fund's rehabilitation program was a unique feature among all welfare systems, and it had won the Fund international acclaim.[71] Finally, he resented that he had not been consulted about the new rule, even though he was responsible for enforcing it. His anger was plainly evident in a memo to Roche which read in part: "The fact that our rehabilitation program could be terminated and such punitive measures imposed upon the miners without my knowledge and the opportunity for discussion of consequences before the action will, in my opinion, destroy the faith and confidence of the area administrators in my ability to administer properly the medical program of the Fund. In these circumstances I cannot but feel that my usefulness to the Fund is at an end."[72] Draper's statement must have startled Roche, because she held a conference with him on the same day that it was sent and she withdrew the directive.[73]

For the rest of the decade, the Fund's leadership attempted no further cuts in the program. By 1961, however, the Fund retrenched its services across the board. Draper attended most of the staff conferences dealing with these problems and knew he was not in a position to protest when the program was scaled back. The Fund reduced its expenses in this instance by limiting the time a miner could receive treatment.[74] Draper accepted the change and directed his activities to securing greater efficiency in diagnostic work.[75] This, however, was the last reduction the rehabilitation program suffered. The program continued operating and was stopped only when the Fund's medical system was terminated in 1977.[76]

Thus, despite the reductions, the rehabilitation program made a continuing effort to improve the quality of life for men seriously injured in the mines by offering them an alternative to indigence. However, the rehabilitation project's impact did not end here. It also gave graphic evidence of the medical profession's failure to address health problems in the coal fields. The embarrassing fact was that without the Fund's initiative, the disabled miners the Fund treated would have remained medically neglected.

In its defense, the medical profession could cite the *Boone Report,* which showed that both low and high quality care existed in the coal fields.[77] Also, physicians could claim that judgments about the quality of care based upon the Fund's rehabilitation case histories were unfair. The general practitioners who originally treated these men had neither the time nor the facilities available for sophisticated rehabilitation work.

Whereas such explanations might have been true, it became increasingly apparent to the Fund's leadership that the medicine in the coal fields had some major problems. Many physicians were rendering inferior care through poor diagnosis, inept surgical technique, or both. At the same time, statistics showed that the Fund's beneficiaries were hospitalized longer and more frequently than any other group of people in the United States.[78] Because organized medicine failed to address these difficulties, the Fund was ultimately forced to take measures to ensure quality medical care for the miners. Relations between the Fund and the AMA became strained on all levels and led to a formal condemnation of the Fund by the AMA's House of Delegates in June 1958. The question was whether a medical third party had the right to judge and control the quality of care its beneficiaries received.

What made the conflict so intense was that neither side could compromise what it regarded as a matter of basic principle. What the Fund viewed as an effort to promote quality practice appeared to the AMA as an attack upon ideas it held as sacred. These included the right of the medical profession to police itself, as well as the individual physician's professional autonomy and standing. Owing to these attitudes, medicine displayed an ethos of all physicians standing together for the sake of the profession.[79] This attitude was exacerbated by changes within the world of medicine. Although general practitioners (GPs) were still the vast majority of physicians at the time, more and more young doctors were choosing to become specialists. Viewing this as a threat, many GPs feared loss of income and status if specialists took over the profession's leadership. Because preventing this trend became a priority, GPs joined the AMA in record numbers, especially after World War II, and used it for their protection.[80] Criticism of a physician's work by another doctor was now unethical. Criticism, or quality control, by outsiders was not to be tolerated.

As mentioned in chapter 4, the Fund had had to deal with underqualified physicians in some areas, especially south-central Appalachia. But, this was only part of the picture. While miners living near larger cities had access to good care, the majority of them lived and worked in a rural setting. Because of this, health care in the coal fields was an aspect of rural medical practice. Looking back, the state of rural practice was not good at the time of the health program's inception in 1948.

The national ratio of physicians to patients stood at an average of 1 doctor for every 831 persons. The ratio for rural areas, however, was much higher. While some counties had 1 doctor for every 1,250 people, others had only 1 for every 1,700.[81] Another factor was the matter of age. It had been postulated that a physician's peak years in terms of effectiveness as a practitioner were ages thirty-five to forty-four. According to this theory, once a physician reached the age of sixty-five, his professional capability declined by 66 percent.[82] The truth of this theory is debatable. It was indisputable, however, that America's rural physicians were aging. In 1923, nearly 25 percent of all physicians practicing in rural areas were aged fifty-eight and older. By 1938 this number had risen to 45 percent.[83] Owing to the demands created by the Second World War, the situation had deteriorated further by the end of the 1940s.

Hand in hand with the increasing age of the doctors was the problem of qualification. Cities, with their wide economic base and diverse quality of life, attracted capable physicians. Faced with such competition, less qualified practitioners, such as those who came out of the two-year schools closed by the Flexner Report, set up practice in rural areas.[84]

Finally, working in rural America in the late 1940s was almost synonymous with isolation. Although some physicians in this setting were able to cope effectively with the demands it presented, many were not. Such isolation resulted in certain practitioners failing to keep up with medical innovation; for others, it translated into depression, marked by drug and alcohol abuse.[85]

Each of these problems was endemic within the coal industry's health delivery system. Stated simply, coal camp check-off practices for the small to medium companies, which made up the majority of coal producers, had become a dumping ground for the incompetent, the unfit, and the unqualified.[86] Aside from the two-year medical school graduates, there were practitioners who had no medical training at all. These were people who knew something about medicine and, because of local needs, had been awarded an M.D. by the state legislature.[87]

These deficiencies violated every AMA standard. But the AMA's national office and local affiliates were keenly interested in preserving established conventions.

Not only did that mean promoting solo practice and fee-for-service payment, it also meant insisting that any licensed physician was capable of practicing medicine in all its branches.[88]

Because of his long association with organized medicine, Dr. Draper sought to work with the AMA's national, state, and local bodies. In 1948, to facilitate cooperation, the association's Council on Industrial Health recommended the formation of liaison committees with the Fund and medical societies of the bituminous coal mining states. The two groups could then work together through the committees to discuss mutual concerns.[89] The proposal was approved by the AMA's House of Delegates, and Draper worked to gain the AMA's confidence through a series of presentations between 1948 and 1949. The program he outlined was enthusiastically received.[90] In addition, Draper recommended that the secretary of the Council on Industrial Health, Dr. Carl M. Peterson, be placed on the Fund's Medical Advisory Board.[91]

Although the advisory board was only window-dressing, the recommendation was significant because of Peterson's views. While Dr. Peterson believed workers deserved quality health care, he insisted that it could only be provided through free competition between physicians. Peterson explicitly stated his views in a printed debate, which appeared in February 1949 under the title "Should Industry Back Compulsory Federal Health Insurance?" According to Dr. Peterson, such a program would only increase bureaucracy, and while the quantity of care would rise, quality would suffer as bureau-run doctors lost their sense of responsibility to their patients.[92] Peterson would never have been appointed if Dr. Draper had fundamentally disagreed with these opinions. For his part, Lewis aided Draper in cultivating good relations with the AMA by having the union move away from its earlier support of national health insurance.

These actions underscored Draper's belief that by cooperating with organized medicine, the Fund's medical service had the opportunity to improve health care in the United States, not only for miners, but for everyone.[93] Draper's vision, however, soon began to encounter difficulties. Late in 1949 he asked the association's Joint Committee for the Coordination of Medical Activities to work on problems associated with the Fund's payment for physician and hospital services. Draper wanted to find a method to control payment in order to avoid the creation of more proprietary hospitals.[94] The committee's chairman, Dr. Ernest Irons, thought Draper's request was too controversial and did not address it.[95]

Another source of trouble was unethical behavior by physicians. In some cases, doctors were charging fees far above accepted prices for common procedures. In other instances, doctors charged reasonable fees but provided excessive and unnecessary office treatment. On the average, a patient visited his or her family physician three and a half times a year. The Fund's records showed that some beneficiaries were seeing their doctors three and four times above the yearly average.[96] Draper understood physicians were not solely to blame for this overusage of the Fund's services. Patients as well as physicians had to behave responsibly. Yet Draper hoped that all such abuse could be solved by the Fund and organized medicine working together.[97]

Cooperation with the AMA not withstanding, before the medical program had completed its first year of operation, health cost inflation necessitated a benefits revision. When the Fund first started operation, the program covered all medical services rendered to its beneficiaries, including home and office care provided by general practitioners. After the 1949–50 suspension period, however, general practitioner office care was discontinued.[98] Originally, Roche wanted to limit the Fund's coverage to all medical care given within the hospital. Members of the Fund's medical staff, including Drs. Draper and Lorin Kerr, protested that the proposed regulation would increase hospital usage. A compromise was then worked out whereby the Fund covered hospitalization and all care given to a beneficiary by a specialist in a hospital, clinic, or office.[99] Ultimately, primary care was also provided through participating clinics that were either established by the Fund, UMWA locals, or by group practice doctors themselves.[100] Also, all tonsillectomies and adenoidectomies needed prior approval before the Fund would pay for them.[101]

While the new restrictions might have been perceived as a lack of confidence in the medical profession, Draper's statements at the time the Fund resumed operation did not show any disappointment. At a meeting of the Conference on Medical Service, held in March 1950, Draper lauded his fellow doctors for their cooperation during the suspension period. Many participating physicians and hospitals had continued to treat Fund beneficiaries on a voluntary basis, and Draper was grateful for their help.[102] Draper added that although some physicians had denounced the Fund as socialized medicine, most realized that the charge was false. To prove the point, he cited an article from the *West Virginia Medical Journal,* whose author said the Fund definitely was not state medicine and offered the greatest defense against the establishment of such a scheme in the United States.[103]

Unfortunately, the goodwill at the conference did not last. Within a year, Draper became concerned about the treatment of the Fund's beneficiaries. By February 1951, the Fund had amassed a large volume of evidence showing that the miners were getting low quality care. In his correspondence with Dr. Peterson, Draper listed four major problem areas: poor treatment of workman's compensation cases, incompetent company doctors, poor hospital care, and inflated fees.[104] Draper believed it was useless to seek disciplinary action for these cases on an individual basis.[105] Rather, he hoped organized medicine would move to correct these abuses once they were made known.

To facilitate movement in that direction, Draper, in March of 1951, arranged for the joint Fund/AMA survey of hospital conditions in Appalachia mentioned in chapter 3.[106] Conducted under the aegis of the Fund's advisory board, the survey team included Dr. Peterson, Dr. George Lull, the AMA's executive director, and Dr. Sayers. During its tour, the team visited a number of hospitals and practice facilities. It also had the opportunity to meet and speak with more than one hundred UMWA local and district officials. The trip provided graphic evidence that something needed to be done.

Aside from influencing the Fund's decision to build the hospital chain, the immediate result of the survey was that the AMA's Councils on Industrial Health and Medical Service created a joint body, the Committee on Health Care for Industrial Workers, to address the problems the Fund was encountering. At the same time, Draper presented the Fund's case to the full membership of the Council on Medical Service in February 1952.[107] By this time, the Fund's difficulties were well known.

Draper started his presentation by emphasizing his longtime membership in the AMA and his work as both a charter member of the Council on Industrial Health and as a senior member of the House of Delegates. He also made it clear that his intention was to inform, not to attack. According to Draper, the vast majority of the AMA's membership, and practicing physicians in general, were honorable people who sought to provide good quality care and followed high professional standards. Yet a minority of unscrupulous physicians were using the association to shield their unethical behavior. Draper implied that if this continued, organized medicine would be discredited, and with it free choice of physician and fee-for-service payment.[108] He also warned that unless the AMA began to discipline unethical practitioners, the Fund would have to take matters into its own hands.[109] Draper hinted that the Fund was willing to consider a shift away from free choice of physician to closed panel organization, where the Fund determined which physicians were and were not eligible to participate.

Closed panel organization was a drastic step and guaranteed vehement opposition from the association on all levels. It is not clear whether Draper would have taken such a step as early as 1952. Certainly he was upset by the unethical behavior the Fund had witnessed, but it is doubtful that he wanted to risk a break with the association at that time. After all, Draper was more than willing a few years later to make an agreement with the Medical Society of the State of Pennsylvania as a method of dealing with the Fund's problems. Thus, it appears that Draper's real purpose was to frighten the association into taking action. He would not have bothered to present the Fund's case if he thought the AMA would do nothing, and he constantly stressed that his intention was to make the AMA understand the Fund's situation.[110]

Regardless of Draper's real purpose, his efforts moved the association to action. A concerned Council on Medical Service decided to do a survey of its own to determine if the Fund's claims had any basis in fact. The council appointed four men to conduct the survey: Dr. W. A. Sayer, who was the council's chairman and medical director for Eastman Kodak Company; Dr. Peterson; Dr. F. H. Arestad, associate secretary of the AMA's Council on Medical Education and Hospitals; and Mr. George Cooley, the council's assistant secretary.[111]

Draper took special care to give advanced notice to the area medical administrators that the survey team planned to interview, such as Drs. Barnes, Winebrenner, and Leslie Falk of Pittsburgh. Because the information the team gathered would ultimately form the basis of any recommendations the council would make to the House of Delegates, Draper advised the area administrators to direct the committee's attention to the quality of home and office care, as well as hospital conditions.[112]

The actual survey was done in May 1952, and as events unfolded, Draper's suggestions to his area administrators proved unnecessary. Because the Fund no longer covered general practitioner office care, the survey team paid particular attention to the subject because it was an important facet in an individual's overall health.[113] The team was shocked by what it found. First, several of the coal camp dispensaries it visited were "incredibly filthy" and deficient in terms of diagnostic aids.[114] Hospital conditions were not much better. Many were overcrowded and "criminally" lacking in ventilation, fire protection, housekeeping, records keeping, and lab services. In addition, many of the institutions showed patient neglect and were understaffed.[115]

The team also investigated the Fund's accusations about overcharging, overhospitalization, and other ethical questions. The records of the area offices were opened to the team for this purpose, and it had to conclude that the Fund was not exaggerating. The records were backed up by pathology reports and showed repeated hospitalization, unnecessary operations, and incompetent surgery. Evidence also existed of duplicate billing and billing for services which had not been performed.[116]

The most striking aspect of the team's report was its discovery that relations between the Fund and organized medicine were breaking down because state liaison committees rarely met with the Fund's representatives. The survey team deplored the situation and stressed that the state societies needed to review all complaints received and to meet regularly with the Fund's personnel to discuss mutual problems.[117]

Based on this information, the team offered moderate recommendations. The report it issued to the council called for a strengthening of general practice, especially with physicians who were independent of the coal companies and the union. Such a change could only be accomplished by bringing new doctors into the coal fields, which necessitated making the mining areas more attractive by improving living conditions. The report failed to specify how the improvement was to be done or who would pay for it. The liaison mechanism of all state medical societies needed to be upgraded. In order to devise corrective methods, the team recommended that a conference of all interested parties meet to exchange ideas.[118]

It is obvious from the report's contents that the survey team had been upset by what it saw. Although its recommendations were not extreme, the team was disturbed by the evidence that organized medicine had neglected its responsibility to maintain standards within the profession. The team advised against releasing the report or its contents to the general public for that reason.[119] At the same time, however, the team made it clear that the AMA had an obligation to correct the problems they had encountered, especially since the Fund was working within the AMA's rules. Failure to address the Fund's legitimate concerns meant that the Fund would possibly seek a solution outside those rules, and thereby discredit the association with the general public.[120]

Draper was pleased with the report's contents. It appeared that the ills the team described had been allowed to exist because the association had not been aware of them. It now looked as if the AMA planned to take corrective action. To facilitate the process, the Fund sponsored the recommended conference and held it in September 1952 at Charleston, West Virginia. The Charleston meeting became the first of four such gatherings the Fund convened between 1952 and 1956.[121]

The results of the 1952 Charleston conference were inconclusive. The general consensus among the participants was that the liaison between the Fund and state medical societies needed to be improved, but the delegates agreed on little else. The most constructive comments came from Dr. B. M. Overholt, representing the Tennessee State Medical Association. Dr. Overholt suggested that the quality of care could be upgraded by greater postgraduate training and continuing education for doctors. The training could be provided through the AMA, which would periodically send instructors out into the field to demonstrate new techniques to physicians and hospital staffs.[122]

Overholt's suggestion was resented. His proposal was similar to ideas articulated by health reformers in the 1920s and 1930s.[123] Because of this, and what it implied, the idea was distinctly unwelcome. Despite this and the conference's failure to address any immediate difficulties, it seemed to show that organized medicine wanted to solve basic problems in health care, and left the door open to future action.

But, solutions for the Fund's concerns were not forthcoming. Despite the AMA's imposing facade, organized medicine was becoming disorganized and incapable of taking the decisive action which Draper needed. Part of the problem was the association's structure. Although its House of Delegates was the

AMA's official rule-making body, state societies could, and did, violate its directives.[124] On the state level, while governing committees were given the authority to set policy, their decisions could be voided by that society's state House of Delegates.

Another major handicap was ideological confusion within the profession. Essentially, organized medicine was a corporate entity, covered by a veneer of individualism. On the one hand, the profession upheld free competition as the only acceptable method of maintaining high service standards. But, when solo practitioners were confronted with real competition, especially by group practices, they shunned their rivals and used the association's mechanisms to persecute them. Although such coercion for economic motives violated AMA ethical standards, the association was reluctant at all levels to use its authority to enforce its rules. Further, unethical practitioners were not disciplined with any severity. These contradictions were frustrating, yet Draper attempted to reconcile them between 1952 and 1955. But his position was becoming increasingly difficult. He needed a settlement with the AMA not only to ensure quality, but to limit expenses.

The budget constraints of the early 1950s had already forced the Fund to discontinue coverage for all tonsillectomies and essential dental care. These measures alone were not adequate to meet the budget shortfalls. Therefore, the Fund's staff developed various other solutions. One such measure, discussed as early as 1951, was the concept of fee-for-time, or retainer. Despite whatever else could be said, fee-for-service was an expensive method of purchasing health care. This point was underscored by health reformers who, during the debate of the 1930s, sought alternatives. One suggestion was the use of capitation payment, where physicians received a flat fee for each patient seen, regardless of treatment rendered.[125]

It is not clear whether capitation had been discussed by the Fund's staff. For its part, the retainer concept had been developed by Dr. Allen Koplin, who was the Fund's AMO for Birmingham, Alabama. Like many of his associates, Koplin had originally worked for the USPHS before coming to the Fund.[126] In terms of how it worked, retainer, or "block-fee-for-service," was a monthly payment negotiated between the AMO and the physician. The payment reflected three factors: the physician's annual income, expenses, and how many Fund beneficiaries he treated as a percentage of his practice.[127] Using a hypothetical case, a physician might have a yearly income of $15,000. His overhead runs at $5,000 a year, and Fund beneficiaries make up 30 percent of his practice. With the retainer, the income and expense figures would be added together and multiplied by 30 percent. The product represented the annual retainer, in this case $6,000. That figure would then be divided by twelve, resulting in a monthly payment of $500. Quality and treatment levels were tracked through a series of forms, and the retainer itself was open to periodic renegotiation by either side whenever the physician's beneficiary load changed.[128]

There were many benefits to retainer payment. First, it relieved the physician of the need for billing. Second, it contained costs since it was based on paying for a physician's time, as opposed to paying for each individual service. Third, since payment was guaranteed, the mechanism worked to attract new and younger physicians into rural areas that had been medically underserved.[129]

This was particularly important since it dovetailed with a second initiative the Fund undertook to cut costs while improving the quality of care: the development of group practices. Unlike the MMHA, the group practice initiative did not come out of the Fund's headquarters, but was started in the field by various AMOs working with other interested parties in their localities. Group practice offered access to a more sophisticated variety of care than what had been available before, especially in isolated coal camps served by a check-off physician.[130] Moreover, group practice was more cost effective, especially since treatment could be rendered within a clinic setting, avoiding the expense of hospitalization. Because of these benefits, group practice had originally been promoted by the health reform movement as a more effective method of providing health services than traditional solo practice.[131]

Although myriad miners' group practice clinics were eventually created throughout the coal fields, the originals were established during the early 1950s in the following communities: Pruden Valley, Tennessee; Russelton, Pennsylvania; Bellaire, Ohio; and Fairmont, West Virginia. In the case of the Pruden Valley and Russelton clinics, the centers were established to replace old company check-off practices. Also, in both cases the clinics were formed by a broad-based community effort, which included the Fund, local branches of the UMWA, as well as various social and fraternal organizations.[132] As a result, the clinics were viewed as community institutions for the good of all. But, since they served the miners, the clinics would have the benefit of a Fund retainer. This combination of a new and up-to-date workplace with financial security was instrumental in attracting young and well-qualified physicians to what had been medical backwaters.[133]

Of these early efforts, the most striking was the Pruden Valley project. What made it so distinctive was that the impetus for it did not come from either the Fund or the UMWA, but the Tennessee State Medical Association (TSMA).[134] Considering the growing tension between the Fund and organized medicine at the time, the question must be asked why the Fund and the TSMA were able to work together. First, there was the influence of Dr. B. M. Overholt. An internist by specialty, Overholt was president of the TSMA's largest county-level affiliate: the Knoxville Academy of Medicine.[135] Through this position he was able to influence the state society's attitudes. While Overholt was certainly committed to preserving a physician's professional rights, there is no question that he also believed organized medicine had an obligation to uphold high standards of practice while making care accessible to all.

Second, the situation was helped by the personality of Knoxville AMO Dr. John Winebrenner. Although he had stood up to various county affiliates of the Kentucky State Medical Association, he was not inclined to view organized medicine as the enemy. Like a number of his colleagues in the field, Winebrenner was a public health specialist. But he had spent most of his early career in the military, rather than the USPHS or the FSA, before joining the Fund. With this, he had the opportunity to view various state-supported medical programs in Europe, especially the German system. As a result, he developed serious doubts about whether such a system was appropriate for the United States.[136] This, in turn, allowed Winebrenner to be more receptive to the TSMA's concerns. Through this combination, the Fund and the TSMA were able to work together to their mutual benefit. This was in stark contrast to the Fund problems with the rest of organized medicine.

By the time the second Charleston conference was held in 1953, relations with the AMA were again showing signs of strain. But, an accommodation was still possible, depending upon the attitudes of the people on either side. During the course of the second conference, the clinic idea was discussed at length. Most participants seemed receptive to the concept and liked the community approach that was being taken.[137] However, the rest of the conference was concerned with the issue of liaison between the Fund and organized medicine in relation to disciplinary action. Representatives of the state medical societies believed that questions of unethical or incompetent practice had to be investigated by the liaison committees, who would then recommend appropriate action.

But, this approach had proven to be completely ineffective as illustrated by a case in Carbon County, Utah, which involved unethical behavior by a physician/operator of a local proprietary hospital. Disgusted by the situation, the Fund's AMO for Denver, Dr. William Dorsey, decided in 1951 to require prior approval through specialist consultations before elective surgery was performed at the institution. To enforce his requirement, Dr. Dorsey secured the cooperation of the Utah State Medical School. The Carbon County Medical Society protested strenuously against the new policy, and the medical school withdrew its cooperation as a result.[138]

Frustrated, Dr. Dorsey requested the Utah State Medical Association to conduct an investigation of the hospital. The matter was turned over to the state society's disciplinary body, the Board of Censors, which looked into the case and cleared the hospital's owner of all charges.[139] Dorsey immediately appealed the decision directly to the state society's president, who reinvestigated the case. The second inquiry substantiated the charges and a confidential letter of censure was issued to the hospital's physician/operator. No further action was taken, since the state society wished to avoid the legal problems attendant to revoking the physician's license to practice.[140]

The matter would have ended there, but the letter which the state society had sent became public. It is not clear how it happened, but upon the letter's release, the UMWA local called a strike demanding better medical care for its members. The strike was settled only after United States Steel, which had an important coal mine in the area, purchased the hospital and donated it to the Permanente hospital group, which brought in a new staff.[141]

For its part, the AMA's national office decided to send its own investigative team into Carbon County to determine what had gone wrong. Dr. Draper was certain the inquiry would reveal that Dr. Dorsey had given the Utah state society every opportunity to work out a fair solution.[142] Without saying so directly, the team determined that the Utah society had mishandled the affair from beginning to end. The original investigation of the hospital had been incomplete, and subsequent action taken by the society was not conclusive. Even at the time when the survey team conducted its inquiry there was widespread confusion over the state society's position on the issue.[143] From its reading of the evidence, the team believed too much authority had been delegated to too many committees and that the bodies had worked at cross-purposes.[144] To address the problem, the team recommended only that the Utah state society strengthen its liaison mechanism for dealing with union health plans.[145]

It is obvious from the report that the survey team wanted to gather all of the facts and to make an honest assessment. Yet, while the report showed where the Utah State Medical Association had failed, it was not overtly critical of the society. It also ignored the fact that the offending physician retained his license despite the evidence against him. Finally, like participants of the Charleston conferences, the survey team believed that effective liaison would solve all difficulties that arose. In reality, Utah's Board of Censors had acted in a liaison capacity as a disciplinary agency and failed in its assignment. There was no guarantee that a specifically designated liaison committee would have behaved any differently, especially since it probably would have been composed of the same physicians who had done the first investigation.

With the AMA proving itself incapable of dealing with these concerns, Dr. Draper began in April 1954 to take matters into his own hands. He ordered the Fund's area administrators to implement a new set of guidelines. First, the offices were to review each physician on the participation lists and limit work authorizations only to those area of medicine for which a doctor was officially qualified. Second, participation itself was limited to physicians willing to arrange for adequate diagnostic work on an office or outpatient basis. Third, all hospitals were to be reviewed for both quality and cost of service. Fourth, area offices were to conduct detailed medical audits of all hospital referrals to determine both the incidence of unnecessary surgery and methods of stopping it. As part of the new guidelines, Dr. Draper directed the area administrators to review reports listing the percentages of normal tissue removed during surgical work and to suspend surgeons who did not meet acceptable standards.[146]

The results of these new policies convinced Dr. Draper that he was moving in the right direction. Prior to April 1954, 65 percent of all surgery which the Fund covered had been performed by general practitioners, at a rate of 66 operations per 1,000 patients. After the new policies went into effect, only 25 percent of all surgery covered was done by general practitioners, and the rate had declined to 30 operations per 1,000 patients. The same was true of hospital admissions. In 1953, the Denver area office reported a total of 263 admissions per 1,000 beneficiaries. By the following year that figure had been cut in half, with a corresponding reduction in the average length of stay.[147]

Experience was showing that when physician participation was restricted on the basis of qualifications, the quality of care increased, while costs decreased. In order to continue the trend, Draper decided to elaborate on the new plan. He directed the area offices to reevaluate all participating hospitals and to discontinue those which did not meet the standards of the Joint Commission on Hospital Accreditation. For individual physicians, the area administrators were to use only those who were broadly competent and responsible in their fields. In cases where a participating doctor was not qualified, the area offices were to get a consultant's opinion before approving any hospital admissions. Dr. Draper added that the administrators were to keep the AMA's liaison committees informed of the Fund's actions.[148]

None of these measures were acceptable to the AMA since they constituted an intrusion into the traditional methods of medical practice. Any physician was assumed to be competent until proven otherwise. If the doctor could not handle a given case, it was his prerogative to refer the individual to another physician. Draper defended his action to the AMA's general manager, Dr. George Lull, by pointing out that the Fund had always sought the best medical care for its beneficiaries and was prepared to pay the cost. Since 1946, the Fund had paid out a total of $205 million to individual physicians and hospitals. Experience had shown that the interests of the miners were best served when they received treatment from doctors widely qualified in surgery and other practice areas.[149] The medical profession recognized the validity of this approach, since it was standard operating procedure for any public hospital to make staff appointments on the basis of physician qualifications.[150]

The most pointed opposition to the new policy though did not come from the AMA's national office, but from its state affiliates. In accordance with Draper's directive, the area offices for Pittsburgh, Johnstown, and Morgantown issued a letter to all participating physicians in March 1955. It required all doctors to seek specialist consultation prior to hospitalizing a Fund beneficiary.[151] The state medical societies of Pennsylvania and West Virginia resented the order and presented resolutions against it at the June 1955 meeting of the AMA's House of Delegates.[152] Pennsylvania took an even more drastic measure by withdrawing its participation from the Fund's program.[153] Draper refused to be intimidated and enforced the new rule.

On June 8, 1955, however, the AMA's House of Delegates passed a resolution against any compulsory specialist consultations.[154] Refusal to comply would have meant breaking relations with the AMA, and Draper was not prepared to take such a step. Although he complied with the association's decision, Draper was not left without some recourse. The same resolution stated that if any unresolvable controversies arose between the Fund and a state medical society in the future, the state society involved should not take any action on its own. Rather, the question was to be referred to the association's Committee on Health Care for Industrial Workers.[155]

At the same time, the Pennsylvania state society's leadership was anxious to arrive at a settlement with the Fund. Four days after the House of Delegates reached its decision on consultations, a meeting was held with representatives of the Fund, including Draper, and the Pennsylvania society's Committee on Medical Economics, chaired by Dr. Edgar W. Meiser. The meeting initiated a series of negotiations between the Fund and the Committee which lasted over four months, and culminated in November 1955 with a formal agreement.[156]

Under the terms of the agreement, organized medicine did not concede to the Fund, or any third party, the right to pass judgment on any treatment a physician rendered. This included decisions involving hospitalization and length of stay.[157] In return, the Pennsylvania society agreed that it was the duty of all doctors to expose any dishonest or unethical behavior among their colleagues.[158] Hospitals were directed to form medical audit committees that recorded the quality of care and the number of admissions. It was also agreed that the state society should endorse a uniform policy whereby any physician received staff privileges at a given hospital when he sought them. The Fund retained the right to classify physicians according to general practice and specialist categories, and to remove doctors from its participation list who violated the rules of medical ethics.[159] The agreement also addressed how the Fund was to pay participating doctors, by putting forward fee-for-time as an acceptable alternative to fee-for-service.[160]

Finally, to prevent the agreement from breaking down, the Fund and the committee included two arbitration clauses. The first stated that if an unsolvable question arose, it would be referred to the AMA's Committee on Health Care for Industrial Workers. The second read as follows: "Should either party become dissatisfied with this agreement, in whole or in part, he shall request a meeting with the other party to discuss points of difference. Such meeting will be held within 30 days of the request. If the points of difference cannot be resolved, then that portion of this agreement affected thereby shall be considered inoperative until such differences are resolved to the satisfaction of both parties."[161]

The Pennsylvania Agreement went into effect on January 1, 1956, and was published in the May 12, 1956, edition of the *Journal of the American Medical Association*.[162] To all parties concerned, it seemed that the Fund and the AMA had reached a milestone. Not only did the agreement meet the AMA's objections, it also solved many of the Fund's problems and committed organized medicine to policing its membership. In addition, the situation looked hopeful since other state medical societies were studying the agreement with the idea of using it as a model for their own relations with the Fund.[163]

Unfortunately, this early optimism was dashed in October 1956 when the House of Delegates of the Medical Society of the State of Pennsylvania voided the agreement. This was done on the pretext that the Committee on Medical Economics had overstepped its authority in coming to a settlement with the Fund without consulting the society's membership.[164] The president of the Pennsylvania society, Dr. Elmer Hess, pleaded with his associates not to abrogate the agreement. It had been made in good faith and was being voided without just cause.[165] Dr. Hess realized that if the Pennsylvania society voided the agreement, the action would certainly poison relations between the Fund and organized medicine. Dr. Draper would be forced to place the Fund's medical service on a closed panel basis. Regardless of Dr. Hess's position as the society's president, his associates booed him.[166]

The House had been moved by a speech given by a member of the Westmoreland County Medical Society. The following year, this county society would be severely criticized in the *Pittsburgh Press* and Westmoreland County's largest newspaper, the Greensburg *Tribune-Review,* for its opposition to administering the Salk polio vaccine through free clinics.[167] The immediate problem over the agreement for both the Westmoreland County Medical Society, and ultimately all of organized medicine in Pennsylvania, grew out of the creation of the clinics mentioned above. The institution in question here was the Miner's Health Center in Russelton, Pennsylvania.

The AMA's president had lauded the clinic effort in an address to the association, and the clinic's directors were careful to ensure that they operated in strict accordance with the AMA's Principles of Medical Ethics.[168] Nevertheless, the Russelton facility was harassed by local physicians, particularly the staff of Citizen's General Hospital in New Kensington. Regarding the clinic as unwanted competition, these individuals sent a petition to the state medical society's president, asking that the clinic be investigated for possible ethical violations.[169] The state society complied and conducted a thorough investigation in

1953. The Fund and the clinic's staff offered their full cooperation during the process.

When they were finished, the investigators reported that the Russelton facility not only provided high quality service, but also the best care the miners in the New Kensington area had probably ever received. But the state society refused to give the clinic any official sanction because it worked independently of the county medical society. In a letter to Dr. Draper, Dr. Dudley P. Walker, then chairman of Pennsylvania's Committee on Medical Economics, wrote that despite the clinic's high practice standards, the state society could not endorse any facility operated by a third party which did not have organized medicine represented on its board.[170] Similar intransigence toward the Fund was clearly expressed by the members of Pennsylvania's House of Delegates.[171]

Dr. Draper viewed this attitude, as well as the abrupt ending of the Pennsylvania Agreement, as a betrayal. The Fund had not been given any prior warning and had been denied the opportunity to present its case. In addition, the ramifications of the termination went beyond Pennsylvania.[172] At the time when the agreement was finalized, Dr. Draper and the Illinois State Medical Association were holding discussions about possibly coming to a similar arrangement. Once the Pennsylvania society voided the agreement, Draper was reluctant to negotiate another for a different state, since it was obvious that a state society's membership would not be bound to follow it.

The Illinois society retaliated by sending a circular letter to every UMWA local in the state which informed the miners that as of January 1, 1957, Illinois physicians would no longer bill the Fund's area office. Instead, the miners would be billed directly and could send their invoices to the Fund themselves if they wished.[173] The state society claimed that the new billing method would ensure the miners received a free choice of physician instead of being forced to use doctors chosen for them by the Fund.[174] To further enforce the action, the Illinois society informed its members that it now disapproved of any doctor working through the Fund to provide medical care to anyone.[175] Each of these measures violated the June 1955 directive about referring state level problems to the Committee on Medical Care for Industrial Workers.[176] However, the AMA's national office failed to protest because the Fund and organized medicine were near a break in relations.

Draper refused to be frightened by such actions and was determined that the Fund would provide union miners with health services. One way or another the Fund would limit participation to physicians qualified to perform surgery. Organized medicine on all of its levels now subjected the Fund to a campaign of vilification, which included the AMA's endorsement of a thirty-one-page pamphlet entitled "Monopoly Power as Exercised by Unions." Published by the National Association of Manufacturers, the pamphlet recommended limitation of the federal government's role in labor relations and an effective end of industrywide collective bargaining.[177]

In a matter of months, relations between organized medicine and the Fund deteriorated rapidly and gave rise to extremism in a large section of the medical profession. However, one factor which had been a source of trouble for the Fund now worked in its favor, the AMA's decentralized structure. If the association had been a united and disciplined body, it could have denied service until the Fund agreed to its demands, but local autonomy prevented this from happening. The Williamson County Medical Society in Illinois, for example, flatly refused to carry out the orders of its state society.[178] Also, the Fund and the Tennessee State Medical Association continued to cooperate throughout the entire controversy.

Regardless of extremists in the AMA, Dr. Draper hoped to repair the situation and asked for the assistance of the Committee on Health Care for Industrial Workers to help settle the dispute. The committee held a special meeting with the Fund and representatives of the various contentious state societies. The meeting's purpose was to gather evidence so that the committee could prepare a set of guidelines to be followed by the state societies and the Fund.

Representatives of the various state societies who attended the meeting repeated the same themes of unfair competition from the Fund and its denial of free choice of physician. As the representative for the Fund, Dr. Draper pointed out that "free choice of physician" had never been clarified. Did it mean that a third party was obligated to assume that any physician was competent to render any service that a patient needed? If it did not, then what did it mean?[179]

The committee's answer came with its creation of the Suggested Guides to Relations between State and County Medical Societies and the United Mine Workers of America Welfare and Retirement Fund. The guides did stipulate that medical societies had a responsibility to correct any wrongdoing by their members.[180] Other than that, the guides made no concessions to the Fund's point of view. As a third party, the Fund was obligated to regard all licensed doctors as competent to practice medicine in all of its branches, unless a physician was proven otherwise by the judgment of his peers.[181] Also, fee-for-service payment was deemed to be the only acceptable form of remuneration.[182]

The guides came as a shock to Dr. Draper. Although he was a member of the committee, he had voluntarily disqualified himself from its deliberations on the issue as gesture of fairness.[183] Taking advantage of the situation, the committee said nothing to Draper until the guides were ready to be presented to the House of Delegates at its June 1957 meeting. In this way, Draper was denied the opportunity to examine the guides and make comments.

When they were finally presented to him, Draper stated flatly that the guides as written were unacceptable. He did not believe that it was proper for the committee to require the Fund to regard all licensed physicians as competent to practice all forms of medicine, since no doctor could be so qualified.[184] Draper also objected to the notion that the only people capable of judging a doctor's performance were his peers. When he questioned the committee about the meaning of this term, the committee told Draper that it meant a physician's county medical society.[185] Draper responded by saying that it would fail because organized medicine had shown itself reluctant to discipline its unethical members in any meaningful way.[186] The committee disregarded Draper's arguments and adopted the guides, which were approved by the House of Delegates the following day.[187]

The guides were now official AMA policy and held the same position as The Principles of Medical Ethics. Draper decided that the guides could not be used and prepared for a fight.[188] As a result, the Fund came under constant attack during the following year. The campaign reached its climax when the AMA's House of Delegates voted to condemn the Fund in June 1958. By late September 1957, the Medical Society of the State of Pennsylvania threatened members with possible expulsion for unethical practice if anyone continued to participate in the Fund's program.[189] The AMA went so far as to victimize Draper by discontinuing his membership on the Committee on Health Care for Industrial Workers.[190]

The most extreme action came from states that sought legislation to force third parties away from closed panel operation. As mentioned previously, such an effort was mounted in Kentucky, although the primary motive was resentment of the Miners' Memorial Hospital Association, as well as the Fund's conflict with the AMA. Although Kentucky's bill failed to pass, similar pieces of legislation were introduced in Texas, Colorado, and Iowa. While such laws were probably unconstitutional, they presented a genuine threat. As it was, the Texas bill passed, which forced the closure of three established workers' hospitals that had been created years before through arrangements between unions and local employers, such as Humble Oil and the Southern Pacific Railroad.[191]

The reason for the conflict's intensity was twofold: first, no other major medical third party had ever attempted what the Fund was doing. Second, because of the Fund's size, as well as its status as the first industrywide program of its kind, it was a leader in the area of industrial benefits. While never overtly stated, the AMA was probably afraid that other major medical payers, such as Blue Cross/Blue Shield, would adopt closed panel themselves if the Fund successfully defied organized medicine's dictates.

Ironically, such fears also accounted for why a minority within the AMA wanted to take a softer line with the Fund. One representative of this group was Dr. James Klump of West Virginia. In a presentation before a special AMA commission on third parties, Dr. Klump criticized the association for its failure to correct fraud and maintain professional standards.[192] Dr. Klump also believed that the association needed to redefine free choice of physician in a fairer and precise manner.[193] Through its laxity, organized medicine had left the Fund with no recourse but to restrict participation to individuals and institutions that behaved responsibly. Since it paid the medical bills of its beneficiaries, Dr. Klump asserted that the Fund had a right to expect good quality care at a reasonable cost, and unless the association corrected its weaknesses, other third parties would follow the Fund's example.

The clash between the two groups in organized medicine was most evident when the AMA's House of Delegates convened for its June 1958 meeting at San Francisco. The floor discussion between the delegates about the Fund was heated, and at times openly insulting. Bitter denunciations of the Fund's program came from the Colorado, Kentucky, Illinois, and Pennsylvania delegations, some of whose members demanded that the House condemn the Fund and begin an educational campaign against it.[194] Other delegates countered by pointing out that the AMA's national and state branches needed to rid their memberships of chiseling doctors before taking action against an outside group.[195] Among the Fund's defenders were Dr. Elmer Hess, who recounted his experience before the Pennsylvania House of Delegates, Dr. Frank Holyrod of West Virginia, and Dr. B. M. Overholt.[196] At the debate's conclusion, the House voted in favor of the condemnation by a margin of 110 to 72.[197]

While the hard-liners won, it was a Pyrrhic victory. Not only had a large minority of the House's members voted against the resolution, events were moving against the extremist's position. Magazines as diverse as *Fortune, Commonwheel,* and *The Nation* either editorialized against the association or presented the story from the Fund's point of view.[198] In addition, the AMA would soon face an adversary more powerful than the Fund. In December 1958, Morgan Beaty of NBC radio reported that the newly elected Congress would be considering a bill introduced by Representative Forman of Rhode Island. The bill called for the government to provide medical care for the elderly.[199] Forman had introduced the bill twice before in previous sessions, but he expected a favorable hearing now because of the liberal majority that had been elected.[200]

With public opinion against it, and the possibility of government intervention into medical care, the AMA suddenly needed to distance itself from its condemnation of the Fund. The one way to do this was for the association to take a second look at the Fund and reassess whether or not a fundamental conflict actually existed. Fortunately for the association, its Special Commission on Medical Third Parties, which it had formed in 1955, gave it the opportunity to make such a reassessment. [201]

Two months before the commission made its final report, it sponsored a conference with several different third parties in Chicago, including the Fund.

Among the other groups attending were the Detroit Community Health Association, the Kaiser-Permanente Medical Group, and the Union Health Center of the International Ladies Garment Workers Union.[202] Speaking for the Fund, Dr. Draper recounted his difficulties with organized medicine, emphasizing the pain the conflict had caused him.[203] As a member of the AMA, he had been proud of the association's achievements. But, he added that the Fund's program was running smoothly and achieving greater cost containment and quality of service than when it attempted to maintain ties with organized medicine.[204]

The commission made its report in December 1958 and gave a favorable assessment of the Fund. The mood of the House of Delegates had markedly changed since its June meeting. The members were more subdued, with the Pennsylvania and Illinois delegations displaying a more flexible attitude.[205] The commission's report documented that the closed panel systems it investigated did not show a deterioration of medical practice. These plans might have limited physician free choice, but they used well-qualified doctors and offered broader and more extensive care than most commercial insurance carriers.[206] The report recommended that the association take a more tolerant and progressive attitude vis-à-vis these plans.

The association did not follow all of the commission's recommendations, and in fact it could not. To accept the closed panel approach as legitimate would have meant a repudiation of the association's basic policies. It is for this reason that when the House of Delegates reassembled in June 1959, it reaffirmed its stand on physician free choice. Meanwhile, the AMA's national office stopped its fight with the Fund. At the same meeting, Dr. Draper was allowed to present a paper showing that the Fund actually increased a miner's free choice by making specialist care available to people who had never had such services before.

Appearances aside, the Fund had managed to win a major victory for itself and other medical third parties. Its experience had dispelled the old myths concerning closed panel arrangements, fee-for-service payment, and free choice of physician. Despite the AMA's claims to the contrary, fee-for-service and physician free choice did not guarantee good medical practice or treatment, nor did closed panel organization automatically cause a deterioration of standards.

This was also a victory for the miners. By taking a less combative attitude, the AMA had been forced to admit that the Fund's beneficiaries were entitled to good medical care, which meant the Fund as a third party had the right to ensure quality and to control costs by whatever measures it deemed necessary. With the AMA conflict at an end, the Fund's medical program continued operating and elaborating on its methods until the late 1970s. In this context, the interests of the miners, the Fund's humanitarian mission, and the need for solvency neatly converged. While he was concerned about reducing costs, there is no question that Dr. Draper was sincerely concerned about providing the Fund's beneficiaries with the best medical care available. Thus, the Fund's leadership was responsive and committed to meeting the needs of the people they served, and the conflict with the AMA proved it.

Tragically, the victory came just before a period of crisis during which financial difficulties would force massive cuts in the Fund's services. The cuts created an image of the Fund's leadership as insensitive toward the miners. Also, during the 1960s the entire system Lewis had built within the industry began to break down. A major contributing factor was the ineptitude of the man who eventually succeeded Lewis as the UMWA's president, W. A. (Tony) Boyle. These problems had a terrible impact upon the Fund. In the short term, it would be embroiled in the charges of corruption associated with Boyle's administration and the investigations they produced. In the long run, these events would provide the preconditions that ultimately caused the destruction of the Fund's medical service.

Chapter 6
The Decade of Crisis

In 1959 John L. Lewis announced his decision to retire from the UMWA's presidency. Named as president emeritus, Lewis remained chairman of the Fund's trustee board, which meant the Fund and the union now had different leaders. Despite continuing as the Fund's chairman, Lewis's retirement signified the end of an era. At the start of his tenure in 1919, Lewis's administration was marked by controversy and failure. The union's radicals opposed his policies, and they believed that Lewis lacked the militancy needed to deal effectively with the operators.[1]

Added to this infighting were the effects of the coal industry's first major decline. Between 1920 and 1929, the union's membership plummeted from 400,000 to less than 100,000, with Lewis's reputation suffering as a result. Lewis's image recovered, however, with the success of the massive organizing campaign he initiated with the passage of the National Industrial Recovery Act in 1933. Thereafter, his influence grew, reaching its height when he founded the CIO. After he resigned the CIO's presidency in 1940, his position as a national figure gradually waned, but his prestige among the UMWA rank and file remained high.

Under Lewis's leadership, miners who remained in the industry not only enjoyed higher wages but also excellent benefits provided by the Fund. Although restrictions had been placed upon pension eligibility in 1953, the Fund remained the most generous benefit program in basic industry. This was especially true of its medical program. Unlike other union systems, such as the USW Blue Cross plan, the Fund covered all union miners and their families, regardless of employment status. The Fund's only limitation was that a miner lost his coverage when he found a full-time job outside the industry. This, however, would soon change.

Lewis's retirement coincided with the start of a prolonged crisis for both the union and the Fund. Because of poor economic conditions in the wider economy, and especially the coal industry, the Fund was forced to make a series of major cuts. As mentioned previously, when the Fund opened the MMHA hospitals in 1956, coal had just recovered from a production decline. Demand, however, remained unstable, and in 1958 production fell dramatically again. Whereas in 1956, approximately 500 million tons were mined, the industry's output dropped to 410 million tons by 1958 and fell by another 8 million tons by 1961.[2] At the same time, total earnings in the bituminous industry had fallen from $1.986 billion in 1951 to $1.315 billion in 1961. A drop of nearly 34 percent.[3] This was the second major recession in the industry since 1950, and production did not begin to recover until 1962.[4]

The production shortfall's impact upon the Fund was devastating. Not only was the Fund's income cut, but many smaller operators defaulted on their royalty payments in a scramble to cut costs. Because neither the union's leadership nor the major operators were in a position to stabilize the industry, the recession's effects could not be contained. Considering the Fund's problems with the hospital chain, this could not have come at a worse time. By the end of fiscal year 1959, the Fund's expenses exceeded income by $18 million, and the deficit was covered by withdrawals from the Fund's assets.[5] By the beginning of 1960, the Fund's financial condition appeared to be serious, and its leadership had no choice but to retrench. The first major cut came in the area of health care. Roche and her staff decided in early 1960 to end medical coverage for any miner unemployed for a year or longer. The tentative date for the new policy was set for July 1, 1960, but Roche decided not to announce the change until it was ready to go into effect. This was done to avoid a sudden rush of people seeking elective surgery.[6]

To prepare for the change, the Fund sent out a questionnaire for distribution by the UMWA district and local offices. The document inquired about the miner's work status, how long he had been unemployed, and whether or not he had received worker's compensation.[7] According to the figures which the Fund gathered, the new policy dropped 59,550 miners from the program, an average of 25 percent of all the Fund's 85 HS card holders.[8] In individual union districts, however, the percentages differed. Districts 8, 10, and 28 reported percentage losses 11 to 15 points below the union's average, but a total of eight districts reported a percentage loss above the average. The hardest hit were Districts 19, 21, 17, 31, and 30, representing primarily south-central Appalachia, which reported a total loss of 20,221.[9]

Roche informed the AMOs of the new policy during a conference she held on April 13. According to Roche, the trustees had examined all of the available data and decided that they had no choice but to approve the reduction. She added that Lewis supported the change and realized that it would cause a great deal of protest.[10] The Fund's central office planned to take the responsibility for sending out the announcements, but it was the duty of the area offices to ensure that no one who became ineligible continued to receive medical assistance.[11] In the meantime, the area offices were ordered to keep the decision in strict confidence in order to avoid a rush of people seeking medical attention before their eligibility ended. Roche implied that the decision was a painful one to make, but that the Fund had a duty to serve the interests of working miners above all others.[12]

The AMOs accepted the new policy as necessary and did not oppose it. Dr. Arestad, however, who had left the AMA to run the Fund's Johnstown office, predicted that the cuts would be bitterly resented. Pittsburgh AMO Dr. Leslie Falk disliked Roche's approach. Falk argued that instead of keeping the decision quiet for as long as possible, it would be better for the Fund to publicize what it was doing and why.[13] Roche disregarded Falk's suggestion and readied the form letter announcing the policy change. The letter was set for distribution by the end of June without any prior warning.[14]

Roche's insistence upon secrecy not only damaged the Fund's prestige, but hers and Lewis's as well. Like with the handling of the Thirty-Year Rule, it created the impression that she and Lewis were aloof and remote. It appeared as if they had ceased to care about the average miner and his family. As predicted, the decision sparked a major outpouring of protest from union members, tinged with a strong sense of betrayal. By failing to take Dr. Falk's advice, Roche cut off the Fund from the union's rank and file, and so precluded the Fund from maintaining a reservoir of goodwill. Nevertheless, Roche sincerely believed that what she did, and how she did it, worked to the best interests of the vast majority of the Fund's beneficiaries. From her perspective, while 50,000 miners were dropped from the Fund's program, more than 180,000 HS 85 health card holders and their dependents continued to receive coverage.[15] Judging from her correspondence with Lewis, Roche believed that if Fund resources were limited, working miners and pensioners had to be given priority in allocation.[16]

Unfortunately, the health care revisions were not enough. During the first four months of fiscal 1960, the Fund lost another $10 million, and projections indicated that an additional $5 million would be lost by January 1, 1961. According to Roche, the Fund needed to cut an additional $16 million to $20 million from its budget.[17] After making an intensive study of the Fund's operating expenses for the previous two years, Roche recommended that the trustees should cut the pension by 20 to 25 percent. The only alternative was another reduction in the medical program, which would have made it inoperative.[18] Lewis agreed that no other option existed, and the trustees discussed the idea during a meeting held on December 2, 1961. In response to a question from the industry trustee, Henry Schmidt, Roche assured her associates that the cut met the income shortfall.[19]

The pension reduction was scheduled to take effect in February 1961, and the Fund sent official notices to all pensioners on December 30, 1960. The letter, signed by Roche, blamed economic conditions in the industry for the cut and stressed that unless the Fund controlled expenses a financial disaster would result.[20] A similar notice was sent by Dr. Draper to all of the area medical administrators. Draper expressed his hope that the pension revision was only a temporary measure, but added that the industry showed signs of a very slow recovery.[21]

Roche and her associates undoubtedly acted in good faith when they ordered the reductions. The recession was serious and no one could possibly have predicted when business conditions would improve. The question that must now be asked is, Did the Fund have alternatives at its disposal other than benefit reductions? On first inspection, the answer is no. The most obvious solution would have been a royalty increase. The last time royalties increased was 1952, when the payment rose from thirty cents to forty cents a ton. When Lewis met with the industry's leadership again in 1956, the Fund's tonnage rate remained the same. Because of this, it is tempting to argue that if an increase for 1956 had been negotiated, the 1960–61 benefit cuts could have been avoided. However, due to the economic circumstances that prevailed in the industry at the time, a royalty increase would have made a bad situation worse.

As previously mentioned, the recession was so severe that when smaller operators used nonunion labor, or broke their contracts, the larger unionized firms could do nothing to correct the problem. Because the larger firms paid into the Fund, and the union wage scale, they risked bankruptcy if they reduced their prices to undercut the smaller operators. In this context, a higher royalty would have placed the Fund in an area of diminishing marginal returns. The larger firms would still have been unable to force the smaller companies out of business, with the higher royalty prompting even more firms to repudiate their contracts.

As it is, Ivana Krajcinovic addresses this and related issues in her study of the Fund's medical program, *From Company Doctors to Managed Care,* and is very critical of Lewis. Essentially, her contentions center around three points. First, while granting the 1958–61 recession's severity, she criticizes Lewis for not seeking a royalty increase after 1962, despite a steady rise in coal production. Second, she asks why the union's treasury was not used to shore up the Fund's financial position. Third, she points to Lewis's failure to make occupational safety and health a priority in his negotiations with the major coal operators.[22]

While Krajcinovic's analysis is well taken, she fails to take into account certain facts that make Lewis's decisions in some of these matters not only understandable but even defensible. First, it must be remembered that after his retirement from the union's presidency in 1959, Lewis's ability to impact upon the Fund's income was severely limited. Negotiating the royalty was the sole prerogative of the union's president. However, even if Lewis could have sought an increase on his own authority as the Fund's chairman, he probably would have been reluctant to do it.

While it is true that the industry steadily recovered after 1962, we know this courtesy of hindsight. Lewis would not have been in a position to see the trend unless he had had a crystal ball. Looking at coal production during the Fund's first thirteen years (1948–61), the industry's performance was marked

THE DECADE OF CRISIS

by a steep overall decline. While there were brief recoveries, none of these lasted longer than two years.[23] Since future action relative to policy is based upon past performance, a decision not to seek a royalty increase seemed to be the right thing to do.

On the issue of using the union's treasury to stabilize the Fund, Krajcinovic is correct when she writes that Lewis had not shown much concern for various legalities in the past. Certainly, Roche's presence on the Fund's board as neutral trustee violated both the letter and spirit of the Taft-Hartley Act. Use of the National Bank of Washington as the Fund's sole depository did the same for the estate and trust laws. However, both of these arrangements dated from 1950. Truman was still president, and while his relations with organized labor were strained, he nevertheless had been an ally. This was demonstrated by his veto of the Taft-Hartley Act when it came across his desk. In addition, early protests from industry trustee Charles Owen notwithstanding, the people who had the standing to object to these arrangements in court, the major coal operators, accepted them.

By 1953, the situation had changed. Eisenhower was president. Although the rabidly antilabor atmosphere that had pervaded Washington in 1947 during the 80th Congress was missing, a small-bore disdain for unions, under the guise of concern about labor racketeering, was now fashionable. Worse, this attitude was not confined to Republicans, but was shared by several up-and-coming Democrats, including John F. Kennedy. This mentality ultimately produced the Labor-Management Reporting and Disclosure Act of 1959 (also known as the Landrum-Griffin Act).

In such a setting, Lewis, ever the astute political observer, was not about to do anything that would call undue attention to the Fund by prying and possibly hostile eyes. To that end, Lewis maintained a policy of strict separation between the Fund and the union. This included housing the Fund's headquarters in a different building from the union and eventually enjoining the union's and Fund's staffs from socializing, or even speaking to one another.[24] Thus, it should come as no surprise that the union's treasury was never tapped to assist the Fund in any way.

This assertion does not deny that Lewis at times used the union's financial assets for questionable purposes. For example, Lewis provided $25 million in union monies to assist railroad millionaire, and ally, Cyrus Eaton to buy control of the Western Kentucky Coal Company. Western Kentucky had successfully resisted unionization to this point, and the maneuver was intended to place the company under a management that would sign the National Bituminous Coal Wage Agreement. This it would ultimately do when Eaton assumed chairmanship of the company's board. The actual purchase, however, was done in 1952, *prior* to Eisenhower's entry to the White House.[25]

132

Finally, it is undeniable that Lewis faltered in the area of occupational health and safety. Although he did strive during his career to achieve a safer workplace, Lewis failed to address the rise in coal dust inhalation among miners, which was directly attributable to the industry's mechanization. This matter, and its ramifications, will be discussed more thoroughly below.

With the disappointment the cuts engendered, the response was swift and bitter. The *Johnstown Tribune Democrat* reported that a protest rally was held by five hundred miners, representing thirty local unions in District 2, ten days after the Fund dropped unemployed miners from its medical program. The men threatened to strike unless full medical benefits were restored in three days.[26] District officials attempted to explain why the trustees needed to make the reductions, but the explanations were not effective. In an attempt to settle the problem, a committee representing seventeen locals came to Washington to meet with Lewis. The meeting failed to calm the situation when Lewis insisted that the cuts could not be restored. One angry committee member compared the former UMWA president to Nikita Khrushchev.[27]

Aside from the *Tribune-Democrat,* the cuts also received coverage from larger media organizations in the coal fields such as the *Pittsburgh Press,* Pittsburgh radio and television station KDKA, and the *Louisville Courier-Journal.*[28] All three of these outlets were noted for their antilabor bias. The Fund's difficulties provided hostile editors with an opportunity to attack the Fund, the UMWA, and their leadership. In one instance, the *Lexington Herald* ran a scathing editorial on the Fund's policies. It went on to describe the UMWA as rich, insensitive, and incorrectly asserted that it was getting richer from coal royalties which went directly into its treasury.[29]

In response to its critics, the Fund's leadership attempted to point out that despite the cuts, the Fund was still the most liberal benefit program in basic industry. They stressed that unemployed miners kept their medical benefits for a year and did not lose their pension rights.[30] But, these statements were too little, too late. The damage had been done. With it, the mass media, as well as so-called thoughtful writers, promoted the idea that the Fund had lost touch with the miners and ceased to care. For example, Harry M. Caudill's influential study *Night Comes to the Cumberlands* dripped with this message. Moreover, in an updated edition of the book, Caudill pointed to the Fund's decision to sell the hospital chain as a prime example of yet another outside organization abandoning the Appalachian region.[31] Although Caudill was mistaken, especially after the lengths the Fund went to keep the hospitals open, his characterization helped confirm the view that the Fund's leadership was calloused and indifferent.

What made the situation worse was a decision in 1962 to try to force defaulting operators to pay their royalties by discontinuing medical benefits for their employees. The benefits would not be restored until the debts were paid.[32]

The policy was a last resort. Since neither the union nor the large operators had the power to compel the defaulting firms to pay, some other coercive method had to be found. In looking for this solution, the Fund's leadership probably decided to borrow from the Progressive Mine Workers. A similar royalty-default policy had been used by the Progressives in the management of their fund for a number of years.[33] The theory was that miners who worked for defaulting companies would strike and thereby force their employers to pay.

Instead, the Fund's leadership was harshly criticized for punishing the miners. Embarrassed, the trustees discontinued the policy in 1967.[34] Despite the policy's failure and discontinuation, it became an issue raised in the *Blankenship* vs. *Boyle* class-action suit filed against the Fund in 1969. It was cited as a prime example of how the Fund had ceased to serve the interests of the miners.[35]

Fortunately, the 1962 health card cancellation was the last reduction made in the Fund's program. By the end of 1962, the coal industry was beginning to recover from the recession. Over the course of the next three years, production increased by an average of 28.5 million tons annually, with total output once again exceeding 500 million tons by 1965.[36] With the recovery well under way, the Fund's leadership began work on repairing the damage the recession had caused. Near the end of 1964, Roche decided to increase pensions, and restoration of the full $100-a-month payment became a top priority.[37]

According to the Fund's statistics, an increase of $15 would cost an additional $9 million over current expenses, whereas an increase of $10 would cost $7.7 million.[38] Although Roche and her staff moved cautiously, they realized that a simple $10 increase was not adequate. The Fund needed to demonstrate that it was still committed to the miners. As an alternative to the immediate restoration of the full payment, Roche and her associates sought to create a formula that included a modest increase while lifting some eligibility restrictions. A consensus eventually developed around the following package: a $10-a-month pension increase combined with a discontinuation of the thirty-year rule for all miners retiring on or after the date the new regulations went into effect. The package also reduced the minimum retirement age to fifty-five.[39] The package's total cost was set at $18.4 million.

While the figure was much higher than what was originally thought desirable, Thomas Ryan provided Roche with some additional facts. The most important fact was that 74 percent of the men working in union mines were less than fifty years of age, and royalty income had risen substantially in the past year and a half.[40] Not only could the Fund meet the increased cost, but Ryan's analysis indicated that the pension program would not be overwhelmed by miners taking early retirement.[41]

The increase and the new regulations went into effect on February 1, 1965. As business conditions continued to improve, Roche decided that the Fund could afford to restore the full $100-a-month payment. It would cost an additional $11 million, and would bring the total pension bill to $84 million a year.[42] Based on income projections, the Fund could pay for the increase without touching any of its reserves. Moreover, Medicare was scheduled to begin operation in July 1966, and Ryan believed that the Fund's total expenses would go down as a result.[43]

From the perspective of the Fund's leadership, restoration of the full pension was a notable achievement. Not only had the Fund survived the recession, it was now in a position to expand one major benefit by liberalizing eligibility rules. Once again, the effort's impact was limited. The $100-a-month payment had been in effect since the trustees created the pension system in 1948, and the recent efforts by the Fund only returned it to the status quo. Obviously, living costs had risen since 1948, and if the Fund hoped to convince the miners that it had not forgotten them, another increase would be necessary.

Originally, Roche and her staff considered a raise of twenty dollars a month, but the income data indicated that the figure was too high. While the income the Fund received at the time could cover the added expense, little would remain for shoring up the Fund's reserves. Taking into account the erratic performance of the industry since 1950, the Fund needed a safety margin of excess annual income in case of an emergency.[44] Therefore, Roche and Lewis decided that it would be impossible to offer more than fifteen dollars a month.[45]

Although the Fund could afford the increase, Roche was primarily concerned with improving the Fund's image with the union's rank and file. While the protests arising from the health care eligibility changes may have been expected, they were still unsettling. The last mass protest in the rank and file had surfaced in the late 1920s and early 1930s over dissatisfaction with Lewis's leadership.[46] Efforts to unseat Lewis had failed, but the memory of rank-and-file insurgency remained, and it seemed possible in the early 1960s that a similar rebellion could break out. As it was, rank-and-file dissension resurfaced when the Fund announced its plan to sell or close four of the ten MMHA hospitals. As the sale deadline approached, angry miners held protest meetings and threatened to destroy the institutions if they closed.[47] Fortunately, as described in chapter 4, the Fund managed to sell the hospitals to the Board of National Missions, Presbyterian Church U.S.A.

By selling the hospitals, the Fund dispelled one immediate manifestation of rank-and-file anger. It is not clear whether the pension increases did the same. On the one hand, the Fund ceased to be the primary focus of protest for the moment. On the other hand, an opposition movement, eventually becoming the Miners for Democracy, grew during the 1960s. Aside from the Fund, the opposition was concerned by the union's lack of militancy in dealing with the operators on health and safety issues, sick pay, and wage increases. However, the opposition remained divided since it lacked a single galvanizing issue and a capable leader who was known throughout the union. Nevertheless, discontent within the union was registered during the 1964 UMWA presidential election when an obscure local official from western Pennsylvania, "Cadillac" Steve Kochis, won 20 percent of the vote.[48]

Despite the discontent, the union's internal structure remained strong. However, the opposition was correct in its belief that the union had come under the control of an ineffective leadership. This weakened the UMWA's position in the industry relative to the operators. Such a debilitation of the union's strength held grave consequences for the Fund, since its position depended not only on the industry's health, but the health of the union as well. This situation might explain why the Fund's leadership decided to follow financial policies in the 1960s which were criticized later; in particular, the maintenance of a large percentage of Fund assets as cash in the union's bank and major investment in utility stocks. Each of these maneuvers contributed to the same goal: enhancing the union's standing within the industry.

Through the 1950s and 1960s, demand for coal changed radically. While purchases from traditionally large coal consumers such as the railroads and the steel industry declined or disappeared completely, consumption by electric utilities rose rapidly. By 1962, utilities used half of all coal produced in the United States.[49] The Fund's leadership noted the change, and in 1962 it began investing heavily in utility stocks. The industry trustee, Henry G. Schmidt, supported and encouraged the new policy. Prior to the change, Lewis had directed the Fund's investments into government securities.[50] Although Schmidt did not recommend speculation, he believed the old investment plan was too cautious. Diversifying into utilities would increase the Fund's earnings while offering some security in low-risk utility stocks.[51] Schmidt also discounted advice against purchasing utility stock given in a report by Bache & Co. The industry trustee insisted that other reputable investment analysts regarded utilities as a solid alternative to traditional low-risk investments.[52]

Thus, from 1962 to 1969, the Fund purchased shares in seventeen different utilities at a price of nearly $44 million. Among the companies included in the Fund's portfolio were such major energy producers as Consolidated Edison, Duquesne Light, Kansas City Power and Light, the Philadelphia Electric Company, and Southern California Edison.[53] All of the utility stocks purchased by the Fund were on the approved list of acceptable investments for trusts published by the District Court of the United States for the District of Columbia. Moreover, with the exception of one firm, all of the companies received an "A" rating on the Standard & Poor securities list.[54]

While the Fund's leadership had taken every precaution to ensure a successful investment strategy, the plan backfired. The actual value of nearly all of the stock purchased declined, amounting to a paper loss of over $10 million.[55]

Undoubtedly, the Fund's leaders made a mistake to invest so heavily in utilities, but did they violate their fiduciary obligations? As trustees, Lewis, Roche, and Schmidt had a duty to exercise their authority solely in the best interests of the beneficiaries. Therefore, in theory, purchasing the utility stock was arguably a breach of trust. Realistically, it was nearly impossible to make such a distinction. The ability of the Fund to offer benefits depended, at least in part, upon the union's ability to enforce its contracts and ensure continued payment of royalties. If the union was weakened, the Fund was weakened.

A related, and more complex, issue involved whether or not Roche and Lewis purchased a large block of shares in Cleveland Electric Illuminating to benefit both the union and the industry trustee's company, North American Coal. During the *Blankenship* case, Harry Huge, attorney for the plaintiffs, pointed to the fact that in 1960, CEI negotiated a contract with North American Coal to purchase 60,000 tons a month. This was at the very time Schmidt recommended that the Fund invest in utilities. Huge's opponents countered by showing that the Fund first purchased stock in CEI in 1955, two years before Schmidt became a trustee.[56] Although the Fund purchased additional shares of CEI between 1963 and 1964, the sale took place long after the Cleveland utility concluded its contract with Schmidt's company. Also, while Schmidt recommended investment in utilities, he never mentioned CEI by name.[57]

Union attorneys denied any connection between the purchase of CEI stock by the Fund and UMWA organization programs. According to their rendering of the facts, the union was engaged in a campaign during the 1960s to persuade CEI to purchase coal from firms that had signed the National Bituminous Coal Wage Agreement. The union was supported in its effort by the Ohio branch of the AFL-CIO and by Cyrus Eaton, who was a member of CEI's board.[58] The board refused to listen to Eaton, and its refusal prevented any further attempts to effect a policy change. Although the Fund owned 150,000 shares of CEI, it did not qualify as a major stockholder since it controlled only 1 percent of the shares the utility issued.[59]

The arguments presented by union lawyers were convincing and cast doubt that any conflict of interest existed between North American Coal and Fund stock purchases and between the Fund and the union. But, in their zeal to show that the Fund's leadership had not violated their fiduciary obligations, the attorneys concluded their presentation with the following statement:

> Even if the plaintiffs' contentions find support in the evidence, they would not advance the action a scintilla. The contentions are that C.E.I. was purchased to further the Union and Trustee Schmidt's corporation and to dissipate the Fund's assets. This logical relationship is impossible. Both the success of the Union's

campaign and North American's increased sales meant that more union mined coal would be sold and . . . that more royalty payments would be made to the Fund. The success of the Union and North American would not dissipate but enlarge the assets of the Fund by the collection of additional royalties.[60]

Their reasoning was clear: A simplistic reading of the law was not appropriate.

Turning to the issue of the Fund's cash holdings, these deposits had usually been kept to the equivalency of one month's expenses.[61] The only irregularity here was that, as mentioned before, the National Bank of Washington, wholly owned by the UMWA, acted as the Fund's sole depository. During the 1950s, this special relationship between the bank, the union, and the Fund was barely noticed. What bothered critics during the 1960s, however, was that between 1961 and 1967, the Fund's cash deposits with the bank grew from 14 percent of the Fund's total holdings to 44 percent.[62]

Lewis's reasons for using the bank have already been offered. His primary concern was to keep the Fund's holdings as far as possible from management's potential interference. Moreover, Lewis's attitude about financial matters had been conditioned by the harsh reality of the unregulated frontier-style economics seen in the United States prior to the New Deal. Viewed in this light, Lewis's use of the bank appears to be similar to stuffing a mattress.[63] Regardless of Lewis's motives, Huge and other critics assailed the use of the union's bank in this manner as inherently detrimental to the Fund and its beneficiaries. Instead of maintaining such high concentrations of cash, these critics argued that the monies should have been invested to yield additional revenues.[64] Because so much was deposited in non-interest-bearing accounts, the bank and the union were benefiting at the Fund's expense.

From a strictly legal standpoint, the critics were correct. The Fund's relationship with the bank was a conflict of interest. However, Lewis probably viewed the Fund, the union, and the bank as allied organizations with a set of goals in common. Therefore, whatever the Fund might have lost in immediate income was marginal compared to what it gained from assuring the union's long-term strength. Because the UMWA had come under the control of an ineffective leader after Lewis retired, the need to enhance the position of the union was greater than ever. This might account for why Lewis allowed the Fund's cash deposit level to rise so high.

At the center of the problem was the union itself. When Lewis retired, he was succeeded by Thomas Kennedy. A former Democratic lieutenant governor of Pennsylvania, Lewis appointed Kennedy as union vice-president in 1942 to replace Philip Murray. Murray had worked with Lewis for years and succeeded the union chief as head of the CIO in 1940. But, the two men quarreled shortly thereafter over Murray's continued support for FDR, which culminated in Lewis purging Murray from the UMWA. Taking over for Murray, Kennedy faithfully served as UMWA vice-president until 1960, when he replaced Lewis. No estimate of Kennedy as president of the union is possible because he died three years after coming to power.

Upon Kennedy's death, the presidency of the union officially went to W. A. (Tony) Boyle, who served as vice-president under Kennedy. Unlike most of the men who had risen through the union's upper echelons, Boyle did not come from the eastern or midwestern coal fields. He was born in Montana, the son of an Irish immigrant miner who had worked in the Scottish mines before coming to the United States. Just when Boyle joined the union is unclear, but he ultimately rose to the presidency of District 27 headquartered in Billings, Montana.[65] Boyle served in that position for eight years, until Lewis brought him to work in the UMWA national office in 1948.[66]

Why Lewis brought Boyle to Washington remains unclear and will never be completely answered, since Lewis never explained his decisions to anyone. Both Boyle and his critics maintained that he was Lewis's hand-chosen successor, whom Lewis had trained for the position. If true, Lewis was not only a poor judge of character, but of ability as well. Boyle did not possess any of Lewis's strengths, and he magnified weaknesses of both Lewis and the system he created for the union during his forty-year tenure as its president. A man of limited intelligence, Boyle's public statements were often incoherent. To compensate for his inadequate rhetorical skills, Boyle bellowed his speeches and tried to project a tough image.

In one well-known instance of this, Boyle displayed his anger over comments made by West Virginia congressman Ken Heckler, who criticized the union's record on mine safety issues. During one such speech, given in Charleston, West Virginia, Congressman Heckler waved a large bologna as a snide comment on the union's position. Boyle was incensed and referred to the incident later when he testified before a congressional committee. In a rambling statement, Boyle said that he was ready to meet a certain congressman in a dark alley any time and stuff a bologna down his throat.[67]

Boyle displayed the same lack of finesse in how he managed the union. While Lewis had been coercive, he had tried to maintain appearances and used force only when necessary. Boyle, on the other hand, was always quick to use goon-squad tactics, without any thought as to consequences. The best example of this difference in style was seen during the union's 1964 convention, held one year after Boyle assumed the union's presidency. At previous conventions Lewis ensured a tightly managed floor by using the credentials committee, as well as his position as convention chairman. During the 1964 meeting, however, Boyle decided he needed additional safeguards and used a squad to manhandle dissenting delegates. The men wore white hardhats, with "District 19, Tony Boyle" written on them. Their activities were described later by Louis Antal, a Miners for Democracy leader from Pittsburgh, when the U.S. Senate investigated the union's 1969 presidential election.[68] Since Boyle was associated with Lewis, his mishandling of the union has cast a shadow on Lewis's career as a labor leader, and the system he built within the union and the coal industry. Because the Fund was part of that system, and due to the impact Boyle's rise ultimately had on the Fund, it is necessary to determine what went wrong and how.

To begin, there is no solid evidence to show that Lewis had ever actually chosen Boyle as his heir. By appointing Boyle to the Washington office, Lewis probably wanted to ensure that the UMWA's western section was represented at union headquarters. As president of District 27, Boyle appeared useful for that function. Not only did District 27 cover a wide geographic area, but it also ranked as the largest western district in the UMWA in terms of membership.[69] In addition, Boyle was not a man to threaten or question the established order. In that context, Lewis used Boyle as his representative in the field to enforce union discipline in the 1950s.

While critics have pointed to this fact to show that Boyle occupied a special position, the claim does not follow.[70] During these same years, similar tasks were performed for Lewis by Joseph A. Yablonski, who opposed Boyle in the 1969 election.[71]

Even Boyle's rise to the union's vice-presidency loses significance when the following is considered: under Lewis, the office did not guarantee any special status. Like most of the offices in the UMWA above the subdistrict level at this time, the vice-presidency was appointive. Phil Murray served in this position under Lewis for nearly twenty years and was one of the union chief's closest allies. Yet Lewis did not hesitate to fire Murray when Murray contradicted him. As Murray's replacement, Kennedy was probably Lewis's real choice as successor. When Boyle was appointed vice-president, it is likely that he was being rewarded for his loyalty and good work. Under Lewis's system, Kennedy could remove Boyle at any time if he became a liability.[72] In effect, it is possible Boyle became the union's president by accident, rather than by design.

Responsibility for the creation of the preconditions which lead to such an accident, however, falls directly upon the system Lewis created within the union and, hence, upon Lewis himself. Through most of his tenure, Lewis provided the UMWA with strong leadership, but his style emasculated the process whereby future leaders were created. Lewis made a fundamental error in confusing firmness, decisiveness, and strength with willfulness and a refusal to tolerate criticism. Although able men, such as Yablonski, could rise within the system by not making waves, the system more readily facilitated the promotion of individuals like Boyle, who simply followed orders. Because of his long time in office and his attitudes concerning authority, Lewis created an administrative structure that could not survive his retirement.

In addition to the all-powerful presidency, Lewis created another problem by placing the UMWA in a contradictory position with his program to restructure the coal industry. To meet his goals, Lewis entered into a quasi-corporate arrangement with the major operators. With this, it is arguable that the arrangement benefited the miners who continued working in the industry. The large mining firms recognized the union, paid its wage scale, accepted the Fund, and worked to eliminate smaller and unsafe operations. Nevertheless, the various components of Lewis's system started working at cross-purposes.

For example, after 1950 the Fund became increasingly involved in mine health and safety issues, especially with the rising incidence of Coal Workers' Pneumoconiosis (CWP), or black lung.[73] In this respect, the Fund was a force to raise consciousness about black lung to facilitate treatment and its recognition as a compensable work-related disease.[74] Yet, the increase in the number of black lung cases noted in the early 1950s was directly attributable to the general mechanization of the industry beginning in 1950. After 1952, Lewis became lax about furthering mine safety legislation.[75] Thus, while the Fund was advancing and fighting for the good of the miner, the union was gradually retreating from the field.

The contradiction, however, was not openly apparent to the public during the last ten years Lewis served in the UMWA's presidency. According to historian Alan Derickson, Lewis understood the basic relationship between CWP and the dusty environment mechanization created, and he cynically decided to do nothing about it.[76] Despite this claim, Lewis's problem here was not cynicism. Rather, throughout his career Lewis successfully acted as both the concerned labor leader and the clever business unionist, and was thereby able to reconcile conflicting positions. In doing so, Lewis was the essential pragmatist. Unfortunately, the contradiction of mechanization versus black lung was so fundamental that a neat solution, which allowed Lewis to have his cake and eat it too, could not be found. Painted into a corner in this way, Lewis was simply immobilized by the issue. Tragically, Boyle, a man of limited ability, inherited Lewis's system, as well as the responsibility of holding it together while finding solutions for its problems.

In pursuing these goals, Boyle's administration of the UMWA amounted to nothing more than a clumsy attempt to continue Lewis's policies. During his first year as president, Boyle used the mechanisms of authority which Lewis created and assigned his supporters to major union offices. This included the appointment of nine district presidents, two of whom also received seats on the union's International Executive Board.[77] At the same time, Boyle began calling for changes in the federal coal mine safety laws. Testifying before the General

Subcommittee on Labor of the U.S. House of Representatives, Boyle requested that all mines, especially those employing fourteen men or less, be brought under the jurisdiction of the safety codes.[78] According to his testimony, 12 percent of all coal tonnage produced in the United States came out of these small operations, but they also accounted for 34 percent of all injuries reported.[79] Boyle added in the same statement that he supported the union's established policy on mechanization, but went on to say he believed that the industry was mechanizing past the point of safety.[80]

Most of the contents of Boyle's statement followed Lewis's ideas concerning the industry. While advocating greater safety, Boyle realized that if smaller operations were placed under stricter regulation, they would be bankrupted. Since most of these mines were probably nonunion, their disappearance would enhance the UMWA's position. Boyle's comments about the level of mechanization in the mines, though, stands out. While his remarks can be disregarded as mere rhetoric, they contained an implied criticism of the Lewis program and displayed some concern about work conditions, but his record on the Fund and other benefit concerns was weak.

Between 1964 and 1968, Boyle negotiated a total of three contracts. Following the pattern Lewis created, the negotiations for all three were conducted secretly with the final product accepted for the union without reference to the membership. With the exception of the third, none of them contained an acceptable wage increase, nor did any of them offer any better grievance mechanisms. Boyle also ignored the Fund, since none of the agreements increased royalty payments. For its part, the rank and file expressed disappointment with these contracts through wildcat strikes. After Boyle negotiated his first contract, the Peabody Agreement, in 1964 18,000 miners walked off their jobs in protest for eighteen days.[81] The same thing happened in 1966 with the second Boyle contract, but the number of strikers increased to 40,000 and then to 66,000 when the union announced Boyle's third agreement.[82]

In addition to his failure to secure greater benefits, Boyle also entered into a series of sweetheart contracts with certain producers. From available evidence, Boyle made a total of fifteen such arrangements with operators engaged in mining sub-bituminous and lignite coal. In each case, the Fund royalty was reduced from forty to twenty cents a ton. These arrangements came to light in the summer of 1969, when the branch of welfare and pensions of the Department of Labor looked into the question. Under law, the Fund was required to file a regular description of its program with the branch, which included all of its related contracts. The agreements had never been mentioned before, and the branch now demanded an updated description listing all operators paying less than the agreed rate. Boyle complied with the demand but never offered an explanation as to why such exemptions had been granted.[83]

The issue of union/operator collusion was one of the points raised during the *Blankenship* case, and the question must be asked whether Boyle originated the idea or was continuing a standard practice used by Lewis. In his book *Death and the Mines* Brit Hume described such arrangements as verbal and hints broadly that Lewis used the practice during the 1950s in response to the sluggish performance in the industry.[84] Harry Huge made a similar accusation in his trial brief and claimed that it was impossible to determine how much money the Fund had lost through such arrangements.[85] Huge went on to affirm that Miss Roche admitted that some local union representatives made unauthorized agreements and that, except for canceling health cards, the Fund had made no attempt to collect back payments.[86]

Union lawyers denied that any sweetheart agreements had ever been knowingly made by the leadership and stressed that Huge failed to give specific evidence indicating that Lewis or Roche ever conspired with any firm to defraud the Fund, even after having examined the Fund's records.[87] Rumors about such agreements had circulated for many years, but the evidence was hearsay and therefore inadmissible. The only proof that could be cited was that a total of 155 companies had failed to pay their obligations on time between 1962 and 1964. But the record also showed that the Fund had worked aggressively to collect all monies owed and had succeeded in doing so by 1966.[88] In his final opinion, Judge Gerhard Gessel agreed that no evidence existed to show that Lewis or Roche ever made sweetheart agreements. Gessel went on to say that in some cases, the legal costs of pursuing certain operators were greater than the royalty bills owed.[89]

Because Boyle never offered an explanation as to why he made the arrangement with the fifteen companies, it is impossible to determine his exact reasoning. But, all of his actions pointed to an attempt to continue Lewis's dual pattern of business unionist and labor leader. Due to the contradictory nature of the situation, and Boyle's personal limitations, his stewardship of the union was marked by confusion and ineptitude. In order to avoid the consequences arising from these problems, Boyle resorted to a twin policy of outright repression and official adulation for his leadership. Such avoidance could not continue indefinitely, and between 1968 and 1969 Boyle's position began to collapse. The issues that started the process of Boyle's fall were those of mine safety and health, especially black lung.

Although Boyle and the union were severely criticized by Ralph Nader and Ken Heckler over an apparent failure to address black lung, no such comments could be truthfully made about the Fund. Long before concern about black lung became fashionable, the Fund had worked to gain recognition for the condition as a real disease. From the early 1950s, the Fund's medical staff had been concerned about the growing incidence of black lung cases reported by the area medical offices.

The Fund's resident expert on the disease was Dr. Lorin E. Kerr. Originally the Fund's AMO for Morgantown, West Virginia, Dr. Kerr was transferred to the Fund's Washington office in 1951 and worked directly under Dr. Draper. It was during his tenure in Morgantown that Dr. Kerr first became interested in the disease. At the time, Kerr read the research papers presented by British physicians on coal workers' pneumoconiosis (CWP), and he noted that some of the beneficiaries his office handled displayed the same symptoms.[90] After he came to Washington, Dr. Kerr, with support from Dr. Draper, pursued a program designed to ensure that Fund beneficiaries who had the disease received treatment and that the symptoms could be identified by participating physicians.[91]

When Kerr began his work, CWP was not recognized as a disease in the United States. CWP had first been identified in the nineteenth century as a possible work-related disease afflicting coal miners. Originally dubbed anthracosis, dissection of affected lung tissue revealed an extensive coating of the lung with coal dust, and the presence of a black, inklike fluid. Miners suffering from the condition displayed a given set of symptoms that included shortness of breath and the expectoration of the black fluid. However, as the study of dust inhalation progressed into the twentieth century, a school of thought developed which viewed coal dust as harmless, with anthracosis becoming a simple discoloration of the lung. According to this point of view, there was one, and only one, dust inhalation disease which afflicted miners: silicosis.[92]

In terms of mechanics, CWP and silicosis were distinct and different varieties of the same general condition afflicting people employed in industries that exposed them to high levels of dust in the work environment. The term *pneumoconiosis* itself means "dust on the lung," and other respiratory conditions that come under the heading include asbestosis, bagassosis, and siderosis. In a poorly ventilated workplace, such as a mine, a worker will inhale dust, which ultimately clogs the bronchial tubes in the lungs and prevents the gas transfer of oxygen for carbon dioxide. Breathing is impaired, blood oxidation does not take place effectively, and a greater strain is placed on the heart. Also, once the condition is created, it is irreversible.[93]

The difference between silicosis and CWP is the kind of dust inhaled and its effects. Silicosis, which afflicted some coal miners, is a lung condition arising from the sustained inhalation of free silica dioxide, or sand, and has been recognized in the United States as a compensable disease since the 1930s.[94] Basically, the minute sand particles that are inhaled are sharp and cut into the lung tissue. Not only does this interfere with breathing, it increases susceptibility to infectious diseases involving the lungs, such as tuberculosis.[95]

CWP is the direct result of coal dust inhalation. In this case, the coal dust coats the lung tissue, clogging the bronchial tubes. Not only does this interfere with breathing, but the lungs eventually lose their elasticity. Unfortunately, the condition did not have silicosis's clear-cut radiological features. In addition, because coal dust was smooth and not sharp-edged like sand, it was seen as harmless.[96] This belief eventually fueled a reductionist tendency in medical science to view silicosis as the one and only dust disease afflicting miners. This point of view was so influential that most American physicians subscribed to it, including Dr. Royd R. Sayers during his tenure with the U.S. Bureau of Mines.[97] However, due to work done in Great Britain during the 1930s, CWP was recognized by the British Medical Research Council as an actual disease in 1942.[98]

The fact that CWP received any recognition in the United States at all was due mostly to efforts by Kerr and the Fund, which focused on a dual program of education and treatment. Under education, a broad-line strategy was used. To begin, Kerr went through the available literature and wrote one of the first scholarly articles on the disease published in an American medical journal in modern times. Appearing in the August 1956 edition of *Industrial Medicine and Surgery* under the title "Coal Workers' Pneumoconiosis," the article described the disease, its effects, and how to recognize it.[99] This and other similar publications were reprinted and distributed to participating physicians throughout the coal fields. At the same time, the Fund assisted in governmental surveys on dust diseases among miners. It also held conferences on CWP by internationally known experts on the disease and sponsored an international X-ray classification for black lung to facilitate diagnosis.

In terms of treatment, the Fund sent miners with the disease to special teaching hospitals and provided drugs, oxygen, and other therapeutic aids for both hospital and ambulatory patients.[100] Kerr's efforts also included testifying before the Senate Subcommittee on Labor in the summer of 1968 about the effects of CWP as part of a Fund drive in support of federal health legislation for the coal industry.[101]

Boyle, as president of the union, was not directly involved with any of the work on CWP, and from an administrative point of view, his behavior was understandable since Lewis continued as chairman of the Fund's trustee board. In his limited correspondence with Roche, Boyle expressed his satisfaction with Dr. Kerr's work, but these notes were short and perfunctory.[102] Kerr's efforts, however, made an impression on Boyle so much so that he asked Dr. Kerr to give an address on black lung to the union's 1968 convention in Denver. Kerr agreed, and the speech was entitled "Coal Workers' Pneumoconiosis: The Road to Dusty Death." It contained descriptions of the disease, its causes and effects, the work done by the British, and the failure of the American medical community to take action on it.[103] As part of the speech, Kerr presented a program to lower mine dust levels and to gain recognition of CWP as a compensable condition.[104]

145

The speech brought the convention's delegates to their feet in a standing ovation.[105] Boyle expressed his enthusiastic support, and the convention passed a resolution calling for a massive lobbying effort to have black lung included in workers' compensation programs.[106] Flushed with excitement, the delegates left Denver prepared to begin a grassroots campaign on CWP.[107] These efforts, however, were ended by the district offices. In District 29, for example, local union presidents were informed by their superiors that the *district* would handle all problems concerning black lung and went on to forbid all locals from calling any meetings about CWP on their own initiative.[108]

Only two explanations for such a reversal are possible. Either Boyle simply engaged in an exercise in public relations at the convention, or he wanted to resolve the problem of black lung in a manner which reflected well on him. Boyle was certainly aware that he had failed to energize or rally the union in any meaningful way, despite his posturing. Black lung represented an opportunity for Boyle to co-opt an issue and further his reputation by making a stand. After all, Lewis had managed to do the same thing twenty years before with the Fund. If Boyle had only wanted to pay lip service to CWP, he simply would have made a short reference to it when he addressed the convention, rather than asking Dr. Kerr to give a full speech.

But, to achieve his goal, Boyle had to take the lead on CWP. Any progress on the matter could not be viewed as a result of rank and file efforts. This meant Boyle would have to be firm about dust levels not only in smaller mines, but in large operations as well. To do so, however, meant possibly offending the large companies that were a cornerstone of Lewis's system. This was an unsolvable dilemma, and Boyle wavered as a result. It is probable Boyle hoped to find a solution that would fit Lewis's model and thereby sought to keep the initiative with himself instead of the rank and file.

As for the Fund, Dr. Kerr's speech was the only part it played at the 1968 convention. Although Roche attended the meeting and was praised for her work, she kept the Fund out of the proceedings. A few weeks earlier, a Fund staff member suggested in a memo to Roche that the Fund should print sample checks made out to each of the delegates for $26,772. The idea was to show the delegates in a dollar amount how much they, and all union members, could statistically expect to receive from the Fund during their lifetime.[109] Roche rejected the scheme.[110]

The convention was held between September 4 and 13, and nearly all of its activities were directed toward celebrating Boyle as leader. Joseph A. Yablonski lauded Boyle's record from the podium, and the delegates received numerous souvenirs of the meeting, including clocks, ashtrays, and cigarette lighters that displayed either Boyle's name or picture. In addition, the *United Mine Workers Journal* devoted an entire issue to the convention. It printed a total of thirty-one pictures, twenty-five of which included Boyle.[111] The most interesting section of the special edition was its editorial page. On the left side, the *Journal* ran a picture of Lewis with a short tribute to him, and on the opposite side appeared "The Ballad of Tony Boyle."

Songs had been written about Lewis during the 1930s, which came out of the great 1933 UMWA organizing drive and later CIO campaigns. [112] "The Ballad of Tony Boyle" was a transparent attempt to invoke that era in order to pass Lewis's mystique of the fighting labor leader to Boyle. Sung to the melody of "The Foggy, Foggy Dew," the offering read as follows:

When Tony was a young man he went underground;
He worked at the miner's trade.
And many, many times the bosses passed the word,
"He's a dangerous renegade."

For he fought for the men in the winter time,
and all summer too, and many, many times
he heard the bosses say: "Pack up Tony, you're
all through."

One day he talked to the union man when the boss
was fast asleep. They asked to run him for
committee man, and he won in a sweep.

The bosses cursed and then proclaimed:
"This plot we've got to foil,"
and many, many long nights they planned to get
rid of Tony Boyle

Now Tony is President of the Mine Workers Union.
And today we offer him praise. And every now
and then he takes a look at those early days

He recalls Montana's summertime and the Hazy
winter too. And many, many times they said
"Tony, you're all through."

So here's to the miner who digs down below,
and here's to his family too.
For he never knows if he'll come up alive,
when his daily shift is through.

He digs coal in the winter time
and in the summer too, and when he gets his
pension from the welfare fund, he says:
"God bless the Union, and Tony too."

The convention was a success for Boyle and his associates. Unlike the 1964 meeting, none of the delegates were manhandled and there was no visible opposition. With a union election about a year away, Boyle seemed assured of another term. Nine weeks after the convention ended, however, Boyle's abilities were severely tested when the number 9 mine of Pittsburgh Consolidated Coal at Farmington, West Virginia, exploded on the morning of November 20. A total of seventy-eight men lost their lives in the explosion, which was caused by a high concentration of coal dust and methane. The gas had seeped through the coal face in the mine due to recent cold weather, and the company had been negligent about rock dusting work areas to reduce the amount of coal dust present in the facility.[113]

The day after the blast, Boyle came to inspect the scene. At a hurried news conference held at a local company store, Boyle expressed his sympathies to the families of the dead men, adding that he had lost family members in mine explosions. Then Boyle made the single greatest mistake of his career. Instead of posturing like Lewis in outrage over the tragedy, he assumed a more dispassionate stance, saying: "as long as we mine coal, there is always this inherent danger of explosion . . . [Consol] . . . happens to be one of the better companies *as far as cooperation with our union* [italics mine] and safety is concerned."[114]

This statement has been widely quoted and interpreted to mean that the UMWA had ceased to be concerned, even rhetorically, with miner safety. While not denying that Boyle gave a weak response, a more accurate characterization would be confusion. Boyle faced a no-win situation: as leader of the union, he had the responsibility to say something about the tragedy. But if he denounced Consol in ringing terms, he would be attacking one of the most important parties to Lewis's 1950 settlement with management. The contradictions basic to that settlement had finally come to the surface. Confronted with that contradiction, Boyle did not know what to say or do.

Outrage over the Farmington disaster and Boyle's weak response bolstered dissent within the union. First, as the new year opened, union miners in West Virginia took matters into their own hands and formed a rank and file group named the Black Lung Association. Denounced by the UMWA as a dual organization, the association, with help of Drs. Donald Rasmussen and Isadore Buff, who had worked with the Fund on CWP, lobbied the West Virginia legislature for a strong compensation bill that included black lung. The effort culminated in a statewide wildcat strike which forced the bill's passage.[115] Two months later, Boyle suddenly faced a challenge for the UMWA's presidency from an associate who had been one of his staunch public supporters: Joseph A. Yablonski. Yablonski made his announcement on May 29, 1969, and invoked Lewis's reputation and memory while attacking Boyle's administration.[116] Under Boyle, Yablonski said, the union had failed to ensure mine safety, to produce a better grievance procedure, and had been inept in securing black lung legislation.[117] After he finished his indictment of Boyle's administration, Yablonski outlined his program: once elected he would take immediate action to allow all districts to elect their officers. He would also liberalize Fund benefits and increase royalties, seek greater occupational safety, demand mandatory retirement for all UMWA officers, and put an end to nepotism.[118] As part of his announcement, Yablonski referred to his own participation in the leadership he now attacked. He said that he had tolerated their behavior, but now he had had enough.[119]

As a reform candidate, Yablonski had a great deal to live down. Not only was he saddled with past statements of support for Boyle, but he also had a reputation for self-enrichment.[120] Growing up in Washington County, Pennsylvania, Yablonski had risen through the ranks of District 5, headquartered in Pittsburgh. In 1933, he successfully organized the Vesta number 6 mine, owned by Jones and Laughlin Steel.[121] Although his honesty was questionable, Yablonski's popularity in District 5 could not be doubted. Unlike most of the districts under the Lewis regime, District 5 never lost the right to elect its own officers. In 1942, the district's members elected Yablonski to the union's International Executive Board. He would hold this position until his death in 1969. He was later elected the district's president in 1958.[122]

During his rise, Yablonski loyally served the union's administration and, as mentioned above, represented Lewis on occasion to enforce the union's discipline in the field, as had Boyle. When Boyle took over, Yablonski continued to serve, and between 1963 and 1969 he made speeches that heaped great praise on Boyle.[123] Public statements aside, relations between the two men were strained at several points. Yablonski criticized the use of intimidation at the 1964 convention and threatened to walk out over it.[124] Boyle retaliated in 1966 by forcing Yablonski to resign either his IEB seat or his district presidency.[125] Yet Yablonski did not become completely alienated from the union hierarchy. Not only did he continue to make speeches for Boyle, but he also received two appointments. The first was to an organizing committee Boyle created, and the second as head of the UMWA's political action group, Labor's Nonpartisan League.

It goes beyond the scope of this study to cover the election in any detail. The campaign was bitter. Boyle and his supporters used every means at their disposal to discredit Yablonski. This included a flood of hate literature about Yablonski's legal problems during the 1930s taken from the Allegheny and Washington County court dockets. Yablonski was also accused of being in league with elements seeking to destroy the union, including the Atomic Energy Commission, the American Communist Party, the oil industry, and large coal operators.[126] The campaign was marred by abuse, fraud, and vituperation.

For her part, Roche watched the campaign closely and received copies of the hate literature the Boyle camp issued. However, Roche avoided the subject. Except for a note which she sent to Lewis, informing the former president of the Yablonski candidacy, no mention of the contest appears in her correspondence.[127] It is apparent that Roche hoped to keep the Fund out of the election. But, as the campaign continued, her goal became increasingly difficult to achieve. For example, Yablonski promised retired anthracite miners, whose Fund was separate from the bituminous, that if elected he would combine the anthracite and bituminous trusts and raise their pensions to $200 a month.[128] The anthracite trust had been established at the same time as the bituminous but was much smaller. Although it too had originally paid a $100-a-month pension, the amount over time had to be reduced to $30 a month because of the anthracite industry's rapid decline after 1948.

Yablonski's promise here was little better than pie in the sky. Because the anthracite industry was in such poor condition, joining the two trusts would have amounted to the bituminous industry's subsidizing the anthracite miners. The bituminous operators would not have accepted such an arrangement.

As disturbing as these developments were, there was a possibility that Lewis and Roche could prevent the Fund from becoming a political football. This depended, however, on their keeping control of the Fund's trustee board. But, even before the election even started, they were confronted with finding a new industry trustee when Schmidt decided to tender his resignation in February 1969.[129] Unlike his predecessors, Schmidt had cooperated closely with Roche and Lewis from the start and viewed himself as their partner. Upon becoming a trustee, Schmidt severed ties with his fellow operators and refused to work with them. In one instance, George Judy, president of the Bituminous Coal Operators Association, wrote to Schmidt asking for an age group breakdown of the miners receiving a Fund pension. Schmidt replied that he was a trustee and not simply the BCOA's representative on the Fund's board. As a trustee, he was responsible to the Fund only and could not send the information.[130]

In his letter of resignation, Schmidt claimed his reasons for leaving were personal and that he needed to reduce his workload.[131] In the weeks prior to his resignation, though, Schmidt occasionally sent news clippings to Roche about the union's problems and criticism of the Fund.[132] It is possible Schmidt was expecting trouble and wanted to steer clear of it.

After Schmidt resigned his position, the BCOA did not move to fill the vacancy until June, and the man it appointed was George Judy. The length of time which the association took to appoint Judy upset Roche, and her anxiety over finally placing the new industry trustee on the board was plainly evident when she wrote the following to Lewis: "At long last the operators have certified Mr. George Judy as their trustee to succeed Mr. Schmidt. The letter of certification . . . to you is attached. *It is imperative that we immediately hold a trustee meeting to formally accept and qualify Mr. Judy. Other vitally pressing matters also require immediate attention by our board* [italics mine]."[133] Roche did not specify what the other matters were. From the content and tone of her letter, and with the union's election campaign already under way, Roche probably hoped to seat Judy on the board as a means to prevent the Fund from becoming politicized.

The first meeting with Judy as the new industry trustee took place at Lewis's home in Alexandria, Virginia, due to Lewis's deteriorating health, but Roche was not present to direct it. A day or so after Judy was appointed, Roche fell and broke her hip, which necessitated her hospitalization. Then, a week later, on June 11, 1969, Lewis died.

Yablonski's candidacy was only two weeks old, and he had hoped to receive Lewis's endorsement. Now his position would be made more complicated, since the UMWA's official mourning became part of the Boyle campaign. Boyle now more than ever stressed his claim as the hand-chosen successor to the fallen labor leader. Even more important, with Lewis dead, Boyle now could be appointed to the Fund's board as union trustee. After a twelve-day interval, the IEB named Boyle to replace Lewis on June 23, and the following day Boyle held his first trustee meeting. Without contacting Roche, who was still recovering, Boyle and Judy voted to boost pensions from $115 to $150 a month. Judy later claimed that Boyle had a proxy from Roche approving the action.[134]

Immediately thereafter, the Fund released a notice about the increase to its pensioners that listed Boyle as chairman of the board of trustees.[135] Previous notices, except for the form letters that carried Roche's signature, never included the names of Fund officers.[136] Clearly, Boyle wanted to capture the union's pension vote by engineering the increase and making sure that the retired miners understood who was responsible for it. At the time, about 70,000 men were on the Fund's pension list, and all of them were eligible to vote in the election.[137] Moreover, many of the men were members of 292 so-called bogus, or pensioner, local unions, which did not contain the minimum of ten working members required by the union's constitution.[138] Except for the retirees in the anthracite region, Boyle won an overwhelming majority of the votes cast by the union's pensioned miners.[139]

The election took place on December 9, 1969, and the official returns listed Boyle as the winner by a two-to-one margin. Convinced that Boyle had stolen the contest, Yablonski had decided to pursue the issue in the courts. During the campaign, Yablonski requested the intervention of the Department of Labor a total of five times, charging that his opponents were using corrupt practices to win. Under the Landrum-Griffin Act, the secretary of labor had the right to intervene in union affairs if he suspected illegality. However, George Schultz, secretary of labor under President Nixon, consistently refused to consider Yablonski's requests. Schultz did so on the grounds that the department had never intervened in a union election while it was in progress. An investigation would only be conducted after the election was over. Despite these rebuffs, Yablonski was confident that the election would eventually be invalidated.[140]

On the last day of the year, however, Yablonski, his wife, Margaret, and daughter Charlotte were murdered in their home in Clarksville, Pennsylvania. The authorities eventually apprehended three men and charged them with the slayings: Paul Gilley, Claude Vealy, and Auburn "Buddy" Martin. Outrage over the crime refocused what had been a marginally important story of a union power struggle into front-page news. Secretary of Labor Schultz now decided to investigate the election, as did the Senate Subcommittee on Labor.

Chaired by Sen. Harrison Williams, the committee decided to investigate the UMWA about one month after the Yablonski murders. The committee wanted to determine whether or not the pension increase had been engineered by Boyle to assist his reelection. The first witness who appeared before the committee on the question was George Judy. Judy was no longer connected with either the Fund or the BCOA, since he resigned his positions with both organizations on July 14, 1969.[141] Judy testified that before the trustee meeting took place, he had met with Boyle in an anteroom of Boyle's office at UMWA headquarters. There, Boyle told Judy that he wanted to increase pensions by thirty-five dollars a month. Judy questioned the idea's wisdom since coal royalties were still at forty cents a ton. Boyle responded that he had a proxy from Roche in his pocket supporting the move and that any opposition would be useless.[142]

The trustee meeting took place immediately thereafter. With Boyle and Judy, the people present included: Edward L. Carey, now the union's general counsel; John Owens, UMWA secretary treasurer; Thomas Ryan, Fund comptroller; and the general counsel for the Fund, Welly K. Hopkins, who had replaced Val J. Mitch in 1966. According to Judy's testimony, both Hopkins and Ryan presented the facts concerning increased costs if pensions were raised and mentioned that Roche was available by phone for consultation.[143] Hopkins reiterated that fact when he testified later with Roche and Ryan.[144]

Once he finished presenting his account of the June 24 trustee meeting, Judy became evasive when the committee members asked him direct questions. For example, Judy said he did not know if it was standard practice for union officials to attend Fund trustee meetings (it was not). Likewise, Judy claimed that he did not know if all three trustees attended every meeting (they did). Although none of the senators questioned him about failing to call Roche,

Judy covered himself by saying two things: first, he expressed the opinion that even if Roche had been present, he would have voted for the increase regardless of her attitude because he believed it was necessary. Second, Judy claimed that "everyone" connected with the BCOA knew that the board had been "stacked" in Lewis's favor. The obvious implication was that Roche had faithfully supported Lewis in the past, and therefore no reason existed to believe she planned to oppose Boyle. In further support of the stacked board statement, Judy cited his experience with Henry G. Schmidt.[145]

From the tone of Judy's testimony, the operators resented Schmidt's attitude and were enraged when Judy voted with Boyle to increase pensions. A few days after the trustee meeting, Judy faced the BCOA's executive committee. In an unprecedented move, the committee decided not to allow the industry trustee any further independence of action. The industry representative would continue to attend trustee meetings, but now the BCOA required him to seek the advice of its general counsel before voting on any measure which materially affected the Fund.

Soon after that meeting, Judy resigned from the BCOA and the Fund. His temporary replacement as industry trustee was BCOA general counsel Guy Farmer. Farmer testified that when Judy introduced him to Boyle, Boyle commented about Roche and indicated that he had her support. But instead of saying that he had her proxy, Boyle said that he had Roche "in his pocket." When pressed by members of the committee, Farmer affirmed that Boyle was speaking in all seriousness and did not use the term *proxy*.[146]

The next person to testify was Roche, assisted by Welly K. Hopkins and Thomas Ryan. Most of her testimony concerned her reaction to the pension increase, and she told the committee that she opposed it because it cut into the Fund's reserves by $30 million a year.[147] In fact, Roche resented that she was not consulted before the June 24 meeting and that Boyle had ignored her subsequently. By the fall of 1969, Guy Farmer had been replaced by the industry's permanent trustee, C. W. Davis. In October, Boyle sent Roche a message that he and Davis had decided to commission an actuarial study of the Fund, and ordered her not to hire any additional personnel until the study was completed.[148] Roche was furious and vented her anger in a lengthy memo intended for Boyle only. Roche pointed out that nothing was said to her about the study at previous trustee meetings, and she was not accustomed to receiving directives. She reminded Boyle of her long association with the Fund, both as director and neutral trustee, and that she had always been solely responsible for its administration. In conclusion, she wrote, this was not the first time a decision had been made without her knowledge, a pointed reference to the June 24 meeting. If such behavior continued, Roche warned that it would give credence to charges of collusion between the union, coal operators, and the Fund's trustees.[149]

Roche affirmed before the committee that union officers never attended trustee meetings, and that she never missed a trustee meeting before breaking her hip. She explained that the accident was due to carelessness on her part, since she was hurrying to have Lewis approve the appointment of Judy.[150] Mentally, Lewis was in full control of his faculties, but his physical condition was very frail.[151] Roche implied that she was attempting to have Judy placed on the board and briefed before Lewis died. In this way, Boyle could have been outmaneuvered, and Roche stressed that she wished to keep the Fund out of politics.

When questioned about the election, Roche at first refused to consider that the pension increase had been politically motivated. In response to a question from Senator Williams on the subject, Roche replied that she believed both Judy and Boyle were sincere in their concern for the miners, and their concern was the principle motive for the increase. Senator Williams did not accept Roche's initial response, however, and pressed further. Roche answered: "My opinion, of course, is that it [the pension increase] had a part to play in the election. Everything does. Doesn't it? I don't know of anything that doesn't, really. If we are really going to have something by election, you want to do things that make people want you in."[152] Roche's answer displayed a deep ambivalence which she could not reconcile. She disliked Boyle intensely and was willing to criticize his behavior as rash. She could not, however, bring herself to admit publicly that Boyle might have been dishonest. Such an admission reflected badly upon the UMWA and Lewis, an institution and man to which she had been devoted for most of her life.

After Roche completed her testimony, Boyle came to tell his side of the story. By far, his was the longest testimony taken in the course of the investigation. Boyle rambled through most of his appearance, but he made one pointed denial: no connection existed between his reelection and the pension increase. According to his version of the affair, he had sought to liberalize Fund benefits from the beginning of his tenure as the UMWA president, but Lewis would not consider his requests.[153] Frustrated by Lewis's refusals, Boyle told the committee that he had decided to increase benefits immediately if he ever became the union's trustee.[154]

Boyle's comments about the proxy issue were less direct. At the beginning of his testimony about the question, Boyle flatly denied that he ever told Judy that he had a proxy from Roche. But in the next sentence, Boyle added that if he ever said such a thing, it was meant as a joke. According to Boyle, everyone knew that he and Roche were not friendly. Also, Judy was a mature business man and should have walked out of the meeting if he suspected anything was wrong.[155] To substantiate his testimony, Boyle produced a witness: Suzanne Richards.

Richards was a lawyer and worked as Boyle's administrative assistant. More importantly, she was Boyle's confidante much in the same manner that Roche had been for Lewis.[156] Although she was not present for the private meeting between Boyle and Judy, Richards presented a story that disputed Judy's testimony. Once the trustee meeting was over, Boyle left Washington for the West Coast, supposedly to organize additional coal companies. While Boyle was away, Miss Richards received several telephone calls from Judy, who was worried about his upcoming meeting with the BCOA's executive committee. Finally, Judy informed Richards that he intended to tell the executive committee that Boyle had a proxy from Roche and asked Richards to verify the story if anyone called.[157] The upshot was that Judy supposedly lied to the BCOA about the proxy to protect himself, and hoped Boyle would substantiate the claim.

After Richards presented the story, her testimony became confused. No precise date was given as to when she informed Boyle about the phone calls from Judy, and the session became embroiled in an argument over the testimony given by Guy Farmer. When asked how Farmer's statement about his meeting with Boyle could be reconciled with Richards's comments, Carey offered a semantical explanation. Farmer had testified that Boyle claimed to have Roche "in his pocket." Carey said that this was a street expression and therefore distinct from *proxy,* which was a legal term.[158] In further denial that he ever said anything to Farmer indicating he had support from Roche, Boyle cited the fact that John Cocran and Heath Lang of U.S. Steel and Consolidated Coal visited Roche on July 8. There Roche informed both men that she never authorized Boyle to vote for her. Boyle asked the committee why he would tell the BCOA's attorney that he possessed a proxy from Roche when a week earlier she told two of its principle members that no such arrangement existed.[159]

The proxy issue proved to be the central concern of the committee during Boyle's appearance. Surprisingly, Boyle managed to defend himself on this issue with some success. However, his overall performance was poor, especially when questioned about the Fund's financial condition and why he raised pensions. Boyle only reiterated his claim that he always wanted to increase benefits. But Senator Williams confronted Boyle with a speech he made to the effect that if union members wanted increased benefits, they would have to organize additional coal companies themselves. Boyle admitted he made the statement, but added he had formed an organizing committee for that purpose.[160] When asked how much tonnage had been organized, Boyle did not know.[161]

It was clear from Williams's line of questioning that he believed Boyle raised pensions only to win reelection. The exchange between the two men became heated, with Boyle protesting that he had worked behind the scenes for years to secure an increase. Williams remained unconvinced, since at no time prior to June 24, 1969, had Boyle ever indicated publicly that he would raise benefits if he became a trustee.[162]

Boyle's treatment by Senator Pell, who concerned himself with the Fund's financial condition, was even more pointed. Farmer testified that the Fund was sound prior to June 24, but its reserves were adequate to continue operation for only one year if all royalty income stopped.[163] Pell asked what percentage of the Fund's assets were kept in cash, stocks, bonds, and the like. Boyle either did not know or referred Pell to the Fund's comptroller. Pell criticized Boyle's lack of knowledge about the Fund's fiscal status, especially since he had been a trustee for nine months and had a chance to familiarize himself with the information.[164] Pell went on to say that he thought Boyle was derelict in his duties as a trustee and risked being sued by the beneficiaries for not carrying out his fiduciary obligations.[165] Boyle's position was made even more difficult when the findings of an actuarial report on the Fund were released showing that because of the pension increase, the Fund would be bankrupted by 1975 unless royalties were increased.

By any standard, Boyle did not fare well before the committee. His failure to deal effectively with questions from Pell and Williams, and their comments during the hearings, gave further legitimacy to the *Blankenship* suit, which had been filed in August 1969. Unquestionably the pension increase was politically motivated, but judging from the evidence presented, the raise might have been only part of a larger agreement between Boyle and Judy.

Judy's story about Boyle supposedly having Roche's proxy has been generally accepted on face value, since it appeared as a continuation of the Lewis-Roche era. In actuality, when Lewis died, that arrangement ceased to exist. Roche's antagonism for Boyle ran deep, and there was no way that she would have cooperated with him. For his part, Boyle wanted to exercise the same authority over the Fund as Lewis had, but Roche worked against him. In order to settle the problem, Boyle and Judy might have come to an understanding.

During the course of his testimony, Judy did say that Boyle made a vague offer to prevent wildcat strikes in return for the pension increase.[166] Moreover, Richards said during her appearance that Boyle wanted to have her replace Roche.[167] It is possible that before the June 24 trustee meeting, Boyle and Judy made a deal. In return for greater discipline within the union, Judy would support the pension increase and the removal of Roche from the board. Although Richards was dedicated to Boyle, Roche's departure from the board offered the possibility of greater influence for the BCOA over the Fund's administration. Such an agreement would have been consistent with Boyle's "back-room" managerial style and would explain why he bypassed Roche after becoming the Fund's chairman.

Coupled with the personal rift between Boyle and Roche, and Richards's story, a major flaw appears in Judy's testimony. Although Judy claimed that the raise was needed, the thrust of his story was that he had no choice but to vote with Boyle. But Judy did not explain, and the committee did not ask, why he failed to telephone Roche if he had any doubts. Both Ryan and Hopkins testified that they told the board Roche was available by phone, and their testimony was supported by the minutes of the meeting.[168] Thus, Richard's testimony about the proxy is probably the most accurate: a story Judy invented to protect himself. Considering Boyle's behavior in office, it would have been in character for him to lie to Farmer in order to assist Judy.

Due to the turmoil within the union, the committee hearings were televised, and the strained relationship between Roche and Boyle was clearly evident to all who watched. Because of the restrictions the BCOA now placed upon the industry trustee, and because the 1968 contract would not expire for another year, Boyle could not immediately force Roche from the Fund's board. Nevertheless, a campaign was mounted within the union to induce Roche to resign.[169] Between April and June 1970, Roche received letters from district presidents as well as approximately ninety locals demanding that she step down.

The vast majority of the letters were critical, and many were openly insulting. The drive was conducted independently by the individual districts of the union and not by the national office. Therefore, the level of organization varied. The most well-planned and vituperative effort came out of District 2. Local unions received a form letter, which the local officers simply signed. The letter praised Boyle's record and referred to Roche as a liar. In all, the letters represented a total of approximately 16,400 miners, 6,044 of whom were retirees.[170] Roche ignored the campaign and continued both as the Fund's neutral trustee and director. By resigning, she would have yielded to Boyle and confirmed the belief that the Fund had been mismanaged.

The second consideration was most important because of the *Blankenship* case. Although the litigation was named for Willie Ray Blankenship, the suit was actually brought by the Disabled Miners and Widows Association on the grounds of breach of trust. A West Virginia–based group similar to the Black Lung Association, the Disabled Miners and Widows directed its attention toward securing benefits for individuals the Fund declared ineligible. As stated above, the plaintiffs were represented by Harry Huge, an associate of the Washington, D.C., law firm of Arnold and Porter. The group argued that the Fund's regulations were unjust and deprived approximately seventy thousand people, both miners and dependents, of benefits to which they were entitled.[171] The case was argued in the District Court of the United States for the District of Columbia before Judge Gerhard Gessel.

As a breach of trust suit, the case involved two broad categories of action: First, whether or not Fund eligibility regulations for pensions and medical assistance were arbitrary and capricious. Second, whether or not the trustees managed Fund assets in the best interests of the beneficiaries. When the action was originally filed, the first category appeared to be paramount. Willie

Blankenship had applied for a pension, but was denied. Although Blankenship had worked for more than twenty years in the industry, a large block of that time could not be accepted because he had been self-employed as a partner in several small mining operations.[172] However, as the litigation progressed, Huge adopted a different strategy and concentrated on the second category.

Of the two, the second category was more important since it centered upon how the Fund had been administered. Huge listed eight items for consideration under the second heading: Maintenance of excessive sums of money in non-interest-bearing accounts; failure to collect delinquent royalty payments; the 1969 pension increase; excessive administrative expenses; denial or withholding of benefits to assist the union in labor disputes; delegation of certain administrative functions to the union, which enabled it to collect "welfare fund dues"; and allowing the union to determine royalty payment delinquencies, which enabled it to enter into sweetheart contracts.[173]

To investigate these charges, Huge requested the court to order the Fund to open its records to his inspection. Huge presented a list of what he wanted, which included all writings concerning assets of the Fund, as well as all trustee minutes.[174] The Fund argued that the request was impracticable since it involved the transfer and organization of a huge amount of material. The Fund had approximately 340,000 separate benefit files, including 153,000 thousand for pensions. Each file contained from one to one hundred pieces of paper. Also, the financial records, books, and related materials Huge wanted to inspect represented the Fund's working files and were needed to conduct daily business.[175] These objections were disregarded and the records had to be made available to Huge.

Because Huge finally focused his attention on how the Fund was managed, the question of the Fund's liquidity became the central issue in the case. Union attorneys maintained that the large cash reserves existed because the trustees acted prudently. The reserve provided a ready source of money in case of an emergency, and the Fund's tax status dictated a high liquidity level.[176] In 1954, the IRS denied the Fund tax-exempt status as a charitable trust. Under the advice of independent counsel, the Fund's leadership had decided upon a low-profile investment policy, where nonroyalty income would not exceed expenses. In that way, total income, both royalty and investment, would be nontaxable.[177] Also, as mentioned above, the lawyers denied that any conspiracy existed among the trustees to use Fund assets to aid the union, the bank, or the North American Coal Company.

Union arguments were vitiated by the testimony of Roche during the hearings before Judge Gessel. Roche said that she became concerned about the size of the cash reserve between 1967 and 1968 while Lewis was focusing his attention on the tax issue. Finally, in 1968 she convinced Lewis that some portion of the money needed to be invested, and he agreed. Roche then admitted that the Fund's cash holdings had become too large and were not justifiable from the point of view of meeting immediate needs.

Roche's testimony flatly contradicted a public statement which the Fund prepared in April 1969, four months before the *Blankenship* suit was filed. Signed by Roche, Ryan, and Hopkins, the statement was a rebuttal of criticism leveled at the Fund's administration. It denied that the Fund was overly liquid by citing the fact that benefit costs had increased by $45 million a year, which meant that the cash balance was actually no greater in relation to the Fund's monthly and annual expenses than had been in the past.

The inconsistency between the statement and Roche's testimony convinced Judge Gessel that there had been a breach of trust, and he mentioned the contradiction in his opinion. The overall analysis contained in the decision was based upon a strict interpretation of trust and labor laws. As trustees, the Fund's leadership had a responsibility to work for the good of the Fund without reference to any other group. Therefore, the idea that the Fund, the union, and the bank could derive collateral advantages through Fund investment policies was not allowable.[178] Although the judge admitted that no direct evidence of conspiracy existed, Gessel wrote that Lewis's system created a conflict of interest, which the judge believed was inherently detrimental to the best interests of the Fund's beneficiaries. In reference to this opinion, Gessel was particularly scathing when he wrote the following:

> The inference is also unavoidable that Lewis made more than a mistake of judgement as a trustee. He acted to benefit the bank and to enhance its prestige and indirectly the prestige of the union, not simply to keep the money in a safe place. The minutes show that he knew the large demand deposits were unnecessary for any legitimate purpose of the Fund. Moreover, he was not lacking in financial sophistication . . . as president of the Union, he utilized the considerable financial resources of the Union for the Union's benefit. The evidence is clear that Lewis, in concert with Roche, used the Fund's resources to benefit the Union's bank and to expand the Union's economic power in disregard to the paramount and exclusive needs of the beneficiaries which he was charged as Chairman of the Board of Trustees to protect.

Gessel dismissed the arguments union attorneys presented. Although the Fund's prior experience justified a large liquid reserve, Gessel believed the Fund could have invested in short-term government securities to meet that purpose. They offered some return and could be redeemed on a half hour's notice.[179]

Gessel addressed the tax issue by pointing out that the question concerning tax assessment of royalties had been settled for the anthracite trust when the IRS declared that the hard coal assessment was not income. A similar ruling could have been sought for the bituminous trust, but no one pursued the idea.[180] The judge further stated that the trustees realized their actions were not proper since the minutes of their meetings were altered. According to evidence presented during the hearing, Val J. Mitch, when still working as general counsel for the Fund, took extensive notes of trustee meetings. Mitch then prepared stenographic drafts of the proceedings, which Roche edited extensively before the final versions were prepared. From Gessel's perspective, Roche excluded informative detail which concealed embarrassing discussions.[181]

In all, Gessel devoted twenty pages of a forty-five-page opinion to the conflict of interest issue and related issues of trustee conduct. As written, the opinion represented a powerful legal indictment of the Lewis system and cast a pall of disgrace over the Fund's administration. In the remainder of his opinion, Gessel directed his attention to the other points included under the second category. From the opinion's content, Gessel obviously regarded these problems as secondary and did not spend a great deal of time on them. For example, he agreed the application forms the Fund used were misleading and that some applicants had mistakenly paid back union dues. Since the trustees were not aware of the problem and no specific action had been brought against the union on the question, Gessel simply issued an injunction ordering the Fund to stop using the forms.[182]

The only other sizable subsection within the opinion was the judgment concerning the 1969 pension increase. The judge agreed that the evidence showed Boyle acted recklessly and for political gain.[183] As a result, Gessel ordered a basic change in the Fund's administration. Sole usage of the National Bank of Washington by the Fund was to end, as well as the Fund's high level of liquidity. Roche and Boyle were to resign their trusteeships, and in the future the director of the Fund could not also serve as a trustee.

Gessel did not address whether Fund eligibility rules were arbitrary. Judging not only from the content of his opinion, but also his behavior afterward, Gessel believed the rules were unfair and should be changed as part of a reorganization. This attitude was best displayed when he refused to grant a stay of execution on his order while union attorneys appealed the decision. This meant that both Boyle and Roche had no choice but to resign from the trustee board.

Although the union would continue to be embroiled in controversy for another year, the decision meant the end of Lewis's system. In a strict sense, Judge Gessel was correct in his perception that a legal conflict of interest existed, especially where Lewis was concerned. However, the judge argued from the premise that there was no other way to serve the best interests of the beneficiaries, except overseeing the Fund without reference to any other agency. Considering his temperament and beliefs, Lewis could not have fulfilled such a demand. As shown throughout this study, Lewis was motivated by the acquisition and exercise of power, so that even his financial dealings were designed to increase the union's and his own position in the coal industry, rather than personal wealth.

Essentially, Lewis was a corporatist. While he was willing to cooperate with large operators to meet common goals, he vehemently fought any intrusion into what he regarded as the union's prerogative or responsibility. Similarly, because it served the needs of the rank and file, Lewis saw the Fund as the union's companion. While separate, the two institutions worked together to advance a common set of goals. Roche agreed with Lewis's assessment, and she acted accordingly. Undoubtedly, Lewis and Roche made mistakes, and the record shows that at times they were less than forthright. However, the assessment Gessel made was far too harsh. As fiduciaries, Lewis and Roche had a responsibility to keep the Fund solvent. They did that while supporting the Fund's efforts to improve medical and hospital care. Some of their policies were mistaken, but Lewis and Roche always acted in good faith. The real problem was that Lewis's system could not survive its creator's death. As long as the UMWA cooperated with the major operators for the good of the industry, it could not fully meet the needs of the individual miner. At some point in time, the contradiction would have surfaced. Although acceptance of the Fund by the major operators depended, in part, upon the union's relationship with them, the end of that cooperation did not necessarily mean the end of the Fund.

However, there was another change which did have serious implications. Between 1950 and 1969, a new generation of leaders had taken over the major coal companies.[184] As a group, they were more aggressive than their predecessors and unwilling to be bound by the 1950 settlement. This was clearly evident with the BCOA's reaction to the 1969 increase. Never before had the major operators ever limited the authority of the industry trustee in such a way. Resentful of the independence exhibited by Schmidt, the industry would not tolerate similar behavior from Judy or anyone who succeeded him. Moreover, the operators probably suspected no one in the union was capable of replacing Lewis. Boyle had proven to be a monumental failure, and Arnold Miller would not be much better.

As will be seen, union infighting increased after Miller's election in 1972. Whereas Miller headed a so-called reform administration, the reformers were unfamiliar with both the coal industry and the Fund, thereby weakening the union. This weakening presented the operators with an opportunity to roll back union gains. As a result, within six years of the *Blankenship* decision, the Fund's medical program would be terminated in basic industry's first give-back contract.

Chapter 7
Reform, Reorganization, and Disaster

Judge Gessel's decision did not end the *Blankenship* case, and litigation continued for another two years before a final settlement. In the meantime, the Fund operated against a backdrop of negative publicity. This included the invalidation of Boyle's 1969 reelection by the federal government, his loss to Arnold Miller in the 1972 special election, and especially Boyle's trial and conviction for conspiring to murder Joseph A. Yablonski.

After Gessel's ruling, the Fund's immediate task was to appoint a new board. Both Roche and Boyle had resigned their trusteeships, and Roche left the Fund's directorship as well. When Boyle resigned, his rank-and-file supporters staged a wildcat strike in protest under the slogan "Loyal to Boyle." Threatened with contempt, Boyle ordered the miners back to work.[1] A similar attitude pervaded the union's International Executive Board. Although Boyle was coming under increasing attack, his supporters hoped to reestablish control by defeating the Miners for Democracy (MFD), and clearing Boyle of any wrongdoing. In that spirit, the IEB appointed UMWA general counsel Edward L. Carey to replace Boyle as the union's trustee on June 15, 1972.[2]

As the union's general counsel, Carey had served Boyle faithfully and supported him during the 1972 campaign. But, leaving his political connections aside, Carey had experience as secretary for the Fund and the MMHA. Carey, therefore, understood the Fund's programs and was able to provide continuity in their management. This was further assured by the elevation of Thomas Ryan to the Fund's directorship.[3] Ryan would hold this office until his death in 1973.

With the new administration in place, work began on complying with Judge Gessel's ruling. Carey created a set of guidelines as a first step to prevent any violation of the judge's orders and imposed a salary/hiring freeze.[4] For the remainder of 1971, Carey worked constantly to ensure that no further suspicion would be cast on management of the Fund. An example was his endorsement of Prof. Paul R. Dean of Georgetown University Law School as Roche's replacement on the Fund's board.[5] In the weeks that followed, Carey dismantled Lewis's entire administrative apparatus.

By September 1, 1971, all Fund holdings had been withdrawn from the National Bank of Washington. New benefit forms were issued. While similar to ones used in the past, the new documents contained a boldfaced disclaimer near the signature space informing the applicant that neither current union membership nor the payment of dues was necessary for eligibility.[6] Problems with operators who defaulted on royalty payments were now referred to the courts, while the Fund continued to cover the employees of the offending companies. Finally, no one from the union worked for the Fund's staff in any position that paid a salary greater than $8,000 a year.[7]

Another important change came when the union negotiated an entirely new contract. The National Bituminous Coal Wage Agreement of 1971 offered a substantial increase in coal royalties. Set to run for three years, the 1971 accord immediately raised royalty payments from forty to sixty cents a ton. Additional increases were scheduled to take place automatically for each year of the life of the contract. This meant that signatory operators would be paying eighty cents a ton by 1974.[8]

The agreement looked like a good one, securing a doubling of the prevailing royalty in three years. But, three factors canceled most of the gains. First, the 1969 pension hike forced the Fund to seek additional income. Evidence had been presented during the Senate investigation showing that the Fund would be bankrupted if its income remained unchanged. Second, there was the impact of an increasing inflation rate upon the American economy as a whole. In August of 1971, President Nixon ordered a three-month wage-price freeze as the first of a multiphase program to deal with the problem. Third, there were the expenses arising from the *Blankenship* case. This factor was by far the largest, at least in the short term. Although the *Blankenship* suit received the most publicity, other less publicized actions had been filed against the Fund at approximately the same time. Because they all involved similar issues, the litigation was consolidated into one package. Through 1972, the Fund's staff worked on estimating the settlement's costs, and the figures were staggering.

One schedule placed the Fund's income at roughly $201 million. This was $31 million less than what was needed to meet basic obligations and did not include the additional expenses arising from the settlement. Taking into account the added beneficiary load and retroactive payments, the litigation would cost the Fund an additional $52 million.[9] Another cost schedule, which took the estimates through 1975, indicated that the total settlement could run as high as $64.7 million, or as low as $38.2 million.[10] Fortunately, these expenses would begin to decline by 1974, when retroactive payments would no longer be necessary once the new beneficiaries were on the Fund's roles.[11] Judging from the correspondence, Ryan handled most of these details. Because he had served as the Fund's comptroller since 1947, he was best qualified to oversee the preparations.

As for Carey, he divided his time between the Fund and the union. Viewed in hindsight, the 1972 campaign can be called the MFD election. But, the MFD was only a part of a broader coalition which sought to unseat Boyle and reform the union. In addition to the MFD, which originally had been Miners for Yablonski, the coalition included the Black Lung Association and the association of Disabled Miners and Widows. Rhetorically, the coalition presented a goal of re-creating the UMWA in such a way that it was less bureaucratic and functioned more as a social movement.

While the circumstances were different, this argument over the nature of unionism was an old one within the UMWA. A similar clash had taken place at the start of the twentieth century between UMWA president John Mitchell and the union's most well-known organizer, Mary Harris "Mother" Jones. Whereas Mitchell was concerned about creating an organization that could last for the long-range benefit of its members, Mother Jones believed Mitchell lacked vision. From her perspective, a union needed to inspire it members and retain rank-and-file spontaneity. Such a philosophy was necessarily more radical than Mitchell's, and it was not an accident that Mother Jones also was one of the original founders of the Industrial Workers of the World (IWW).[12]

This difference of opinion was also at the heart of the struggle between Lewis and his critics in the 1920s. Owing to his corporate views, Lewis believed a union needed to function on bureaucratic lines if it was to provide a disciplined labor force, as well as represent the needs of its membership. This opinion was based upon the premise that the major operators and the union had a mutual interest in restructuring the industry. Lewis's critics, including John Brophy and John Walker, sharply disagreed. Both men had served as UMWA district presidents, and neither believed that Lewis's program would work. Eventually, Walker and Brophy became vocal opponents of Lewis. They attempted to unseat him in the 1920s through a Save the Union committee and the creation of a rival organization: the Reorganized United Mine Workers of America (RUMWA).[13]

Although the MFD did not mirror the radicalism of either Mother Jones or the RUMWA, it represented a carryover of similar ideas. Unfortunately, none of its leaders had any administrative experience.[14] The MFD's election slate was nominated by a special convention held at Wheeling, West Virginia, in late May 1972. Most of the union's districts were represented, but the convention consisted almost exclusively of the union's eastern and midwestern sections.[15] Aside from Miller, the men nominated for the ticket's top positions were Mike Trobvich for vice-president and Henry Patrick for secretary treasurer. Whereas Trobvich was an established member of the MFD, Miller had risen to prominence in the anti-Boyle coalition as president of the Black Lung Association.[16] Other than his work for the association, the only offices Miller ever held were the presidency of his local union and membership on a mine safety committee.[17]

In addition to his lack of administrative experience, Miller also appeared to harbor resentment toward the Fund. This hostility was most apparent when, during a preelection interview on the *Today Show,* Miller flatly denied the Fund was still the most generous benefit program in basic industry.[18] This statement was wrong. Certainly, inflation had taken its toll on the Fund's pension, but the Fund's health care system was still a leader in the area of industrial benefits. It continued to offer nearly complete coverage without any payroll contributions, deductibles, or other form of out-of-pocket expenses.

The precise reasons for Miller's hostility toward the Fund are unclear and probably will never be fully known. According to Dr. John Newdorp, Miller, who was a heavy smoker, was originally rejected for a black lung award by a Fund-participating physician. When Miller lobbied to have this particular physician dropped from the participation list, the Fund's leadership refused.[19] According to another member of the Fund's senior staff, Miller simply resented the program because he did not create it.[20] Whatever the reasons, Miller's attitude did not bode well.

Miller won the 1972 election, but it was not a rousing victory, despite the media's pro-MFD bias and the news of Boyle's incarceration for fraud.[21] Winning by a margin of slightly more than fourteen thousand votes, Miller and his supporters maintained that they had a mandate for change. Upon taking office, Miller fired as many Boyle appointees as he could. Although Miller argued that a thorough housecleaning was necessary, he nevertheless used the very mechanisms of power he had decried during the campaign. This high-handedness finally involved the Fund on January 8, 1973, when without even the nominal approval of the IEB, Miller dismissed Carey as union trustee.[22] The move was not formally ratified until ten days later.[23]

Fighting back, Carey refused to recognize Miller's authority, and the dispute was referred to Judge Gessel. The union argued that Carey's removal was dictated by public policy. A supporter of the old administration, Carey had campaigned for Boyle in 1969 and 1972.[24] Moreover, the circumstances behind Carey's appointment also demonstrated his unfitness for the position. To support the claim, union attorneys presented a press release announcing Carey's appointment, which said the arrangement was temporary until Boyle was cleared.[25] Because Miller represented a force for change, it was intolerable for the union to be represented by "Boyle's surrogate" on the Fund board.[26] In the same vein, the plaintiffs also raised the issue of Carey's hostility toward the union's new leadership. During the 1972 election, Carey had referred to Miller, Trobvich, and Patrick as "The Three Stooges" and warned that they would sell out the membership.[27]

Carey's counterarguments were based upon a strict reading of the law. The only way he could be removed was by negotiation of a new contract or dereliction of his duties as a trustee.[28] The record, however, showed that Carey had consistently acted in good faith. In particular, he had complied unquestioningly with all of the specifics contained within Gessel's original order.[29]

Owing to these facts, when Gessel handed down his first decision on the matter in mid-February 1973, he found no evidence to warrant Carey's removal. Using impartiality as the standard of performance, Gessel wrote that Carey's outside activities had not placed him in a conflicting position.[30] No sooner had Gessel rendered the decision, though, than the union requested a reconsideration since it had additional evidence to present. According to the union, Carey could not be impartial because he had continuing associations with people hostile to the union's new administration. To support this claim, the union stated that Carey had joined the law firm of Foster and Perkins, which was handling the various suits filed against the UMWA by its former leadership.[31] Carey denied the charge by arguing that although he had joined this firm, he was not involved with any litigation concerning the union.[32]

Based on this new evidence, Gessel reversed himself and ordered Carey to resign. The new order showed that the issues concerning the Fund's litigation were complex. The judge ordered Carey's removal since credible evidence existed to prove an antagonistic attitude toward the union's new administration. In this context, the issue again was conflict of interest, since, as Gessel put it, "[c]lose collaboration with the union is required in an atmosphere of mutual confidence to further the objective and effectiveness of the Fund."[33] By itself this was logical, but the judge did not precisely delineate where close collaboration ended and something like Lewis's system began. Thus, in order to force Carey out, Gessel partially retreated from the uncompromising stand he had taken in 1971.[34]

With Carey out of the way, Miller took over as chairman of the Fund's board. He resigned the position in August 1973 to concentrate on union affairs.[35] Miller's term as a trustee was short, but he had a profound impact upon the Fund, both in terms of how he led the union and who he supported to replace him as the new union trustee: Harry Huge. At the time Huge assumed the trusteeship, the *Blankenship* case had been settled. Since the litigation primarily focused on benefit eligibility and the Fund's financial arrangements, little or nothing had been said about how the Fund operated in terms of actually providing benefits. This meant the Fund's various mechanisms to provide health care and pensions had remained in place. Miller and Huge had decided that basic change in this area was necessary.[36] Their efforts, while intended to restore the social contract with the miners, were disastrous.

The initial rearrangement involved not only the benefits the Fund offered, but its basic structure as well. These were outlined in the National Bituminous Coal Wage Agreement of 1974. Hailed as a major victory for the union, the contract increased coal royalties dramatically.[37] Under its terms, coal royalties would start at $1.18 a ton in 1974 and top out at $1.55 a ton by December 1977.[38] These were the single largest rate hikes in the Fund's history. But, the contract's language differed markedly from previous agreements and created a legal nightmare.

The Fund had always operated as a single trust, with its terms purposely vague. Starting with the 1950 agreement, the contracts simply listed the Fund's trustee board and the royalty. Matters of eligibility and benefits were left to the discretion of the trustees. The 1974 contract, however, broke the Fund into four separate legal entities: the 1950 Benefit Trust, the 1950 Pension Trust, the 1974 Benefit Trust, and the 1974 Pension Trust. Percentages of the royalty were allocated to each, and each had to meet specific requirements concerning benefit eligibility.[39]

These measures placed enormous limits upon the Fund's ability to act in emergencies. First, by breaking the Fund into four separate trusts, the board could no longer reallocate resources at will. Any transfer of monies from one of the four trusts to another constituted a contractual violation and was only allowed if all the interested parties agreed to it. For the first time since 1950, coal companies could legitimately intrude upon the Fund's operations.

To a degree, some change was unavoidable. Prior to the 1974 agreement, Congress passed the Employee Retirement Income Security Act (ERISA), which required all pension programs be guaranteed. Huge testified in its favor.[40] Because the Fund continued using the pay-as-you-go method, the pension system had to be separated from the medical service and given a distinct income.[41] Nevertheless, the 1974 contract's language clearly showed that union negotiators had not fully considered the ramifications of the Fund's restructuring, nor did they consider the Fund's history. The negotiators based the divisions on function and time limits. Basically, the 1950 trusts handled all beneficiaries who worked and/or retired prior to 1976, with the 1974 Funds handling all those who retired or entered the industry thereafter.[42] In addition, there was a marked increase in benefits and beneficiaries. All retirees covered by the 1950 pension trust saw their payments increased from $150 to $200 a month during the contract's first year. If a beneficiary received black lung benefits over and above his pension, he was awarded a final increase of $25 a month during the agreement's third year, and $50 a month if he did not receive black lung benefits.[43]

The 1974 pension trust was even more generous. Instead of offering a flat payment to its retirees, the 1974 pension fund used a sliding scale based on a miner's age and years of service in the industry. The contract set the minimum retirement age at 55, with at least ten years' service with a signatory operator. During the first ten years of employment, a miner was given a credit of $12 a month toward his pension. The credit rose by fifty cents for each additional ten years worked, up to a maximum of forty years. According to the assessment table printed in the contract, a miner retiring at fifty-five with ten years of service received $98.80 a month, whereas one retiring at sixty-two with forty years of service was entitled to $510 a month.[44]

Moreover, the 1974 agreement declared widows and disabled miners eligible for Fund benefits. At the very least, a miner's widow continued to be fully covered by the Fund's medical service. If she had been married to a pensioner, she continued to receive half of her husband's pension until her death or remarriage. Disabled miners now received full health coverage and a $125-a-month pension.[45]

Death benefits were also increased and varied according to whether the miner was retired, disabled, or active. Prior to 1974, dependents of retirees received $2,000, and those of an active miner were awarded $5,000 upon the miner's death. Dependents of disabled miners were not included. While the new contract increased the payment to the survivors of a retiree by only $500, the payments made to the families of disabled and active miners were far larger. An active miner's family was now entitled to anywhere from $7,500 to $20,000 in the event of the breadwinner's death. Families of disabled miners received anywhere from $2,500 to $10,000.[46]

The motive behind the increases was understandable. The Fund was intended to assist all miners and their families. However, the limitations which Roche and Lewis had imposed were not meant simply to exclude. They were solutions to the continuing problem of periodic drops in coal demand and, hence, production. The UMWA negotiators who handled the 1974 contract talks overestimated expected increases in coal demand that arose from the acute petroleum shortage caused by the 1973 OPEC oil embargo.[47] The negotiators also underestimated the rate of inflation for medical costs. Coupled with the Fund's new organizational structure, such a lack of foresight helped set the stage for a catastrophe. If royalty income did not meet expectations, the Fund's administration would not have the authority to reallocate resources as needed.

The same lack of foresight was present when Huge became union trustee and Fund chairman. Despite having no experience in either the coal industry or fringe benefit programs, Huge began to redefine the Fund's activities. At the time of his appointment, Huge met with the Fund's staff only once,[48] at a dinner held during the union's 1973 convention in Pittsburgh.[49] While thanking the staff for its work, Huge had already decided to bring in an expert to study the Fund's operations.

The man Huge chose was a personal friend, Dr. C. Arden Miller, a professor of pediatric medicine at the University of North Carolina at Chapel Hill.[50] Miller had a reputation for social activism, and his work had branched out into the area of public health. In fact, not long after doing his study of the Fund, Miller would be elected president of the American Public Health Association. These credentials notwithstanding, Miller's final report was a major disappointment since what it said had little or no practical use.

In researching his study, Dr. Miller visited a number of sites throughout the bituminous coal fields between the fall of 1973 and the spring of 1974. His report was supposedly based upon on his observations. In the words of one senior staff member, the report damned the Fund with faint praise.[51] It also articulated a pseudo-liberalism. First, Miller stressed the need to improve the miner's "quality of life." As part of that observation, he chided the Fund for not having taken an active role to improve Appalachia's housing conditions.[52] Miller claimed such a project was possible through the creation of local housing co-operatives that utilized the skills of its members and purchased materials on a group basis.[53] Turning to health care, Miller stated that the quality of medical treatment should be controlled through greater beneficiary participation and the use of data banks to follow each patient's treatment.[54] Miller believed the Fund's manual review system was antiquated and needed to be brought up to modern standards.[55]

To anyone familiar with the Fund's history, the flaws in Miller's report were obvious and myriad. To begin, Miller's comments about the state of housing for miners in Appalachia was not the great revelation he thought it was. The *Boone Report* had commented extensively on the problem in 1947. Moreover, the Fund's staff, from the executive medical officer down, realized a problem existed and knew about its negative impact on individual health. The problem was that the Fund did not have the resources to engage in home construction. In this respect, Miller's observations were simply trite and of no consequence.

These liberal generalities, however, camouflaged Miller's conservatism in the area of medical economics. This became apparent when Miller commented about the Fund's physician participation and retainer system. While admitting the Fund had improved miner health care by promoting group practice, Miller claimed that the retainer "functioned more as a bookkeeping convenience than as a device to improve the traditional pattern of medical care."[56] In order for Miller to have written this and meant it, he had to have believed fee-for-service was the best way to pay for health services while ignoring the Fund's experience to the contrary.

As it was, the validity of the Fund's experience in this area was documented later by a study done on the impact of retainer payment upon general medical care. This Department of Community Medicine of West Virginia University study looked at various primary care and multispecialty clinics operating in the state. The origins of each of these facilities varied. Some, such as the clinic at Fairmont, West Virginia, had been established through UMWA local unions. Others, like the Man Community Heath Foundation, had originally been operated as outpatient facilities for the MMHA hospital chain. Each of these facilities had retainer agreements with the Fund, as did at least twenty-three other West Virginia clinics.[57]

The retainer provided these institutions with a secure financial base, and its flexibility allowed them to expand their operations. Most importantly, while assuring quality treatment, the retainer allowed the facilities to be more liberal in their treatment policies.[58] In some instances, 25 percent of the beneficiaries who received treatment were actually ineligible.[59] Under fee-for-service, these individuals could not have received any medical care.

Since Dr. Miller had traveled through the coal fields, he presumably visited some of the clinics mentioned above and had the opportunity not only to view their work, but also to speak with their staffs. The fact that Miller made such a statement about the retainer meant that either he had not been very thorough in his investigation or he was prejudiced against using the retainer from the start. As a concerned physician, Miller should have understood what using the retainer meant in terms of making health services more accessible. Therefore, by writing off the retainer as a bookkeeping device, Miller failed to comprehend what the Fund was doing and was ignorant of the needs of the program's beneficiaries.

Despite these weaknesses, Miller's report became the basis for redesigning the Fund's programs. Tragically, at the time the report was nearing completion, Thomas Ryan, who was still serving as director, suddenly died. To replace him, Huge hired Martin B. Danzinger. Like Huge, Danzinger had no experience with either the coal industry or medical third parties.[60] But, his selection reflected the "reforming" mentality which pervaded the union's new administration. He would be given carte blanche to modernize the Fund's operations.

Prior to joining the Fund's staff, Danzinger had worked as a lawyer in the Department of Justice. Although he had no experience in any area of social policy, Danzinger was confident that he could come in, shake up the Fund, and have it operate more efficiently. The basis of his thinking was grounded in scientific management, whereby a manager did not have to know anything about the system he was overseeing in order to succeed. Regardless of whether the system was making shoes or offering health services, as long as the correct administrative procedures were followed, things would run smoothly to the benefit of all.[61]

In this setting, previous experience was devalued. For example, in one of his first acts as director, Danzinger established a hiring policy where new staff members had to be "bright" and "energetic," but did not need any previous experience.[62] In another instance, the new director told an AMO that he had to stop thinking like a physician and function as a professional bureaucrat.[63] It is clear from this, and the bulk of evidence, that Danzinger wanted both the Fund's physician-administrator model and the human touch in how the Fund did its work.[64]

A good example of this can be seen in how the Fund's headquarters reacted to a beneficiary problem in the Fund's Johnstown office. In April 1976, a fifty-year-old woman was in a Johnstown hospital suffering from a gangrenous foot. An amputation was an absolute necessity. However, the woman was fearful and refused treatment. At the behest of the attending physicians, the Fund's staff intervened to convince the woman to accept treatment. One staff member, Eleanor Wehere, recounted her father's successful rehabilitation experience after having undergone an amputation. With this, the woman agreed to be treated. While this was going on, another member of the Johnstown office, Helen Jacobs, explained the Fund's policies relative to nursing care and rehabilitation to the woman's husband in his native language, Slovak. According to the attending physicians, the Fund's intervention in this case made the difference. Not only had their attempts at persuasion failed, but the woman had not been swayed even by her parish priest.

Although this case was unusual, it represented the kind of service the Fund was capable of providing and, in fact, provided. The Washington office, however, viewed this approach with disdain. Writing to the Johnstown staff about a month after this incident, the Washington office said simply that the service provided the woman was a perfect example of the sort of "handholding" the program would no longer waste its time doing.[65]

In addition to this desire to end the human touch, Danzinger's managerial style was marked by rigidity of thinking and arrogance in his dealings with subordinates.[66] According to one veteran staff member, Danzinger had his own ideas, and one either did it his way or did not do it.[67] A telling example of this managerial style can be seen in an early exchange between Danzinger and Dr. Newdorp, who had succeeded Dr. Draper as the Fund's Executive Medical Officer after Draper's retirement in 1969. The issue in the correspondence between Danzinger and Newdorp involved the transfer of certain beneficiary cases from the Washington office to various area medical offices. Newdorp was concerned that many of the people whose cases were handled by the Washington office were elderly and lived far from the coal fields. Also, some of these people needed special attention that only the Washington office could provide. Newdorp asked, therefore, that the old arrangement remain in place. Danzinger not only refused the request, but also returned the memo to Newdorp covered with critical and insulting comments.[68]

Confronted with such an attitude, the Fund's veteran staff quickly became demoralized and embittered.[69] The situation was made worse by Danzinger's reorganization of the area offices in 1974. Within a year, three were closed, one was moved, and the rest were transformed into regional centers served by a network of twenty satellite offices.[70] But, the biggest change was in function. Whereas the medical program had worked out of the area offices, and the pension system out of Washington, the roles were suddenly reversed. This decision involved extensive personnel transfers as well as layoffs. With it, people who had worked out of certain offices for many years were given a simple choice: either accept the transfer or be fired. When area offices were closed, such as Pittsburgh's, no prior warning was given.[71]

The purpose of the change was twofold. First, Danzinger hoped to achieve a thorough standardization of all Fund medical benefits.[72] Second, he could have believed that if area office personnel were freed from processing medical claims, they could devote their full attention to clinic organization and the like.[73] Unfortunately, an absolute standardization of the Fund's medical benefits was not possible. In fact, a similar effort had been made several years earlier when Roche was still the Fund's director. Although some uniformity was achieved, variations in functions of area offices remained.

This was due to the nature of America's health delivery system. Although the quality of rural medical practice had vastly improved, due in no small part to the Fund's efforts, it was nevertheless different from urban practice. A miner living near an urban area with access to a major medical center received a different type of medical care than one who did not.[74] Because the AMOs were autonomous, the Fund's medical program as a whole had the flexibility necessary to address these differences. Also, because the AMOs were the Fund's principle defense against medical fraud, an entire system had been created over time whereby physicians and other providers presented medical audits, and other supportive documentation, to justify their charges.[75] While assisted by a staff of medical professionals, it was the physician administrator who could speak authoritatively about what was and was not fraudulent.[76] With Danzinger's reorganization, this all-important quality and cost control feature was lost.

Although cost containment had always been a major concern for the Fund, the matter took on special urgency during the late 1960s. The problem was an unforeseen side-effect of Medicare. Described by Prof. Paul Starr as a bonanza for providers, Medicare acted simply as a bill payer.[77] Based upon the fee-for-service approach, and using the "usual and customary fee" concept as its payment basis, the program failed to take note of regional price differences. Instead, providers in lower cost areas increased their fees to match those charged in higher cost regions.[78]

Even worse, because Medicare did not require medical audits, hospitals began financing physical expansion and new equipment by passing the costs to the program via increased per-diem charges. Medical charges spiraled as a result. From 1969 to 1973, the Fund's annual disbursements for health care rose from $55 million to $109 million, an average increase of roughly 25 percent a year. If anything, these figures should have underscored a need for caution. Nevertheless, Danzinger had Huge's confidence and so pressed ahead with his efforts to reorganize the Fund's operations.

What became a centerpiece of those efforts was a plan to computerize all of the Fund's services. Arising out of the Miller Report, a study of the Fund by the Touche Ross & Co consulting firm was authorized by the trustees. The firm reviewed Fund procedures and presented its findings in an eight-page report.

The report contended that the Fund's system of benefit review was outdated, since application processing was done by hand. A computer was used, but only to issue checks, health cards, and "limited statistical reports."[79] Because the work was done manually, and without a computer database, Touche Ross claimed the Fund could not monitor beneficiary eligibility, since it lacked up-to-date information on which to base actuarial projections. Also, the report claimed the Fund's current methods unnecessarily duplicated processing work. These problems would be solved by using a central database.[80]

The firm then turned its attention to medical payments. Once again the old system, where payment arrangements were handled manually by the area offices, was characterized as outmoded and inefficient. Touche-Ross insisted that manual processing delayed payment to health service providers and criticized the lack of diagnosis codes, provider numbers, and the like.[81] If the medical service used a central database, however, all of these supposed problems would be solved. The report asserted that the providers would be paid more quickly and the database would assure greater quality control, since all detailed information on treatment could be fed into the system.[82]

From the start, members of the Fund's veteran staff had their doubts about the report's efficacy. This is not to say that these people rejected the idea of a modern database out of hand. In fact, there were those who favored such a move.[83] But, this was a far cry from computerizing the entire medical program. An initial warning that such an effort might not be possible was sounded by a senior Fund consultant: Dr. Paul Cornely. A former president of the American Public Health Association, Cornely had also served as chair of the Department of Public Health of the Howard University Medical School. Cornely stressed the need for caution, since he believed the Touche-Ross study had not clearly defined its goals and objectives. Shortly thereafter, Cornely was abruptly dismissed from the Fund's staff by Danzinger.[84]

Although Danzinger claimed Cornely was fired because of poor job performance, Cornely effectively disputed the claim in a presentation to the trustees. Cornely showed in this presentation that he had been complimented on the quality of his work by Danzinger on at least one occasion.[85] This evidence of unjust treatment notwithstanding, the trustees allowed the dismissal to stand. In a letter sent to Cornely two days after his presentation, the board thanked him for meeting with them. The letter then went on to say that the past few months had been difficult for all involved, but that change was necessary.[86] Nowhere in the letter did the board dispute any of the facts Dr. Cornely presented, but it was clear the board had no intention of overruling Danzinger's decision.[87] If nothing else, these events showed that the Fund's leaders had made up their minds. The Touche-Ross study was going to be implemented; any doubts or objections were unwelcome.

As for implementing the plan, the computerization was organized around the creation of two major database systems: BENEFITS and MINES. "BENEFITS" stood for Beneficiary Information and Tracking System. According to the Fund's 1975 *Annual Report,* the system handled all pension applications. Through it, a miner's application was entered into the computer and subjected to an eligibility examination, which enabled the Fund to monitor a miner's eligibility status more closely.[88] No information is available on whether the system worked.

"MINES" was short for Medical Information and Evaluation System. It was intended to speed up payment for medical care while ensuring lower costs by using billing standards for all medical procedures. If a bill fed into the system met the standards, payment would be made automatically. If not, the bill would be pended for closer examination. The system would also gather information on work being done by individual health service providers by examining how much treatment was given, the rate of hospitalization, and its cost.

This, at least, is how the system was supposed to work and how its virtues were presented to the beneficiaries by the Fund's leadership.[89] The reality was far different. As mentioned above, Danzinger wanted to take the human factor out of how the Fund did its work, especially in the medical field. MINES was the vehicle for this approach. But, Danzinger and his associates failed to grasp that health care delivery was a complex matter. Even if an absolute uniformity of medical benefits could be achieved, there were myriad other factors involved that necessitated human judgment. Nothing else was its equal.[90]

This became obvious after MINES went online in October 1976. By that time, nearly two years of effort had been poured into creating the system, during which a mountain of evidence accumulated showing it would not work as planned. Aside from various glitches within the system, all medical procedures had to be converted into numerical codes to serve as its working vocabulary. This alone was a daunting task.[91] Work proceeded on the system, however, and it was given a preliminary test in September 1975 at the Johnstown office. This test failed and showed that major obstacles still existed. One of the most difficult problems was the forms the system used. In order for bills to clear MINES, they had to be itemized. This was difficult for hospitals and laboratories.[92] At the same time, forms designed to cover retained physicians were too complex. During the test, a physician on retainer attempted to fill out the form and could not do it. Disgusted, he finally requested a fee-for-service form, which was easier to complete.[93]

This, however, was only the tip of the iceberg. There were many other difficulties, all of which significantly increased the Fund's costs and diluted quality control. For example, MINES took over control of the Fund's hospital and physician participation lists. Originally, providers who wished to be included on the list had to meet the Fund's treatment and cost standards. Now all that a provider needed to do was to treat enough beneficiaries to meet a billing threshold. Once that threshold was met, inclusion on the list was automatic.[94] Another example was that under the old billing method, a physician could not charge for incidental surgery arising from a procedure. MINES, however, read incidental surgery as something distinct, separate, and billable.

Just as maddening was the system's rigidity. Owing to MINES's design requirements, the codes for its billing standards were very specific. This meant that the slightest discrepancy from the standard resulted in a pended bill. According to one source, MINES, when it finally went online, pended 70 percent of the bills presented.[95] Since pended bills were then sent back to the area offices for closer examination, the system actually resulted in increased paperwork and slower payment. According to a monthly report dated December 1976 from the Johnstown Office, that office had 122 pended bills left over from November. In December MINES generated 1,154 new pends. Of those, 762 had been processed, 93 had been sent to other Fund offices, leaving 421 which still needed to be processed by the month's end.[96] In a similar vein, if a physician lost or added a partner in his or her practice, the participation and payment codes would be outdated. New codes would have to be generated, which meant even more paperwork and delay in payment.[97]

Finally, MINES failed at what was supposed to be one of its primary tasks: beneficiary tracking. The Fund's leadership had made much of this feature in the program's annual report for 1975. Supposedly, MINES would track each individual beneficiary's treatment record and make it readily available for evaluation. In reality, the only way this information could be generated was by printing out a hard copy of the entire database and then going through it by hand.[98] By every available standard, MINES was a failure. Yet the system was never scrapped. This meant that because of the system's problems, the Fund lost all control over costs.[99] While no actual figures are currently available, former Washington staff member Henry C. Daniels maintains that the losses were staggering.[100]

These losses could not have come at a worse time. When Miller first assumed office in 1972, it appeared that the UMWA had weathered its troubles and was stronger. Although Miller did not seem to be an inspiring figure, but he projected an image of a dedicated reformer who would be responsive to the needs of the rank and file. Moreover, his staff was characterized as dedicated and able.[101] But, as Miller's first term progressed, the union was weakened by infighting and Miller's erratic behavior. In one instance, Miller became convinced that his secretary was plotting against him. He went so far as to take her office door off its hinges to prevent her from speaking to anyone in private.[102] As the infighting worsened, Miller publicly broke with his vice-president, Mike Trobvich, which culminated in the 1977 union election with Miller opposed by two rivals. Isolated from his associates in the union's hierarchy, Miller became increasingly dependent upon Huge as his principle advisor.[103]

By itself, the union's debilitation placed the Fund in jeopardy. However, the danger was heightened by the more aggressive posture taken by the BCOA. Controlled by a new generation of leaders who had little or no use for either Lewis or his legacy, they were especially dissatisfied with the 1974 contract's generosity.[104] The root cause of this attitudinal shift probably dated back to Schmidt's behavior as industry trustee and crystallized when Judy voted with Boyle to increase the Fund's pension in 1969. Judy had resented Schmidt's refusal to confer with his fellow operators, and this attitude probably reflected general opinion within the BCOA as a whole. Judy's decision to side with Boyle so soon after becoming industry trustee added insult to injury. The BCOA became determined not to be shut out in this manner again.

At the same time, the major coal companies had become increasingly upset with a structural inequity arising out of how the Fund was financed. As highly capitalized mining operations, companies such as Consolidated, Peabody, and Pitston had fewer working miners as a percentage of their payrolls than did smaller, more labor intensive firms. But, because the larger companies were producing more coal, their royalty payments were higher. This meant that they were partially subsidizing the rest of the industry to its health care.[105] Anxious to change this situation, the major coal companies of the BCOA became convinced that purchasing traditional group coverage for their miners through either commercial plans or Blue Cross would be substantially cheaper than continuing the Fund's health program.[106] With this in mind, the major operators began looking for an opportunity to end that program. They received their chance in 1977.

At the close of fiscal year 1975, the Fund listed total net assets of $108 million and reported totals of $232 million and $346 million in the next two years.[107] However, most of these monies belonged to the 1974 Pension Trust. Starting in 1975, the other three trusts either listed a simple deficit or negative assets.[108] The problem, aside from the impact of MINES, was that the Fund's total beneficiary load jumped from 548,000 people in 1973 to 787,000 by 1976, an increase of 43.6 percent.[109] Meanwhile, the Fund's total income did not meet expectations. After the industry recovered from the 1958–62 recession, coal output rose steadily and reached a peak in 1970 of 603 million tons.[110] The following year, however, production dropped and remained unstable until 1974, when the industry began a period of strong recovery.[111] In 1975 alone, a total output of 648.5 million tons was reported, which broke the old production record set in 1947.[112] Undoubtedly, coal demand was on the rise due to America's oil shortage. Substantial as the increase was, it fell short of the Fund's needs.

At the time when the union's membership was voting on the National Bituminous Coal Wage Agreement of 1974, the *UMWA Journal* published an open letter from Arnold Miller. In the letter, Miller urged ratification, claiming that the contract would earn the Fund a total of $1.876 billion in royalties between 1975 and 1977.[113] This projection proved to be wrong. Counting both royalties and earnings from investments, the Fund's total income for the contract's three years was 1.686 billion.[114]

Although the shortfall was considerable, the Fund would have had enough income to cope with the problem had it not been thwarted by its division into four different trusts. Because of tax requirements and ERISA, some restructuring was inevitable. But, the four-way division deprived the Fund's leadership of any flexibility in terms of reallocating the Fund's resources. Considering the context in which the 1974 agreement was negotiated, as well as the preconceived notions MFD appointees probably brought to their work, this could have been what the union's negotiators wanted. To them, previous benefit cuts might have appeared to be arbitrary and lacking in any sense of accountability to the beneficiaries. But, it was this flexibility which had helped keep the Fund solvent over the years.

Union negotiators also made a terrible mistake by underestimating the rate of inflation for health care. As mentioned above, health costs had risen an average of 25 percent a year between 1969 and 1973. This fact was clearly outlined in the Fund's annual reports for these years, and union negotiators presumably had access to this information. Yet, despite this evidence, the negotiators optimistically projected that medical costs would rise an average of 12.5 percent a year for the life of the 1974 contract.[115] The real annual increase turned out to be 20 percent.[116]

One other contributing factor to the Fund's difficulties at the time remains to be examined: the rash of wildcat strikes seen between 1975 and 1977. Janet Ploss, in an extensive master of science thesis written for the Johns Hopkins University School of Public Health, concludes that the strikes did not materially contribute to the Fund's financial problems. Going further, Ploss shows that the operators caused the walkouts through their efforts to avoid compliance with the 1974 contract. Their tactics ranged from obstructionism, such as using the contract's complex grievance machinery to settle minor disputes, to failure to pay royalty obligations.[117] Since the miners were forced to strike illegally, Ploss maintains that holding the miners responsible for the Fund's difficulties amounts to blaming the victim.[118]

Ploss is correct that the BCOA was aggressively working to end the Fund's medical program. Also, it is clear that the strikes really did not impact upon the Fund. Figures for 1976 and 1977 show the Fund had adequate resources to cover its obligations if those resources had been allocated correctly by the contract. Yet, the miners must assume part of the responsibility for what finally happened. The effect of the strikes might have been minimal, and the grievances real, but by taking matters into its own hands, the membership inadvertently legitimized the operators' position. The walkouts seemed to show that the UMWA could no longer control its membership, nor fulfill its contractual obligations.[119] In such a situation where media perceptions, and thereby public support, were at stake, the union needed greater discipline rather than misguided militancy.

As the financial crisis continued, it became apparent that income reallocations were necessary. Since this involved momentarily transferring income from one trust to another, all interested parties on the trustee boards had to agree. In 1976, two such reallocations were made, but none of them involved tapping the 1974 pension trust's resources. With the second reallocation, the situation appeared to have stabilized.[120] But, the crisis was reignited when the Fund lost $20 million due to a severe winter that forced a number of mines to close.[121]

This proved to be the straw that broke the camel's back. Having no other recourse, Miller contacted Joseph Brennan, president of the BCOA, and requested an income transfer from the 1974 pension trust. Brennan refused.[122] Considering the issues involved, one would have expected a strong reaction from the union's leadership. Although the BCOA had the right to refuse a transfer of either income or assets from one trust to another, the union had the option of fighting the refusal in the courts. Despite the Fund's financial difficulties, there had not been a breach of trust. Moreover the union could have argued that the refusal vitiated one of the Fund's basic purposes: to meet the medical needs of miners, active and retired, and those of their families. Instead, Miller did nothing, and Huge, as union trustee and chairman of the board, simply cut the Fund's program.

Huge announced his decision on July 20, 1977.[123] The news was shocking, especially since Miller had narrowly won reelection as president of the union just three days before.[124] As it was, Miller's opponents raised the issue of the Fund's solvency during the campaign and went so far as to say that a disaster was in the offing.[125] Miller, aware of the extent of the crisis, nevertheless insisted that nothing was wrong and assured the membership the Fund was in no danger.[126] The changes in coverage Huge put through were dramatic. Whereas all medical care which the Fund covered had been free, Huge's plan established a $250 deductible for all professional services, with 40 percent co-insurance to a maximum of $500 per family. The plan meant that all miners now had an out-of-pocket expense ranging from a minimum of $250 to a maximum of $750 a year for their family's health care. In addition, medical services were placed on a fee-for-service basis, with all Fund retainer agreements terminated.[127]

The new plan had two primary effects. The clinics which had depended upon the retainers for most of their cash flow now saw that source of income cut off. Immediately afterward, the clinics rushed to find alternative sources of funding. Services at some of them were diminished and a few eventually closed.

The majority, however, did manage to find other sources of income and continued operating.[128] The impact upon the miners was far greater. With the introduction of the co-payment and deductible features, the usage levels reported at the primary care clinics in West Virginia dropped by half. Since medical care was no longer free, the miners displayed a greater reluctance to use the facilities. Although the reduction in usage can be attributed in part to the loss of individual income during the long strike of 1977–78, the reported usage levels did not rebound to what they had been prior to the July 1977 decision.[129]

Health care for miners also suffered when the federal government ceased to recognize the Fund as a Group Practice Prepayment Program. Under GPPP, the Fund acted as an intermediary between its retirees and Medicare by processing their claims.[130] As part of the arrangement, the Fund received Medicare monies, which it then distributed to its participating physicians, clinics, and hospitals. When the Fund lost its GPPP recognition, retirees were forced to file Medicare claims on their own. Unfamiliar with the forms and procedures involved, pensioners were not able to get the assistance to which they were entitled, and they went without treatment.[131]

Response to the new situation within the union was swift. Immediately after the change was announced, there were more wildcat strikes involving nearly 80,000 union members. At the same time, the UMWA International Executive Board demanded Huge's resignation, and in fact voted to fire him on several occasions. Huge, however, refused to step down or recognize the IEB's authority to remove him. Miller supported Huge in his refusal and used Huge as a principle advisor during the 1978 contract talks.[132] These negotiations were crucial, since they would finally decide the medical program's fate.

The talks began in October 1978, but neither side reached an agreement when the 1974 contract expired on December 6. With the contract's expiration, the union struck and remained off the job for 111 days. Despite rank and file militancy, the union did not have the strength to enforce its will, since only 50 percent of the nation's coal tonnage now came out of UMWA organized mines. During the course of the strike, nonunion operators worked around the clock and were able to fill 80 percent of the nation's coal needs.[133] The union's position was weakened further by Miller's seeming inability to grasp the issues being discussed in the contract negotiations, and by his erratic behavior. During the course of the talks, Miller was accused of delaying discussions with the BCOA while he rode around the Washington Beltway in his limousine, leaving a negotiating session for two hours to be photographed by *Time* magazine and leaving another negotiating session to fill out his expense vouchers.[134] Miller's conduct at the time was so poor that he was ultimately compared to Lt. Comdr. Philip Francis Queeg, the emotionally disturbed Navy ship's captain in Herman Wouk's novel *The Caine Mutiny*.[135]

Obviously, because of the union's diminished position within the industry and its ineffective leadership, the chances of a complete restoration of the Fund's medical program were slim. Yet, the end of the medical service can be attributed to Harry Huge. Because of Miller's limitations, responsibility for the talks fell to Huge by default. As the de facto chief negotiator for the UMWA, Huge blocked all suggestions from the Fund's staff and simply put forward his own ideas. From the beginning, he told the operators that he was willing to include deductibles and co-insurance in the contract.[136]

For people who had longstanding connections with the Fund, such as Dr. Lorin E. Kerr, there was no question but that Huge was in league with the BCOA and sold out the miners.[137] While there is no evidence to substantiate the charge, Huge's behavior was certainly infuriating for people like Dr. Kerr. After all, the Fund's history, at least in part, had been marked by struggle and controversy, all in the name of improving the miners' quality of life. Now it appeared that Huge, an outsider to the mining industry, was giving away, without a second thought, something for which the miners had fought so hard. Not only that, but as one author pointed out in the *New Republic*, the Fund's 85 HS health card represented more than access to medical care. It symbolized a union miners' independence from the coal operators.[138] According to Janet Ploss, the operators wanted to end that independence and won their goal with the new agreement.[139] Considering his role in the negotiations, Huge was certainly complicit in that outcome.

Under the 1978 contract, working miners would now receive their health care through private insurance programs purchased by their employers. The implications of the new situation were enormous, and Huge should have been aware of them. Immediately after Dr. C. Arden Miller presented his report in 1974, a task force was created to study Fund operations in light of Miller's analysis. One of the subjects investigated was the use of retainers by the Fund, as opposed to alternative methods of payment. The task force stated flatly that private insurance schemes could not provide the medical coverage the Fund offered.[140] All of them, Blue Cross/Blue Shield as well as commercial plans, contained coverage limitations which would have required the Fund's beneficiaries to make substantial out-of-pocket payments. Also, if it used private insurance, the Fund lost its ability to monitor the quality of care rendered and the beneficiaries would be left on their own in the health care marketplace without any guidance.[141] Since experience had shown that quality control had a direct impact upon cost containment, the retainer was the most effective means for the Fund to provide health care.[142]

With the new contract, the Fund's retainer was a thing of the past. Although the new medical system's cost sharing features were less expensive than the changes Huge made in 1977, they showed where the coal industry was heading in terms of coverage. All working miners now paid $7.50 each time they received professional services; retirees paid $5. The co-insurance liability was reduced from $500 to $200 for working miners and to $150 for widows and retirees. Also, all prescription drugs were now subject to a $5 co-payment. At the same time, while the operators assumed responsibility for providing medical care for working miners, the Fund continued handling the health needs of retirees. However, the Fund lost its right to monitor the quality of care. Its work was strictly limited to determining eligibility and paying bills. All payment was done on a fee-for-service basis.[143]

Clearly, while the MFD responded to legitimate problems within the UMWA, its stewardship of the union and the Fund was a disaster. The problem was the organization's reformist mentality, which disregarded previous experience. This, combined with the technocratic fascination that marked Danzinger's tenure as the Fund's director, were primary causes for the program's collapse. Although outside forces—such as health cost inflation—were beyond their control, much that happened to the Fund was due to inexperience and possible incompetence at the top. As for Huge, after the medical program was terminated, he left the Fund to return to a private law practice. Danzinger eventually left the Fund as well, taking a position with New Jersey to oversee its state lottery. With the demise of the Fund's medical program, a thirty-year period of American labor relations had ended. A new one was just beginning.

Conclusions

During the thirty-year span the Fund's medical program was in operation, it appeared as if management and organized labor had achieved a permanent settlement. In return for labor's recognition of managerial prerogatives, such as control over long-term investment decisions, management agreed to negotiate with labor in good faith over issues of compensation, hours, and work rules.[1] Underlying this was the assumption that management had accepted organized labor as a junior partner in a corporate economy, creating the terms of a social contract between management and labor eventually dubbed the "New Deal Formula." The Fund's creation, as well as Lewis's approach to its management, anticipated this settlement and was a prime example of it.

In terms of how the Fund was managed, Lewis and Roche were effective in meeting crises and keeping the Fund solvent, but their methods, especially Roche's secretiveness, were self-defeating in the long run. They failed to consider the sensibilities of those the Fund served. Although many union miners praised Lewis's leadership, there were probably many others who viewed the Fund as something they had earned, not as Lewis's gift to them. This sense of ownership would have arisen not only from the sacrifices made by the rank and file to build the union, but also from their demands for something better prior to World War II. As mentioned before, Lewis was prompted to seek the Fund's creation only when more and more local unions began demanding better health care arrangements at UMWA conventions during the middle to late 1930s.[2] Because of this, and because of the sense of commitment the Fund's leadership projected, benefit reductions and claim rejections were not viewed simply as bad luck, but also as profound betrayal.

Much the same can be said about Lewis's 1950 settlement with the major coal operators. On the one hand, it provided the Fund with an assured existence; yet it ultimately worked against the miners by placing the UMWA in a contradictory position. Although this contradiction was obscured for a long time, it finally came to a head with the black lung issue and the Farmington disaster. Faced with such a terrible dilemma, both Lewis and Tony Boyle, each in his own way, simply opted not to act. Although in Boyle's case this was due, in part, to his considerable limitations as a labor leader, the problem was that a neat solution, which addressed the issue while leaving the 1950 settlement in place, was not possible.

The saddest aspect of this is that the union's moral authority was sacrificed here to preserve an edifice built on sand. With the advantage of hindsight, it now appears that the settlement, both in the coal fields and the rest of basic industry, was a mirage. True to an individualist ideology, management never accepted the idea that unions could fill a useful role.[3] Far from being a necessary evil for maintaining labor peace, unions were an unwanted nuisance. Thus, while maintaining an appearance of cooperation, corporate America sought and developed methods to outmaneuver the labor movement. The tactics created ranged from gradual disinvestment in unionized facilities to developing new methods of addressing worker alienation, as well as taking advantage of changes in the labor market.[4] The cumulative effect of such a methodical and broad-based assault was the undermining of organized labor's position within the American economy.

Given this context, the UMWA's decline, and with it the collapse of the Fund's health care program, can be viewed simply as an aspect of a much larger trend. Nevertheless, the cancellation of the Fund's medical program stands out. In effect, the UMWA's 1978 agreement with the BCOA amounted to labor's first major "give back" contract. It showed conclusively that it was possible for management, under the right conditions, to recapture hard-won wage and benefit gains unions had made in the years prior.

Even more heartening for management was the fact that no major union bothered to protest what had happened to the Fund. Although it is true that the UMWA had been an independent organization since 1947, when it withdrew from the AFL, the end of the Fund's medical program was a major loss in the area of industrial benefits as a whole. The fact that no major union, let alone the AFL-CIO itself, responded to this in any significant way bespoke a lack of cohesion and a lack of foresight, which management used to its advantage. Aided by Ronald Reagan's election to the presidency, as well as the conventional wisdom created by the recession of 1979–81, management was able to turn back the clock significantly. Not only did union membership plummet, give-back contracts became the norm rather than the exception.

Taking these points into account, the question must be asked whether the Fund's problems could have been avoided. The answer is probably not, but the impact might have been limited. As has been seen, many of the Fund's difficulties were the result of the inexperience of Arnold Miller and the people who took over the program during his tenure as the UMWA's president. Seen in this light, the loss of Joseph A. Yablonski stands out not only as a personal tragedy but an institutional disaster.

Yet, despite his strengths as a leader, Yablonski would have been one man against myriad problems that defied solution. First, health care cost inflation, fueled by Medicare, was continuing. Although the Fund's organizational structure and payment mechanisms contained costs, some reduction in services might have been necessary at some point because of the spiral's impact.

Second, there was still the matter of management's attitude toward the program. George Love and his associates may have, in fact, made their settlement with Lewis in good faith. However, by the time Lewis died in 1969, he had been predeceased by all of the men with whom he had negotiated over the years. One by one, they had been replaced by a new and more aggressive generation who did not feel bound by any arrangements made by their predecessors. Certainly, Yablonski would have been more effective in dealing with this group than Miller. But, it is doubtful he could have held them off indefinitely. The labor movement's general decline would have taken its toll, with the Fund always being a prime target.

Viewed in this light, it is fortunate that the Fund's pension program has survived. Just how fortunate becomes evident when one considers the fact that the inequity which moved the large coal companies to seek the medical program's termination also applies to the pension system. Specifically, due to the program's financing via a tonnage royalty, the efficient firms who have few miners per ton of coal produced are partially subsidizing more labor-intensive companies to their employees' retirement.[5] Because of this, the pension's continuation has been a bone of contention in negotiations subsequent to 1978.[6] In that time, the union has managed to hold firm while seeking ways to give the program greater stability. For example, Richard Trumka worked very hard to make the 1950 Pension Trust self-supporting. Notable as this may be, Trumka's drive to achieve this goal was aided by the fact that the Trust had, and continues to have, its own distinct income, as well as a declining beneficiary population. The real issue is the 1974 Pension Trust's future.

If current trends in other industries are any sort of an indicator, the major coal operators would like to do two things: first, assume control over their employees' pensions. Second, move from the current pension model, which is based upon what is referred to as a "defined benefit," to a method using a so-called defined contribution. Under defined benefit, a specific income is guaranteed to the pensioner from retirement to death. The amount is based upon such variables as length of service, size of income, and the like.[7] Defined contribution, on the other hand, is the approach used by 401 K and similar plans. Under it, an employee contributes into a pension fund that is converted into an annuity at retirement. With this method, an employer may or may not elect to make matching contributions.[8]

The problems with this method are myriad. First, returns from the financial and bond markets, where such contributions are invested, are by no means guaranteed. Due to the element of risk involved, as well as the specialized skills required to invest effectively, many people would be in jeopardy of losing their

185

accumulations. Second, and as serious, many of these plans, including those with a joint employee/employer contribution, are voluntary and allow early withdrawal of funds at a substantial penalty. Since everyday life is demanding, the temptation to either put off participation or to withdraw funds to meet current needs, would be tremendous. In either case, the retiree would face destitution in his or her old age. Also, even if a retiree did all the right things, an adequate retirement income would not be assured.[9]

At present, there is a great deal of discussion about "reforming" social security along these very lines. Because the Fund has served in the past as a barometer in terms of where labor relations and social policy are headed, it may tell the future in this case. If the major coal operators ever manage to re-create the Fund's pension as a defined contribution program, then the so-called reform of Social Security could be next. Fortunately, there are indications that such an effort would fail. A good case in point is the 1997 strike involving United Parcel Service and the International Brotherhood of Teamsters.

Although it goes beyond the scope of this study to address all of the strike's major issues in detail, the dispute focused on the Teamster's pension program. Specifically, UPS wanted to separate from the Teamster pension fund, claiming that the company was partially subsidizing the employees of their less efficient competitors. As everyone knows, UPS lost. This was not only due to the strength of the Teamsters as a union, but also because the AFL-CIO was far more aware and vigilant than it was in 1978.

Looking at the Fund as it currently stands in light of this, the question has to be asked whether it was an entity which could not survive the end of the era which created it. The answer is yes and no. Certainly, the medical program's collapse heralded the end of the New Deal Order. This notwithstanding, the Fund, especially its pension program, has shown considerable durability and so demonstrates that management has not been able to turn back the clock entirely. Moreover, the Fund has left a considerable legacy. This is seen with the group practice clinics it helped create, as well as with Appalachian Regional Health Care. This legacy also includes the Fund's collective experience, which will continue as an example of what can be achieved in the area of social policy.

Notes

Introduction

1. See the following: Saul D. Alinksy, *John L. Lewis: An Unauthorized Biography* (New York: Putnam, 1949), Cecil Carnes, *John L. Lewis: Leader of Labor* (New York: Robert Speller Publishing Co., 1936), Cyrus L. Sulzberger, *Sit Down with John L. Lewis* (New York: Random House, 1939), David F. Selvin, *The Thundering Voice of John L. Lewis* (New York: Lanthrop, Lee, & Shepard Co., 1969), Mary Heaton Vorse, *Labor's New Millions* (New York: Putnam, 1939)

2. Barton J. Bernstein, "America in War and Peace: The Test of Liberalism," in *Towards a New Past: Dissenting Essays in American History,* ed. Barton J. Bernstein (New York: Random House, 1967; paperback ed., New York: Vintage Press, 1969), 290.

3. See Nelson Lichtenstein, "From Corporatism to Collective Bargaining: Organized Labor and the Eclipse of Social Democracy in the Post-War Era," in *The Rise and Fall of the New Deal Order, 1930–1980,* ed. Steve Fraser and Gary Gerstle (Princeton: Princeton Univ. Press, 1989), 122–52.

4. Taped interview with Lorin E. Kerr, M.D., May 30, 1988. Hereafter referred to as Kerr Interview. Dr. Kerr was a specialist in public health and originally served as an officer in the U.S. Public Health Service (USPHS). Leaving the USPHS shortly after the close of World War II, Kerr joined the Fund's staff at the time when the program was first being organized. Originally working as the Fund's Area Medical Officer (AMO) for Morgantown, West Virginia, Kerr eventually came to work in the Fund's headquarters in Washington, D.C. While there, he became an expert on coal workers' pneumoconiosis (black lung) and became a leading proponent for the condition's recognition as a compensable, work-related disease afflicting miners or anyone who worked around coal dust. Traditionally, scholars have claimed that government efforts influenced the private sector relative to social policy. However, recent scholarship in this area contradicts this claim. Thus, Kerr's idea that a private program like the Fund influencing governmental policy is not at all far-fetched. In fact, according to social analyst Beth Stevens, the private sector has been the place where social policy innovation has taken place, thereby influencing government policy. For a complete presentation on this idea, see Beth Stevens, "Blurring the Boundaries: How the Federal Government Has Influenced Welfare Benefits in the Private Sector," in *The Politics of Social Welfare in the United States* (Princeton: Princeton Univ. Press, 1988), 125ff.

5. See Janet E. Ploss, "A History of the Medical Care Program of the United Mine Workers of America Health and Retirement Funds" (master's thesis, Johns Hopkins Univ., 1981); Ivana Krajcinovic, *From Company Doctors to Managed Care: The United Mine Workers' Noble Experiment* (Ithaca, N.Y.: ILR Press, 1997).

Chapter 1. Establishing the Fund

1. Taped interview with Ada Kruger, R.N., June 18, 1993; Taped interview with Robert Boylan, M.D., July 16, 1993 (hereafter referred to as Boylan Interview); Kerr Interview. Each of the people listed above were health professionals who worked for the Fund, either in the Washington office or in the field. Miss Kruger had been assistant area medical officer for the Fund's Denver office. As mentioned previously, Dr. Kerr had served as the Fund's AMO for Morgantown, West Virginia, and later became the Fund's deputy executive medical officer in Washington. Dr. Boylan took over as the Fund's AMO in Pittsburgh in the late 1960s when the original Pittsburgh AMO, Dr. Leslie Falk, retired.

2. Alan Derickson, *Black Lung: Anatomy of a Public Health Disaster* (Ithaca, N.Y.: Cornell Univ. Press, 1998), 114.

3. John L. Lewis, *The Miner's Fight for American Standards* (Indianapolis: Bell Publishing Co., 1925), 24–25.

4. Morton S. Baratz, *The Union and the Coal Industry* (1955; rpt. Westport: Greenwood Press, 1983), 70–74.

5. Ibid.

6. Melvyn Dubofsky and Warren Van Tine, *John L. Lewis: A Biography* (New York: Quadrangle/New York Times Book Co., 1977), 121–30.

7. Ibid., 133–36.

8. Baratz, *The Union and the Coal Industry,* 47–48.

9. Janet E. Ploss, *A History of the Medical Care Program of the United Mine Workers of America Welfare and Retirement Fund* (master's thesis, Johns Hopkins Univ. School of Hygiene and Public Health, 1981), 17–18.

10. *Mine People,* 1–3, F.F. British Miners Welfare, box 2 of 2, Actuary and Insurance Company Data, Series II, Office of the Director Records (hereafter referred to as Director's Records), United Mine Workers of America Welfare and Retirement Fund (hereafter referred to as Fund Papers), West Virginia Collection, West Virginia Univ., Morgantown. The Fund's files were opened in 1981 and are fully available for researchers to use.

11. U.S. Dept. of the Interior, *A Medical Survey of the Bituminous Coal Industry, Report of the Coal Mines Administrator (The Boone Report)* (Washington D.C.: GPO, 1947), 91, 100, box 1 of 1, "Bibliography-UMWA Health and Retirement Fund."

12. Ibid., 76.

13. Ploss, *A History of the Medical Care Program,* 12.

14. Daniel P. Harrington, "Review of Safety in Coal Mining in 1945," 1–2; Walter A. Thurmond, "Statement of Walter A. Thurmond before Senate Sub-Committee on Public Lands, RE Senate Joint Resolution 133 [on Coal Mine Safety], 1–5, box 2, Walter P. Thurmond Papers (hereafter referred to as Thurmond Papers), A & M 2141, West Virginia Collection, West Virginia Univ.

15. Alan Derickson, "Part of the Yellow Dog: U.S. Coal Miner Opposition to the Company

Doctor System, 1936–1946," *International Journal of Health Sciences* 19, no. 4 (1989): 714–18; Marlene Huff, "The Effect of the UMWA upon Reform of the Company Doctor System," 8–9, 11–12, Paper presented at the Sixteenth Annual Appalachian Studies Conference, Mar. 21, 1993; *Proceedings of the National Health Conference*, Interdepartmental Committee to Coordinate Health and Welfare Activities, Josephine Roche, Chairman (Washington: GPO, 1938), 68–70.

16. Ploss, *A History of the Medical Care Program,* 16–17; Kerr Interview; taped interview with Dr. John Winebrenner, Sept. 10, 1993 (hereafter referred to as Winebrenner Interview #1). Dr. Winebrenner worked for the Fund for twenty-five years, working primarily as AMO for Knoxville, Tennessee. Since his retirement in 1972, Dr. Winebrenner has remained active in health care delivery. The author wishes to thank Dr. Winebrenner for his interest and contribution to this project.

17. Jere A. Wysang and Sherman R. Williams, *Health Services for Miners: Development and Evolution of the United Mine Workers Health Care Program* (Washington, D.C.: National Center for Health Service Research, U.S. Dept. of Health and Human Services, Office of Health Research, Statistics, and Technology, 1981), 3.

18. *Proceedings of the National Health Conference,* 68–69.

19. John Brophy, *A Miner's Life* (Madison: Univ. of Wisconsin Press, 1964), 157–58.

20. Derickson, "Part of the Yellow Dog," 714–18; Huff, "The Effect of the UMWA," 11–12.

21. Dubofsky and Van Tine, *John L. Lewis: A Biography,* 376.

22. Baratz, *The Union and the Coal Industry,* 115–16.

23. Curtis Seltzer, *Fire in the Hole: Miners and Managers in the American Coal Industry* (Lexington: Univ. Press of Kentucky, 1985), 57.

24. Adolf Held, "Report as Submitted to Conference on Union Health Insurance," May 25, 1946, 13, F.F. Health and Welfare Survey, Research Dept., United Steel Workers Papers, box 65, Labor Archives, Patee Library, Pennsylvania State Univ.

25. "Summarized Proceedings: Conference of Labor Research Group," Dec. 10, 11, 1946, appendix B, Federal Security Agency, Social Security Administration, Bureau of Research and Statistics.

26. Ibid., 3b.

27. Ibid., 1–3a.

28. Lichtenstein, "From Corporatism to Collective Bargaining," 123–33.

29. *UE Guide to Group Insurance* (New York: United Electrical, Radio, and Machine Workers of America, CIO, 1944), 7, box Yellow Dot #1, Group 78, Group Insurance, UE Collection, Archives of Industrial Society, Univ. of Pittsburgh.

30. Ibid., 29.

31. Ibid., 64–65.

32. Ibid.

33. Ibid., 8.

34. Murray W. Latimer, "Instructions Relating to Social Insurance Fact Finding," Nov. 14,

1949, 270, F.F. 17, David J. Macdonald Papers, box 68, Labor Archives, Patee Library, Pennsylvania State Univ.

35. Ibid.

36. Ibid.

37. I. S. Falk, "Health Insurance Experience in Basic Industry: Summary of Utilization and Costs Under Blue Cross and Blue Shield Contracts of the United States Steel Corporation for Employees and Their Dependents," 1–3, F.F. Medical Care, 1963–65, National Can Corporation, National Labor Management Panel, 1962–67, box 6, Frank Pollara Papers, Labor Archives, Patee Library, Pennsylvania State Univ.

38. Murray W. Latimer, "Instructions Relating to Social Insurance Fact Finding, Nov. 14, 1949, 5, F.F. 17, Instructions Related to Social Insurance Fact Finding, box 68, David J. MacDonald Papers, Labor Archives, Patee Library, Pennsylvania State Univ.

39. I. S. Falk, "Health Insurance Experience in the Basic Steel Industry: A Summary of Utilization and Costs Under the Blue Cross and Blue Shield Contracts of the United States Steel Corporation for Employees and Their Dependents, 1953–62, 3, F.F. Medical Care, 1963–65, National Can Corporation, 1960–69, National Labor Management Panel, 1962–67, box 6, Frank Pollara Papers, Labor Archives, Patee Library, Pennsylvania State Univ.

40. Beth Stevens, *Complimenting the Welfare State: The Development of Private Pension, Health Insurance, and Other Employee Benefits in the United States,* Labor Management Relations Series No. 5 (Geneva: International Labor Office, 1986), 40–42.

41. Paul Starr, *The Social Transformation of American Medicine* (New York: Basic Books, 1982), 294–98, 306–10.

42. *Proceedings of the National Health Conference,* 58.

43. Daniel M. Fox, *Health Policies, Health Politics: The British and American Experience* (Princeton: Princeton Univ. Press, 1986), 47; Starr, *Social Transformation of American Medicine,* 226–37.

44. Starr, *Social Transformation of American Medicine,* 226–37.

45. "Health Security/Message from the President of the United States Transmitting the Report and Recommendations on National Health Prepared by the Interdepartmental Committee to Coordinate Health and Welfare Activities," 76th Cong., 1st sess., H.R. Doc. 120, 1–2, Josephine Roche Papers, Archives, Univ. of Colorado, Boulder.

46. *Proceedings of the National Health Conference,* 29–64.

47. 76th Cong., 1st sess., S. Doc. 1620, Legislative Day, Feb. 27, 1939, 1ff, F.F. 8, box 16, Roche Papers; Joseph Huthmaker, *Senator Robert F. Wagner: The Rise of an Urban Liberal* (New York: Anthaneum, 1971), 263–66.

48. John H. Warner, "Power, Conflict, and Identity in Mid-Nineteenth Century American Medicine: Therapeutic Change at Commercial Hospital in Cincinnati," *Journal of American History* 73, no. 4 (Mar. 1987): 935–36.

49. Starr, *Social Transformation of American Medicine,* 101–10; Elaine Riska, *Power, Politics, and Health: Forces Shaping American Medicine* (Helsinki: Finnish Society of Science, 1985), 18, 30.

50. Daniel Fox, *Health Policies, Health Politics,* 16–20; Rosemary Stevens, *American Medicine and the Public Interest* (New Haven: Yale Univ. Press, 1971), 417–18.

51. John A. Kingsbury, *Health in Handcuffs: The National Health Crisis—and What Can Be Done About It* (New York: Modern Age Books, 1939), 138–44; *Proceedings of the National Health Conference,* 101–3.

52. "Statement on National Health Insurance Bill (S-1879) by Russ Nixon, Washington Representative of the United Electrical, Radio, and Machine Workers of America—CIO," 1, June 7, 1947, F.F. Health Through 1951, box 336, Red Dot, UE Papers, Archives of Industrial Society, Univ. of Pittsburgh.

53. Clipping from the "P.M." by Albert Deutsch, July 11, 1944, F.F. Murray-Wagner-Dingell Bill, box 78, Yellow Dot, UE Papers.

54. Ibid.

55. "An Address by Senator James E. Murray of Montana before the CIO Committee for Political Action, New York," Jan. 14, 1944, 2–3, F.F. Murray-Wagner-Dingell Bill, box 78, Group Insurance, Yellow Dot, UE Papers.

56. Thurmond Diary, Mar. 22, 1946, Apr. 1, 1946, box 3, Walter E. Thurmond Papers, A & M 2141, West Virginia Collection. Thurmond was one of the founders of, and secretary for, the Southern Coal Producers Association.

57. Press statement of John L. Lewis on retirement fund, May 14, 1946, F.F. 10, box 1 of 3, 1946, 1947 Fund Files, Series II, Director's Records, Fund Papers, ibid.

58. Thurmond Diary, May 14, 1946, box 3, Walter E. Thurmond Papers, West Virginia Collection; Seltzer, *Fire in the Hole,* 58.

59. Press Release, Apr. 9, 1947, F.F. 8, box 1 of 3, 1946, 1947 Fund Files, Series II, Director's Records, Fund Papers, West Virginia Collection.

60. National Bituminous Coal Wage Agreement of 1946, F.F. 6, box 1 of 3, 1946, 1947 Fund Files, Series II, Director's Records.

61. Ibid.

62. *The Boone Report,* 1–2, box 1 of 1, "Bibliography, UMWA Health and Retirement Fund," [no series number], Director's Records.

63. *The Pottsville Republican,* Mar. 13, 1997.

64. *The Boone Report,* 123, 127–31, 168–73, 191–93, box 1 of 1, "Bibliography, UMWA Health and Retirement Fund," [no series number], Fund Papers, West Virginia Collection.

65. Ibid., 59.

66. Ploss, *A History of the Medical Care Program,* 23.

67. Draft petition of Capt. Norman H. Collisson to the Federal District Court of Washington, D.C., to be relieved of his responsibilities as a trustee of the UMWA Welfare and Retirement Fund, 2. F.F. 6, box 1 of 3, 1946, 1947 Fund Files, Series II, Director's Records.

68. Ibid.

69. John L. Lewis to all UMWA District Presidents, Mar. 13, 1947, F.F. 6, box 1 of 3, 1946, 1947 Fund Files.

70. Henry H. Adams, *Harry Hopkins: A Biography* (New York: Putnam, 1977), 34; Robyn Muncy, *Creating a Female Dominion in American Reform, 1890–1935* (New York: Oxford Univ. Press, 1991), 150–53; Eleanor McGinn, "Josephine Roche: Progressive Reformer, 1910–1940," 1–2 (copy of a presented paper written by Dr. McGinn and given to the author in April 1993).

71. McGinn, "Josephine Roche," 1–2.

72. "Josephine Roche," *Current Biography, 1941* (New York: W. W. Wilson Co., 1941), 725.

73. *Proceedings of the National Health Conference,* vii–ix, 1–3.

74. Minutes and Resolutions of the United Mine Workers of America Welfare and Retirement of 1947, 12, Contained in John L. Lewis's Motion to Dismiss Suit brought by Ezra Van Horn, F.F. John L. Lewis Motion to Dismiss, Affidavits and Points and Authorities in Support, box 3 of 3, 1946, 1947 Fund Files, Series II, Director's Records, Fund Papers.

75. Draft Petition of Capt. Norman H. Collisson to the Federal District Court of Washington, D.C., to be relieved of his responsibilities as a trustee of the UMWA Welfare and Retirement Fund, 3., F.F. 6, box 1 of 3, 1946, 1947 Fund Files, Series II, Director's Records UMWA Welfare and Retirement Fund; Minutes and Resolutions of the United Mine Workers of America Welfare and Retirement Fund of 1947, 12 passim, contained in John L. Lewis's Motion to Dismiss Suit brought by Ezra Van Horn, F.F. JLL Motion to Dismiss, Affidavit and Points and Authorities in Support, box 3 of 3, 1946, 1947 Fund Files, Series II, Director's Records, Fund Papers

76. Press release, Apr. 9, 1947, F.F. 6, box 1 of 3, 1946, 1947 Fund Files, box 1 of 3.

77. Ibid.

78. Memo to Thomas Murray from Godfrey Schmidt, Apr. 21, 1947, F.F. 9.

79. Memo from Percy Tetlow to the board of trustees, June 13, 1947.

80. Memo to Thomas Murray from Godfrey Schmidt, Apr. 21, 1947.

81. Percy Tetlow to all district presidents of the UMWA, Aug. 6, 1947, F.F. 9.

82. Memo from D. L. Henneke to Thomas Ryan, Apr. 30, 1947, F.F. Retainer Fee and Expense Correspondence, box 5 of 8, Board of Trustees Correspondence, 1946–71, Series II.

83. William L. P. Burke to John L. Lewis, Nov. 2, 1949, F.F. William L. P. Burke: Miscellaneous Correspondence.

84. Thurmond Diary, June 27, 1947, box 4, Thurmond Papers.

85. G. H. Scott, "A Study of the United Mine Workers of America Welfare and Retirement Fund" (master's thesis, West Virginia Univ., Morgantown, 1951), 26.

86. *In the District Court of the United States for the District of Columbia. Ezra Van Horn Individually and as Representative of the Operators Signatory to the National Bituminous Coal Wage Agreement of 1947, on the Board of Trustees of the United Mine Workers of America Welfare and Retirement Fund, Petitioner, v. John L. Lewis, as Trustee of the United Mine Workers of America Welfare and Retirement Fund and as Representative of the United Mine Workers of America, and H. Styles Bridges, Third and Neutral Trustee of the United Mine Workers of America Welfare and Retirement Fund, 48–49,*

F.F. John L. Lewis, Trustee 1947 Fund (1948), box 1 of 8, Board of Trustees Correspondence, 1946–71, Series II, Director's Records, Fund Papers.

87. Statement of John L. Lewis, President of the United Mine Workers of America, Washington, D.C., before Senate Committee on Labor and Public Welfare, Mar. 7, 1947, F.F. 10, box 1 of 3, 1946, 1947 Fund Files, Series II, Director's Records.

88. Draft Petition of Capt. Norman H. Collisson to the Federal District Court of Washington, D.C., to be relieved of his responsibilities as a trustee of the UMWA Welfare and Retirement Fund, 1, 4., F.F. 6.

89. Memos from William L. P. Burke to the board of trustees, July 15, 1947, and Sept. 2, 1947.

90. Ibid.

91. Ibid.

92. Ibid.

93. Draft Petition of Capt. Norman H. Collisson to the Federal District Court of Washington, D.C., to be relieved of his responsibilities as a trustee of the United Mine Workers of America Welfare and Retirement Fund, 4.

94. Krajcinovic, *From Company Doctors to Managed Care,* 37.

95. Memo to Lewis from Roche, Dec. 19, 1947, box 8 of 11, United Mine Workers of America Correspondence, 1946–72, Series II, Director's Records, Fund Papers.

96. Minutes and Resolutions of the United Mine Workers of America Welfare and Retirement Fund of 1947, 1, contained in John L. Lewis's Motion to Dismiss suit brought by Ezra Van Horn, F.F. JLL Motion to Dismiss, Affidavit and Points and Authorities in Support, box 3 of 3, 1946, 1947 Fund Files, Series II, Director's Records, Fund Papers.

97. Memo from Lewis to Francis Fitzgerald, Dec. 20, 1947, F.F. 10, box 1 of 3, 1946 1947 Fund Files.

98. Van Horn to Lewis, June 5, 1948; Roche to Van Horn, Mar. 17, 1949, F.F. Correspondence: E. Van Horn, box 2 of 8, Board of Trustees Correspondence, Series II, Director's Records. In this particular case Roche denied Van Horn's request for several back copies of the Fund's official minutes. Although Van Horn could not be kept from having them ultimately, Roche told him politely to wait until the next trustee meeting to make his request formally there.

99. Van Horn to Lewis, June 5, 1948.

100. Memo to Lewis from Roche, Aug. 30, 1949, F.F. JLL, Audits, CPA Reports, Memos 1950 and 1947 Funds, box 2 of 11, United Mine Workers Correspondence, 1946–72, Series II, Director's Records, Fund Papers.

101. Ibid.

102. Minutes and Resolutions of the United Mine Workers of America Welfare and Retirement Fund of 1947, 1, 4–6, contained in John L. Lewis's Motion to Dismiss suit brought by Ezra Van Horn, F.F. JLL Motion to Dismiss, Affidavit and Points and Authorities in Support, box 3 of 3, 1947, 1947 Fund Files, Series II, Director's Records, Fund Papers.

103. Ibid.; Memo from Roche to Lewis May 5, 1948, F.F. JLL Trustee 1947 Fund (1948), box 1 of 8, Board of Trustees Correspondence, 1946–71, Series II, Director's Records.

104. Minutes and Resolutions of the United Mine Workers of America Welfare and Retirement Fund of 1947, 4–6, contained in John L. Lewis's Motion to Dismiss suit brought by Ezra Van Horn, F.F. JLL Motion to Dismiss, Affidavit and Points and Authorities in Support, box 3 of 3, 1946, 1947 Fund Files, Series II, Director's Records. Tentative draft of Haskins and Sells Accounting Report for Apr. 8 to July 22, 1947, 3–4, F.F. Haskins and Sells—1946 Fund (Reports), box 1 of 2, 1946 Fund, Actuary and Insurance Company Data, 1947–48, Series II, Director's Records.

105. Minutes and Resolutions of the United Mine Workers of America Welfare and Retirement Fund of 1947, 6., contained in John L. Lewis's Motion to Dismiss suit brought by Ezra Van Horn, F.F. John L. Lewis Motion to Dismiss, Affidavit and Points and Authorities in Support, box 3 of 3; Letters to Lewis: UMWA Local 753, District 2, Apr. 1946; Local 762, undated; Local 5835, July 26, 1946; Local 7323, Nov. 3, 1947; F.F. 2, box 2 of 3, 1946, 1947 Fund Files, Series II, Director's Records.

106. Minutes and Resolutions of the United Mine Workers of America Welfare and Retirement Fund of 1947, 7, contained in John L. Lewis's Motion to Dismiss suit brought by Ezra Van Horn, F.F. JLL Motion to Dismiss, Affidavit and Points and Authorities in Support, box 3 of 3.

107. Ibid.

108. *Preliminary Report to United Mine Workers of America Welfare and Retirement Fund on Industrial Benefits,* Nov. 6, 1947, title page, F.F. T.-P.F.C. Incorporated, box 1 of 2, 1946 Fund, Actuary and Insurance Company Data, 1947–48, Series II, Director's Records.

109. J. H. Sherner, vice-president of Towers-Perrin, Forster, & Crosby, to Van Horn, Sept. 26, 1947.

110. *Report to the Bituminous Coal Operators on Welfare and Retirement Fund for Employees,* Mar. 12, 1948.

111. *Preliminary Report to United Mine Workers of America Welfare and Retirement Fund on Industrial Benefits,* 1.

112. Ibid. 2.

113. Ibid.

114. Ibid., 3.

115. Ibid.

116. Ibid., 3–4.

117. Ibid., 4.

118. Ibid.

119. Ibid., 5–6.

120. Ibid., 7.

121. Ibid.

122. *Report to the Bituminous Coal Operators on Welfare and Retirement Fund for Employees,* 5.

123. Ibid., 6–7.

124. Ibid.

125. *Employment and Training: Report to the President* (Washington: GPO, 1979), 323.

126. Murray W. Latimer, "Instructions Relating to Social Insurance Fact Finding," Nov. 1949, 270, F.F. 17, Instructions Relating to Social Insurance Fact Finding, Nov. 1949; "Report on Insurance and Pensions by Joint Committee on Insurance of the United States Steel Corporation, vol. 1., Insurance and Pension Programs of the United States Steel Corporation," May 1954, Part III, 2–7, F.F. 20, Insurance and Pension Programs, vol. 1, May 1954, box 68, David J. MacDonald Papers, Patee Library, Pennsylvania State Univ.

127. *Preliminary Report,* 3, *Report to the Bituminous Coal Operators,* 2, F.F. T-PFC Incorporated, box 1 of 2, 1946 Fund, Actuary and Insurance Company Data, 1947–48, Series II, Director's Records, Fund Papers.

128. Memo from Lewis to Roche, May 20 1948, F.F. JLL Trustee 1947 Fund (1948), box 1 of 8, Board of Trustees Correspondence, 1946–71, Series II, Director's Records.

129. *Minutes and Resolutions of the United Mine Workers of America Welfare and Retirement Fund of 1947,* 11, contained in John L. Lewis's Motion to Dismiss suit brought by Ezra Van Horn, F.F. JLL Motion to Dismiss, Affidavit and Points and Authorities in Support, box 3 of 3, 1946, 1947 Fund Files, Series II, Director's Records.

130. *In the District Court of the United States for the District of Columbia. Ezra Van Horn . . . v. John L. Lewis . . . and H. Styles Bridges,* 46, F.F. John L. Lewis, Trustee, 1947 Fund (1948), box 1 of 8, Board of Trustees Correspondence, 1946–71, Series II, Director's Records.

131. Ibid.

132. *Minutes and Resolutions of the United Mine Workers of America Welfare and Retirement Fund of 1947,* contained in John L. Lewis's Motion to Dismiss, F.F. JLL Motion to Dismiss, Affidavit and Points and Authorities in Support, box 3 of 3, 1946, 1947 Fund Files, Series II, Director's Records.

133. Ibid., 12–13.

134. Ibid., 14

135. Ibid., 33–37.

136. Ibid., 18.

137. Ibid., 17.

138. Joseph E. Finley, *The Corrupt Kingdom: The Rise and Fall of the United Mine Workers* (New York: Simon & Schuster, 1972), 180–81.

Chapter 2. The Struggle for Control

1. *Minutes and Resolutions of the United Mine Workers of America Welfare and Retirement Fund of 1947,* 18, contained in John L. Lewis's Motion to Dismiss suit brought by Ezra Van Horn, F.F. John L. Lewis Motion to Dismiss, Affidavit and Points and Authorities

in Support, box 3 of 3, 1946, 1947 Fund Files; Van Horn to Lewis, Mar. 16, 1948, F.F. Van Horn Murray, Operators Letters, box 2 of 8, Board of Trustees Correspondence, 1946–71, Series II, Director's Records, Fund Papers.

2. *In the District Court of the United States for the District of Columbia: United States of America, Plaintiff, v. International Union, United Mine Workers of America et al.*, Motion to Dissolve and Vacate Restraining Order, 2, F.F. Motion to Dissolve, Restraining Order Apr. 3, 1948, box 3 of 3, 1946, 1947 Fund Files, Series II, Director's Records.

3. Ibid.

4. Ibid.

5. Ibid.

6. Ibid.

7. Finley, *The Corrupt Kingdom,* 181.

8. Ibid.

9. Van Horn to Lewis, Mar. 16, 1948, F.F. Van Horn Murray Operator Letters, box 2 of 8, Board of Trustees Correspondence, 1946–71, Series II, Director's Records, Fund Papers.

10. Ibid.

11. Love, O'Neil, et al. to Lewis, Mar. 19, 1948, F.F. Van Horn Murray Operator Letters.

12. Ibid.

13. *In the District Court of the United States for the District of Columbia: United States of America, Plaintiff, v. International Union United Mine Workers of America, et al.*, Motion to Dissolve and Vacate Restraining Order, 2., F.F. Motion to Dissolve, Restraining Order Apr. 3, 1948, box 3 of 3, 1946, 1947 Fund Files, Series II, Director's Records.

14. Ibid., 2–3.

15. *Minutes and Resolutions of the United Mine Workers of America Welfare and Retirement Fund of 1947,* 19, contained in John L. Lewis's Motion to Dismiss suit brought by Ezra Van Horn, F.F. John L. Lewis Motion to Dismiss, Affidavit and Points and Authorities in Support.

16. See Robert Newman, *Owen Lattimore and the "Loss" of China* (Berkeley: Univ. of California Press, 1992), 173, 213.

17. Lewis to all district union presidents, Mar. 13, 1947 F.F. 8, box 1 of 3, 1946 Fund Files, Series II, Director's Records, Fund Papers.

18. *Minutes and Resolutions of the United Mine Workers of America Welfare and Retirement Fund of 1947,* 19, contained in John L. Lewis's Motion to Dismiss suit brought by Ezra Van Horn, F.F. John L. Lewis Motion to Dismiss, Affidavit and Points and Authorities in Support, box 3 of 3, 1946, 1947 Fund Files, Series II, Director's Records.

19. Statement of United States Senator H. Styles Bridges at the Meeting of the Trustees of the 1947 United Mine Workers of America Welfare and Retirement Fund, Apr. 12, 1948, F.F. Correspondence H. Styles Bridges, box 4 of 8, Board of Trustees Correspondence, 1946–71, Series II, Director's Records.

20. Ibid.

21. Ibid.

22. The minutes make no mention of this presentation; however, the study is dated April 11, 1948, the day of the first trustee meeting attended by Bridges.

23. Latimer Biography, F.F. Latimer, Murray W. Biographical Notes, box 1 of 2, 1946 Fund, Actuary and Insurance Company Data, 1947–48.

24. Memo to the Members of the Advisory Board of the Office of War Reconversion from Murray W. Latimer, undated, 1–6, F.F. Guaranteed Annual Wage, Government Studies, 1938–55, box 64, Research Dept. Office Files, United Steel Workers of America Papers, Patee Library, Pennsylvania State Univ.

25. Report of Murray W. Latimer to the Board of Trustees of the UMWA Welfare and Retirement Fund, Apr. 11, 1948, 1–2, F.F. Latimer Report, box 1 of 2, Actuary and Insurance Company Data 1946–48, Series II, Director's Records, Fund Papers.

26. Ibid., 3.

27. Ibid., 3–4.

28. Ibid., 5.

29. Ibid., 10.

30. Ibid., 12.

31. *Minutes and Resolutions of the United Mine Workers of America Welfare and Retirement Fund of 1947,* 20, contained in John L. Lewis's Motion to Dismiss suit brought by Ezra Van Horn, F.F. John L. Lewis Motion to Dismiss, Affidavit and Points and Authorities in Support, box 3 of 3, 1946, 1947 Fund Files, Series II, Director's Records.

32. Ibid.

33. Ibid., 21.

34. F. C. Schlundt to Van Horn, President Central National Bank of Cleveland, May 5, 1948; National Savings and Trust Company of Washington, D.C., to Van Horn, May 5, 1848; Van Horn to American Security and Trust, June 5, 1948, F.F. Correspondence E. Van Horn, box 2 of 8, Board of Trustees Correspondence, 1946–71, Series II, Director's Records.

35. Senator Bridges to Lewis, May 15, 1948, F.F. John L. Lewis Trustee 1947 Fund (1948), box 1 of 8, Board of Trustees Correspondence, 1946–71.

36. Lewis to F. C. Schlundt, President of the Central National Bank of Cleveland, May 24, 1948, F.F. Correspondence Senator Bridges, box 4 of 8, Board of Trustees Correspondence, 1946–71.

37. Senator Bridges to Lewis, May 15, 1948.

38. *In the District Court of the United States for the District of Columbia: Ezra Van Horn, . . . Petitioner v. John L. Lewis, . . . and H. Styles Bridges . . . ,* 1, F.F. John L. Lewis Trustee 1947 Fund (1948), box 1 of 8, Board of Trustees Correspondence, 1946–71.

39. Dubofsky and Van Tine, *John L. Lewis: A Biography,* 466–67.

40. *In the District Court of the United States for the District of Columbia: Ezra Van Horn, . . . Petitioner v. John L. Lewis, . . . and H. Styles Bridges . . . ,* 41, F.F. John L. Lewis,

Trustee 1947 Fund (1948), box 1 of 8, Board of Trustees Correspondence, 1946–71, Series II, Director's Records, Fund Papers.

41. Ibid., 21, 42–43.

42. Ibid., 47.

43. Memorandum of Law Relative to the Possible Personal Liability of H. Styles Bridges as "Neutral Trustee" of United Mine Workers of America Welfare and Retirement Fund, by Edward R. Hale, 8.

44. Ibid., 5.

45. Ibid.

46. *In the District Court of the United States for the District of Columbia: Ezra Van Horn, . . . Petitioner v. John L. Lewis, . . . and H. Styles Bridges, . . .* , 10.

47. Ibid., 10–12.

48. Ibid., 21.

49. Ibid., 46.

50. *John L. Lewis Affidavit to Judge Goldsborough in Response to Civil Action 1651–48,* 1– 3, F.F. John L. Lewis Motion to Dismiss, Affidavit and Points and Authorities in Support, box 3 of 3, 1946, 1947 Fund Files, Series II, Director's Records.

51. *In the District Court of the United States for the District of Columbia: Ezra Van Horn, . . . Petitioner v. John L. Lewis, . . . and H. Styles Bridges, . . .* , 79–80, F.F. John L. Lewis Trustee 1947 Fund (1948), box 1 of 8, Board of Trustees Correspondence, 1946–71, Series II, Director's Records.

52. Ibid., 82.

53. Ibid., 80, 86–87.

54. Board of Trustee Minutes of the United Mine Workers of America Welfare and Retirement Fund for 1946 (handwritten notes of meeting taken by F. Fitzgerald acting as Secretary).

55. Thurmond Diary, June 9, 1948, box 4, Walter Thurmond Papers.

56. Statement of Policy Made at Bituminous Wage Conference, June 9, 1948, 5, F.F. O'Neil Statement and Operators Resolutions for 1948 Retirement Plan June 9, 1948, Bituminous Wage Conference, box 2 of 2, 1946 Fund, Actuary and Insurance Company Data, 1947–48, Series II, Director's Records, Fund Papers.

57. National Coal Association, June 15, 1948, Industrial Bulletin No. 2563.

58. Thurmond Diary, June 23, 1948, box 4, Walter Thurmond Papers.

59. *A Chronology of the United Mine Workers of America Welfare and Retirement Fund between January 1, 1945, to April 26, 1951,* 8, Control Folder for A & M 2769, Fund Papers.

60. Dubofsky and Van Tine, *John L. Lewis: A Biography,* 483.

61. Pension Progress Report, 1, F.F. John L. Lewis Trustee 1947 Fund (1948), box 1 of 8, Board of Trustees Correspondence, 1946–71, Series II, Director's Records, Fund Papers.

62. Memo from Roche to Lewis, May 20, 1948.

63. Undated Memo from William L. P. Burke to Lewis on *Van Horn* vs. *Lewis,* F.F. Burke, William L. Memos and Letters, 1950 Fund, box 5 of 8, Board of Trustees Correspondence, 1946–71.

64. Ibid.

65. Bridges to Lewis, July 15, 1948, F.F. John L. Lewis Trustee 1947 Fund (1948), box 1 of 8, Board of Trustees Correspondence, 1946–71.

66. Edward R. Hale to Bridges, July 15, 1948.

67. Memo from Roche to Lewis, July 13, 1948, F.F. Actuaries Miscellaneous, JLL Memos, box 2 of 2, 1946 Fund, Actuary and Insurance Company Data, 1947–48, Series II, Director's Records.

68. Ibid.

69. Memo from Roche to Lewis, Oct. 28, 1948.

70. Memo from Roche to Lewis July 13, 1948.

71. Memo from Roche to Lewis, Oct. 28, 1948.

72. Ibid.

73. Ibid.

74. Report of Russel B. Reagh Submitted to Senator H. Styles Bridges, F.F. Actuarial Data (Senator Bridges), box 4 of 8, Board of Trustees Correspondence, 1946–71, Series II, Director's Records.

75. Ibid., 1.

76. Ibid., 8.; see also Stevens, *American Medicine and the Public Interest,* 8.

77. Report of Russel B. Reagh Submitted to Senator H. Styles Bridges, 10–12, F.F. Actuarial Data (Senator Bridges), box 4 of 8, Board of Trustees Correspondence, 1946–71, Series II, Director's Records, Fund Papers.

78. Ibid., 20.

79. Mayberry Report, 3, F.F. L. M. Mayberry Actuary, box 2 of 2, 1946 Fund, Actuary and Insurance Company Data, 1947–48, Series II, Director's Records.

80. Ibid., 2–3.

81. Memo from Roche to Lewis, Nov. 18, 1948, F.F. Actuaries Miscellaneous, JLL Memos.

82. Memo from Roche to Lewis, Dec. 6, 1948.

83. Memos from Roche to Lewis, Jan. 22, 1949, Feb. 28, 1949, Mar. 30, 1949, July 22, 1949, Aug. 8, 1949, F.F. John L. Lewis Trustee 1947 Fund 1949, 50 Correspondence, box 1 of 8, Board of Trustees Correspondence, 1946–71, Series II, Director's Records.

84. Senator Bridges to Roche, May 4, 1949, F.F. Correspondence H. Styles Bridges, box 4 of 8, Board of Trustees Correspondence, 1946–71.

85. Memo from Roche to Lewis, May 9, 1949, F.F. John L. Lewis Trustee 1947 Fund 1949, 50 Correspondence, box 1 of 8, Board of Trustees Correspondence, 1946–71.

86. Bridges to Lewis, Jan. 4, 1949, F.F. Correspondence H. Styles Bridges, box 4 of 8, Board of Trustees Correspondence, 1946–71.

87. Memo from Roche to Lewis, Mar. 30, 1949, F.F. John L. Lewis Trustee 1947 Fund 1949, 50 Correspondence, box 1 of 8, Board of Trustees Correspondence, 1946–71.

88. Statement of Trustee H. Styles Bridges at the Meeting of the United Mine Workers of America Welfare and Retirement Fund, Apr. 7, 1949, F.F. Correspondence H. Styles Bridges, box 4 of 8, Board of Trustees Correspondence, 1946–71.

89. Memo of a conversation between Senator Bridges, Miss Roche, and Val J. Mitch, July 27, 1949.

90. Thurmond Diary, July 5, 1949, box 4, Thurmond Papers.

91. Dubofsky and Van Tine, *John L. Lewis: A Biography,* 483–85.

92. Ibid.

93. Memo of a conversation between Senator Bridges, Miss Roche, and Val J. Mitch, July 27, 1949, F.F. Correspondence H. Styles Bridges, box 4 of 8, Board of Trustees Correspondence, 1946–71, Series II, Director's Records, Fund Papers.

94. Ibid.

95. Van Horn to Roche, Aug. 3, 1949, F.F. Correspondence Ezra Van Horn, box 2 of 8, Board of Trustees Correspondence, 1946–71.

96. Memo from Roche to Lewis, Oct. 27, 1948, F.F. CPA Report Memos (1950 and 1947 Funds).

97. Record of a meeting between Chairman Lewis and Joseph Moody, President of the Southern Coal Producers Association, held on Apr. 29, 1949, 11:15 A.M. to 12:15 P.M.

98. See letter sent to Lewis as Chairman of the Fund from West Virginia Coal & Coke Co., Sept. 20, 1949, Harlan Coal & Coke Co., Sept. 20, 1949, Pocahontas Fuel Co., undated, Warner Colliers Co., Sept. 20, 1949, F.F. Ezra Van Horn Correspondence.

99. Van Horn to Bridges, Sept. 16, 1949, F.F. Letters to or by Van Horn 1946 Fund.

100. Resolutions 26 and 27, Sept. 16, 1949, F.F. Correspondence Senator Bridges, box 4 of 8, Board of Trustees Correspondence.

101. Van Horn to Roche, Sept. 27, 1949, F.F. Letters to or by Van Horn 1946 Fund, box 2 of 8, Board of Trustees Correspondence, 1946–71.

102. Ibid.

103. Ibid.

104. *New York Times,* July 30, 1951.

105. Bridges to Roche, Sept. 27, 1949, F.F. Correspondence Senator Bridges, box 4 of 8, Board of Trustees Correspondence, 1946–71, Series II, Director's Records, Fund Papers.

106. Roche to Van Horn and Bridges, Oct. 5, 1949.

107. Bridges to Van Horn and Lewis, Oct. 24, 1949.

108. Lewis to Bridges, Oct. 27, 1949.

109. Van Horn to Bridges, Oct. 31, 1949.

110. Senator Bridges to Van Horn, Nov. 7, 1949, F.F. E. Van Horn Correspondence, box 2 of 8, Board of Trustees Correspondence, 1956–71.

111. Van Horn to Lewis, Aug. 25, 1949.

112. The United Mine Workers of America Welfare and Retirement Fund of 1947 Washington, D.C., Report for the Fiscal Year Beginning July 1, 1948, and ending June 30, 1949.

113. Van Horn to Lewis, Oct. 26, 1949.

114. Lewis to Van Horn, Oct. 27, 1949, Bridges to Van Horn, Nov. 7, 1949.

115. Van Horn to Coal Operators, Sept. 14, 1949, F.F. Letters to or by E. Van Horn.

116. Telegram from Lewis to Van Horn, Nov. 14, 1949, F.F. Correspondence E. Van Horn.

117. Biography of Charles I. Dawson, F.F. Correspondence Judge Dawson, box 3 of 8, Board of Trustees Correspondence, 1946–71. See also John W. Hevener, *Which Side Are You On? The Harlan County Coal Miners, 1931–1939* (Urbana: Univ. of Illinois Press, 1978).

118. See Hevener, *Which Side are You On?*

119. Telegram from Dawson to Roche, Nov. 23, 1949, F.F. Correspondence Judge Dawson, box 3 of 8, Board of Trustees Correspondence, 1946–71, Series II, Director's Records, Fund Papers.

120. Telegram from Dawson to Roche, Nov. 22, 1949.

121. Telegram from Lewis to Dawson, Nov. 23, 1949; Van Horn to Truman E. Johnson, Dec. 16, 1949.

122. *In the District Court of the United States for the District of Columbia, Charles I. Dawson, Individually, v. John L. Lewis, Individually,* 1–3, F.F. Dawson Suit, F.F. Correspondence Judge Dawson.

123. Ibid.

124. Ibid.

125. Ibid., 8.

126. Ibid., 14–15.

127. Bridges to Roche, Nov. 8, 1949; office memo of a phone conversation between Lewis and Senator Bridges, Bridges to Lewis, Nov. 22, 1949; press release Dec. 2, 20, 1949; Bridges to Lewis, Dec. 28, 1949; Lewis to Senator Bridges, Dec. 30, 1949; Senator Bridges to Lewis, Jan. 23, 1950; Senator Bridges to Lewis, Feb. 21, 1950; F.F. Correspondence Senator Bridges, box 4 of 8, Board of Trustees Correspondence, 1946–71.

128. *Indianapolis Times,* Nov. 13, 1949, Clipping, F.F. John L. Lewis Trustee Fund 1949, 50, box 1 of 8, Board of Trustees Correspondence.

129. Thurmond Diary, Dec. 7, 1949, box 4, Thurmond Papers.

130. Dubofsky and Van Tine, *John L. Lewis: A Biography,* 486–87.

131. Ibid., 488.

132. Dubofsky and Van Tine, *John L. Lewis: A Biography,* 489; Ploss, *A History of the Medical Care Program,* 27–28.

133. National Bituminous Coal Wage Agreement of 1950, 3, F.F. Contracts NBCWA 1950, box 1 of 2, Contracts, 1946–71, Series II, Director's Records, Fund Papers.

134. Ploss, *A History of the Medical Care Program,* 27–28.

135. Seltzer, *Fire in the Hole,* 63–64.

136. Dubofsky and Van Tine, *John L. Lewis: A Biography,* 496.

137. Thurmond Diary, Mar. 3, Mar. 5, 1950, box 4, Thurmond Papers.

138. Kruger Interview.

Chapter 3. Retreat and Advance

1. National Bituminous Coal Wage Agreement of 1950, 4, F.F. Contracts NBCWA 1950, box 1 of 2, Contracts, 1946–71, Series II, Director's Records, Fund Papers.

2. Ibid., 5.

3. Ezra Van Horn to John L. Lewis, Aug. 28, Sept. 18, and Sept. 19, 1950; telegram from Van Horn to Lewis, Sept. 22, 1950; John L. Lewis to Van Horn, Sept. 20, 1950; Val J. Mitch to Van Horn, Oct. 2, 1950, F.F. Correspondence, Ezra Van Horn, box 2 of 8, Board of Trustees Correspondence, 1946–71, Series II, Director's Records.

4. Lewis to Owen, Mar. 7, 1950; Owen to Roche and Lewis, Mar. 15, 1950; F.F. Charles A. Owen, Trustee 1950, box 6 of 8, Board of Trustees Correspondence, 1946–71.

5. Unsigned and undated notes by Owen.

6. Ibid.

7. Ibid.

8. Roche to "Nickie," June 19, 1950.

9. Ibid.

10. Ibid.

11. Letters from Roche to Lewis, Apr. 19, May 6, 1950, F.F. JLL Trustee 1950 Fund, box 1 of 8, Board of Trustees Correspondence, 1946–71.

12. Letters from Roche to Lewis, Apr. 19, May 6, 1950, F.F. JLL Trustee 1950 Fund, box 1 of 8; Owen to Roche, May 2, 1950, June 8, 1950, Sept. 26, 1950, Oct. 20, 1950, Jan. 21, 1951, Feb. 24, 1951, May 6, 1951, F.F. Charles A. Owen Trustee 1950, box 6 of 8, Board of Trustees Correspondence, 1946–71, Series II, Director's Records, Fund Papers; Finley, *The Corrupt Kingdom,* 163.

13. Finley, *The Corrupt Kingdom,* chap. 8, "The Fabulous Fund: Pioneering and Passivity," 178ff; Brit Hume, *Death and the Mines: Rebellion and Murder in the United Mine Workers* (New York: Grossman Publishers, 1971)

14. Newdorp Interview, Apr. 23, 1993.

15. Newdorp Interview, June 4, 1993; Interviews with Mr. Henry Daniels, hereafter referred to as Daniels Interview, Sept. 21, 1995; Interview with Dr. John Winebrenner

(hereafter referred to as Winebrenner Interview), Sept. 10, 1993; Kerr Interview; Kruger Interview; Interview with W. Philip Palmer (hereafter referred to as Palmer Interview), Oct. 4, 1993.

16. Kerr Interview; Palmer Interview.

17. Unsigned and undated notes by Owen, F.F. Charles A. Owen, Trustee, 1950, box 6 of 8, Board of Trustees Correspondence, 1946–71, Series II, Director's Records, Fund Papers.

18. Maier Fox, *United We Stand: The United Mine Workers of America, 1890–1990* (Washington, D.C.: United Mine Workers of America, 1990), 300–303.

19. Ibid., 303–34.

20. "Contract between the Coal Producers' Association of Illinois and the Progressive Mine Workers of America, District No. 1, in Effect 12:01 July 1, 1947, Expires, June 30, 1948," 84–85, F.F. A & M 2609, box 5, PMWA Printed Contracts, 1941–48, 1952, 1965, 1972, box 5, Series I, Minutes and Contracts, Progressive Mine Workers of America Papers, A & M 2609, West Virginia Collection.

21. "Contract between the Coal Producers' Association of Illinois and the Progressive Mine Workers of America, District No. 1, in effect 12:01 July 1, 1947, Expires June 30, 1948," 86; "General Agreement dated April 1, 1950, between Wisconsin Steel Coal Mines of International Harvester Company and the Progressive Mine Workers of America, District No. 4," 13; "Contract between the Coal Producers' Association of Illinois and the Progressive Mine Workers of America, District No. 1, Oct. 1, 1952," 81.

22. Letter to All Recording Secretaries of All Local Unions, from W. C. Bell and Earl Evans, Co-Trustees, Sept. 3, 1947, F.F. Circular, New Welfare and Retirement Fund Plan, Sept. 4, 1947, box 26, Series V, Office Files, Fund Papers.

23. Ibid.

24. John McCann, President, PMWA from E. E. Brill, vice-president, General American Life Insurance Company, June 17, 1948; H. R. Maples to John McCann, Assistant Manager, Group Service Section [General American Life Insurance Company], Aug. 5, 1948, F.F. Insurance Company Welfare, box 9, Series III, President's Office Files, 1947–49, Progressive Mine Workers of America Papers.

25. Memo from Roche to Lewis, May 23, 1950, F.F. JLL Trustee, 1950 Fund, box 1 of 8, Roche to "Nickie," June 19, 1950, F.F. Charles A. Owen, Trustee, 1950, box 6 of 8, Board of Trustees Correspondence, 1946–71, Correspondence, Series II, Director's Records, Fund Papers.

26. Lewis to Owen, Mar. 17, 1950, F.F. Charles A. Owen Trustee, 1950, box 6 of 8, Board of Trustees Correspondence; Memo from Roche to Lewis, Apr. 19, 1950, Owen to Lewis and Roche, Mar. 20, 1950, May 16, 1950, May 20, 1950, telegram from Owen to Roche, July 17, 1950, F.F. JLL Trustee, 1950 Fund, box 1 of 8, Board of Trustees Correspondence, 1946–71.

27. Statement by Charles A. Owen at Board of Trustees meeting, June 19, 1950, F.F. JLL Trustee, 1950 Fund, box 1 of 8, Board of Trustees Correspondence.

28. Roche to William E. Blizzard and A. O. Lewis, Jan. 10, 1951, F.F. JLL Medical and

Hospital District 17, Hospital and Medical Benefits, Hospital at Whitesville, 85 H.S. Data, Benefits in Compensation Cases, box 6 of 11, United Mine Workers of America Correspondence, 1946–72, Series II, Director's Records.

29. Clipping from the *Johnstown Democrat,* undated, F.F. Charles A. Owen Trustee, 1950 Fund, box 6 of 8, Board of Trustees Correspondence, 1946–71, Series II, Director's Records.

30. Roche to John Owen, F.F. JLL Medical and Hospital District 17, Hospital and Medical Benefits, Hospital at Whitesville, 85 H.S. Data, Benefits in Compensation Cases, box 6 of 11, United Mine Workers General Correspondence, Series II, Director's Records.

31. Paul F. Clark, *The Miners' Fight for Democracy: Arnold Miller and the Reform of the UMWA* (Ithaca: Cornell Univ. Press, 1981), viii, see UMWA district map; Finley, *The Corrupt Kingdom,* 109–11.

32. Finley, *The Corrupt Kingdom,* 109–11.

33. Ibid.

34. Palmer Interview.

35. Kerr Interview; Winebrenner Interview, Sept. 10, 1993.

36. Memo from Robert Kaplan to Roche, Dec. 29, 1950, F.F. JLL Medical and Hospital District 17, Hospital and Medical Benefits, Hospital at Whitesville, 85 H.S. Data, Benefits in Compensation Cases, box 6 of 11, United Mine Workers of America Correspondence, 1946–72, Series II, Director's Records, Fund Papers.

37. Ibid.

38. Memo from Dr. Draper to Roche, Jan. 2, 1951.

39. Finley, *The Corrupt Kingdom,* 129.

40. Roche to Blizzard and A. O. Lewis, Jan. 10, 1951, F.F. JLL Medical and Hospital Benefits, Hospital at Whitesville, 85 H.S. Data, Benefits in Compensation Cases, box 6 of 11, United Mine Workers of America Correspondence, 1946–72, Series II, Director's Records, Fund Papers.

41. Prepared chronology of events concerning difficulties with District 17 over form 85 H.S.

42. Winebrenner Interview, Sept. 10, 15, 1993; Alan Brinkley, "For Their Own Good," *New York Review of Books* 41, no. 10 (May 29, 1994): 40–43.

43. Taped interview with Robert Boylan, July 16, 1993. Mr. Boylan was a senior member of the Fund's staff who worked in the program's pension division. A veteran member of that staff, he eventually served for a few months as the Fund's director during the early 1970s.

44. Chronology, record of January 1951 meeting between Roche and A. O. Lewis, F.F. JLL Medical and Hospital Benefits, Hospital at Whitesville, 85 HS Data, Benefits in Compensation Cases, box 6 of 11, United Mine Workers Correspondence, 1946–72, Series II, Director's Records, Fund Papers.

45. Ibid.

46. Ibid.

47. A. O. Lewis to John Owens, June 18, 1951.

48. Chronology, record of January 1951 meeting between Roche and A. O. Lewis.

49. A. O. Lewis to John Owens, June 18, 1951.

50. Roche to Owens, Aug. 23, 1951.

51. Ibid.

52. William E. Blizzard to Roche, Sept. 26, 1951.

53. "Report on Insurance and Pensions by Joint Committee on Insurance and Pensions of the United Steel Workers of America and the United States Steel Corporation," May 1954, Part II, 2, F.F. Insurance and Pension Programs (vol. 1), May 1954, box 68, David J. MacDonald Papers, Labor Archives, Patee Library, Pennsylvania State Univ.

54. I. S. Falk (preliminary draft), "Health Insurance Experience in the Basic Steel Industry: A Summary of Utilization and Costs Under the Blue Cross and Blue Shield Contracts of the United States Steel Corporation for Employees and Their Dependents, 1953–1962," dated Aug. 1963, 4, F.F. Medical Care 1963–65, National Can Corporation, 1960–69, National Labor Management Panel, 1962–67, box 6, Frank Pollara Papers, Patee Library, Pennsylvania State Univ.

55. *Statistical Abstract, Welfare and Retirement Fund, United Mine Workers of America,* Jan. 10, 1949, 29–30, F.F. Statistical Abstracts, 1947 Fund July 1, 1948 through June 30, 1950, box 1 of 7, Statistical Reports, 1952–74, Series V, Office of Research and Statistics, Fund Papers.

56. Ibid.

57. *Statistical Abstract, Welfare and Retirement Fund, United Mine Workers of America,* Dec. 10, 1951, 11, *Statistical Abstract, Welfare and Retirement Fund, United Mine Workers of America,* Dec. 10, 1952, 11–12.

58. Ibid.

59. National Coal Association, *Bituminous Coal Facts, 1960* (Washington: National Coal Association, 1960), 80.

60. See *Proceedings of the Forty-second Convention United Mine Workers of America, 1956,* 124–27; and *Proceedings of the Forty-third Convention United Mine Workers of America, 1960,* 32–38.

61. Roche to all district presidents, Jan. 29, 1953, Binder "Pension Regulations," box 6 of 7, Administrative Files, 1948–71, Series II, Director's Records, Fund Papers.

62. Union to all district presidents, Jan. 25, 1954.

63. Roche to all district presidents, Jan. 29, 1953, Binder "Pension Regulations," box 6 of 7, Administrative Files, 1948–71, Series II, Director's Records, Fund Papers.

64. *Proceedings of the Forty-second Convention United Mine Workers of America, 1956,* vol. 2, 12, 14, 17, 18, 21.

65. A. O. Lewis to Roche, Mar. 25, 1953. F.F. JLL Medical and Hospital District 17, Hospital and Medical Benefits, Hospital at Whitesville, 85 H.S. Data, Benefits in Compensation Cases,

box 6 of 11, United Mine Workers of America Correspondence, 1946–72, Series II, Director's Records, Fund Papers.

66. Undated Notice from Local 677 calling for a meeting to be held on March 29, 1953, Notice from Local 6013 to all District 17 locals, Mar. 17, 1953, F.F. JLL Medical and Hospital District 17, Hospital and Medical Benefits, Hospital at Whitesville, 85 H.S. Data, Benefits in Compensation Cases, box 6 of 11, United Mine Workers of America Correspondence, 1946–72, Series II, Director's Records, Fund Papers.

67. Ibid.

68. *Statistical Abstract, Welfare and Retirement Fund, United Mine Workers of America,* Jan. 10, 1955, 11–13, box 1 of 7, Statistical Reports, Series V, Office of Research and Statistics.

69. Daniel Fox, *Health Policies, Health Politics,* 18; Charles E. Rosenburg, ed., *Caring for the Working Man: The Rise and Fall of the Dispensary, An Anthology of Sources* (New York, 1989), 1–3.

70. Dr. John Winebrenner to author, Aug. 17, 1993. Dr. Winebrenner was the Fund's area medical administrator for Knoxville, Tennessee, and later Louisville, Kentucky. A specialist in public health, Dr. Winebrenner served in the military for six years. During this time, Winebrenner met Dr. Draper when he was a member of General Eisenhower's staff, overseeing all hospitals in the European Theater of Military Operations. It was because of this connection that Dr. Winebrenner was later recruited for the Fund by Dr. Draper.

71. Dr. John D. Winebrenner to author, Aug. 17, 1993.

72. *A Medical Survey of the Bituminous Coal Industry,* 170, box 1 of 1, Bibliography-UMWA Health and Retirement Fund, Fund Papers.

73. Wysang and Williams, *Health Services for Miners,* 16; Remarks Given by Dr. Warren Draper at the Groundbreaking Ceremonies at Man Memorial Hospital, Man, West Virginia, Oct. 31, 1953, F.F. MMHA Publicity-Publications, box 2 of 5, Construction/Administration, Series IV, Miners' Memorial Hospital Association.

74. *A Medical Survey of the Bituminous Coal Industry,* 171–75, 176–80, 180–86, box 1 of 1, Bibliography-UMWA Health and Retirement Fund.

75. Ibid., 227.

76. Ibid.

77. Brochure, Raleigh-Boone Hospital Association, Inc., Whitesville, West Virginia, 1–2, F.F. JLL Medical and Hospital District 17, Hospital and Medical Benefits, Hospital at Whitesville, 85 H.S. Data, Benefits in Compensation Cases, box 6 of 11, United Mine Workers of America Correspondence, 1946–72, Series II, Director's Records.

78. Ibid., 1.

79. Ibid., 2.

80. Dr. Draper to Roche, July 19, 1950.

81. Telegram from Owen to Blizzard, May 3, 1949.

82. John L. Lewis to Blizzard, May 3, 1949.

83. Blizzard to John L. Lewis, May 6, 1949.

84. Remarks Given by Dr. Warren Draper at Groundbreaking Ceremonies at Man Memorial Hospital, Man, West Virginia, Oct. 31, 1953, F.F. MMHA Publicity, Publications, box 2 of 5, Construction/Administration, Series IV, Miners' Memorial Hospital Association.

85. Fox, *Health Policies, Health Politics,* 86–87, 153–56.

86. Remarks Given by Dr. Warren Draper at Groundbreaking Ceremonies at Man Memorial Hospital, Man, West Virginia, Oct. 31, 1953, F.F. MMHA Publicity, Publications, box 2 of 5, Construction/Administration, Series IV, Miners' Memorial Hospital Association, Fund Papers.

87. Newdorp Interview, Jan. 22, 1993.

88. Ibid.

89. Ibid.

90. Ibid.

91. Dr. John D. Winebrenner to author, Aug. 17, 1993.

92. Dr. John Morrison to Dr. John Newdorp, Oct. 5, 1951, F.F. MMHA General Correspondence, Loans, box 6 of 11, United Mine Workers of America Correspondence, 1946–72, Series II, Director's Records; Excerpts from the Minutes of the 12th Meeting of the Board of Trustees of the United Mine Workers of America Welfare and Retirement Fund of 1950, 35, F.F. Minutes of Welfare and Retirement Fund Trustees Meetings with Respect to the Miners' Memorial Hospital Association, box 2 of 7, Legal and Contracts, Series IV, Miners Memorial Hospital Association, Fund Papers.

93. Excerpts from the Minutes of the 12th Meeting of the Board of Trustees of the United Mine Workers of America Welfare and Retirement Fund of 1950, 35, F.F. Minutes of Welfare and Retirement Fund Trustees Meetings with Respect to the Miners' Memorial Hospital Association, box 2 of 7, Legal and Contracts, Series IV, Miners Memorial Hospital Association, Miners Memorial Hospital Association.

94. Ibid., 32–40.

95. Roche to Lewis, Sept. 14, 1951, F.F. JLL Miners' Memorial Hospital Association, box 6 of 8, Board of Trustees Correspondence, 1946–71, Series II, Director's Records.

96. Ibid.

97. E. L. Carey to Dr. Mott, Dec. 17, 1952, F.F. MMHA Finance, box 2 of 7, Legal and Contracts, Series IV, Miners' Memorial Hospital Association.

98. Memo from Val J. Mitch to E. L. Carey, Mar. 10, 1955; memo to Val J. Mitch from E. L. Carey, Mar. 28, 1955.

99. Excerpts from the Minutes of the 12th Meeting of the Board of Trustees of the United Mine Workers of America Welfare and Retirement Fund of 1950, 55, F.F. Minutes of Welfare and Retirement Fund Trustee Meetings with Respect to the Miners' Memorial Hospital Association.

100. National Coal Association Industry Bulletin, Nov. 6, 1951, 3, F.F. JLL Trustee (1950 Fund), 1950, 1951, box 1 of 8, Board of Trustees Correspondence, 1946–71, Series II, Director's Records.

101. See Frederick W. Mott, M.D., and Milton I. Roemer, M.D., *Rural Health and Medical Care* (New York: McGraw, Hill, 1948).

102. *Building America's Health,* vol. 2, *America's Health Status, Needs, and Resources* (Washington: GPO, 1952), 307.

103. Ibid., 308.

104. Dr. John Winebrenner to author, Aug. 17, 1993.

105. Newdorp Interview, Dec. 3, 1992; John Newdorp, M.D., "Planning for Medical Care in the Post-War Period: With Reference to Alabama," rpt. from *Journal of the Medical Association of the State of Alabama* (Feb./Mar./Apr. 1945): 3–5, F.F. "Reprint of Article, Post-War Medical Plan, *Journal of the Medical Association of the State of Alabama,"* box 1, Private Papers of Dr. John Newdorp.

Dr. Newdorp worked for the Fund for about thirty years, ultimately rising to the post of executive medical officer. He kept a small archive of papers dealing with his career in public medicine, which he generously gave me access to in the summer of 1993. Dr. Newdorp currently resides in Wayne, Pennsylvania, and plans to eventually turn his papers over to the West Virginia Collection of West Virginia University. The author wishes to thank Dr. Newdorp for his help and interest in this project.

106. *Health and Medical Care in Alabama: An Inventory of Conditions and a Proposed Hospital Plan* (Alabama State Planning Board in Cooperation with the Post-War Planning Commission of the Medical Association of Alabama and the Alabama Dept. of Health, May 1945), iii–iv, F.F. Health and Medical Care in Alabama (St. Hosp Report, 1945, May).

107. Fox, *Health Policies, Health Politics,* 18ff.

108. Newdorp Interview, Jan. 22, 1993.

109. Ibid.

110. Booklet for the Dedication of Three State Network of Ten Memorial Hospitals, June 2, 1956, 5, box 2 of 7, Legal and Contracts, Series IV, Miners' Memorial Hospital Association, Fund Papers.

111. Newdorp Interviews, Jan. 22, 1993.

112. Remarks Given by Dr. Warren Draper at the Groundbreaking Ceremonies at Man Memorial Hospital, Man, West Virginia, Oct. 31, 1953, F.F. MMHA Publicity, Publications, box 2 of 5, Construction/Administration, Series IV, Miners' Memorial Hospital Association, Fund Papers.

113. Minutes of the 7th Meeting of the Memorial Hospital Association of Kentucky, Inc., Nov. 7, 1953, 3–5, Memorial Hospital Association of Kentucky, Inc., binder 2, vol. 1, Minutes, 1951–54.

114. Questionnaire of the General Memorial Hospital Project, Kentucky, West Virginia, and

Virginia, Oct. 9, 1952, Miners' Memorial Hospital Association, Inc., binder vol. 7, exhibits 1, 1951–56.

115. Telegram to Lewis, Nov. 13, 1952, memo from Roche to Lewis, Oct. 3, 1952, F.F. JLL-MMHA, box 6 of 11, United Mine Workers of America Correspondence, Series II, Director's Records.

116. Finley, *The Corrupt Kingdom,* 104; memo from Roche to Lewis, Jan. 1, 1952, F.F. JLL-MMHA, box 6 of 11, United Mine Workers of America Correspondence, Series II, Director's Records, Fund Papers.

117. Memo from Roche to Lewis, Feb. 18, 1953, F.F. JLL-MMHA, box 6 of 11, United Mine Workers of America Correspondence, Series II, Director's Records, Fund Papers.

118. Ibid.

119. Dubofsky and Van Tine, *John L. Lewis: A Biography,* 448–49.

120. Summary of Conference between Val J. Mitch, Dr. Mott, Miss Roche, and Personal Representative of the Jones Construction Company, Mar. 16, 1953, F.F. JLL-MMHA, box 6 of 11, United Mine Workers of America Correspondence, Series II, Director's Records, Fund Papers.

121. Ibid.

122. Ibid.

123. Undated handwritten notes by Roche, F.F. JLL-MMHA.

124. Excerpts from the Minutes of the 12th Meeting of the Board of Trustees of the United Mine Workers of America Welfare and Retirement Fund of 1950, 32–40, F.F. Minutes of Welfare and Retirement Fund Trustee Meetings with Respect to the Miners' Memorial Hospital Association, box 2 of 7, Legal and Contracts, Series IV, Miners' Memorial Hospital Association.

125. Minutes of the 24th Meeting of the Memorial Hospital Association of Kentucky, Inc., Jan. 26, 1956, 3–7, binder 2, vol. 3, Minutes 1955–58.

126. Minutes of the 11th Meeting of the Memorial Hospital Association of Kentucky, Inc., 5.

127. Ibid., 7–8.

128. Ibid., 12–17.

129. Ibid., 17–19.

130. Memo from E. Todd Wheeler to Dr. Draper, Oct. 12, 1954, F.F. MMHA Reports by E. Todd Wheeler, box 1 of 5, Construction/Administration, Series IV, Miners' Memorial Hospital Association.

131. Memo from Roche to Draper, Oct. 12, 1954, F.F. MMHA Schedule of Hospital Completion.

132. Memo from Wheeler to Draper, June 9, 1955; memo from Wheeler to Draper, Oct. 12, 1954; memo from Wheeler to Val J. Mitch, Apr. 8, 1955, F.F. MMHA Reports by E. Todd Wheeler.

133. Memo from Wheeler to Draper, June 16, 1955; memo from Wheeler to Draper, July 8, 1955.

134. Memo to Draper, July 12, 1954, F.F. JLL-MMHA, box 6 of 11, United Mine Workers of America Correspondence, Series II, Director's Records.

135. Report by Roche, July 17, 1954; Ralph Courtly, District 50 Regional Director, to A. D. Lewis, July 17, 1954; memo from Draper to Roche, undated; memo from Roche to John L. Lewis, July 13, 1954.

136. Memo from Roche to Lewis, July 17, 1954; memo from Dr. Mott to Dr. Draper, July 12, 1954.

137. Memo from Ralph Courtly to A. D. Lewis, July 17, 1954.

138. "Memorial Hospital Project, Harlan and Williamson Groups, May 26, 1952, E. Todd Wheeler, Hospital Consultant," F.F. MMHA Proposed Building Program, box 1 of 5, Construction/Administration, Series IV, Miners' Memorial Hospital Association.

139. Memo from Wheeler to Draper, Apr. 23, 1956.

140. Memo from Newdorp to Draper, Oct. 21, 1952.

141. Memo from Wheeler to Draper, Aug. 25, 1954.

142. Memo from Wheeler to Draper, Nov. 2, 1954.

143. Ibid.

144. Memo from Wheeler to Draper, June 2, 1955; memo from Mott to Draper, June 7, 1955; J. A. Jones Construction Company to Mott, Aug. 8, 1955.

145. Memo from Wheeler to Draper, Aug. 18, 1955; memo from Wheeler to Draper, Sept. 3, 1955.

146. Memo from Wheeler to Draper, Aug. 20, 1955.

147. Memo from Wheeler to Draper, Sept. 3, 1955; memo from Wheeler to Draper, Oct. 6, 1955, F.F. Proposed Building Program.

148. Memo from Mott to Draper, Nov. 23, 1955, F.F. Reports by E. Todd Wheeler.

149. Memo from Mott to Draper, Dec. 8, 1955.

150. Memo from Wheeler to Draper, Oct. 15, 1955.

151. Memo from Mott to Draper, Jan. 31, 1956.

152. "A Hospital Chain 250 Miles Long," excerpt editorial from the *Engineering News-Record,* Mar. 17, 1955, box 2 of 5, Construction/Administration, Series IV, Miners' Memorial Hospital Association.

153. Clipping from the *Morgantown (W.Va.) Dominion News* Sept. 6, 1956, F.F. MMHA Publicity Publications.

154. Draper to D. W. Wallace, Aug. 28, 1956; Draper to Vest, Aug. 31, 1956.

155. Vest to Draper, Sept. 5, 1956, clipping from the *Charleston (W.Va.) Gazette,* Sept. 18, 1956.

156. Program for the Rip Van Winkle Foundation for July 2, 1956.

157. "High Quality Care Is the Keystone," address given by Dr. Mott at the Fourth Annual Group Health Institute of the Cooperative Health Federation of America.

158. Speech given by Moody quoted in a memo from Roche to Draper, Sept. 14, 1953.

159. Clipping of an editorial entitled "Between Us," *Pineville (Ky.) Sun,* Sept. 10, 1953.

160. Jane Jacobs to the *Pineville (Ky.) Sun,* Oct. 20, 1953.

161. See dedication booklet for the Three State Network of Ten Memorial Hospitals.

162. Ibid., 1.

Chapter 4. The Noble Failure

1. *United Mine Workers Journal,* June 1, 1956.

2. "A Pension Plan in Trouble," *U.S. News and World Report,* Apr. 30, 1954, 77–80.

3. Robert J. Meyers, "Experience of the UMWA Welfare and Retirement Fund," *Industrial Labor Relations Review,* Oct. 1956, 96.

4. Ibid.

5. Ibid.

6. See the following: Ben Pearse, "Milestones for Miners: Pensions, Welfare, Hospitals," *The Nation,* Aug. 28, 1954, 170–72; "How Welfare Fund Aids Miners," *U.S. News and World Report,* Oct. 15, 1948, 49–50; "John L. Lewis's 250-Mile Chain of Hospitals," *U.S. News and World Report,* June 29, 1956, 98–100; "Lewis's Billion-Dollar Fund," *U.S. News and World Report,* Sept. 23, 1955, 108–13; "Miners' Bonanza Free Medical Care, from the Cradle to the Grave," *Scholastic,* Oct. 20, 1948, 13; "Miners' Hospital Chain," *Fortune,* Mar. 1954, 70; "Miners' Welfare," *Newsweek,* Sept. 7, 1953, 76–79; "Welfare Fund Keeping Solvent," *U.S. News and World Report,* Sept. 10, 1954, 113–14; Ira Wolfert, "Miners' Fund, a Tribute to Good Management," *Readers' Digest,* Sept. 1956, 173–80; "I'm Awful Thankful: United Mine Workers' Welfare and Retirement Fund," *Time,* Aug. 15, 1949, 17.

7. Remarks of Charles Owen, Industry Trustee at the Dedication of the Miners Memorial Hospitals, box 6 of 8, Board of Trustees Correspondence, 1946–71, Series II, Director's Records, Fund Papers.

8. Ibid.

9. Ibid.

10. *United Mine Workers Journal,* Jan. 1, 1956.

11. Ibid., Feb. 1, 1956.

12. Newdorp Interview, Mar. 26, 1993.

13. See Richard Mulcahy, "Working Against the Odds: Josephine Roche, the New Deal, and the Drive for National Health Insurance," *Maryland Historian* 25, no. 2 (Fall–Winter 1994): 1–21.

14. Remarks of Charles Owen at the Dedication of Miners Memorial Hospitals, box 6 of 8, Board of Trustees Correspondence, 1946–71, Series II, Director's Records, Fund Papers.

15. Ibid.

16. Memo dated Mar. 6, 1958, box 7 of 8, Board of Trustees Correspondence, 1946–71.

17. Bituminous Coal Operators Association Release, Mar. 10, 1958.

18. Memo from Draper to Medical Health and Hospital Service, Miners' Memorial Hospital Association, Dec. 5, 1956, F.F. MMHA Integration of Operation and Medical Service of the Fund, box 5 of 12, Clinical Operations Series IV, Miners' Memorial Hospital Association.

19. Newdorp Interview, Dec. 10, 1992; Winebrenner Interview, Sept. 10, 1993; Kerr Interview; Palmer Interview; taped interview with Warfield Garson, M.D., July 14, 1993 (hereafter referred to as Garson Interview).

20. Dr. Asa Barnes to Draper, July 26, 1956, Dr. John Winebrenner to Draper, Nov. 19, 1956, notes of a conference between Draper and Drs. Barnes, Marshal, and Riheldaffer on Memorial Hospitals, Responsibilities of Hospital Staffs, Nov. 1956, box 5 of 12, Clinical Operations, Series IV, Miners' Memorial Hospital Association, Fund Papers.

21. Memo from Draper to Medical Health and Hospital Service Miners' Memorial Hospital Association, Dec. 5, 1956, box 5 of 12, Clinical Operations.

22. Ibid.

23. Ibid.

24. Mott to Draper, 1953, F.F. A-II-2 Relationship between Fund Medical Service and the MMHA, box 6 of 16, Subject Files, Series IV, Miners' Memorial Hospital Association.

25. Record of two-day joint conference between the MMHA and the Area Medical Administrators, May 23, 24, 1955.

26. Dr. Asa Barnes to Dr. Draper, Aug. 8, 1956.

27. F. G. Schmidt to Roche, May 20, 1958, F.F. F. G. Schmidt, Trustee 1950 Fund (1958), box 7 of 8, Board of Trustees Correspondence, 1946–71, Series II, Director's Records.

28. Starr, *Social Transformation of American Medicine,* 213.

29. *Report of a Survey of the Group Practice Medical Centers Serving Beneficiaries of the United Mine Workers of America Welfare and Retirement Fund in the Pittsburgh Area,* Oct. 12–17, 1957, F.F. A-II-3, box 6 of 16, Subject Files, Series IV, Miners' Memorial Hospital Association, Fund Papers.

30. Wysang and Williams, *Health Services for Miners,* 7–10.

31. Dr. Barnes to Draper, Aug. 8, 1956, F.F. Integration of the MMHA and the Medical Service of the Fund, box 5 of 12, Clinical Operations, Series IV, Miners' Memorial Hospital Association, Subject Files, Fund Papers.

32. Ibid.

33. Notes of a conference between Draper and Drs. Barnes, Marshal, and Riheldaffer on Memorial Hospitals, Responsibilities of Hospital Staffs, Nov. 1956, Winebrenner to Draper, Nov. 19, 1956, Asa Barnes to Draper, Aug. 8, 1956.

34. Memo from Draper to Medical Service and Hospital Service, Miners' Memorial Hospital Association, Dec. 5, 1956.

35. Dr. Mott to Draper, Dec. 7, 1956, Jan. 22, 1957.

36. Wysang and Williams, *Health Services for Miners,* 7.

37. Dr. Mott to Draper, Dec. 7, 1956, Jan. 22, 1957, F.F. Integration of MMHA and Area Offices, box 5 of 12, Clinical Operations, Series IV, Miners' Memorial Hospital Association, Fund Papers.

38. Dr. Mott to Draper, Jan. 22, 1957.

39. Memo from Dr. Morrison to Draper, Nov. 18, 1956.

40. Ibid.

41. Winebrenner Interview, Sept. 15, 1993.

42. "Third Party Medicine in Kentucky," paper presented by Dr. Asa Barnes before the Jefferson County Medical Society, Oct. 19, 1959, 4–5, F.F. A-II-6, Relations with Medical Societies, box 6 of 16, Subject Files, Series IV, Miners' Memorial Hospital Association, Fund Papers.

43. Riska, *Power, Politics, and Health,* 31.

44. Merle Wertz to Dr. Asa Barnes, Dec. 7, 1955, F.F. A-II-6 Relations with Medical Societies, box 6 of 16, Subject Files, Series IV, Miners' Memorial Hospital Association, Fund Papers.

45. Ibid.

46. Memo from Dr. Newdorp to Draper, Oct. 28, 1959.

47. Memo from Dr. Newdorp to Draper, Oct. 28, 1959; memo from Dr. Keeny to Dr. Meade, Mar. 18, 1957.

48. Winebrenner Interview, Sept. 10, 1993.

49. Asa Barnes to Richard M. Shecker, M.D., President of the Kentucky State Medical Association, Oct. 18, 1956, F.F. A-II-6 Relations with Medical Societies, box 6 of 16, Subject Files, Series IV, Miners' Memorial Hospital Association, Fund Papers.

50. Francis Hodges to Asa Barnes, May 2, 1956.

51. Ibid.

52. Ibid.

53. Ibid.

54. Dr. Winebrenner to Draper, Nov. 19, 1956, F.F. MMHA Integration of Operation of the MMHA and the Medical Service of the Fund, box 5 of 12, Clinical Operations, Series IV, Miners' Memorial Association.

55. Statement of Kentucky delegation, Carl Fortune, M.D., F.F. A-II-6, Relations with Medical Societies, box 6 of 16, Subject Files, Series IV, Miners' Memorial Association.

56. Ibid.

57. "The Hearing," Mar. 27, 1958, F.F. A-II-6.1, Dr. Fred Zuspan vs. Floyd County.

58. Letter to Dr. Newdorp from Dr. Meade, Jan. 29, 1959.

59. An example is Kentucky House Bill 343. Introduced during the 1958 session, it would have barred the Fund from operating in the state; see "In House, Regular Session, 1958, House Bill No. 343."

60. Dr. McGuiness to Dr. Mott, June 29, 1956; memo to Roche from Draper, undated, F.F. A-II-6.

61. "Before the Council of the Kentucky State Medical Association: Matter of Frederick P.

Zuspan, M.D., McDowell, Kentucky, Statement on Appeal on Dec. 12, 1957, from Denial of Membership by Floyd County Society," F.F. A-II-6.1, *Dr. Fred Zuspan vs. Floyd County.*

62. Ibid.

63. Ibid.

64. J. R. Sanford, M.D., to Zuspan, Aug. 13, 1957, F.F. Zuspan and the KSMA.

65. Law firm Hanson, Hazard, and Lynch to Zuspan, Nov. 1, 1957.

66. Zuspan to W. B. Troutman, M.D., Nov. 13, 1957.

67. "Before the Council of the Kentucky State Medical Association: Matter of Dr. Frederick Zuspan, M.D."

68. Ibid.

69. Ibid.

70. Ibid.

71. "The Hearing," Mar. 27, 1958. According to Zuspan's statements here, the hospitals did allow their patients a free choice of physicians.

72. Excerpt from the *Washington Report on Medical Sciences,* no. 555, Feb. 10, 1958.

73. Asa Barnes to Walter O'Nan, Feb. 19, 1958.

74. In the House of Delegates of the State of Kentucky, Regular Session, 1958, Regular Session, House Bill No. 343, Monday, Feb. 17, 1958.

75. Ibid.

76. Editorial entitled "This Is Wise 'Medical' Advice to Physicians," clipping from Jan. 23, 1960, edition of the *Louisville Courier,* F.F. A-II-6, Relations with Medical Societies.

77. Union and Fund teletype, Aug. 1, 1958; Dr. Sanford to Zuspan.

78. Dr. Sanford to Zuspan.

79. Dr. Gordon Meade to Newdorp, Jan. 29, 1959.

80. Ibid.

81. Newdorp Interview, Jan. 22, 1993.

82. Memo from Gordon Meade to file, July 9, 1959, F.F. A-II-6, Relations with County Medical Societies, box 6 of 16.

83. Memo from Draper to Dr. Newdorp, Oct. 28, 1959.

84. Memo from Gordon Meade to file, Oct. 21, 1959; letter to Drs. Clark, Judd, Wishman, and Owens, Nov. 28, 1959.

85. Meade to J. H. Westmer, Dec. 31, 1959.

86. Draft letter to chairman of the board of trustees of the American Medical Association, F.F. A-II-7, Society of Medicine of Pike County.

87. Ibid.

88. Ibid.

89. Undated form letter announcing Dr. Butler's lecture for Nov. 2, 1960, Newdorp to Draper, May 19, 1960; Dr. Leslie Falk to Draper, undated.

90. Meeting of the Associate Administrators, Hospital Administrators, Chiefs of Clinical Services, Medical Administrators' Staff, Sept. 27, 1956, F.F. A-III-3.1, box 7 of 16.

91. Ibid.

92. Annual Report for 1958 from Dr. John Newdorp, Medical Administrator, to Dr. John Morrison, President of the Miners' Memorial Hospital Association, F.F. Annual Reports, box 4 of 16.

93. Gordon Meade to Dr. E. D. Rosenfeld, F.F. A-VI-5.2, E. D. Rosenfeld & Associates, box 14 of 16.

94. Annual Report for 1957, from Dr. John Newdorp, Medical Director, to Dr. John Morrison, President of the Miners' Memorial Hospital Association, F.F. Annual Reports, box 4 of 16.

95. Annual Report for 1958, from Dr. John Newdorp, Medical Director, to Dr. John Morrison, President of the Miners' Memorial Hospital Association.

96. Annual Report for 1960, from Dr. John Newdorp, Medical Administrator, to Dr. John Morrison, President of the Miners' Memorial Hospital Association.

97. Dr. Newdorp to Dr. Morrison, June 12, 1962, exhibit 149, vol. 12, exhibits no. 6., Minutes and Resolutions of the Miners' Memorial Hospital Association, Series IV, Miners' Memorial Hospital Association.

98. Ibid.

99. Ibid.

100. Ibid.

101. American Hospital Association, Hospital Rate Questionnaire (1956), American Hospital Association, Survey of Employee Starting Salaries and Benefits, F.F. A-IV-6, box 12 of 16, Subject Files, Series IV, Miners' Memorial Hospital Association.

102. For Agenda: General Administrative Committee, May 23, 1957 F.F. A-III-4.1, Agenda and Minutes, box 7 of 16.

103. Annual Report for 1957, from Dr. John Newdorp, Medical Director, to Dr. John Morrison, President of the Miners' Memorial Hospital Association, F.F. Annual Reports, box 4 of 16.

104. Miners' Memorial Hospital Association, Minutes and Exhibits of the Board of Directors, exhibits 3, 1956–60, vol. 9, Series IV, Miners' Memorial Hospital Association.

105. Annual Report for 1959, from Dr. John Newdorp, Medical Administrator, to Dr. John Morrison, President of the Miners' Memorial Hospital Association, F.F. Annual Reports, box 4 of 16, Subject Files, Series IV, Miners' Memorial Hospital Association.

106. "Miners' Memorial Hospital Association Fiscal Year Consolidated Statement of Receipts and Disbursements," F.F. A-VI-5.2, E. D. Rosenfeld & Associates, box 14 of 16.

107. Rayburn to Newdorp, June 28, 1958, F.F. A-V-1 Utilization of Beds, box 12 of 16.

108. Wysang and Williams, *Health Services for Miners,* 8.

109. Letter to Dr. Mott, Apr. 29, 1957, F.F. A-V-I Utilization of Beds, box 12 of 16, Subject Files, Series IV, Miners Memorial Hospital Association, Fund Papers.

110. Memo from W. R. McNutt to Draper, May 14, 1956.

111. Report on a meeting with local unions on Sept. 20, 1957, F.F. A-II-5, Relations with Local Unions, box 6 of 16.

112. Memo from Newdorp to David Mc.L. Greeley and Robert Black, F.F. Measures to Increase Utilization of Memorial Hospitals, box 12 of 16.

113. Ibid.

114. "Pikeville Memorial Hospital, Memorial Hospital Association, Pikeville, Kentucky, Information for the Patient."

115. Memo from Newdorp to Dresdener, Nov. 13, 1958.

116. Memo from Dresdener to Newdorp, Nov. 14, 1958; memo to Newdorp from A. H. Robertson, Nov. 14, 1958.

117. Newdorp to A.H. Robertson, Dec. 5, 1958.

118. A. H. Robertson to Newdorp, Nov. 14, 1958, Newdorp to A. H. Robertson, Dec. 5, 1958.

119. Newdorp to A. H. Robertson, Dec. 5, 1958.

120. Memo from Roche to Draper, Dec. 1, 1958.

121. Ibid.

122. Ibid.

123. Memo from Newdorp to Draper, Dec. 18, 1958.

124. Ibid.

125. Ibid.

126. Report from Morrison to Draper, July 11, 1958, F.F. A-II-2 Relationship of the Fund's Medical Service to the MMHA, box 6 of 16.

127. Ibid.

128. Ibid.

129. Ibid.

130. "Chaos in the Coal Fields," The Nation, Jan. 26, 1963, 70–72.

131. Albert Reese, The Economics of Trade Unions (Chicago: Univ. of Chicago Press, 1989), 197.

132. Ibid.

133. Notes of a conference held between Miss Roche, Dr. Draper, Mitch, Ryan, officers of the MMHA, and all area administrators on Apr. 13, 1960, F.F. Revised Regulations, Policy, and Procedure, (Conferences), box 2 of 7, Administrative Files, Series II, Director's Records, Fund Papers.

134. Notes of a conference held between Miss Roche, Dr. Draper, Dr. Newdorp, Dr. Striet, Mr. Ryan, Henry Daniels, Harold Meyers, and Mrs. Lea, Feb. 4–6 and 9–12, F.F. A-V-I Utilization of Beds, box 12 of 16, Subject Files, Series IV, Miners Memorial Hospital Association.

135. Notice from administrator of Norton General Hospital to his staff, letter to St. Mary's Hospital, Jan. 10, 1961.

136. Notes of a meeting between Roche, Draper, Newdorp, and the MMHA's leadership, and

all Fund area administrators, Apr. 13, 1960, F.F. Revised Regulations, Policy, and Procedure, (Conferences), box 2 of 7, Administrative Files, Series II, Director's Records.

137. Undated and unsigned memo, F.F. MMHA, Utilization of Hospitals, box 6 of 12, Clinical Operations; memo from Draper to all area administrators, Aug. 25, 1961, F.F. A-V-I, Utilization of Beds, box 12 of 16, Subject Files, Series VI, Miners' Memorial Hospital Association.

138. Memo from Draper to Roche, F.F. Utilization of Hospitals, box 6 of 12, Clinical Operations, Series IV, Miners' Memorial Hospital Association.

139. Factual material put together for Dr. Draper in preparation for a meeting with Miss Roche, Dec. 29, 1961, F.F. MMHA, Utilization of Beds, box 6 of 12, Clinical Operations; Roche to Draper, Oct. 12, 1961, box 12 of 16, Subject Files, Series IV, Miners' Memorial Hospital Association.

140. Memo from Draper to the file, Jan. 5, 1962; memo to Draper from Roche, Mar. 22, 1962, F.F. MMHA Utilization of the Hospitals, box 12 of 16, Subject Files, Series IV, Miners' Memorial Hospital Association.

141. Memo from Newdorp to Draper, Aug. 14, 1962; memo from Draper to Newdorp, Aug. 15, 1962.

142. Undated notes of a radio broadcast made from a station in Huntington, West Virginia, referring to an Associated Press release, F.F. Transfer of Hospitals, box 13 of 16.

143. Unsigned memo to Roche, Oct. 1962.

144. Ibid.

145. Memo from Harold Ward to Newdorp, Dec. 15, 1961, F.F. Use of Hospitals, box 6 of 12, Clinical Operations, Series IV, Miners' Memorial Hospital Association.

146. Letters from Greeley to Newdorp, Sept. 13, 1962, and Sept. 21, 1962, F.F. Transfer of Hospitals, Greeley to Newdorp, Sept. 21, 1962, F.F. A-VI-1, Prospective Purchasers, box 13 of 16, Subject Files, Series IV, Miners' Memorial Hospital Association.

147. Harry M. Caudill, *Night Comes to the Cumberlands: A Biography of a Depressed Area,* with a foreword by Stewart L. Udall (Boston: Little, Brown, & Co., 1962; paperback ed., Boston: Atlantic Monthly Press, 1963), 212.

148. Draper to John Wishman, Special Assistant to Gov. B. T. Combs, Nov. 2, 1962; Wishman to Draper, Oct. 31, 1962; public statement of Governor Combs, F.F. A-VI-2, State of Kentucky and Governor Combs' Meeting, box 13 of 16, Subject Files, Series IV, Miners' Memorial Hospital Association, Fund Papers.

149. Memo from Asa Barnes to Draper, Dec. 14, 1962.

150. Undated memo to file on governor's meeting.

151. Dr. Newdorp's handwritten notes of the governor's meeting, Jan. 11, 1963.

152. Undated memo to file on the governor's meeting; Dr. Newdorp's handwritten notes on the governor's meeting, Jan. 11, 1963.

153. For a description of this rivalry, see Caudill, *Night Comes to the Cumberlands,* 206–15.

154. See F.F. A-VI-1, Prospective Purchasers, box 13 of 16, Subject Files, Series IV, Miners'

Memorial Hospital Association, Fund Papers. This file contains all of the correspondence with prospective buyers, and a typed report that lists all of them and the problems encountered. Judging from this correspondence and the report, the Fund's problem was that none of the possible buyers were willing to pay what the hospitals were worth. At the same time, several of the interested parties would not guarantee that the hospitals would continue to be used for their intended purpose. Aside from the Presbyterian Mission Board, the only potential buyer who could have offered a reasonable price, and would have kept the institutions working as hospitals, was the Kaiser Health Plan.

155. Memo from Draper to Roche, Jan. 4, 1963, information requested from the UMWA Welfare and Retirement Fund for the Kaiser Health Plan Inc.

156. "Private Welfare State in Trouble," *U.S. News and World Report* 53, Dec. 3, 1962; see also "One Pension Plan Where Things Are Going from Bad to Worse," *U.S. News and World Report* 53, Mar. 25, 1963, 121–23. The second article deals with massive cuts made in the separate welfare fund for anthracite coal miners.

157. Dan Wakefield, "In Hazard," in *Appalachia in the Sixties,* ed. Daniel S. Wall and John B. Stephenson (Lexington: Univ. Press of Kentucky, 1972), 23.

158. Rev. McMaster Kerr to UMWA Washington Office, Oct. 31, 1962, Roche to Kerr, Nov. 2, 1962, F.F. A-VI-5.1, Presbyterian Church, box 13 of 16, Subject Files, Series IV, Miners Memorial Hospital Association, Fund Papers.

159. Undated and unsigned report on first contacts with Board of National Missions, United Presbyterian Church, U.S.A., F.F. A-VI-1, Prospective Purchasers.

160. Memo from Dr. Newdorp to Blackendecker, F.F. A-VI-5.2, E. D. Rosenfeld & Associates, box 14 of 16, Subject Files.

161. Memo from Dr. Newdorp to Dr. Rosenfeld, Mar. 4, 1963; memo from R. E. Selwyn to Dr. Rosenfeld, Mar. 13, 1963; memo from E. L. King to Dr. Rosenfeld, Mar. 22, 1963.

162. Memo from Dr. Newdorp to Dr. Rosenfeld, May 10, 1963, Miners' Memorial Hospital Association Fiscal Year Consolidated Statement of Receipts and Disbursements, appendix 13.

163. Pamphlet "U.S. Department of Commerce, Area Redevelopment Administration, Washington, D.C.," June 9, 1963, F.F. A-VI-3, Outside Financing Possibilities and By-Laws for Community Hospital.

164. Finley, *The Corrupt Kingdom,* 195.

165. Memo from Harold W. Ward to Roche, Apr. 16, 1963, F.F. A-VI-3, Outside Financing Possibilities & By-Laws for Community Hospital, box 13 of 16, Subject Files, Series IV, Miners' Memorial Hospital Association, Fund Papers.

166. Newdorp Interview, Mar. 17, 1993.

167. Ibid.

168. Finely, *The Corrupt Kingdom,* 196–97.

169. Newdorp Interview, Mar. 17, 1993.

170. Starr, *Social Transformation of American Medicine,* 368–70, 381–87; taped interview with Domanic Raino, Sept. 8, 1993 (hereafter referred to as Raino Interview). Mr. Raino is cur-

rently an investment counselor, overseeing portfolios amounting to $20 million in value. An expert in medical economics, he originally worked for Blue Cross–Blue Shield. Later, Mr. Raino went to work for the Fund in its Washington office.

171. *Compendium: Appalachian Regional Health Care,* special issue (Summer 1995): 16–17.

172. Dr. John D. Winebrenner to the author, Aug. 16, 1993.

173. Ibid.; Winebrenner Interview, Sept. 10, 15, 1993.

174. Newdorp Interview, Jan. 22, 1993.

Chapter 5. The National Conflict

1. Newdorp Interview, Dec. 10, 1992, June 4, 1993; Daniels Interview, Sept. 21, 1995; Kerr Interview.

2. *United Mine Workers Journal,* Aug. 1, 1947.

3. Ibid., Apr. 1, 1947.

4. Ibid., Aug. 1, 1947.

5. Ibid., Mar. 15, 1947.

6. Ibid., Aug. 1, 1947.

7. See Derickson, *Black Lung,* chap. 5, "To Bits," 87–111.

8. Memos from Roche to Lewis, Apr. 24, 1948, and May 19, 1948, F.F. JLL Medical and Hospital, Dr. Sayers Memorandums, box 6 of 11, United Mine Workers of America Correspondence, 1946–72, Series II, Director's Records, Fund Papers.

9. Memos from Roche to Lewis, Mar. 29, 1948, May 18, 1948.

10. Memo from Roche to Lewis, May 19, 1948.

11. Memos from Roche to Lewis, Mar. 29, 1948, May 18, 1948.

12. Newdorp Interview, Dec. 10, 1992; Kerr Interview.

13. *United Mine Workers Journal,* Sept. 1, 1948.

14. Kerr Interview.

15. Ploss, *A History of the Medical Care Program,* 53.

16. Kerr Interview.

17. Memo from Draper to Roche, Nov. 1, 1948, F.F. AMA Council on Industrial Health, 1948 and 1949, box 6 of 52, Subject Files, Series III, Executive Medical Officer, Fund Papers.

18. Winebrenner Interview, Sept. 10, 1993, Palmer Interview, Garson Interview, Raino Interview.

19. Kerr Interview; Newdorp Interview, Dec. 10, 1992.

20. Dr. Cecil A. Z. Sharp to Draper, Aug. 8, 1949; Dr. S. B. Brinkley to Draper, July 31, 1949, F.F. Office of the Director Records, MMHS Correspondence, 1947 Fund Area

Reports, box 1 of 4, Medical, Hospital, and Health Service Correspondence, Series II, Director's Records, Fund Papers.

21. Dr. S. B. Brinkley to Dr. Draper, July 31, 1949; Dr. Allen Koplin to Draper, Aug. 31, 1949.

22. Dr. Allen Koplin to Dr. Draper, Aug. 16, 1949.

23. Dr. Loin Kerr to Dr. Draper, Aug. 19, 1949.

24. Dr. Cecil A. Z. Sharp to Dr. Draper, Aug. 8, 1949.

25. Dr. Loin Kerr to Dr. Draper, Aug. 19, 1949.

26. Ibid.

27. Dr. Dorsey to Dr. Draper, Aug. 11, 1949.

28. "Trip Report—Visit to Rehabilitation Wards of New York Hospitals, July 15–16, 1949 (Dr. Draper)," F.F. JLL Medical and Hospital, Memos and Correspondence, box 6 of 11, United Mine Workers of America Correspondence, 1946–72.

29. Dr. Howard Rusk to Dr. Draper, Mar. 13, 1956.

30. Newdorp Interview, Dec. 10, 1992.

31. Carlton Jackson, *The Dreadful Month,* foreword by Harry M. Caudill (Bowling Green, Ohio: Bowling Green Univ. Popular Press, 1982), 28; William Graebner, *Coal-Mining Safety in the Progressive Period: The Political Economy of Reform* (Lexington: Univ. Press of Kentucky, 1976), 6–7; see also William Graebner, "Coal Mining Safety: National Solutions in the Progressive Period" (Ph.D. diss., Univ. of Illinois, 1970), 4–6.

32. Newdorp Interview, Dec. 10, 1992.

33. Edward D. Berkowitz, "and the Emergence of Rehabilitation Medicine," *Historian* 43, no. 4 (Aug. 1981): 530–31.

34. Berkowitz, "The Federal Government," 533; Newdorp Interview, Dec. 10, 1992.

35. Memo from Dr. Sayers to Roche, June 28, 1948, F.F. Office of the Director Records, 1946–71, MHHS Correspondence—Rehabilitation, 1948, box 1 of 4, Medical, Hospital, and Health Service Correspondence, Series II, Director's Records, Fund Papers.

36. Memo from Thomas Ryan to Francis Fitzgerald, May 26, 1948; Memo to Roche from Dr. Sayers, May 29, 1948.

37. Memo from Dr. Draper to Val J. Mitch, Apr. 29, 1952, F.F. Special Centers, box 29 of 52, Subject Files, Series III, Executive Medical Officer.

38. Kenneth E. Pohlman, "Rehabilitation of the Severely Disabled: UMWA Welfare and Retirement Fund Experience," 445, Rpt. from *Journal of Public Health* (Apr. 1953), F.F. Office of the Director Records, MMHS Correspondence, 1947 Fund Area Reports, box 1 of 4, Medical, Hospital, and Health Service Records.

39. Memo from Pohlman to Roche, July 9, 1948, F.F. Office of the Director Records, 1946–71, MHHS Correspondence, Rehabilitation, 1949–61.

40. Dr. Rusk to Dr. Draper, Mar. 13, 1956, F.F. Office of the Director Records, 1946–71, Medical, MHHS Correspondence, Rehabilitation, Kabat-Kaiser.

41. Ibid.

42. Ibid.

43. Dr. Draper to All Area Medical Administrators, May 20, 1949, F.F. Rehabilitation (1 of 2 folders), box 21 of 21, Health Care Delivery, Series III, Executive Medical Officer.

44. Report by Dr. John Morrison and Dr. William H. Timer, Sept. 9, 1949.

45. Ibid.

46. Ibid.

47. Ibid.

48. Ibid.

49. Ibid.

50. Ibid.

51. Ibid.

52. Dr. Draper to Dr. Morrison, Oct. 18, 1948.

53. Report from Pohlman to Harmon Kelly on Successful Rehabilitation Cases, Nov. 9, 1951, F.F. Office of the Director Records, 1946–71, Rehabilitation, Case Studies, box 4 of 4, Medical, Hospital, and Health Service Correspondence, Series II, Director's Records.

54. Pohlman, "Rehabilitation of the Severely Disabled," 445–46, F.F. Office of the Director Records, MMHS Correspondence, 1947 Fund Area Reports, box 1 of 4.

55. Petition to Lewis from a meeting of miner patients at the Kabat-Kaiser Institute, Sept. 27, 1947, F.F. Office of the Director Records, MMHS Correspondence, Rehabilitation Kabat-Kaiser.

56. Undated copy of a telegram from miner patients at Vallejo, California, with transmittal memo to Roche, Mar. 9, 1950.

57. Memo from Dr. Herman Kabat to Lewis, July 3, 1950, F.F. JLL Medical and Hospital, Memos and Correspondence, Re: Hospital and Med. Care and Center Rehabilitation, box 6 of 11, United Mine Workers of America Correspondence, Series II, Director's Records.

58. "Proposed Policy and Procedure for Rehabilitation Services for Guidance of Area Medical Administrators/Vocational Rehabilitation," by Kenneth Pohlman, June 30, 1949, F.F. Rehabilitation, General, UMWA Health and Retirement Funds, box 21 of 21, Health Care Delivery, Series III, Executive Medical Officer.

59. Dr. Draper to All Area Medical Administrators, July 11, 1951, F.F. Rehabilitation (1 of 2 folders).

60. Ibid.

61. Ibid.

62. Ibid.

63. Dr. Howard Rusk to Draper, Mar. 13, 1956, F.F. Office of the Director Records, MMHS Correspondence, Rehabilitation, Kabat-Kaiser, box 1 of 4, Medical, Hospital, and Health Service Correspondence, Series II, Director's Records.

64. Pohlman, "Rehabilitation of the Severely Disabled," 449.

65. Dr. Draper to All Area Medical Administrators, July 22, 1953, F.F. Special Centers, General, box 29 of 52, Subject Files, Series III, Executive Medical Officer.

66. Memo from Draper to Roche, June 1, 1953, F.F. Rehabilitation (1 of 2), box 21 of 21, Health Care Delivery, Series III, Executive Medical Officer.

67. Ibid.

68. Drafts of Draper to Roche, Feb. 17, 1956, F.F. Rehabilitation (2 of 2).

69. Ibid.

70. Ibid.

71. Ibid.

72. Memo from Draper to Roche, Feb. 20, 1956.

73. Memo from Dr. Draper to Dr. Morrison and Staff, Feb. 20, 1956.

74. Draper to all Area Medical Administrators, Mar. 10, 1961.

75. Ibid.

76. Newdorp Interview, Dec. 10, 1992.

77. *A Medical Survey of the Bituminous Coal Industry (The Boone Report),* see 115–36; 165–93, box 1 of 1, Bibliography, UMWA Health and Retirement Fund, Fund Papers.

78. "The Medical Care Program of the United Mine Workers of America Welfare and Retirement Fund," by Warren F. Draper, 7, presented at the New England Hospital Assembly, Hotel Statler, Mar. 25, 1958, box Addendum, July 1981, Annual Reports and Misc. Medical Staff Publications, Gift of Yale Univ. Library.

79. Winebrenner Interview, Sept. 10, 15, 1993; Palmer Interview.

80. Stevens, *American Medicine and the Public Interest,* 417–18.

81. Mott and Roemer, *Rural Health and Medical Care,* 152.

82. Ibid., 156.

83. Ibid., 167.

84. Ibid., 172.

85. Ibid., 182–85.

86. Kerr Interview; Warren F. Draper, "Conference on Medical Care in the Bituminous Coal Mining Area: Views and Suggestions," rpt. with additions from *Journal of the American Medical Association* 151 (Mar. 7, 1953): 848–49, in "Medical Hospital Problems in the Bituminous Coal Mining Area: Report of a Conference Sponsored by the Committee on Medical Care for Industrial Workers of the Council on Medical Service and the Council on Industrial Health," Charleston, W.Va., Sept. 6–7, 1952 (rpt. from *Journal of the American Medical Association* [Jan. 31, 1953]: 23–25), F.F. C-X-2 Newdorp, John, MD 1953–54, box 1, Private Papers of John Newdorp.

87. Winebrenner Interview, Sept. 10, 1993.

88. *Suggested Guide to Relations between State and County Medical Societies and the United Mine Workers of America Welfare and Retirement Fund* (hereafter referred to as *Suggested Guide*), 1958, 8, F.F. American Medical Association, Committee on Medical Care for Industrial Workers, 1957-1958-1960, box 7 of 52 Subject Files, Series III, Executive Medical Officer, Fund Papers.

89. "Problems of the United Mine Workers of America Welfare and Retirement Fund in Providing Medical Care to Its Beneficiaries," by Warren F. Draper, 2, F.F. American Medical Association Meetings in 1957, box 12 of 52.

90. Memo from Draper to Roche, Nov. 11, 1948, F.F. AMA Council on Industrial Health, box 6 of 52.

91. Memo from Draper to Roche, Dec. 4, 1948.

92. Clipping of article entitled "Should Industry Back Compulsory Federal Health Insurance?"

93. "Problems of the United Mine Workers of America Welfare and Retirement Fund in Providing Medical Care for Its Beneficiaries," by Warren Draper, 2, F.F. American Medical Association Meetings in 1957.

94. Draper to Dr. Ernest E. Irons, F.F. American Medical Association, Joint Committee for Coordination of Medical Activities, box 17 of 52.

95. Letters from Dr. Irons to Draper, Dec. 30, 1949, and Jan. 6, 1950.

96. Outline of a speech given by Draper at Annual Conference on Medical Health Service at the Palmer House, Chicago, Feb. 5, 1950, F.F. AMA Council on Industrial Health, box 6 of 52.

97. Ibid.

98. Wysang and Williams, *Health Services for Miners,* 8.

99. Kerr Interview

100. See "The Impact of Changes in Health Care Coverage Provided by the United Mine Workers of America Health and Retirement Funds in West Virginia Primary Care Clinics and Multi-Specialty Clinics Having Extensive Miner Case Loads," final report, Bettina T. Durmaskin, Ronald C. Althouse, William Wyant, and Edward Bosnar, unpublished report, West Virginia Univ., Dept. of Community Medicine, Office of Health Services Research, 1982 (hereafter referred to as West Virginia Clinic Report).

101. Wysang and Williams, *Health Services for Miners,* 7.

102. Outline of a speech given by Draper at Annual Conference on Medical Health Service at the Palmer House, Chicago, Feb. 5, 1950, F.F. AMA Council on Industrial Health, box 6 of 52, Subject Files, Series III, Executive Medical Officer, Fund Papers.

103. Ibid.

104. Draper to Dr. Carl Peterson, Jan. 5, Feb. 12, 1951, F.F. AMA Dr. Draper (Correspondence), box 39 of 52.

105. Draper to Dr. Peterson, Feb. 12, 1951.

106. Dr. John D. Winebrenner to author, Aug. 1993.

107. Report from Dr. Draper to Miss Roche, Feb. 12, 1952, F.F. American Medical Association Survey, May 25, 1952, box 13 of 52, Subject Files, Series III, Executive Medical Officer, Fund Papers.

108. Ibid.

109. Ibid.

110. Ibid.

111. Memo from Draper to Drs. Barnes, Winebrenner, Falk, Marshal, and Riheldaffer, Apr. 11, 1952, box 13 of 52, "Medical Hospitals in the Bituminous Coal Mining Areas of Kentucky-Tennessee-West Virginia, Preliminary Study to Survey Extent of Problems," 2, F.F. Council on Medical Service, UMW Survey Report, box 7 of 52, Subject Files, Series III, Executive Medical Officer.

112. Memo from Draper to Drs. Barnes, Winebrenner, Falk, Marshal, and Riheldaffer, Apr. 11, 1952, box 13 of 52, Subject Files, Series III, Executive Medical Officer.

113. "Medical Hospitals in the Bituminous Coal Mining Areas of Kentucky-Tennessee-West Virginia, Preliminary Study to Survey Extent of Problems," 5, F.F. Council on Medical Service, UMW Survey Report, box 7 of 52.

114. Ibid., 5–6.

115. Ibid.

116. Ibid.

117. Ibid., 7–8.

118. Ibid., 9–12.

119. Ibid., 8–9.

120. Ibid.

121. "Problems of the United Mine Workers of America Welfare and Retirement Fund in Providing Medical Care to Its Beneficiaries, 2–5, F.F. American Medical Association Meetings in 1957, box 12 of 52.

122. Conference on Medical Care in the Bituminous Coal Mining Areas, Charleston, W.Va., Sept. 6–7, 1952, 3–4, F.F. American Medical Association, Committee on Health Care for Industrial Workers, box 17 of 52.

123. Fox, *Health Policies, Health Politics*, 45–49.

124. "Problems of the United Mine Workers of America Welfare and Retirement Fund in Providing Medical Care to Its Beneficiaries," by Warren F. Draper, 4–8, F.F. American Medical Association Meetings in 1957, box 12 of 52, Subject Files, Series III, Executive Medical Officer, Fund Papers.

125. Kingsbury, *Health in Handcuffs*, 61–62.

126. Daniels Interview, Sept. 21, 1995.

127. Allen Koplin, "Retainer Payment for Physician Services," 4–5, box Addendum, Annual Reports and Misc. Medical Staff Publications, July 1981, Gift Yale Univ. Library, Fund Papers.

128. Ibid., 3.

129. Ibid., 10–12.

130. Winebrenner Interview, Sept. 10, 1993.

131. Kingsbury, *Health in Handcuffs*, 35.

132. William A. Massie, *Medical Services for Rural Areas* (Cambridge: Harvard Univ. Press, 1957), 17ff.

133. Allen Koplin, "Retainer Payment for Physician Services," 10–12, box Addendum, Annual Reports, Misc. Medical Staff Publications, Gift Yale Univ. Library, Fund Papers.

134. Massie, *Medical Services for Rural Areas,* 11–12.

135. Winebrenner Interview, Sept. 15, 1993.

136. Ibid.

137. "Report of Group III, Medical and Hospital Facilities," F.F. AMA Charleston Conference, Sept. 13–14, 1953, 2 of 2, Reports of Groups I, II, III, IV, and V, box 13 of 52, Subject Files, Series III, Executive Medical Officer, Fund Papers.

138. Report of Survey Team to the Committee on Medical Care for Industrial Workers of the Council on Medical Service and Industrial Health, American Medical Association, Apr. 15–16, 1953, 2, F.F. American Medical Association, Council on Industrial Health, box 17 of 52.

139. Ibid.

140. Ibid.

141. Ibid., 3–5.

142. Telegram from Dr. Dorsey to Dr. C. M. Peterson, Apr. 10, 1953.

143. "Report of Survey Team to the Committee on Medical Care for Industrial Workers of the Councils on Medical Service and Industrial Health, American Medical Association, Apr. 15–16, 1953, 2, 11.

144. Ibid., 12

145. Ibid., 10

146. Dr. Draper to all area administrators, Apr. 6, 1954, F.F. American Medical Association, General 1952–55, box 6 of 52.

147. Draper to all area administrators, Dec. 30, 1954.

148. Ibid.

149. Draper to Dr. George Lull, Dec. 9, 1954.

150. Ibid.

151. Dr. William A. Sawyer to Draper, Apr. 26, 1955.

152. Resolutions of the Pennsylvania and West Virginia Delegations to the House of Delegates of the American Medical Association, June 1955 meeting held in Atlantic City.

153. Resolution of the Pennsylvania Delegation to the House of Delegates of the American Medical Association, June 1955 meeting.

154. *Report of the Fourth Conference on Medical Care in the Bituminous Coal Mine Area,* Charleston, W.Va., May 6, 1956, 9, box Addendum, 1981, July 9: Annual Reports 1952–79, and Misc. Medical Staff Publications, Gift, Yale Univ. Library, Fund Papers.

155. Ibid., 9–10.

156. Ibid.

157. "Agreement between the Medical Service, UMWA Welfare and Retirement Fund and the Medical Society of the State of Pennsylvania," F.F. Agreement, UMWA Welfare and

Retirement Fund and the Medical Society of the State of Pennsylvania, box 40 of 52, Subject Files, Series III, Executive Medical Officer.

158. Ibid.

159. Ibid.

160. Wysang and Williams, *Health Services for Miners,* 20; "Agreement between the Medical Service, UMWA Welfare and Retirement Fund and the Medical Society of the State of Pennsylvania," F.F. Agreement, UMWA Welfare and Retirement Fund and the Medical Society of the State of Pennsylvania, box 40 of 52, Subject Files, Series III, Executive Medical Officer, Fund Papers.

161. "Agreement between the Medical Service, UMWA Welfare and Retirement Fund and the Medical Society of the State of Pennsylvania," F.F. Agreement, UMWA Welfare and Retirement Fund and the Medical Society of the State of Pennsylvania, box 40 of 52, Subject Files, Series III, Executive Medical Officer, Fund Papers.

162. "Problems of the United Mine Workers of America Welfare and Retirement Fund in Providing Medical Care to Its Beneficiaries," by Warren F. Draper, 5, F.F. American Medical Association, Meetings in 1957, box 12 of 52.

163. Ibid.

164. Ibid.; see also Report of the Meeting of the House of Delegates of the American Medical Association, San Francisco, June 23–26, 1958, F.F. AMA General, box 5 of 52.

165. Report of the Meeting of the House of Delegates of the American Medical Association, San Francisco, June 23–26, 1958.

166. Ibid.

167. Statement of Pittsburgh Area Administrator Leslie A. Falk to Medical Advisory Committee, Medical Service, UMWA Welfare and Retirement Fund, meeting of Mar. 1–2, 1957, see appendix 3, F.F. AMA Summit Meeting, Oct. 17, 1958, Publications and Reference Material, box 12 of 52.

168. Ibid., 1–2, 7.

169. Undated letter submitted by S. M. Fleeger et al., petition to the Medical Society of the State of Pennsylvania.

170. Letter to Draper from Dr. Dudley P. Walker.

171. "Minutes of the One Hundred Sixth Annual Session [of the House of Delegates of the Medical Society of the State of Pennsylvania]," *Pennsylvania Medical Journal* 60, no. 2 (Feb. 1957): 242–49, 267–71.

172. "Problems of the United Mine Workers of America Welfare and Retirement Fund in Providing Medical Care to Its Beneficiaries," by Warren Draper, 6, F.F. American Medical Association Meetings in 1957, box 6 of 52, Subject Files, Series III, Executive Medical Officer, Fund Papers.

173. Draper to Dr. William A. Sawyer, Jan. 9, 1957, F.F. American Medical Association, Committee on Medical Care for Industrial Workers, 1957, 1958–59, box 7 of 52.

174. Ibid.

175. Ibid.

176. Ibid.

177. "Monopoly Power as Exercised by Labor Unions," 30–31, see also American Medical Association Secretary's Letter to Members, Mar. 20, 1957, F.F. American Medical Association Correspondence, box 39 of 52, Subject Files.

178. Draper to Dr. William Sawyer, Jan. 23, 1957, F.F. American Medical Association Committee on Medical Care for Industrial Workers, box 7 of 52.

179. Committee on Medical Care for Industrial Workers, Chicago meeting, Mar. 21–22, 1957, questions presented to AMA Special Committee Mar. 21 and 22 by Dr. Draper, F.F. American Medical Association, Committee on Medical Care for Industrial Workers, 1957–1958–1960.

180. *Suggested Guide,* 7.

181. Ibid., 6.

182. Ibid., 3–4.

183. Minutes of the Meeting of the Committee on Medical Care for Industrial Workers, 15.

184. Minutes of the Meeting of the Committee on Medical Care for Industrial Workers, June 4, 1957.

185. Ibid.

186. Ibid.

187. "The Quest of the United Mine Workers of America Welfare and Retirement Fund for the Best Medical Care Obtainable for Its Beneficiaries," by Warren Draper, 13.

188. Draper to Dr. William Sawyer, Sept. 18, 1957.

189. Clipping from the *Pittsburgh Post-Gazette,* Sept. 18, 1957.

190. Dr. B. Holland to Draper, Jan. 23, 1958.

191. Clipping from the *Minnesota Union Advocate,* undated, published by the St. Paul AFL-CIO Trade Assembly, entitled "That Humane AMA," F.F. American Medical Association, 1958, box 12 of 52.

192. James S. Klump, "Third Party Problems," 1–3, presented to AMA Board of Trustees Commission on Third Party Payers.

193. Ibid.

194. Report of the Meeting of the House of Delegates of the American Medical Association, San Francisco, June 26, 1958.

195. Ibid.

196. Ibid.

197. Ibid.

198. Clipping from *Fortune,* Sept. 19, 1958; "AMA vs. The Miners," clipping from *Commonwheel,* Sept. 19, 1958. See also Dan Wakefield, "Dr. Jeckle and the AMA," *Nation,* June 22, 1957, 539–41. Wakefield wrote this scathing and satirical article one year prior to the AMA's decision to condemn the Fund, when he attended the June 1957

meeting of the House of Delegates. In it, he captured the association's true character: trade protection.

199. Transcript of Report of Morgan Beaty, NBC Radio News, Dec. 4, 1958.

200. Ibid.

201. Selig Perlman, "Bitter Pill for the AMA," clipping from *Progressive,* May 1959.

202. *Proceedings of Conference with Third Parties,* Oct. 17, 1958, 1, no F.F., box 12 of 52.

203. Ibid., 27–30.

204. Ibid.

205. Dr. Draper to Miss Roche, Dec. 8, 1958, F.F. American Medical Association, 1958.

206. Perlman, "Bitter Pill for the AMA."

Chapter 6. The Decade of Crisis

1. Paul Nyden, "Miners for Democracy: Struggle in the Coal Fields" (unpublished manuscript, 1974), 100–106; See also Alan J. Singer, "'Which Side Are You On?' Ideological Conflict in the United Mine Workers of America, 1919–1928" (Ph.D. diss., Rutgers Univ., New Brunswick, N.J., 1982).

2. National Coal Association, *Bituminous Coal Facts, 1972,* 54.

3. Memo to Participants in PARC [President's Appalachian Regional Commission] Conference, Oct. 30, 1963, F.F. 2, Appendix Data, 1963–64, box 2, Frank Pollara Papers.

4. Ibid.

5. Memo from Roche to Lewis, Dec. 21, 1960, F.F. Pension, Revised Regulations Effective 1/1/61, box 2 of 7, Administrative Files, Series II, Director's Records, Fund Papers.

6. Notes of a conference between Miss Roche, Mr. Ryan, Mr. Boylan, Mr. Kelly, et al., F.F. 7/1/60 Revised Regulations, Corres. Policy and Procedures, (Confs.).

7. Notes of a conference between Miss Roche, Mr. Ryan, Mr. Kelly, Mr. Boylan, et al., Apr. 13, 1960.

8. Table 1, 85 H.S. Form by District, attached to notes of a Conference between Miss Roche, Mr. Mitch, Mr. Ryan, Mr. Kelly, Mrs. Lea, Drs. Draper, Striet, Morrison, Kerr, Arestad, Barnes, Brooke, Brother, Dorsey, Falk, Kaplan, Marshal, Riheldaffer, Winebrenner, and Newdorp, Apr. 13, 1960.

9. Ibid.

10. Ibid.

11. Ibid.

12. Ibid.

13. Notes of a conference between Roche and the area medical administrators, Apr. 14, 1960.

14. Notes of a conference between Roche and her staff, May 4, 1960.

15. Memo to Lewis from Roche, June 3, 1960.

16. Ibid.

17. Memo from Roche to Lewis, Nov. 21, 1961, F.F. Pension, Revised Regulations, effective Jan. 1, 1961.

18. Ibid.

19. Excerpt from the 60th Meeting of the Board of Trustees of the United Mine Workers of America Welfare and Retirement Fund, Dec. 2, 1961.

20. Office notice to all pensioners from Roche, Dec. 30, 1961.

21. Notice from Draper to all area medical administrators, Dec. 28, 1960.

22. Krajcinovic, *From Company Doctors to Managed Care,* 158–61.

23. See National Coal Association, *Coal Facts, 1978–1979,* 56.

24. Kerr Interview.

25. Finley, *The Corrupt Kingdom,* 164.

26. H. Younkers, vice-president, District 2, UMWA to Roche, July 11, 1960, clipping from *Johnstown Tribune-Democrat,* July 11, 1960, F.F. 7,1,60, Revised Regulations, Clippings and Publicity, box 2 of 7, Administrative Files, Series II, Director's Records, Fund Papers.

27. Clipping from the *Johnstown Tribune-Democrat,* July 23, 1960.

28. Memo from Warren Williams to Roche, July 7, 1960.

29. Fund's Washington office to H. Evans, editor of the *Lexington Herald,* Aug. 19, 1960.

30. Roche to Harold C. Ward, July 1, 1960.

31. Caudill, *Night Comes to the Cumberlands,* 393–94.

32. *In the United States District Court for the District of Columbia: Willie Ray Blankenship, et al, Plaintiffs, v. W. A. Boyle, et al., Defendants,* Reply Brief of Defendants United Mine Workers of America, W. A. (Tony) Boyle, George Titler, and Edward L. Carey, 35, F.F. Blankenship Reply Brief, W. A. Boyle, George Titler, and Edward L. Carey, box 2 of 3, Blankenship, Series II, Director's Records, Fund Papers.

33. "Contract between the Coal Producers' Association of Illinois and the Progressive Mine Workers of America, District no. 1, in effect 12:01, A.M. Oct. 1, 1952," 85, F.F., A & M 2609, PMWA Printed Contracts, 1941–48, 1952, 1965, 1972, Box 5, Progressive Mine Workers of America Papers.

34. *In the United States District Court for the District of Columbia: Willie Ray Blankenship, et al., Plaintiffs, v. W. A. Boyle, et al., Defendants,* Reply Brief of Defendants United Mine Workers of America, W. A. (Tony) Boyle, George Titler, and Edward L. Carey, 35, F.F. Blankenship Reply Brief, W. A. Boyle, George Titler, and Edward L. Carey, box 2 of 3, Blankenship, Series II, Director's Records, Fund Papers; see also George W. Hopkins, "The Miners for Democracy: Insurgency in the United Mine Workers of America, 1970–1972" (Ph.D. diss., Univ. of North Carolina, Chapel Hill, 1976), 23–42. In his first chapter, Hopkins gives a brief description of the Fund. Starting with the thirty-year rule, he presents a picture of total insensitivity. Not only is this presentation mistaken in some of its facts, but it also lacks depth. However, it does present a good example of how the Fund came to be viewed as a result of the benefit cuts.

35. Hopkins, "The Miners for Democracy," 35–36; see also Hume, *Death and the Mines,* 32.

36. National Coal Association, *Bituminous Coal Facts, 1972,* 52.

37. Unsigned memo to Roche, Dec. 17, 1964, F.F. Pension Rev. Regulation Change Effective 2/1/65, box 3 of 7, Administrative Files, Series II, Director's Records, Fund Papers.

38. Ibid.

39. Memo from Robert Kaplan to Roche, Dec. 31, 1964.

40. Memo from Thomas Ryan to Roche, Dec. 29, 1964.

41. Ibid.

42. Memo from Thomas Ryan to Miss Roche, Aug. 31, 1965, F.F. Pension Reg Change, effective Oct. 11, 1965.

43. Ibid.

44. Unsigned memo to Roche, Apr. 25, 1967.

45. Ibid.

46. Dubofsky and Van Tine, *John L. Lewis: A Biography,* 160–67.

47. Finley, *The Corrupt Kingdom,* 196.

48. Nyden, "Miners for Democracy," 225.

49. National Coal Association, *Bituminous Coal Facts, 1966,* 80.

50. Memo from Schmidt to Lewis, Jan. 24, 1962, F.F. H. G. Schmidt, 1950 Fund Trustee, 1961, 1962, 1963 Corres., box 7 of 8, Board of Trustees Correspondence, 1946–71, Series II, Director's Records, Fund Papers.

51. Ibid.

52. Ibid.

53. "United Mine Workers of America Welfare and Retirement Fund Investments as of the Close of Business July 16, 1969," F.F. W. A. (Tony) Boyle, Trustee, 1950, 1969, 1970, box 8 of 8, Board of Trustees Correspondence, 1946–71.

54. Memo on Alleged Breach of Fiduciary Duty by Trustees, 7, from Frank Robinson, Attorney, attached to letter from Robinson to Welly K. Hopkins, Oct. 14, 1970, F.F. Blankenship Correspondence and Legal Documents, Apr. 18, 1969, box 1 of 3, Blankenship, Series II, Director's Records.

55. United Mine Workers of America Welfare and Retirement Fund Investments as of the Close of Business July 16, 1969, F.F. W. A. (Tony) Boyle, Trustee, 1950, 1969, 1970, box 8 of 8, Board of Trustees Correspondence, Series II, Director's Records.

56. *In the United States District Court for the District of Columbia: Willie Ray Blankenship, et al., Plaintiffs v. W.A. (Tony) Boyle, et al., Defendants,* Reply Brief, 19, F.F. Blankenship, Reply Brief, W. A. Boyle, George Titler, and Edward L. Carey, box 2 of 3, Blankenship, Series II, Director's Records.

57. Ibid., 19–22.

58. Ibid., 59.

59. Ibid., 23.

60. Ibid., 24.

61. Finley, *The Corrupt Kingdom,* 163.

62. *In the United States Court for the District of Columbia: Willie Ray Blankenship, et al. Plaintiffs, v. W. A. Tony Boyle, George Titler, Edward L. Carey, United Mine Workers of America, Bituminous Coal Operators' Association, United Mine Workers of America Welfare and Retirement Fund of 1950, The National Bank of Washington, C. W. Davis, Josephine Roche, George L. Judy, Henry S. Schmidt, Willmer J. Waller, Barnam L. Colton, Defendants,* Memorandum of Opinion, 8, F.F. Blankenship, Memorandum Opinion, box 1 of 3, Blankenship, Series II, Director's Records, Fund Papers.

63. Newdorp Interview, Apr. 23, 1993.

64. *In the United States District Court for the District of Columbia: Willie Ray Blankenship, et al., Plaintiffs, v. W. A. (Tony) Boyle, et al., Defendants,* Defendants Reply Brief, 9., F.F. Blankenship Reply Brief, UMWA, W. A. Boyle, and Edward L. Carey, box 2 of 3, Blankenship, Series II, Director's Records, Fund Papers.

65. Hume, *Death and the Mines,* 23–25.

66. Deposition of W. A. Boyle, Taken Thursday, Jan. 7, 1971, 4–6, F.F. Boyle Deposition, box 2 of 3, Blankenship, Series II, Director's Records, Fund Papers.

67. Hume, *Death and the Mines,* 89–90.

68. U.S. Senate, Subcommittee on Labor of the Committee on Labor and Public Welfare, United Mine Workers Election: Hearing before the Committee on Labor and Public Welfare, 91st Cong., 2d sess., 1971, Investigation of Mine Worker's Election, 122–23 (hereafter referred to as Senate Investigation).

69. Nyden, "Miners for Democracy," 127.

70. Hume, *Death and the Mines,* 25–28; Finley, *The Corrupt Kingdom,* 237.

71. Nyden, "Miners for Democracy," 154.

72. Just how tenuous the union's vice-presidency could be was further illustrated in 1964. When Boyle succeeded Kennedy, Lewis's brother, Raymond was appointed as vice-president. However, he disagreed with Boyle and was forced out a year later in favor of George Titler.

73. Kerr Interview.

74. Ibid.

75. Finley, *The Corrupt Kingdom,* 232–33.

76. Derickson, *Black Lung,* 139.

77. Boyle to the Department Heads, International Headquarters, United Mine Workers of America, Jan. 4, 1963, Feb. 20, 1963, Apr. 10, 1963, Apr. 15, 1963, June 15, 1963, Aug. 11, 1963, Apr. 27, 1964, F.F. Int'l Union—W. A. Boyle, Pres. UMWA (I.E.B. Meetings and Recommendations, Dist. & Int'l Designation), box 1 of 11, United Mine Workers of America Correspondence, 1946–72, Series II, Director's Records, Fund Papers.

78. UMWA news release, Aug. 8, 1963, F.F. International Union, W. A. Boyle, Pres. (Statements and Publicity), F.F. Int'l Union—W. A. Boyle, Pres. UMWA (I.E.B. Meetings and Recommendations, Dist. & Int'l Designation).

79. Ibid.

80. Ibid.

81. Nyden, "Miners for Democracy," 152.

82. Ibid.

83. Roche to Boyle, Sept. 3, 1969; E. F. Daly, Branch of Welfare and Pensions, Division of Compliance Operations, Dept. of Labor, to the Board of Trustees, Aug. 22, 1969; memo to Roche from Boyle, Sept. 4, 1969, F.F. Int'l Union—W. A. Boyle Pres. UMWA Coal Companies and Royalties, box 2 of 11, United Mine Workers Correspondence, 1946–72, Series II, Director's Records, Fund Papers.

84. Hume, *Death and the Mines,* 23–24, 32.

85. *In the United States District Court for the District of Columbia: Willie Ray Blankenship, et al., Plaintiffs, v. W. A. (Tony) Boyle, et al.,* Defendants, Plaintiffs' Trial Brief, 25, F.F. Trial Brief, Harry Huge and Armestead Gilliam, box 2 of 3, Blankenship, Series II, Director's Records, Fund Papers.

86. Ibid., 26.

87. *In the United States District Court for the District of Columbia: Willie Ray Blankenship, et al., Plaintiffs, v. W. A. (Tony) Boyle et al. Defendants,* Reply Brief of Defendants United Mine Workers of America. W. A. (Tony) Boyle, George Titler, and Edward L. Carey, 20, F.F. Blankenship Reply Brief, W. A. Boyle, George Titler, and Edward L. Carey.

88. Ibid., 26–28.

89. *In the United States District Court for the District of Columbia: Willie Ray Blankenship, et al. Plaintiffs v. W. A. (Tony) Boyle, George Titler, Edward L. Carey, United Mine Workers of America, Bituminous Coal Operators' Association, United Mine Workers of America Welfare and Retirement Fund of 1950, The National Bank of Washington, C. W. Davis, Josephine Roche, George L. Judy, Henry S. Schmidt, Willmer J. Waller, and Barnum L. Colton,* 30–31, F.F. Blankenship, Memorandum Opinion, box 1 of 3, Blankenship.

90. Kerr Interview.

91. Ibid.

92. See Derickson, *Black Lung,* chap. 1, "They Spit a Black Substance," and chap. 3, "The Atmosphere of the Mine Is Now Vindicated."

93. Kerr Interview.

94. Ibid.

95. Mark Wyman, *Hard Rock Epic: Western Miners and the Industrial Revolution, 1860–1910* (Berkeley: Univ. of California Press, 1979), 91–92.

96. Derickson, *Black Lung,* 48.

97. Ibid., 81, 94, 98.

98. Lorin E. Kerr, "Coal Workers' Pneumoconiosis," 579, rpt. from the *Archives of Environmental Health,* Apr. 1968, vol. 16, F.F. Pneumoconiosis—Black Lung Legislation, box 2 of 11, United Mine Workers Correspondence, 1946–72, Series II, Director's Records, Fund Papers.

99. Lorin E. Kerr, M.D., M.P.H. "Coal Workers' Pneumoconiosis," *Industrial Medicine and Surgery,* Aug. 1956, 355–62.

100. "Statement by Lorin E. Kerr, M.D., M.P.H. on S 2864 to Subcommittee on Labor of the Senate Committee on Labor and Public Welfare, 1–3, F.F. W. A. Boyle, UMWA Pneumoconiosis—Black Lung, box 2 of 11, United Mine Workers Correspondence, 1946–72, Series II, Director's Records, Fund Papers.

101. Memo from Boyle to Roche, July 9, 1968. In every respect, the efforts of both Kerr and the Fund complimented and matched the work performed by two other West Virginia physicians whose names became synonymous with black lung: Dr. Donald Rasmussen of Beckley and Dr. Isadore Buff of Charleston. Both Buff and Rasmussen called attention to the need for preventative measures in the mines as the only way to stop its spread. Also, Dr. Rasmussen regarded the Fund and its medical staff as allies in the fight for black lung's recognition. Interview with Dr. Donald Rasmussen, June 1988.

102. Memos from Boyle to Roche, May 9, 17, 1968; Memo from Roche to Boyle, June 18, 1968.

103. Lorin E. Kerr, "Coal Workers' Pneumoconiosis: The Road to Dusty Death," paper presented Sept. 10, 1968, at 45th Consecutive Constitutional Convention of the United Mine Workers of America, Sept. 4–13, 1968, Denver, F.F. Office of the Director Records, 1947–71, Conventions, 45 UMWA, Preparation Materials, box 1 of 1, Conventions, Series II, Director's Records.

104. Ibid.

105. Kerr Interview.

106. Hume, *Death and the Mines,* 69.

107. Notes of telephone interview between author and Dr. Donald Rasmussen, given May 26, 1988 (hereafter referred to as Rasmussen Interview).

108. Ibid.

109. Memo from Robert Kaplan to Roche, June 21, 1968, F.F. Office of the Director Records, 1946–71, Conventions, 45 UMWA Preparation Materials, box 1 of 1, Conventions, Series II, Director's Records, Fund Papers.

110. Ibid.

111. See *United Mine Workers Journal* 79, no. 18 (Sept. 15, 1968), special convention issue.

112. Dubofsky and Van Tine, *John L. Lewis: A Biography,* 191.

113. Nyden, "Miners for Democracy," 71–74.

114. Quoted in ibid., 73–74.

115. Ibid., 260–66.

116. "Statement by Joseph A. Yablonski, Member of the International Executive Board of the United Mine Workers of America Concerning His Candidacy for the Presidency of the United Mine Workers of America," 1–2, Washington, D.C., May 29, 1969, F.F. Office of the Director Records, 1946–71, 1969 UMWA Election, Joseph A. Yablonski, Statements Releases, box 1 of 2, 1969 UMWA Election, Series II, Director's Records, Fund Papers.

117. Ibid., 2–3.
118. Ibid., 4–10.
119. Ibid., 3.
120. Nyden, "Miners for Democracy," 153.
121. Ibid., 123.
122. Ibid., 123.
123. Ibid., 155–56.
124. Hume, *Death and the Mines,* 49.
125. Nyden, "Miners for Democracy," 127.
126. Mimeographed notice to "Fellow Coal Miners," July 2, 1969, Charleston, W.Va., F.F. Office of the Director Records, 1946–71, 1969 UMWA elections; Joseph A. Yablonski, Statements Releases, pamphlet entitled "The Two Faces of Joseph Yablonski"; eight-page "Election Bulletin" paid for by the "Miners' Committee for Boyle, Titler, and Owens"; press releases from "Miners' Committee for Boyle, Titler, and Owens," Sept. 15, 19, 23, 29, Oct. 13, and Nov. 14, 1968; *Ammunition,* published by the Miners' Committee for Boyle, Titler, and Owens, Sept. 29, Oct. 15, Oct. 23, Nov. 6, 1968, F.F. Office of the Director Records, 1946–71, 1969 UMWA election, W. A. "Tony" Boyle Statements and Releases, box 1 of 2, 1969 UMWA Election, Series II, Director's Records, Fund Papers. At the beginning of the campaign, Yablonski admitted that he had been in trouble as a young man. The story he recounted was that he had served time in jail for breaking into a slot machine after losing his week's earnings in it. In response, the Boyle campaign issued an eight-page election bulletin that presented a detailed account of Yablonski's police record, including his mug shot. Their version of the story was that the challenger had been arrested for robbing a cash register and an orphan's collection jar belonging to a Loyal Order of Moose lodge. In proof of this charge, the bulletin printed a dated letter, written on the lodge's stationery, which had been sent to the court listing what had been stolen. The bulletin also presented a court docket showing that Yablonski at one point had deserted his wife and child. In conclusion, the bulletin recounted a story in which John L. Lewis supposedly told Yablonski that no man who had ever worn numbers across his chest would ever become president of the union.
127. Note from Roche to Lewis, May 29, 1969.
128. Senate Investigation, 230.
129. Schmidt to Lewis, Feb. 25, 1969, F.F. H. G. Schmidt, 1950 Fund Trustee, 1968, 1969 Correspondence, box 8 of 8, Board of Trustees Correspondence, 1946–71, Series II, Director's Records, Fund Papers.
130. George Judy to H. G. Schmidt, Oct. 16, 1967, H. G. Schmidt to George Judy, Oct. 23, 1967, F.F. H. G. Schmidt, 1950 Fund Trustee (1967, 1968, 1969 Corres.).
131. Schmidt to Lewis, Feb. 25, 1969.
132. Note from Schmidt to Roche, Jan. 27, 1969, undated clipping from the *Cleveland Plain Dealer* attached; note from Schmidt to Roche, Jan. 20, 1969, with clipping from the *Atlanta Mirror* attached, Dec. 5, 1968.

133. Roche to Lewis, June 2, 1969, F.F. Trustee George L. Judy, UMWA Welfare and Retirement Fund. Resigned effective July 14, 1969.

134. Senate Investigation, 165.

135. Ibid., 7–8.

136. Ibid.

137. Ibid., 290–91.

138. Ibid.

139. Ibid.

140. Finley, *The Corrupt Kingdom,* 267–69.

141. A. P. teletype, July 15, 1969, F.F. Trustee George L. Judy, UMWA Welfare and Retirement Fund, Resignation eff. 7/14/69, box 8 of 8, Board of Trustees Correspondence, 1946–71, Series II, Director's Records, Fund Papers.

142. Senate Investigation, 165.

143. Ibid., 186.

144. Ibid.

145. Ibid., 170–73.

146. Ibid., 226.

147. Ibid., 186.

148. Memo from Boyle to Roche, Oct. 24, 1969, F.F. Boyle, W. A. (Tony) Trustee, 1950, 1969, 1970, box 8 of 8, Board of Trustees Correspondence, 1946–71, Series II, Director's Records, Fund Papers.

149. Undated memo draft from Roche to Boyle, F.F. Miss Roche, Trustee and Director, UMWA Welfare and Retirement Fund (1950 Fund).

150. Senate Investigation, 185.

151. Ibid., 184.

152. Ibid., 199.

153. Ibid., 209–10, 221.

154. Ibid., 252–54.

155. Ibid., 220–21.

156. Richard J. Jensen, "Rebellion in the United Mine Workers: The Miners for Democracy, 1970–1972" (Ph.D. diss., Indiana Univ., Bloomington, 1974), 149. In fact, Boyle's relationship with Richards became an issue when the results of the union's 1969 presidential election were voided. During the course of the rematch in 1972, the MFD ridiculed Boyle as being under Richards's "domination."

157. Senate Investigation, 306–8.

158. Ibid., 312.

159. Ibid., 313.

160. Ibid., 223.

161. Ibid., 224.

162. Ibid., 225, 230.

163. Ibid., 228.

164. Ibid., 247–51.

165. Ibid., 252

166. Ibid., 166.

167. Ibid., 308.

168. Ibid., 163.

169. See F.F. Office of the Director Records, 1946–71, Investigation of Fund, Letters, Re J.R.'s Testimony, box 1 of 3, Investigation of the Fund, Series II, Director's Records, Fund Papers.

170. For example, see Local Union 488, District 2 to Roche, Mar. 18, 1970. Also, each letter was checked against the union's membership lists. Thus, the letters include an attached listing of the local's total membership broken down into working members and retirees. If the letter came from a pensioner local, made up solely of retirees, it was reported as such.

171. Nyden, "Miners for Democracy," 274–77; notes of a news conference called by the Disabled Miners and Widows, taken by Warren Williams, Aug. 5, 1969, F.F. Blankenship, Correspondence and Legal Documents, box 1 of 3, Blankenship, Series II, Director's Records, Fund Papers.

172. Robert F. Boylan to Welly K. Hopkins, Aug. 22, 1969, attached, file on Willie Ray Blankenship, F.F. Blankenship, Correspondence and Legal Documents, box 1 of 3, Blankenship, Series II, Director's Records, Fund Papers.

173. *In the United States District Court for the District of Columbia: Willie Ray Blankenship, et al., v. W. A. (Tony) Boyle, et al.,* Motion for Detection, 2–3.

174. Ibid., 3.

175. *In the United States District Court for the District of Columbia: Willie Ray Blankenship, et al., Plaintiffs, v. W. A. (Tony) Boyle, et al., Defendants,* Affidavit of Thomas Ryan, 1–2.

176. *In the United States District Court for the District of Columbia: Willie Ray Blankenship, et al., Plaintiffs, v. W. A. (Tony) Boyle, et al., Defendants,* Reply Brief of Defendants United Mine Workers of America, W. A. (Tony) Boyle, George Titler, and Edward L. Carey, 5–7, F.F. Blankenship Reply Brief UMWA, W. A. Boyle, George Titler, and Edward L. Carey, box 2 of 3, Blankenship.

177. Ibid., 6–7.

178. *In the United States District Court for the District of Columbia: Willie Ray Blankenship, et al., Plaintiffs v. W. A. (Tony) Boyle, George Titler, Edward L. Carey, The United Mine Workers of America, Bituminous Coal Operators Association, United Mine Workers of America Welfare and Retirement Fund of 1950, The National Bank of Washington, C. W. Davis, Josephine Roche, George L. Judy, Henry S. Schmidt, Willmer J. Waller, Barnam S. Colton,* Memorandum Opinion, 5–6, 7–13, F. F. Blankenship Memorandum Opinion, box 1 of 3, Blankenship.

179. Ibid., 10.

180. Ibid., 11–12.

181. Ibid., 16.

182. Ibid., 26–27.

183. Ibid., 31–34, 35–37.

184. Dubofsky and Van Tine, *John L. Lewis: A Biography,* 513–14.

Chapter 7. Reform, Reorganization, and Disaster

1. Clippings from *Washington Evening Star,* June 17, 1971, *Washington Post,* June 18, 1971, F. F. Blankenship, 1971–72, box 1 of 3, Blankenship, Series II, Director's Records, Fund Papers.

2. Unsigned memo from the office of the UMWA's secretary treasurer, June 17, 1971, F.F. Edward L. Carey Chairman Trustees, box 6 of 10, Director's Correspondence, Miscellaneous Files, Thomas Ryan 1973, Series II, Director's Records.

3. General memo to all employees of the United Mine Workers of America Welfare and Retirement Fund, July 15, 1971.

4. Memo from Carey to Roche, June 24, 1971.

5. *United Mine Workers of America Welfare and Retirement Fund Annual Report for 1971– 1972,* 24., box Addendum, 1981, July 8, Annual Reports 1952–79 and Misc. Medical Staff Publications, Gift, Yale Univ. Library.

6. Ibid., 24–26.

7. Ibid.

8. Ibid., 26.

9. Projection of Income and Expenditure of the United Mine Workers of America Welfare and Retirement Fund through 1974, undated, F.F. Edward L. Carey, Chairman, Trustees, box 6 of 10, Director's Correspondence and Miscellaneous Files, Thomas F. Ryan, 1973, Series II, Director's Records.

10. Undated memo to Carey, C. W. Davis, and Paul R. Dean from Ryan, cost schedule attached.

11. Ibid.

12. Melvyn Dubofsky, *We Shall Be All: A History of the I.W.W.* (New York: New York Times/ Quadrangle Books, 1969), 78.

13. Dubofsky and Van Tine, *John L. Lewis: A Biography,* 23–25, 163–67; Singer, "Which Side Are You On?," 112–13, 233.

14. Seltzer, *Fire in the Hole,* 120.

15. Nyden, "Miners for Democracy," 180.

16. Clark, *The Miners' Fight for Democracy,* 27.

17. Nyden, "Miners for Democracy," 191.

18. "An Interview with Arnold Miller," transcript of the *Today Show,* Nov. 28, 1972, 4, F.F. 3, box 85, Miners for Democracy Papers, Wayne State Univ., Detroit, Mich. (hereafter referred to as MFD Papers). It should be noted that the MFD papers are open to all scholars for research without any major restrictions.

19. Newdorp Interview, May 7, 1993.

20. Daniels Interview, Sept. 21, 1995.

21. Nyden, "Miners for Democracy," 193.

22. Letter to C. W. Davis, Paul R. Dean, Harold Brown, and Thomas Ryan from Miller, Jan. 8, 1973, F.F. Edward L. Carey, Chairman, Trustees, box 6 of 10, Director's Correspondence and Miscellaneous Files, Thomas F. Ryan, 1973, Series II, Director's Records, Fund Papers.

23. *In the United States District Court for the District of Columbia: Willie Ray Blankenship, Newman A. Lamb, et al. Plaintiffs, v. United Mine Workers of America Welfare and Retirement Fund of 1950, et al.,* Response of the United Mine Workers of America to the Motion for Immediate Relief, 7, Resolution Approving and Ratifying the Removal of Edward L. Carey as UMWA Trustee and Designating Arnold Miller UMWA Trustee on the UMWA Welfare and Retirement Fund of 1950.

24. *In the United States District Court for the District of Columbia: Willie Ray Blankenship, Newman A. Lamb, et al., Plaintiffs, v. United Mine Workers of America Welfare and Retirement Fund, et al.,* Response of the United Mine Workers of America to the Motion for Immediate Relief, 7.

25. Ibid., 1–3.

26. Ibid., 7.

27. Ibid., 8.

28. *In the United States District Court for the District of Columbia: Willie Ray Blankenship, Newman A. Lamb, et al., Plaintiffs, v. United Mine Workers of America Welfare and Retirement Fund of 1950,* Memorandum of Edward L. Carey in Reply to Motion for Instruction, 1–2.

29. Ibid., 3–4.

30. *United States Court of Appeals for the District of Columbia: Newman A. Lamb, v. Edward L. Carey, Appellant, C. W. Davis and Paul R. Dean, Trustees, United Mine Workers of America Welfare and Retirement Fund,* 9, F.F. Blankenship, box 5 of 10, Trustee Records, Series I, Harry Huge Correspondence.

31. *In the United States District Court for the District of Columbia: Willie Ray Blankenship, Newman Lamb, et al., Plaintiffs, v. United Mine Workers of America Welfare and Retirement Fund, et al.,* Motion for Reconsideration, 1–2.

32. *United States Court of Appeals for the District of Columbia, Newman A. Lamb v. Edward L. Carey, Appellant, C. W. Davis and Paul R. Dean, Trustees, United Mine Workers of America Welfare and Retirement Fund,* 10, F.F. Blankenship.

33. Ibid., 8.

34. Ibid., 10–11.

35. Wysang and Williams, *Health Services for Miners*, 29.

36. Ibid.

37. Clark, *The Miners' Fight for Democracy*, 54; Not everyone in the union, however, was happy about the new contract. After the agreement was concluded, Miller presented it to the union's bargaining council. A product of Miners for Democracy reforms, the council consisted of the union's international executive board and district presidents. The majority of the council's members did not support the agreement, and Miller threatened to take the issue directly to the union's membership unless the council endorsed the new contract to assist in its ratification by the rank and file. See Charles R. Perry, *Collective Bargaining and the Decline of the United Mine Workers* (Philadelphia: Univ. of Pennsylvania Press, 1984), 208.

38. National Bituminous Coal Wage Agreement of 1974, 28–29, F.F. Trustee Files, Contracts, Pensions, and Benefit Plans, box 9 of 10, Trustee Records, Series I, Harry Huge Correspondence, Fund Papers.

39. Ploss, *A History of the Medical Care Program*, 171.

40. Ibid., 166.

41. Nyden, "Miners for Democracy," 358.

42. National Bituminous Coal Wage Agreement of 1974, 27. F.F. Trustee Files, Contracts, Pensions and Benefit Plans, box 9 of 10, Trustee Records, Series I, Harry Huge Correspondence, Fund Papers.

43. Ibid., 31.

44. Ibid., 32.

45. Ibid., 32–33.

46. *United Mine Workers of America Health and Retirement Funds, 1975 Annual Report*, 11.

47. Ploss, *A History of the Medical Care Program*, 178.

48. Interview with Susan Jarworski Rodenbaugh, June 17, 1993 (hereafter referred to as Rodenbaugh Interview). Rodenbaugh worked as a staff member of the Fund's Johnstown office and was in a good position to see how policy decisions by Huge and Danzinger played out in the field. The author wishes to thank Ms. Rodenbaugh for kindness in assisting with this project.

49. Daniels Interview, June 14, 1988.

50. *The United Mine Workers of America Welfare and Retirement Fund Annual Report, 1973–1974*, 18–19, box, Addendum 1981, July 8, Annual Reports 1952–79 and Misc. Medical Staff Publications, Gift, Yale Univ. Library, Fund Papers.

51. Daniels Interview, June 14, 1988.

52. Report to the Trustees: United Mine Workers of America Welfare and Retirement Fund, Representing Impressions from Consultations Recorded from Late 1973 to Apr. 1974, by C. Arden Miller, M.D., 5–8, F.F. Report of C. Arden Miller, M.D., box 51 of 52, Subject Files, Series III, Executive Medical Officer, Fund Papers.

53. Ibid., 8.

54. Ibid., 20–21.

55. Ibid.

56. Ibid., 2.

57. West Virginia Clinic Report, 17.

58. Ibid., 7.

59. Ibid.

60. Ploss, *A History of the Medical Care Program,* 113–14.

61. It should be noted that the statement about making shoes is a paraphrasing of Danzinger's own comments about the blessings of scientific management. See Ploss, *A History of the Medical Care Program,* 133–39.

62. Memo to Dr. John Newdorp from Martin B. Danzinger, June 3, 1974, F.F. Book of M.B.D. [Martin B. Danzinger], Private Papers of John Newdorp.

63. Interview with Warfield Garson, M.D., July 14, 1993. An academic specialist in public health, Dr. Garson worked for the USPHS for twenty-five years. After leaving the public health service, he joined the Fund's staff as AMO for Pittsburgh, Pennsylvania, to replace Dr. Leslie Falk, who was Pittsburgh's original Fund AMO and who left in 1967 for a teaching post.

64. Ploss, *A History of the Medical Care Program,* 133; Daniels Interview, June 14, 1988; Rodenbaugh Interview.

65. Rodenbaugh Interview.

66. Newdorp Interview, May 7, 1993; Kerr Interview; Palmer Interview; Boylan Interview; taped interview with Robert Smith, M.D., June 7, 1994 (hereafter referred to as Smith Interview). A former USPHS physician, Dr. Smith was hired in the early 1970s by the Fund to serve as AMO for Morgantown, West Virginia.

67. Daniels Interview, June 14, 1988.

68. Memo from Dr. Newdorp to Martin B. Danzinger, Apr. 24, 1974, F.F. Reorganization, 1974, Transfer of Washington Beneficiaries to Regional Offices, box 51 of 52, Subject Files, Series III, Executive Medical Officer, Fund Papers.

69. Ploss, *A History of the Medical Care Program,* 115; Kerr Interview. Although a number of the interviewees expressed considerable antipathy toward Danzinger, the late Dr. Lorin E. Kerr was far more explicit about his feelings than most of the others. During the course of our interview in 1988, Dr. Kerr, when questioned about Danzinger, at one point screamed, "I hate the man!"

70. Ploss, *A History of the Medical Care Program,* 115.

71. Ibid.; Palmer Interview. One of the offices closed at this time was Pittsburgh's. According to W. Philip Palmer, who was assistant A.M.O. for the Pittsburgh office, the closing was handled in the following manner: Danzinger informed the office's staff that he was coming to Pittsburgh for a special meeting just prior to the Christmas holiday. When the meeting opened, Danzinger first wished everyone a happy holiday and then announced,

without warning, that the office was to be closed shortly thereafter. Most staff members were stunned, and several broke into tears. According to Palmer, Danzinger did not appear to understand why these people were so upset.

72. Ploss, *A History of the Medical Care Program,* 133; Kerr Interview; Daniels Interview, June 14, 1988; Garson Interview; Raino Interview; Rodenbaugh Interview.

73. Rodenbaugh Interview.

74. Daniels Interview, June 14, 1988.

75. Garson Interview; Palmer Interview; Winebrenner Interview, Sept. 10, 1993.

76. Winebrenner Interview, Sept. 10, 1993; Palmer Interview.

77. Starr, *Social Transformation of American Medicine,* 370.

78. Starr, *Social Transformation of American Medicine,* 381–87; Raino Interview; Palmer Interview; Winebrenner Interview, Sept. 15, 1993.

79. Summary of Systems Review Findings and Recommendations from Study of Touche Ross & Co., 2, F.F. Reorganization, Touche Ross Review Findings of Benefit Eligibility and Medical Payment Systems, box 52 of 52, Subject Files, Series III, Executive Medical Officer, Fund Papers.

80. Ibid., 3.

81. Ibid., 4–5.

82. Ibid., 5–6.

83. Rodenbaugh Interview.

84. Taped interview with Paul Cornely, M.D., July 20, 1993; "Presentation to the Board of Trustees, Wednesday, Dec. 11, 1974, in Reference to the Dismissal of Paul B. Cornely, M.D.," memo made available by Paul Cornely, M.D.

85. "Presentation to the Board of Trustees, Wednesday, Dec. 11, 1974, in Reference to the Dismissal of Paul B. Cornely, M.D.," memo made available by Paul Cornely, M.D.

86. Letter to Dr. Paul B. Cornely from the Board of Trustees, UMWA Welfare and Retirement Fund, Dec. 16, 1974, memo made available by Paul Cornely, M.D.

87. Ibid.

88. *United Mine Workers of America Health and Retirement Funds 1975 Annual Report,* 8.

89. Ibid., 9.

90. Rodenbaugh Interview.

91. Memo from Robert Kaplan to regional offices, Feb. 26, 1975; memo from Dr. Newdorp to Karen Clark, July 30, 1975, F.F. Reorganization, Touche-Ross Review Finds of Benefit Eligibility and Medical Payment Systems, box 52 of 52, Subject Files, Executive Medical Officer, Fund Papers.

92. Memo to file, Sept. 24, 1975.

93. Ibid.

94. Rodenbaugh Interview.

95. Wysang and Williams, *Health Services for Miners,* 33.

96. Rodenbaugh Interview.

97. Ibid.

98. Newdorp Interview, May 21, 1993; Raino Interview; Palmer Interview; Rodenbaugh Interview.

99. Newdorp Interview, May 21, 1993; Raino Interview, Palmer Interview; Rodenbaugh Interview.

100. Daniels Interview, June 14, 1988.

101. Clark, *The Miners' Fight for Democracy*, 93, 105.

102. Ibid.

103. Ploss, *A History of the Medical Care Program*, 194.

104. Ibid., 176.

105. Raino Interview; Albert Reese, *The Economics of Trade Unions*, 3d ed. (Chicago: Univ. of Chicago Press, 1989), 83–84.

106. Raino Interview.

107. *United Mine Workers of America Health and Retirement Funds 1976 Annual Report*, 24–33; *United Mine Workers of America Health and Retirement Funds 1977 Annual Report*, 7–16; *United Mine Workers of America Health and Retirement Funds 1975 Annual Report*, 32.

108. *United Mine Workers of America Health and Retirement Funds 1976 Annual Report*, 25–30, 33.

109. National Coal Association, *Bituminous Coal Facts, 1972*, 54.

110. Ibid.

111. *Minerals Yearbook, 1973*, vol. 1, *Metals, Minerals, and Fuels* (Washington, D.C.: GPO, 1975), 317.

112. *Minerals Yearbook, 1975*, vol. 1, *Metals, Minerals, and Fuels* (Washington, D.C.: GPO, 1977), 387.

113. *United Mine Workers Journal*, Mar. 16, 1975, 8–9.

114. Ploss, *A History of the Medical Care Program*, 189; *United Mine Workers of America Health and Retirement Funds 1975 Annual Report*, 32; *United Mine Workers of America Health and Retirement Funds 1976 Annual Report*, 24–33; *United Mine Workers of America Health and Retirement Funds 1977 Annual Report*, 7–16.

115. Wysang and Williams, *Health Services for Miners*, 35.

116. Ibid.

117. Ploss, *A History of the Medical Care Program*, 176–77.

118. Ibid., 193.

119. Ibid., 192.

120. *United Mine Workers of America Health and Retirement Funds 1977 Annual Report*, 6.

121. Ibid.

122. Ploss, *A History of the Medical Care Program*, 185.

123. *United Mine Workers of America Health and Retirement Funds 1977 Annual Report,* 6.

124. Ploss, *A History of the Medical Care Program,* 194

125. Clark, *The Miners' Fight for Democracy,* 107–8, 116.

126. Ibid.

127. West Virginia Clinic Report, 141–42.

128. Ibid., 169–71.

129. Ibid., 18–30.

130. Wysang and Williams, *Health Services for Miners,* 38.

131. Ibid.

132. Ploss, *A History of the Medical Care Program,* 242–45.

133. Thomas N. Bethell, "U.M.W. in the Pits," *New Republic,* Apr. 1, 1978, 7.

134. Clark, *The Miners' Fight for Democracy,* 123–25; Bethell, "U.M.W. in the Pits," 8.

135. Bethell, "U.M.W. in the Pits," 9.

136. Ploss, *A History of the Medical Care Program,* 245.

137. Kerr Interview.

138. Bethell, "U.M.W. in the Pits," 9.

139. Ploss, *A History of the Medical Care Program,* 256–58.

140. "Fund Payment Options for Health Services," 43–46, F.F. Task Force Reports on the C. Arden Miller, M.D., Report, 2 of 3, box 51 of 52, Subject Files, Series III, Executive Medical Officer, Fund Papers.

141. Ibid., 44.

142. Ploss, *A History of the Medical Care Program,* 257.

143. Wysang and Williams, *Health Services for Miners,* 42.

Conclusions

1. Thomas A. Kockran, Harry C. Hatz, and Robert B. McKenzie, *The Transformation of American Industrial Relations* (New York: Basic Books, 1986), 2–30.

2. Derickson, "Part of the Yellow Dog," 714–18.

3. Ibid.

4. Ibid.

5. Raino Interview, Aug. 17, 1998.

6. Ibid.

7. Ibid.

8. Ibid.

9. Ibid.

Bibliography

Manuscript Collections

MacDonald, David J. Papers. Labor Archives, Patee Library, Pennsylvania State Univ., University Park.

Miners for Democracy. Papers. Walter P. Reuther Library, Wayne State Univ., Detroit, Mich.

Newdorp, John, M.D., Private Papers of John Newdorp, M.D. Arlington, Va.

Ozanic, Joseph. Papers. Archives and Manuscripts 2482, West Virginia Collection, West Virginia Univ., Morgantown.

Peterson, Carl A. Papers. Labor Archives, Patee Library, Pennsylvania State Univ., University Park.

Pollara, Frank. Papers. Labor Archives, Patee Library, Pennsylvania State Univ., University Park.

Progressive Mine Workers of America. Papers. Archives and Manuscripts 2609. West Virginia Collection, West Virginia Univ., Morgantown.

Rice, Father Charles Owen. Papers. Archives of Industrial Society, Univ. of Pittsburgh, Pennsylvania.

Roche, Josephine. Papers. Archives, Univ. of Colorado, Boulder.

Thurmond, Walter A. Papers. Archives and Manuscripts 2141, West Virginia Collection, West Virginia Univ., Morgantown.

United Electrical, Radio, and Machine Workers of America. Papers. Archives of Industrial Society, Univ. of Pittsburgh.

United Mine Workers of America Health and Retirement Funds. Archives and Manuscripts 2769, West Virginia Collection, West Virginia Univ., Morgantown.

Series I. Board of Trustees. Boxes 1, 5, 6, 9.

Series II. Director's Records. Office of the Director. 1946 Fund Files. Boxes 1, 2, 3.

Office of the Director. Actuary and Insurance Company. Data, 1947–48. Boxes 1, 2.

———. Board of Trustees, Correspondence, 1946–71. Boxes, 1–8.

———. Administrative Files, 1948–71. Boxes 2, 3, 6.

———. United Mine Workers of America. Correspondence, 1946–72. Boxes, 1, 2, 6, 8.

———. Contracts, 1946–71. Box 1.

———. Conventions, 1948–68. Box 1.

———. 1969 UMWA Election, 1969–71. Boxes 1, 2.

———. Investigation of the Fund, 1969–71. Box 1.

———. Blankenship, 1969–71. Boxes 1, 2, 3.

———. Medical Hospital, and Health Service Correspondence, 1947–71. Boxes 1, 4.

———. Director's Correspondence and Miscellaneous Files. Box 6.

Series III. Executive Medical Officer. Subject Files. Boxes 6, 7, 11, 12, 13, 14, 17, 29, 39, 40, 49, 50, 51, 52.

Executive Medical Officer, Health Care Delivery. Boxes 20, 21.

Series IV. Miners Memorial Hospital Association. Miners Memorial Hospital Association. Minutes, Resolutions, Bylaws. 18 vols. Volumes consulted:

Vol. 1, Memorial Hospital Association of Kentucky, Inc. No. 2. Minutes, 1951–54.

Vol. 2, Memorial Hospital Association of Kentucky, Inc. No 3. Minutes, 1955–58.

Vol. 7, Miners Memorial Hospital Association, Inc. Exhibits 1, 1951–56.

Vol. 8, Miners Memorial Hospital Association, Inc. Exhibits 2, 1956–58.

Vol. 9, Miners Memorial Hospital Association, Inc. Exhibits 3, 1959–60.

Vol. 12, Miners Memorial Hospital Association, Inc. Exhibits 6, 1962

Vol. 14, Miners Memorial Hospital Association, Inc. Exhibits 8, 1964–68.

Miners Memorial Hospital Association. Construction/Administration. Boxes 1, 2, 5.

Clinical Operations. Boxes 1, 5, 12.

Subject Files. Boxes 4, 5, 6, 7, 12, 13, 14.

Series V. Office of Research and Statistics. Medical Care Statistics, 1951–73. Box 1.

Annual Reports, 1952–79 and Misc. Medical Staff Publications. [No series.] Gift. July 8, 1981. Yale Univ. Library.

United Steel Workers of America. Papers. Labor Archives, Patee Library, Pennsylvania State Univ.

Government and Private Industrial Reports

Employment and Training: Report to the President. Washington, D.C.: GPO, 1979.

Minerals Yearbook, 1973. Vol. 1, *Metals Minerals, and Fuels.* Washington, D.C.: GPO, 1975.

Minerals Yearbook, 1975. Vol. 1, *Metals Minerals, and Fuels.* Washington, D.C.: GPO, 1977.

"Minutes of the One Hundred Sixth Annual Session [of the House of Delegates of the Medical Society of the State of Pennsylvania]." *Pennsylvania Medical Journal* 60, no. 2 (Feb. 1957): 197–280.

Minutes of the 1957 House of Delegates [of the Medical Society of the State of Pennsylvania], Including Reports of Officers and Councilors for 1956–57. Rpt. from *Pennsylvania Medical Journal* (Aug. 1957–Jan. 1958).

National Coal Association. *Bituminous Coal Facts, 1960.* Washington, D.C.: National Coal Association, 1960.

———. *Bituminous Coal Facts, 1964*. Washington, D.C.: National Coal Association, 1964.

———. *Bituminous Coal Facts, 1966*. Washington, D.C.: National Coal Association, 1966.

———. *Bituminous Coal Facts, 1972*. Washington, D.C.: National Coal Association, 1972.

———. *Coal Facts, 1978–1979*. Washington, D.C.: National Coal Association, 1979.

"Official Reports." *Pennsylvania Medical Journal* 59, no. 9 (Sept. 1956): 1099–160.

President's Commission on the Health of the Nation. *Building America's Health: A Report to the President of the United States*. 5 vols. Washington, D.C.: GPO, 1952–53.

Proceedings: National Health Conference, July 18, 19, 20, 1938. Interdepartmental Committee to Coordinate Health and Welfare Activities. Josephine Roche, Chairman. Washington: GPO, 1938.

[United Mine Workers of America.] *Proceedings of the Forty-second Convention United Mine Workers of America, 1956*.

[United Mine Workers of America.] *Proceedings of the Forty-third Convention United Mine Workers of America, 1960*.

[United Steel Workers of America.] *Proceedings of the Fourth Constitutional Convention of the United Steel Workers of America*. May 11–15, 1948.

[United Steel Workers of America.] *Proceedings of the Fifth Constitutional Convention of the United Steel Workers of America*. May 9–12, 1950.

[United Steel Workers of America.] *Proceedings of the Tenth Constitutional Convention of the United Steel Workers of America*. Sept. 19–23, 1960.

U.S. Senate. Subcommittee on Labor of the Committee on Labor and Public Welfare. United Mine Workers Election: Hearing before the Committee on Labor and Public Welfare. 91st Cong., 2d sess., 1971.

Interviews

Boylan, Robert. Interview by author. Tape recording. July 16, 1993.

Chadwick, Donald, M.D. Interview by author. Tape recording. July 14, 1994.

Cornely, Paul, M.D. Interview by author. Tape recording. July 20, 1993.

Daniels, Henry C. Interview by author. Tape recording. June 14, 1988, Sept. 21, 1995.

Falk, Leslie, M.D. Interview by author. Tape recording. Aug. 14, 1998.

Garson, Warfield, M.D. Interview by author. Tape recording. July 14, 1993.

Kerr, Lorin E. Interview by author. Tape recording. May 30, 1988.

Kruger, Ada, R.N. Interview by author. Tape recording. June 18, 1993.

Newdorp, John, M.D. Interview by author. Tape recording. Dec. 2, 10, 1992, Jan. 22, Feb. 5, 26, Mar. 17, 26, Apr. 2, 23, May 7, 21, June 4, 1993.

Palmer, W. Philip. Interview by author. Tape recording. Oct. 7, 1993.

Price, Robert, M.D. Interview by author. Tape recording. June 9, 1994.

Raino, Domanic. Interview by author. Tape recording. Sept. 8, 1993, Aug. 17, 1998.

Rasmussen, Donald, M.D. Interview by author. Handwritten notes. May 26, 1988.

Rodenbaugh, Susan Jarworski. Interview by author. Tape recording. June 17, 1993.

Smith, Robert, M.D. Interview by author. Tape recording. June 7, 29, 1994.

Winebrenner, John, M.D. Interview by author. Tape recording. Sept. 10, 15, 1993.

Correspondence

Bernet, Tom, to Paul Cornely, M.D., Nov. 20, 1974.

Board of Trustees [of the Fund] to Paul Cornely, Dec. 16, 1974.

Cornely, Paul, M.D. "Presentation to the Board of Trustees [of the Fund], Wednesday, December 11, 1974, in Reference to the Dismissal of Paul B. Cornely, M.D."

Cornely, Paul, to Harry Huge, Dec. 16, 1974.

Cornely, Paul, M.D., to Louis Krempasky, Jan. 30, 1975.

David, Will, to Paul Cornely, M.D., Nov. 20, 1974.

Desmarais, M. Virginia, to Paul Cornely, M.D., Dec. 10, 1974.

Doresy, William "Bill," M.D., to Paul Cornely, M.D., undated.

Falk, Leslie, M.D., to Arnold Miller, Dec. 18, 1974.

Falk, Leslie, M.D., to Harry Huge, Jan. 16, 1974.

Falk, Leslie, M.D., to Harry Huge, Jan. 3, 1975.

Falk, Leslie A. "Health Care for All: A Life in Social Medicine." Includes hitherto unpublished correspondence between Dr. Henry Sigerist and Falk. Unpublished manuscript. Aug. 6, 1994.

Fulton, Rose to Paul Cornely, M.D., Dec. 1, 1974.

Palmer, W. Philip, to Paul Cornely, M.D., Nov. 16, 1974.

Rodenbaugh, Susan Jarworski to Tom Berret, Tom Fulton, and Ton Skerl, [Fund] Memo, Jan. 13, 1977.

Sherwood, Robert W., M.D., to Paul Cornely, M.D., Nov. 21, 1974.

Smith, Robert, M.D., to Paul Cornely, M.D., Nov. 18, 1974.

Winebrenner, John, M.D., to author, Aug. 17, 1993.

Reports and Proceedings in West Virginia Collection

"Agreement between the Medical Service, UMWA Welfare and Retirement Fund and the Medical Society of the State of Pennsylvania." F.F. "Agreement, UMWA Welfare and Retirement Fund and the Medical Society of the State of Pennsylvania." Box 4 of 52, Subject Files, Series III, Executive Medical Officer, UMWA Health and Retirement Funds, A & M 2769.

"Before the Council of the Kentucky State Medical Association: Matter of Frederick W. Zuspan, M.D., McDowell, Kentucky, Statement on Appeal on December 12, 1957, from Denial of Membership by Floyd County Society." F.F. A-II-6.1, Dr. Fred Zuspan vs. Floyd County. Box 6 of 16, Subject Files, Series IV, UMWA Health and Retirement Funds, A & M 2769.

"A Chronology of the United Mine Workers of America Welfare and Retirement Fund between January 1, 1945, to April 26, 1951." Control Folder, UMWA Health and Retirement Funds, A & M 2769.

Harrington, Daniel P. "Review of Safety in Coal Mining, 1945." Box 2, Walter R. Thurmond Papers, A & M 2141.

Latimer, Murray W. Report to the Board of Trustees of the UMWA Welfare and Retirement Fund. F.F. Latimer Report, box 1 of 2, Actuary and Insurance Company Data, 1947–48, Series II, Office of the Director, UMWA Health and Retirement Funds, A & M 2769.

Mayberry Report [no formal title]. F.F. L. M. Mayberry Actuary. Box 2 of 2, Actuary and Insurance Company Data, 1947–48. Series II, Office of the Director, UMWA Health and Retirement Funds, A & M 2769.

"Medical Care in the Bituminous Coal Mining Areas." Conference held in Charleston, W.Va., Sept. 6–7, 1952. F.F. American Medical Association, Committee on Health Care for Industrial Workers. Box 17 of 52, Subject Files, Series III, Executive Medical Officer, UMWA Health and Retirement Funds, A & M 2769.

"Medical Hospitals in the Bituminous Coal Mining Areas of Kentucky-Tennessee-West Virginia, Preliminary Study to Survey Extent of Problems" F. F. Council on Medical Service, UMWA Survey Report. Box 7 of 52, Subject Files, Series III, Executive Medical Officer, UMWA Health and Retirement Funds, A & M 2769.

Miller, C. Arden. *Report to the Trustees: United Mine Workers of America Welfare and Retirement Fund, Representing Impressions from Consultations Recorded from Late 1973 to April 1974.* F.F. Report of C. Arden Miller, M.D. Box 51 of 52, Subject Files, Series III, Executive Medical Officer, UMWA Health and Retirement Funds, A & M 2769.

Preliminary Report to United Mine Workers of America Welfare and Retirement Fund on Industrial Benefits. Nov. 6, 1947. F.F. T.-P.F.C., Inc. Box 1 of 2, Actuary and Insurance Company Data, 1947–48, Series II, Office of the Director, UMWA Health and Retirement Funds, A & M 2769.

Proceedings of Conference with Third Parties. Oct. 17, 1957. Box 12 of 52, Series III, Executive Medical Officer, UMWA Health and Retirement Funds, A & M 2769.

Reagh, Russel B. Report submitted to Sen. H. Styles Bridges. F.F. Actuarial Data (Senator Bridges), box 4 of 8, Board of Trustees Correspondence, 1948–71. Series II, Office of the Director, UMWA Health and Retirement Funds, A & M 2769.

Report of a Survey of the Group Practice Medical Centers Serving Beneficiaries of the United Mine Workers of America Welfare and Retirement Fund in the Pittsburgh Area. Oct. 12–17, 1957, F.F. A-II-3. Box 6 of 16, Subject Files, Series IV, Miners Memorial Hospital Association, UMWA Health and Retirement Funds, A & M 2769.

Report of the Fourth Conference on Medical Care in the Bituminous Coal Mining Area. Charleston, W.Va., May 6, 1956. Box Addendum, July 9, 1981, Annual Reports 1952–79 and

Misc. Medical Staff Publications, [no series], UMWA Health and Retirement Funds. A & M 2769.

Report of Group III, Medical Care and Hospital Facilities. F.F. A.M.A. Charleston Conference, Sept. 13–14, 1953, 2 of 2 Report Groups I, II, III, IV, and V. Box 13 of 52, Subject Files, Series III, Executive Medical Officer, UMWA Health and Retirement Funds, A & M 2769.

Report of Survey Team to Committee on Medical Care for Industrial Workers of the Councils on Medical Service and Industrial Health, American Medical Association. Apr. 15–16, 1953, F.F. "American Medical Association Council on Industrial Health," box 17 of 52, Subject Files, Series III, Executive Medical Officer, UMWA Health and Retirement Funds, A & M 2769.

Report to the Bituminous Coal Operators on Welfare and Retirement Fund for Employees. Mar. 12, 1948, F.F. T.-P.F.C. Report, Mar. 1948, box 1 of 2, Actuary and Insurance Company Data, 1947–48, Series II, Office of the Director, UMWA Health and Retirement Funds, A & M 2769.

"Suggested Guide to Relations between State and County Medical Societies and the United Mine Workers of America Welfare and Retirement Fund." 1958, F.F. "American Medical Association, Committee on Medical Care for Industrial Workers, 1957-1958-1960." Box 7 of 52, Subject Files, Series III, Executive Medical Officer, UMWA Health and Retirement Funds, A & M 2769.

Summary of Systems Review Findings and Recommendations from Study of Touche Ross & Co. F.F. Reorganization, Touche Ross Review Findings of Benefit Eligibility and Medical Payment Systems. Box 52 of 52, Subject Files, Series III, Executive Medical Officer, UMWA Health and Retirement Funds, A & M 2769.

Thurmond, Walter R. "Statement of Walter A. Thurmond before Senate Sub Committee on Public Lands, RE Senate Joint Resolution #133 [on Coal Mine Safety]." Box 2, Walter R. Thurmond Papers, A & M 2141.

United Mine Workers of America Welfare and Retirement Fund Annual Report, 1968–1969. Box Addendum, July 9, 1981, Annual Reports 1952–79 and Misc. Medical Staff Publications [no series], UMWA Health and Retirement Funds, A & M 2769.

United Mine Workers of America Welfare and Retirement Fund Annual Report, 1969–1970. Box Addendum, July 9, 1981, Annual Reports 1952–79 and Misc. Medical Staff Publications [no series], UMWA Health and Retirement Funds, A & M 2769.

United Mine Workers of America Welfare and Retirement Fund Annual Report, 1970–1971. Box Addendum, July 9, 1981, Annual Reports 1952–79 and Misc. Medical Staff Publications [no series], UMWA Health and Retirement Funds, A & M 2769.

United Mine Workers of America Welfare and Retirement Fund Annual Report, 1971–1972. Box Addendum, July 9, 1981, Annual Reports 1952–79 and Misc. Medical Staff Publications [no series], UMWA Health and Retirement Funds, A & M 2769.

United Mine Workers of America Welfare and Retirement Fund Annual Report, 1972–1973. Box Addendum, July 9, 1981, Annual Reports 1952–79 and Misc. Medical Staff Publications [no series], UMWA Health and Retirement Funds, A & M 2769.

United Mine Workers of America Welfare and Retirement Fund Annual Report, 1973–1974.

Box Addendum, July 9, 1981, Annual Reports 1952–79 and Misc. Medical Staff Publications [no series], UMWA Health and Retirement Funds, A & M 2769.

U.S. Dept. of the Interior. *Report of the Coal Mines Administrator (Boone Report).* A Medical Survey of the Bituminous Coal Mining Industry. Washington, D.C.: GPO, 1947. Box 1 of 1, Bibliography, UMWA Health and Retirement Funds, A & M 2769.

Reports outside West Virginia Collection

"An Address by Senator James E. Murray of Montana before the CIO Committee for Political Action, New York." Jan. 14, 1944, F.F. "Murray-Wagner-Dingell Bill," box Yellow Dot 78, Group Insurance, United Electrical, Radio, and Machine Workers of America Papers, Archives of Industrial Society, Univ. of Pittsburgh.

Draper, Warren F. "Conference on Medical Care in the Bituminous Coal Mine Area: Views and Suggestions." Rpt. with additions from *Journal of the American Medical Association* 151, Mar. 7, 1953, 848–49. In "Medical Hospital Problems in the Bituminous Coal Mining Area: Report of a Conference Sponsored by the Committee on Medical Care for Industrial Workers of the Council on Medical Service and the Council on Industrial Health," Charleston, W.Va., Sept. 6–7, 1952. (Rpt. from *Journal of the American Medical Association,* Jan. 31, 1953.) F.F. C-X-2–Newdorp, John, M.D., 1953–54, box 1, Private Papers of John Newdorp, M.D., Arlington, Va.

Durmaskin, Bettina T., Ronald C. Althouse, William Wyant, and Edward Bosnar. *The Impact of Changes in Health Care Coverage Provided by the United Mine Workers of America Health and Retirement Funds in West Virginia Primary Care Clinics and Multi-Specialty Clinics Having Extensive Miner Case Loads.* Dept. of Community Medicine, Office of Health Services Research, West Virginia Univ., Unpublished Report, 1982.

Falk, I. S. "Health Insurance Experience in Basic Industry: Summary of Utilization and Costs Under Blue Cross/Shield Contracts of the United States Steel Corporation for Employees and Their Dependents." F.F. "Medical Care 1963–1965, National Can Corporation, National Labor Management Panel, 1962–1967." Box 6, Frank Pollara Papers, Labor Archives, Patee Library, Pennsylvania State Univ.

Health and Medical Care in Alabama: An Inventory of Conditions and a Proposed Hospital Plan. Alabama State Planning Board, in Cooperation with the Post-War Planning Commission of the Medical Association of the State of Alabama and the Alabama Dept. of Health, May 1945. F.F. "Health and Medical Care in Alabama" (St. Hosp Report May 1945). Box 1, Private Papers of John Newdorp, M.D., Arlington, Va.

Held, Adolf. "Report as Submitted to Conference on Union Health Insurance." May 25, 1946, F.F. "Health and Welfare Survey." Research Dept., United Steel Workers of America Papers, box 65, Labor Archives, Patee Library, Pennsylvania State Univ.

"An Interview with Arnold Miller." Transcript of the *Today Show,* Nov. 28, 1972, p. 4, F.F. 3, box 85, Miners for Democracy Papers, Walter P. Reuther Library, Wayne State Univ., Detroit, Mich.

Kessler, Henry, M.D. Manuscript on John L. Lewis, Private Papers of John Newdorp, M.D., Arlington, Va.

Lattimer, Murray W. "Instructions Relating to Social Insurance Fact Finding." Nov. 14, 1949, F.F. 17, box 68, David J. MacDonald Papers, Labor Archives, Patee Library, Pennsylvania State Univ..

Newdorp, John. "Planning for Medical Care in the Post-War Period: With Reference to Alabama." Rpt. from *Journal of the Medical Association of the State of Alabama*" (Feb./Mar./Apr. 1945). F.F. "Reprint of Article, Post-War Medical Plan *Journal of the Medical Association of the State of Alabama.*" Box 1, Private Papers of John Newdorp, M.D., Arlington, Va.

"Report on Insurance and Pensions by Joint Committee on Insurance of the United Steel Workers of America and the United States Steel Corporation, vol. 1, Insurance and Pension Programs of the United States Steel Corporation." Pt. 3. May 1954, F.F. "Insurance and Pension Programs, vol. 1, May 1954." Box 68, David J. MacDonald Papers, Labor Archives, Patee Library, Pennsylvania State Univ.

Rockette, Howard. *Mortality among Coal Miners Covered by the UMWA Health and Retirement Fund.* Morgantown, W.Va.: U.S. Dept. of Health Education and Welfare, Public Health Service, Center for Disease Control, National Institute for Occupational Safety and Health, Appalachian Laboratory for Occupational Safety and Health, Mar. 1977.

"Statement on National Health Insurance Bill (S-1879) by Russ Nixon, Washington Representative of the United Electrical, Radio, and Machine Workers of America, CIO." June 7, 1947, F.F. "Health through 1951." Box Red Dot 336, United Electrical, Radio, and Machine Workers of America Papers, Archives of Industrial Society, Univ. of Pittsburgh.

"Summarized Proceedings: Conference on Labor Research Group, December 10 & 11, 1946." Appendix B, Federal Security Agency, Social Security Administration, Bureau of Research and Statistics. Research Dept., United Steel Workers of America Papers, box 65, Labor Archives, Patee Library, Pennsylvania State Univ.

U[nited] E[lectrical Workers] Guide to Group Insurance. Box Yellow Dot 1, Group 78, Group Insurance, United Electrical, Radio, and Machine Workers of America Papers, Archives of Industrial Society, Univ. of Pittsburgh. United Electrical, Radio, and Machine Workers of America, New York, CIO, 1944.

United Mine Workers of America Health and Retirement Funds 1975 Annual Report. West Virginia Univ. Library.

United Mine Workers of America Health and Retirement Funds 1976 Annual Report. West Virginia Univ. Library.

United Mine Workers of America Health and Retirement Funds 1977 Annual Report. West Virginia Univ. Library.

United Mine Workers of America Health and Retirement Funds 1978 Annual Report. West Virginia Univ. Library.

U.S. Congress. House. *Health Security/Message from the President of the United States Transmitting the Report and Recommendations on National Health Prepared by the Interde-*

partmental Committee to Coordinated Health and Welfare Activities. 76th Cong., 1st sess., H.R. Doc. 120. F.F. 8, Josephine Roche Papers, Archives, Univ. of Colorado, Boulder.

Wysang, Jere A., and Williams, Sherman R. *Health Services for Miners: Development and Evolution of the United Miner Health Care Program.* Washington, D.C.: National Center for Health Service Research, U.S. Dept. of Health and Human Services, Office of Health Research, Statistics, and Technology, 1981.

Books and Articles in West Virginia Collection

Barnes, Asa. "Third Party Medicine in Kentucky." F.F. A-II-6, Relations with Medical Societies. Box 6 of 16, Subject Files, Series IV, Miners Memorial Hospital Association, UMWA Health and Retirement Funds, A & M 2769.

"Coal Workers' Pneumoconiosis: The Road to Dusty Death." F.F. Office of the Director Records, 1947–71, Conventions, 45 UMWA. Box 1 of 1, Conventions, Series II, Office of the Director, UMWA Health and Retirement Funds, A & M 2769.

Draper, Warren F. "The Medical Care Program of the United Mine Workers of America Welfare and Retirement Fund." Box Addendum, July 9, 1981, Annual Reports 1952–79 and Misc. Medical Staff Publications [no series], UMWA Health and Retirement Funds, A & M 2769.

"A Hospital Chain 250 Miles Long." *Engineering News-Records,* Mar. 17, 1955, F.F. MMHA Publicity Publications, box 2 of 5, Construction/Administration, Series IV, Miners Memorial Hospital Association, UMWA Health and Retirement Funds, A & M 2769.

Kerr, Lorin E. "Coal Workers' Pneumoconiosis." *Archives of Environmental Health,* Apr. 1968. F.F. Pneumoconiosis–Black Lung Legislation. Box 2 of 11, United Mine Workers of America Correspondence, 1948–72, UMWA Health and Retirement Funds, A & M 2769.

Koplin, Allen N. "Retainer Payment for Physician Services." Box Addendum, July 9, 1981, Annual Reports 1952–79 and Misc. Medical Staff Publications [no series], UMWA Health and Retirement Funds, A & M 2769.

Mott, Frederick, M.D. "High Quality Care Is the Keystone." F.F. MMHA Publicity Publications. Box 2 of 5, Construction/Administration, Series IV, Miners Memorial Hospital Association, UMWA Health and Retirement Funds, A & M 2769.

Pohlman, Kenneth E. "Rehabilitation of the Severely Disabled: UMWA Welfare and Retirement Fund Experience." *Journal of Public Health,* Apr. 1953. F.F. Office of the Director Records, MMHA Correspondence, 1947 Fund Area Reports. Box 1 of 4, Medical, Hospital, and Health Service Records, Series II, Office of the Director, UMWA Health and Retirement Funds. A & M 2769.

"Problems of the United Mine Workers of America Welfare and Retirement Fund in Providing Medical Care to Its Beneficiaries" F.F. American Medical Association Meetings in 1957. Box 12 of 52, Subject Files, Series III, Executive Medical Officer, UMWA Health and Retirement Funds, A & M 2769.

Books and Articles outside West Virginia Collection

Bethell, Thomas N. "U.M.W. in the Pits." *New Republic,* Apr. 1, 1978, 7–9.

"Chaos in the Coal Fields." *Nation,* Jan. 26, 1963, 70–72.

Falk, I. S. "Content and Administration of a Medical Care Program: Unmet Health Needs." *American Journal of Public Health* 34, no. 12 (Dec. 1944): 1223–30.

Gorman, Michael. "The Impact of National Health Insurance on Delivery of Health Care." *American Journal of Public Health* 61, no. 5 (May 1971): 962–71.

"How Welfare Fund Aids Miners." *U.S. News and World Report,* Oct. 15, 1948, 49–50.

"I'm Awful Thankful: United Mine Workers' Welfare and Retirement Fund." *Time,* Aug. 15, 1949, 17.

"John L. Lewis's 250-Mile Chain of Hospitals." *U.S. News and World Report* 40, June 29, 1956, 98–100.

"Josephine Roche." *Current Biography, 1941.* New York: W. H. Wilson Co., 1941, 725.

Kerr, Lorin E. "Coal Workers' Pneumoconiosis." *Industrial Medicine and Surgery,* Aug. 1956, 355–62.

———. "The United Mine Workers of America Look at Occupational Health." *American Journal of Public Health* 61, no. 5 (May 1971): 972–78.

"Lewis's Billion-Dollar Fund." *U.S. News and World Report,* Sept. 23, 1955, 108–13.

Meyers, Robert J. "Experience of the UMWA Welfare and Retirement Fund." *Industrial Labor Relations Review* (Oct. 1956).

"Miners' Bonanza Free Medical Care: From the Cradle to the Grave." *Scholastic* 53 (Oct. 20, 1948): 13.

"Miners' Hospital Chain." *Fortune* 49, Mar. 1954, 70.

"Miners' Welfare." *Newsweek* 42, Sept. 7, 1953, 76–79.

Pearse, Ben. "Milestones for Miners: Pensions, Welfare, Hospitals." *Nation,* Aug. 28, 1954, 170–72.

"A Pension Plan in Trouble." *U.S. News and World Report,* Apr. 30, 1954, 77–80.

"The Quality of Medical Care in a National Health Program: A Statement by the Subcommittee on Medical Care [of the American Public Health Association]. *American Journal of Public Health* 39, no. 7 (July 1949): 898–924.

Rodenbaugh, Susan Jarworski. "Death by Computer and Contract: The UMWA Health and Retirement Fund." *Crossroads,* July–Aug. 1978, 22–26.

———. "Two Steps Backward: Health Benefit Provisions of the March 1978 UMWA Contract Proposal." Guest editorial published in *The Mountain Eagle, Coalfield Progress,* and *Appalachia Express,* Mar. 16, 1978.

———. Letter to the Editor. *Pittsburgh Post-Gazette, Mountain Eagle, Williamson Daily News,* and *Valley News Dispatch,* July 6, 1977.

Wakefield, Dan. "Dr. Jeckle and the A.M.A." *Nation,* June 22, 1957, 539–41.

——. "In Hazard." In *Appalachia in the Sixties,* ed. Daniel S. Wall and John Stephenson. Lexington: Univ. Press of Kentucky, 1972

"Welfare Fund Keeping Solvent." *U.S. News and World Report,* Sept. 10, 1954, 113–14.

Winebrenner, John, M.D. "An Epic in the Coal Fields." *Journal of Occupational Medicine* 8, no. 8 (Aug. 1966): 403–8.

——. "Medicine into the Sixties." *Tennessee State Medical Journal* 53, no. 10 (Oct. 1960): 431–34.

——. "The Reins of Progress." Paper presented at the Midwestern Regional Meeting, AAMC. Rpt. from *Group Practice* 14, no. 9 (Sept. 1965).

Wolfert, Ira. "Miners' Fund, A Tribute to Good Management." *Readers' Digest* 69, Sept. 1956, 173–80.

Newspapers

New York Times. 1946–50, 1953–58, 1960–62, 1968–73, 1976–79.

United Mine Workers Journal. 1946–50, 1953–57, 1968–79.

All other newspaper references are taken from clippings found in the Fund collection.

Secondary Sources

Adams, Henry H. *Harry Hopkins: A Biography.* New York: Putnam, 1977.

Alinsky, Saul D. *John L. Lewis: An Unauthorized Biography.* New York: Putnam, 1949.

Amenta, Edwin, and Theda Skokpol. "Redefining the New Deal: World War II and the Development of Social Provision in the United States." In *The Politics of Social Policy in the United States,* ed. Margaret Weir, Ann Shola Orloff, and Theda Skokpol, 81–122. Princeton, N.J.: Princeton Univ. Press, 1988.

Arbrestor, Trevor. *Act of Vengeance: The Yablonski Murders and Their Solution.* New York: Saturday Review Press, 1975.

Baratz, Morton S. *The Union and the Coal Industry.* 1955. Rpt. Westport: Greenwood Press, 1983.

Barnum, Darnald T. *The Negro in the Bituminous Coal Mining Industry.* Philadelphia: Industrial Research Unit, Wharton School, Univ. of Pennsylvania, 1969.

Berkowitz, Edward. "The Federal Government and the Emergence of Rehabilitation Medicine." *Historian* 43, no. 4 (Aug. 1981): 530–45.

Bernstein, Barton J. "America in War and Peace: The Test of Liberalism." In *Towards a New Past:*

Dissenting Essays in American History, ed. Barton J. Bernstein, 289–321. New York: Random House, 1967; paperback ed., New York: Vintage Press, 1969.

Bernstein, Irving. *The Lean Years: A History of the American Worker, 1920–1933.* Boston: Houghton Mifflin, 1960.

———. *The Turbulent Years: A History of the American Worker, 1933–1941.* Boston: Houghton Mifflin, 1970.

Brophy, John. *A Miner's Life: An Autobiography.* Edited with supplement by John O. P. Hall. Madison: Univ. of Wisconsin Press, 1964.

Brown, Stuart. *A Man Named Tony: The Story of the Yablonski Murders.* New York: W. W. Norton & Co., 1976.

Carnes, Cecil. *John L. Lewis: Leader of Labor.* New York: Robert Speller Publishing Co., 1936.

Carter, Richard. *The Doctor Business.* Garden City, N.Y: Doubleday., 1958.

Caudill, Harry M. *Night Comes to the Cumberlands: A Biography of a Depressed Area.* Foreword by Stewart L. Udall. Boston: Little, Brown, & Co., 1962; Paperback ed., Boston: Atlantic Monthly Press, 1963.

Clark, Paul. *The Miners' Fight for Democracy: Arnold Miller and the U.M.W.* Ithaca: Cornell Univ. Press, 1981.

Derickson, Alan. "Part of the Yellow Dog: U.S. Coal Miner Opposition to the Company Doctor System." *International Journal of Health Services* 19, no. 4 (Fall 1989): 709–20.

———. *Black Lung: Anatomy of a Public Health Disaster.* Ithaca, N.Y.: Cornell Univ. Press, 1998.

Dubofsky, Melvyn. *We Shall Be All: A History of the I.W.W.* New York: New York Times/Quadrangle Books, 1969.

Dubofsky, Melvyn, and Warren Van Tine. *John L. Lewis: A Biography.* New York: Quadrangle/ New York Times Book Co., 1977.

Edwards, Richard C. *Contested Terrain: The Transformation of the Workplace in the Twentieth Century.* New York: Basic Books, 1979.

Eller, Richard D. *Miners, Millhands, and Mountaineers Industrialization of the Appalachian South, 1880–1930.* Knoxville: Univ. of Tennessee Press, 1982.

Featherling, Dale. *Mother Jones, The Miners' Angel: A Portrait.* Carbondale: Southern Illinois Univ. Press, 1974.

Finley, William. *The Corrupt Kingdom: The Rise and Fall of the United Mine Workers.* New York: Simon & Schuster, 1972.

Form, William. *Divided We Stand: Working Class Consciousness in America.* Urbana: Univ. of Illinois Press, 1986.

Fox, Daniel M. *Health Policies, Health Politics: The British and American Experience.* Princeton: Princeton Univ. Press, 1986.

Fox, Maier. *United We Stand: The United Mine Workers of America, 1890–1990.* Washington, 1990.

Frazer, Steven, and Gary Gerstle, eds. *The Rise and Fall of the New Deal Order, 1930–1980.* Princeton, N.J.: Princeton Univ. Press, 1989.

Gaventa, John. *Power and Powerlessness: Quiescence and Rebellion in an Appalachian Valley.* Urbana: Univ. of Illinois Press, 1980.

Geleman, Walter. *C.I.O. Challenge to the A.F.L.: A History of the American Labor Movement, 1935–1941.* Cambridge, Mass.: Harvard Univ. Press, 1960.

Ginzber, Eli. *From Health Dollars to Health Services: New York City, 1965–1985* Towata, N.J.: Rowman & Allenheld, 1986.

Goodrich, Carter. *The Miner's Freedom: A Study of Working Conditions in a Changing Industry.* 1925. Rpt. New York: Arno Press, 1977.

Gordon, David M., Richard C. Edwards, Michael Reich. *Segmented Divided Workers: The Historical Transformation of Labor in the United States.* Cambridge: Cambridge Univ. Press, 1982.

Graebner, William. *Coal-Mining Safety in the Progressive Period: The Political Economy of Reform.* Univ. Press of Kentucky, 1976.

Green, James R. *The World of the Worker: Labor in Twentieth Century America.* New York: Hill and Wang, 1977.

Hevener, John W. *Which Side Are You On? The Harlan Mine Wars.* Urbana: Univ. of Illinois Press, 1978.

Huff, Merlene. "The Effect of the UMWA upon Reform of the Company Doctor System." Paper presented at the Sixteenth Annual Appalachian Studies Conference. East Tennessee State Univ., Johnson City, Tenn. Mar. 1993.

Hume, Brit. *Death and the Mines: Corruption in the UMWA.* New York: Grossman Publishers, 1971.

Hutchinson, John. *The Imperfect Union: A History of Corruption in American Trade Unions.* New York: Dutton, 1970.

Huthmaker, John. *Senator Robert F. Wagner: The Rise of an Urban Liberal.* New York: Anthaneum, 1971.

Jackson, Carlton. *The Dreadful Month.* Foreword by Harry M. Caudill. Bowling Green, Ohio: Bowling Green Univ. Popular Press, 1982.

Kingsbury, John A. *Health in Handcuffs: The National Health Crisis—And What Can Be Done.* New York: Modern Age Books, 1939.

Kochan, Thomas A., Harry C. Katz, and Robert B. McKersie. *The Transformation of American Industrial Relations.* New York: Basic Books, 1986.

Krajcinovic, Ivana. *From Company Doctors to Managed Care: The United Mine Workers Noble Experiment.* Ithaca, N.Y.: ILR Press, 1997.

Lewis, Arthur H. *Murder by Contract: The People v. "Tough Tony."* New York: Macmillan, 1975.

Lewis, John L. *The Miners' Fight for American Standards.* Indianapolis: Bell Publishing Co., 1925.

Lichtenstein, Nelson. "From Corporatism to Collective Bargaining: Organized Labor and the Eclipse of Social Democracy in the Post War Era." In *The Rise and Fall of the New Deal Order,* ed. Steven Fraser and Gary Gerstle, 121–52. Princeton: Princeton Univ. Press, 1989.

Massie, William A. *Medical Services for Rural Areas.* Cambridge: Harvard Univ. Press, 1957.

McAteer, J. D. *Coal Mine Health and Safety, The Case of West Virginia.* New York: Praeger, 1970.

McGinn, Eleanor. "Josephine Roche—Progressive Reformer, 1910–1940." Copy of presented paper given to author by Dr. McGinn at Colorado State Historical Association. Boulder, 1991.

Morris, James O. *Conflict within the A.F.L.: A Study of Craft versus Industrial Unionism.* Ithaca, N.Y.: Cornell Univ. Press, 1958.

Mott, Frederick W., and Milton I. Roemer. *Rural Health and Medical Care.* New York: McGraw, Hill, 1948.

Mulcahy, Richard. "Working Against the Odds: Josephine Roche, the New Deal, and the Drive for National Health Insurance." *Maryland Historian* 25, no. 2 (Fall–Winter 1994), 1–21.

Muncy, Robyn. *Creating a Female Dominion in American Reform, 1890–1935.* New York: Oxford Univ. Press, 1991.

Newman, Robert P. *Owen Lattimore and the "Loss" of China.* Berkeley: Univ. of California Press, 1992.

Nolan, Robert L., and Jerome L. Schwartz, eds. *Rural and Appalachian Health.* Foreword by Sen. Edward Kennedy. Springfield, Ill.: Thomas, 1973.

Nyden, Paul J. "Miners for Democracy: Struggle in the Coal Fields." Unpublished manuscript. Pittsburgh, 1977.

Orloff, Ann S. "The Political Origins of America's Belated Welfare State." In *The Politics of Social Policy in the United States,* ed. Margaret Weir, Ann S. Orloff, and Theda Skokpol, 61–80. Princeton, N.J.: Princeton Univ. Press, 1988.

Perry, Charles R. *Collective Bargaining and the Decline of the United Mine Workers.* Philadelphia: Univ. of Pennsylvania Press, 1984.

Peterson, Bill. *Coal Town Revisited: An Appalachian Notebook.* Chicago: Regnery, 1972.

Reese, Albert. *The Economics of Trade Unions.* Chicago: Univ. of Chicago Press, 1989.

Riska, Elaine. *Power, Politics, and Health: Forces Shaping American Medicine.* Helsinki: Finnish Society of Science, 1985.

Rosenburg, Charles E. *Caring for the Working Man: The Rise and Fall of the Dispensary, An Anthology of Sources.* New York: privately published, 1989.

Savage, Lon. *Thunder in the Mountains: A History of the Kanawha Mine Wars.* Charleston, W.Va., 1984.

Seltzer, Curtis. *Fire in the Hole.* Lexington: Univ. Press of Kentucky, 1985.

Selvin, David F. *The Thundering Voice of John L. Lewis.* New York: Lanthrop, Lee, & Shepard Co., 1969.

Smith, Barbara E. "Black Lung: The Social Production of Disease." *International Journal of Health Sciences* 11, no. 3, 343–59.

———. "The Politics of Victory: Some Lessons from the Black Lung Movement." Paper presented at the United Mine Workers of America Centennial Conference. Pennsylvania State Univ., University Park. Oct. 19, 1990.

Starr, Paul. *The Social Transformation of American Medicine.* New York: Basic Books, 1982.

Stevens, Beth. *Complementing the Welfare State: The Development of Private Pension, Health Insurance, and Other Employee Benefits in the United States.* Labor-Management Series 65. Geneva: International Labor Office, 1986.

———. "Blurring the Boundaries: How the Federal Government Has Influenced Welfare Benefits in the Private Sector." In *The Politics of Social Policy in the United States,* ed. Margaret Weir, Ann Shola Orloff, and Theda Skokpol, 123–48. Princeton: Princeton Univ. Press, 1988.

Stevens, Rosemary. *American Medicine and the Public Interest.* New Haven: Yale Univ. Press, 1971.

Sulzberger, Cyrus Leo. *Sit Down with John L. Lewis.* New York: Random House, 1939.

Van Tine, Warren R. *The Making of a Labor Bureaucrat, Union Leadership in the United States, 1870–1920.* Amherst: Univ. of Massachusetts Press, 1973.

Vorse, Mary Heaton. *Labor's New Millions.* New York: Putnam, 1939.

Wallace, Anthony F. C. *St. Clair: A Nineteenth Century Coal Town's Experience with a Disaster-Prone Industry.* Ithaca, N.Y.: Cornell Univ. Press, 1985.

Warner, John H. "Power, Conflict, and Identity in Mid-Nineteenth Century Medicine: Therapeutic Change at Commercial Hospital in Cincinnati." *Journal of American History* 73, no. 4 (Mar. 1987): 934–56.

Weir, Margaret, Ann Shola Orloff, and Theda Skokpol, eds. *The Politics of Social Policy in the United States.* Princeton, N.J.: Princeton Univ. Press, 1988.

Wyman, Mark. *Hard Rock Epic: Western Miners and the Industrial Revolution, 1860–1910.* Berkeley: Univ. of California Press, 1979.

Theses and Dissertations

Graebner, William. "Coal Mining Safety: National Solutions in the Progressive Period." Ph.D. diss., Univ. of Illinois, Urbana, 1970.

Hopkins, George William. "The Miners for Democracy: Insurgency in the United Mine Workers of America, 1970–1972." Ph.D. diss., Univ. of North Carolina, Chapel Hill, 1976.

Jensen, Richard Jay. "Rebellion in the United Mine Workers: The Miners for Democracy, 1970–1972." Ph.D. diss., Indiana Univ., Bloomington, 1974.

Nyden, Paul John. "Miners for Democracy: Struggle in the Coal Fields." Ph.D. diss., Columbia Univ., New York, 1974.

Ploss, Janet E. "A History of the Medical Care Program of the United Mine Workers of America Health and Retirement Funds." Ph.D. diss., Johns Hopkins Univ., Baltimore, 1981.

Scott, G. H. "A Study of the United Mine Workers of America Welfare and Retirement Fund." Master's thesis, West Virginia Univ., Morgantown, 1951.

Seltzer, Curtis. "The United Mine Workers and the Coal Operators: The Political Economy of Coal in Appalachia, 1950–1973." Ph.D. diss., Columbia Univ., New York, 1977.

Singer, Alan M. "'Which Side Are You On?' Ideological Conflict in the United Mine Workers of America, 1919–1928." Ph.D. diss., Rutgers Univ., New Brunswick, N.J., 1982.

Index

Kessler Institute of Physical Rehabilitation, 102
Khrushchev, Nikita, John L. Lewis compared to, 133
Klump, Dr. James, 124–25
Knoxville Academy of Medicine, 116
Knoxville, Tenn., 117; location of area medical office, 57
Kochis, "Cadillac" Steve, 1964 Union presidential election, 136
Koplin, Dr. Allen, 100; AMO for Birmingham, Ala., 100; develops fee-for-time concept, 115
Krajcinovic, Ivana, 12, 131–33
Krug, Secretary of the Interior Julius A., 8
Kruger, Miss Ada, RN, 189n
Krug-Lewis agreement, 8, 18, 35, 97; *see also* National Bituminous Coal Wage Agreement of 1946
KSMA (Kentucky State Medical Association), 63–67, 76; decision in Zuspan case, 65–66; impact of its boycott of MMHA, 67; opposition to Fund Medical Program and MMHA, 62–67; use of appeal procedure in denial of membership, 64–66

Labor Management Reporting and Disclosure Act, 132
Labor relations, 9, 132
Labor's Nonpartisan League, Yablonski appointed chair by Boyle, 149
LaFollette, Senator Robert, Jr., 29
Landrum-Griffen Act, 152
Lasker, Dr. Albert, 56
Lasker, Mrs. Albert, 93 (illus.)
Latimer, Murray W., 18, 19, 21, 23, 24
Lecher County (Ky.), 63
Lecher County (Ky.) medical society, 63
Lewis, A. O., 36; failure to distribute Form 85 HS, 36–39; Roche's problems with, 37–39
Lewis, John L., xi, xii, xiii, 7, 8, 10, 11, 12, 24, 36, 37, 40, 45, 83 (illus.), 110, 131–33, 142, 150, 159–61, 162, 176, 183, 234n; activation of Fund pension, 13–16, 17–22; agrees with Draper on Fund Medical Program, 99; AMO dispute with MMHA, 60; and Dr. Sayers' "promotion," 99; authoritarianism, 1–2, 39, 44, 139, 161; background of, 1–2; benefit cuts 1960–1962, 128–34; Boyle's use of power mechanisms created by, 141; brings Tony Boyle to UMWA HQ, 140; choice of actuary, 13; condition prior to death, 154; continuation as Fund chair, 128, 131, 145; contradictions in 1950 settlement, 31–32, 141, 148, 161, 183; control of Fund Board,

9, 31–32, 34; controversy in early career, 2, 35, 128, 135, 164; corporatist views of, 31, 161; creation of thirty year rule, 42–43; crisis in the system he built, 127, 129, 140, 141, 159–61; crisis of coal industry in early '60s, 73–74, 129–35; death, 151, 156, 185; declaration of three day work week, 26, 27; demand for Fund's creation, 3, 4; dual character of Lewis' leadership, 141, 143; early opposition to, 2, 35, 128, 135, 164; effects of Lewis's leadership, 140–41; efforts by Tony Boyle to associate with legacy, 139–40, 147–48; end of trustee cooperation, 27–30; failure to get contract for 1949, 26; fiduciary obligations of, 137–38, 159–61; financial matters, 34, 132, 136, 138; friendship with Roche, 9, 56; Fund 1949 audit, 27; Fund investment decisions, 136–38, 158; Fund, 1949 suspension, 27–31; Fund's 1949 audit, 27; hires Dr. Royd R. Sayers, 97–99; hospital construction bids, 48–49; hospital development, 45, 48–49; initial support for Dr. Sayers, 97–98; interrelationship of Fund, union, and bank, 138; lowering retirement age to 60, 23, 26; management of UMWA conventions, 139; meets with protesters, 133; mine mechanization, xiii, 2, 31, 40, 73, 132, 141; 1948 contract negotiations, 22; 1949 Kentucky "truck" mine agreement, 30–31; 1950 settlement, 31–32, 183; 1961 pension reduction, 130; no evidence of sweetheart contracts, 143; no royalty increase in 1956, 131; non-action on black lung, 141; non-involvement in AMO/MMHA dispute, 61; opening of MMHA, 54, 55, 57; opposes Dawson's appointment, 29–30; payment of legal expenses, 33; pension fight, 13–16, 17–22; pension increases, 135; pragmatism of, 1, 141; praised by Charles Owen, 57; prestige with UMWA rank and file, 3, 105, 128; purchase of National Bank of Washington, 34; purchase of West Kentucky Coal Company, 132; rationalization of the coal industry, 1–2, 40, 56; reasons behind Fund benefit limits, 168; replacement of Schmidt, 150–51; retirement as UMWA president, 128, 131, 139; safety legislation, 133, 141; split with President Franklin Roosevelt, 1, 79–80; status of UMWA vice presidency under, 140; struggle with critics in 1920s, 2, 35, 128, 135; thirty year rule, 42–43; trustee cooperation, 1947 Fund Board, 22–23; union centralization, 2–3, 36–37; use of

A Social Contract for the Coal Fields was designed and typeset on a Macintosh computer system using PageMaker software. The text is set in TimesNewRoman and the chapter openings are set in Industria. This book was designed by David Alcorn, typeset by Kimberly Scarbrough, and manufactured by Thomson-Shore, Inc. The paper used in this book is designed for an effective life of at least three hundred years.